LOVE STORIES

LOVE STORIES

Selected by MARTIN LEVIN

NYT Quadrangle / The New York Times Book Co.

Copyright © 1975 by Martin Levin

To the memory of Irene and Philip Levin

Contents

About Love Stories   ix

Long Walk to Forever, KURT VONNEGUT, JR.   1

Dürling, or the Faithless Wife, SEAN O'FAOLAIN   8

Her Son, ISAAC BASHEVIS SINGER   25

The Admiralty Spire, VLADIMIR NABOKOV   35

Tarzan's First Love, EDGAR RICE BURROUGHS   45

Coming, Aphrodite!, WILLA CATHER   60

Animal Behavior, LAURIE COLWIN   95

The Love-Letters of a Clodhopper, GERTRUDE BROOKE HAMILTON   112

Love: Three Pages From a Sportsman's Book, GUY DE MAUPASSANT   123

The Fourposter, JAN DE HARTOG   128

The Hand, COLETTE   172

The Wheel of Love, JOYCE CAROL OATES   175

The Rider Was Lost, NANCY HALE   190

Boys and Girls Together, WILLIAM SAROYAN   205

A Cure for Love, H. G. WELLS   223

The Offshore Pirate, F. SCOTT FITZGERALD   239

About Two Nice People, SHIRLEY JACKSON   267

L'Elégance, RUMER GODDEN   278

A Short Walk From the Station, JOHN O'HARA   295

An Unposted Love Letter, DORIS LESSING   301

The Actress, KATHARINE BRUSH   310

Make Me Real, VICTORIA LINCOLN   313

The Liberation, JEAN STAFFORD   337

Fifty-Fifty, LEONARD WOLF   353

Maud, LOUIS AUCHINCLOSS   365

A Southern Landscape, ELIZABETH SPENCER   390

Love in the Spring, JESSE STUART   402

The Apple Tree, JOHN GALSWORTHY   415

About Love Stories

I believe in love at first sight. Also in physical attraction and the notion that two people can be uniquely destined for one another. (This also applies to mallard ducks—see page 123.) I believe that love aims at forever (see page 128), although it may not always make it (page 175).

Love is an idea whose time has come back. Even Masters & Johnson got married and closed the lab.

So—in search of love, I went about asking sundry editors, writers, and lovable people, "What is your favorite love story?"

"Love story?" the respondent would mutter, in the midst of a busy day. "What do you mean by *love*?"

"Whatever *you* mean by love."

"Hmmm. Must it be between a man and a woman?"

"Not at all."

"How about two whales?" asked one respondent.

"How about a little boy and his nanny?" asked another.

"How about a necrophile?" asked a third.

I finally included a caveat that a love story must concern two *live* adults and leave at least one survivor. But I was not inflexible. In Guy de Maupassant's "Love: Three Pages from a Sportsman's Book," both

lovers die, and they don't belong to the human species. I also allowed
Tarzan his fling with Teeka.

The tie that binds most of these stories is that they are all about two
creatures who find one another uniquely magnetic. And whose lives are
in some way changed by this feeling. Some are about *falling* in love, the
focus of the romantic love story. Victoria Lincoln's "Make Me Real" is
in this category. Also F. Scott Fitzgerald's "The Offshore Pirate,"
Shirley Jackson's "About Two Nice People," Willa Cather's "Coming,
Aphrodite!"—and, of course, "The Love-Letters of a Clodhopper,"
which I retrieved from a 1917 *Redbook*, for the fun of it.

Some of the stories hinge on *being* in love. Jan de Hartog's fortify-
ing comedy shows that love need not have the short attention span that
open- and contractual-marriage advocates would have you believe. And
some are about having *been* in love, with repercussions delicately comic
(Nabokov's "The Admiralty Spire"), bitter (Doris Lessing's "An
Unposted Love Letter"), or desolate (Joyce Carol Oates's "The Wheel
of Love").

There are also the stories that are love stories only because I say so.
After all, it's *my* book.

"Do the characters in these stories play clearly defined sex roles?" I
hear a concerned voice ask from the balcony.

Damn right they do. So do their bodies. But not their "life styles."
Saroyan's hero hots up the beans for his family's dinner and nurtures
his children. Auchincloss's Maud goes off to war. Willa Cather's opera
singer puts career ahead of love. Leonard Wolf's lovers go Dutch on everything. Laurie Colwin's heroine is the peer of her lover at the museum. John O'Hara's heroine is doing very nicely in her boutique, thank
you. Love is programmed not by society but by the vital juices. If this is
a controversial view, I have 28 expert witnesses here to support my testimony.

MARTIN LEVIN

March 21, 1975

My gratitude for their helpfulness goes to Robie Macauley, Sey
Chassler, Alice Morris, Jane Ogle, Ann Mollegen Smith, Ellen A.
Stoianoff, Robert Stein, Richard Lingeman, Neal Thorpe, Phyllis Levy,
John Kobler, Norman Axelrod, Justine Auerbach, Ann Shanks, Gordon
Lish, and Barbara Dicks. Special thanks go to Edmund Levin for intro-
ducing me to "Tarzan's First Love," and to Andrea Levin whose liter-
ary acuity was invaluable to me in making final selections.

LOVE STORIES

Long Walk to Forever

by KURT VONNEGUT, JR.

They had grown up next door to each other, on the fringe of a city, near fields and woods and orchards, within sight of a lovely bell tower that belonged to a school for the blind.

Now they were twenty, had not seen each other for nearly a year. There had always been playful, comfortable warmth between them, but never any talk of love.

His name was Newt. Her name was Catharine. In the early afternoon, Newt knocked on Catharine's front door.

Catharine came to the door. She was carrying a fat, glossy magazine she had been reading. The magazine was devoted entirely to brides. "Newt!" she said. She was surprised to see him.

"Could you come for a walk?" he said. He was a shy person, even with Catharine. He covered his shyness by speaking absently, as though what really concerned him were far away—as though he were a secret agent pausing briefly on a mission between beautiful, distant, and sinister points. This manner of speaking had always been Newt's style, even in matters that concerned him desperately.

"A walk?" said Catharine.

"One foot in front of the other," said Newt, "through leaves, over bridges——"

"I had no idea you were in town," she said.

"Just this minute got in," he said.

"Still in the Army, I see," she said.

"Seven more months to go," he said. He was a private first class in the Artillery. His uniform was rumpled. His shoes were dusty. He needed a shave. He held out his hand for the magazine. "Let's see the pretty book," he said.

She gave it to him. "I'm getting married, Newt," she said.

"I know," he said. "Let's go for a walk."

"I'm awfully busy, Newt," she said. "The wedding is only a week away."

"If we go for a walk," he said, "it will make you rosy. It will make you a rosy bride." He turned the pages of the magazine. "A rosy bride like her—like her—like her," he said, showing her rosy brides.

Catharine turned rosy, thinking about rosy brides.

"That will be my present to Henry Stewart Chasens," said Newt. "By taking you for a walk, I'll be giving him a rosy bride."

"You know his name?" said Catharine.

"Mother wrote," he said. "From Pittsburgh?"

"Yes," she said. "You'd like him."

"Maybe," he said.

"Can—can you come to the wedding, Newt?" she said.

"That I doubt," he said.

"Your furlough isn't for long enough?" she said.

"Furlough?" said Newt. He was studying a two-page ad for flat silver. "I'm not on furlough," he said.

"Oh?" she said.

"I'm what they call A.W.O.L.," said Newt.

"Oh, Newt! You're not!" she said.

"Sure I am," he said, still looking at the magazine.

"Why, Newt?" she said.

"I had to find out what your silver pattern is," he said. He read names of silver patterns from the magazine. "Albemarle? Heather?" he said. "Legend? Rambler Rose?" He looked up, smiled. "I plan to give you and your husband a spoon," he said.

"Newt, Newt—tell me really," she said.

"I want to go for a walk," he said.

She wrung her hands in sisterly anguish. "Oh, Newt—you're fooling me about being A.W.O.L.," she said.

Newt imitated a police siren softly, raised his eyebrows.

"Where—where from?" she said.

"Fort Bragg," he said.

"North Carolina?" she said.

"That's right," he said. "Near Fayetteville—where Scarlett O'Hara went to school."

"How did you get here, Newt?" she said.

He raised his thumb, jerked it in a hitchhike gesture. "Two days," he said.

"Does your mother know?" she said.

"I didn't come to see my mother," he told her.

"Who did you come to see?" she said.

"You," he said.

"Why me?" she said.

"Because I love you," he said. "Now can we take a walk?" he said. "One foot in front of the other—through leaves, over bridges—"

They were taking the walk now, were in a woods with a brown-leaf floor.

Catharine was angry and rattled, close to tears. "Newt," she said, "this is absolutely crazy."

"How so?" said Newt.

"What a crazy time to tell me you love me," she said. "You never talked that way before." She stopped walking.

"Let's keep walking," he said.

"No," she said. "So far, no farther. I shouldn't have come out with you at all," she said.

"You did," he said.

"To get you out of the house," she said. "If somebody walked in and heard you talking to me that way, a week before the wedding——"

"What would they think?" he said.

"They'd think you were crazy," she said.

"Why?" he said.

Catharine took a deep breath, made a speech. "Let me say that I'm deeply honored by this crazy thing you've done," she said. "I can't believe you're really A.W.O.L., but maybe you are. I can't believe you really love me, but maybe you do. But——"

"I do," said Newt.

"Well, I'm deeply honored," said Catharine, "and I'm very fond of you as a friend, Newt, extremely fond—but it's just too late." She took a step away from him. "You've never even kissed me," she said, and she protected herself with her hands. "I don't mean you should do it now. I just mean this is all so unexpected. I haven't got the remotest idea of how to respond."

"Just walk some more," he said. "Have a nice time."

They started walking again.

"How did you expect me to react?" she said.

"How would I know what to expect?" he said. "I've never done anything like this before."

"Did you think I would throw myself into your arms?" she said.

"Maybe," he said.

"I'm sorry to disappoint you," she said.

"I'm not disappointed," he said. "I wasn't counting on it. This is very nice, just walking."

Catharine stopped again. "You know what happens next?" she said.

"Nope," he said.

"We shake hands," she said. "We shake hands and part friends," she said. "That's what happens next."

Newt nodded. "All right," he said. "Remember me from time to time. Remember how much I loved you."

Involuntarily, Catharine burst into tears. She turned her back to Newt, looked into the infinite colonnade of the woods.

"What does that mean?" said Newt.

"Rage!" said Catharine. She clenched her hands. "You have no right——"

"I had to find out," he said.

"If I'd loved you," she said, "I would have let you know before now."

"You would?" he said.

"Yes," she said. She faced him, looked up at him, her face quite red. "You would have known," she said.

"How?" he said.

"You would have seen it," she said. "Women aren't very clever at hiding it."

Newt looked closely at Catharine's face now. To her consternation, she realized that what she had said was true, that a woman couldn't hide love.

Newt was seeing love now.

And he did what he had to do. He kissed her.

"You're hell to get along with!" she said when Newt let her go.

"I am?" said Newt.

"You shouldn't have done that," she said.

"You didn't like it?" he said.

"What did you expect," she said—"wild, abandoned passion?"

"I keep telling you," he said, "I never know what's going to happen next."

"We say good-by," she said.

He frowned slightly. "All right," he said.

She made another speech. "I'm not sorry we kissed," she said. "That was sweet. We should have kissed, we've been so close. I'll always remember you, Newt, and good luck."

"You too," he said.

"Thank you, Newt," she said.

"Thirty days," he said.

"What?" she said.

"Thirty days in the stockade," he said—"that's what one kiss will cost me."

"I—I'm sorry," she said, "but I didn't ask you to go A.W.O.L."

"I know," he said.

"You certainly don't deserve any hero's reward for doing something as foolish as that," she said.

"Must be nice to be a hero," said Newt. "Is Henry Stewart Chasens a hero?"

"He might be, if he got the chance," said Catharine. She noted uneasily that they had begun to walk again. The farewell had been forgotten.

"You really love him?" he said.

"Certainly I love him!" she said hotly. "I wouldn't marry him if I didn't love him!"

"What's good about him?" said Newt.

"Honestly!" she cried, stopping again. "Do you have any idea how offensive you're being? Many, many, many things are good about Henry! Yes," she said, "and many, many, many things are probably bad too. But that isn't any of your business. I love Henry, and I don't have to argue his merits with you!"

"Sorry," said Newt.

"Honestly!" said Catharine.

Newt kissed her again. He kissed her again because she wanted him to.

They were now in a large orchard.

"How did we get so far from home, Newt?" said Catharine.

"One foot in front of the other—through leaves, over bridges," said Newt.

"They add up—the steps," she said.

Bells rang in the tower of the school for the blind nearby.

"School for the blind," said Newt.

"School for the blind," said Catharine. She shook her head in drowsy wonder. "I've got to go back now," she said.

"Say good-by," said Newt.

"Every time I do," said Catharine, "I seem to get kissed."

Newt sat down on the close-cropped grass under an apple tree. "Sit down," he said.

"No," she said.

"I won't touch you," he said.

"I don't believe you," she said.

She sat down under another tree, twenty feet away from him. She closed her eyes.

"Dream of Henry Stewart Chasens," he said.

"What?" she said.

"Dream of your wonderful husband-to-be," he said.

"All right, I will," she said. She closed her eyes tighter, caught glimpses of her husband-to-be.

Newt yawned.

The bees were humming in the trees, and Catharine almost fell asleep. When she opened her eyes she saw that Newt really was asleep.

He began to snore softly.

Catharine let Newt sleep for an hour, and while he slept she adored him with all her heart.

The shadows of the apple trees grew to the east. The bells in the tower of the school for the blind rang again.

"*Chick-a-dee-dee-dee,*" went a chickadee.

Somewhere far away an automobile starter nagged and failed, nagged and failed, fell still.

Catharine came out from under her tree, knelt by Newt.

"Newt?" she said.

"H'm?" he said. He opened his eyes.

"Late," she said.

"Hello, Catharine," he said.

"Hello, Newt," she said.

"I love you," he said.

"I know," she said.

"Too late," he said.

"Too late," she said.

He stood, stretched groaningly. "A very nice walk," he said.

"I thought so," she said.

"Part company here?" he said.

"Where will you go?" she said.

"Hitch into town, turn myself in," he said.

"Good luck," she said.

"You, too," he said. "Marry me, Catharine?"

"No," she said.

He smiled, stared at her hard for a moment, then walked away quickly.

Catharine watched him grow smaller in the long perspective of shadows and trees, knew that if he stopped and turned now, if he called to her, she would run to him. She would have no choice.

Newt did stop. He did turn. He did call. "Catharine," he called.

She ran to him, put her arms around him, could not speak.

Dürling, or the Faithless Wife

by SEAN O'FAOLAIN

He had now been stalking his beautiful Mlle. O'Murphy, whose real name was Mrs. Meehawl O'Sullivan, for some six weeks, and she had appeared to be so amused at every stage of the hunt, so responsive, *séduisante*, even *entraînante*, that he could already foresee the kill over the next horizon. At their first encounter, during the Saint Patrick's Day cocktail party at the Dutch embassy, accompanied by a husband who had not a word to throw to a cat about anything except the scissors and shears that he manufactured somewhere in the west of Ireland, and who was obviously quite ill at ease and drank too much Irish whisky, what had attracted him to her was not only her splendid Courbet figure (whence his sudden nickname for her, *La Morphée*), or her copper-colored hair, her lime-green Irish eyes and her seemingly poreless skin but her calm, total and subdued elegance: the Balenciaga costume, the peacockskin gloves, the gleaming crocodile handbag, a glimpse of tiny, lace-edged lawn handkerchief and her dry, delicate scent. He had a grateful eye and nose for such things. It was, after all, part of his job. Their second meeting, two weeks later, at his own embassy had opened the doors. She came alone.

Now, at last, inside a week, perhaps less, there would be an end to all
the probationary encounters that followed—mostly her inventions, at
his persistent appeals—those wide-eyed fancy-meeting-you-heres at the
zoo, at race meetings, afternoon cinemas, in art galleries, at more
diplomatic parties (once he had said gaily to her, "The whole diplomacy of Europe seems to circle around our interest in each other"),
those long drives over the Dublin mountains in his sports Renault,
those titillating rural lunches, nose to nose, toe to toe (rural because
she quickly educated him to see Dublin as a stock exchange for gossip,
a casino of scandal), an end, which was rather a pity, to those charming
unforeseen-foreseen, that is to say proposed but in the end just
snatched, afternoon *promenades champêtres* under the budding leaves
and closing skies of the Phoenix Park, with the first lights of the city
springing up below them to mark the end of another boring day for
him in Ailesbury Road, at the embassy, for her another possibly cozier
but, he selfishly hoped, not much more exciting day in her swank boutique on Saint Stephen's Green. Little by little those intimate encounters, those murmured confessions had lifted acquaintance to friendship,
self-mocking smiles over some tiny incident during their last meeting to
eager anticipation of the next, an aimless tenderness twanging to appetite like an arrow. Or, at least, that was how he felt about it all. Any
day now, even any hour, the slow countdown, slower than the slow
movement of Mendelssohn's *Concerto in E Minor*, or the most swoony
sequence from the *Siegfried Idyl*, or that floating spun-sugar balloon of
Mahler's *Song of the Earth*, to the music of which on his gramophone
he would imagine her smiling sidelong at him as she softly disrobed,
and his ingenious playing with her, his teasing and warming of her moment by moment for the roaring, blazing take-off. To the moon!

Only one apprehension remained with him, not a real misgiving,
something nearer to a recurring anxiety. It was that at the last moments, when her mind and her body ought to take leave of each other,
she might take to her heels. It was a fear that flooded him whenever,
with smiles too diffident to reassure him, she would once again mention
that she was a Roman Catholic, or a Cat, a Papist or a Pape, a convent
girl, and once she laughed that during her school days in the convent,
she had actually been made an *enfant de Marie*. The words never
ceased to startle him, dragging him back miserably to his first sexual
frustration with his very pretty but unexpectedly proper cousin Berthe
Ohnet during his *lycée* years in Nancy; a similar icy snub a few years
later in Quebec; repeated still later by that smack on the face in Rio
that almost became a public scandal; memories so painful that when-

ever an attractive woman nowadays mentioned religion, even in so simple a context as, "Thank God I didn't buy that hat, or frock, or stock,
or mare," a red flag at once began to flutter in his belly.

Obsessed, every time she uttered one of those ominous words, he
rushed for the reassurance of what he called The Sherbet Test, which
meant observing the effect on her of some tentatively sexy joke, like the
remark of the young princess on tasting her first sherbet: "Oh, how absolutely delicious! But what a pity it isn't a sin!" To his relief, she not
only always laughed merrily at his stories but always capped them, indeed, at times so startling him by her coarseness that it only occurred to
him quite late in their day that this might be her way of showing her
distaste for his diaphanous indelicacies. He had once or twice observed
that priests, peasants and children will roar with laughter at some scav-
enger joke and growl at even a veiled reference to a thigh. Was she a
child of nature? Still, again and again, back would come those disturbing words. He could have understood them from a prude, but what on
earth did *she* mean by them? Were they so many herbs to season her
desire with pleasure in her naughtiness? Flicks of nasty puritan sen-
suality to whip her body over some last ditch of indecision? It was only
when the final crisis came that he wondered if this might not all along
have been her way of warning him that she was neither a light nor a
lecherous woman, neither a flirt nor a flibbertigibbet, that in matters of
the heart she was *une femme très sérieuse.*

He might have guessed at something like it much earlier. He knew almost from the first day that she was *bien élevée*, her father a judge of
the Supreme Court, her uncle a monsignor at the Vatican, a worldly,
sport-loving, learned, contriving priest who had persuaded her poppa to
send her for a finishing year to Rome with the Sisters of the Sacred
Heart at the top of the Spanish Steps; chiefly, it later appeared, because
the convent was near the *centre hippique* in the Borghese gardens and
it was his right reverend's opinion that no Irish girl could possibly be
said to have completed her education until she had learned enough
about horses to ride to hounds. She had told him a lot, and most amusingly, about this uncle, who, when she had duly returned from Rome to
Dublin, and whenever he came over for the hunting, always rode beside
her. This attention had mightily flattered her until she discovered that
she was being used as a cover for his uncontrollable passion for Lady
Kinvara and Loughrea, then the master, some said the mistress, of the
Clare-Galway hounds.

"How old were you then?" Ferdy asked, fascinated.

"I was at the university. Four blissful, idling years. But I got my degree. I was quick. And," she smiled, "good-looking. It helps, even with professors."

"But riding to hounds as a student?"

"Why not? In Ireland, everybody does. Children do. You could ride to hounds on a plow horse if you had nothing else. So long as you keep out of the way of real hunters. I only stopped after my marriage, when I had a miscarriage. And I swear that was only because I was thrown."

A monsignor who was sport-loving, worldly and contriving. He understood, and approved. It explained many things about her.

The only other ways in which her dash, beauty and gaiety puzzled and beguiled him were trivial. Timid she was not; she was game for any risk. But the coolness of her weather eye often surprised him.

"The Leopardstown Races? Oh, what a good idea, Ferdy! Let's meet there. . . . The Phoenix Park Races? No, not there. Too many doctors showing off their wives and their cars, trying to be noticed. And taking notice. Remember, a lot of my college friends married doctors. . . . No, not *that* cinema. It has become vogueish. . . . In fact, no cinema on the south side of the river. What we want is a good old flea-bitten picture house on the north side where they show nothing but Westerns and horrors and where the kids get in on Saturday mornings for thruppence. . . . Oh, and do, please, only ring the boutique in an emergency. Girls gossip."

Could she be calculating? For a second of jealous heat, he wondered if she could possibly have another lover. Cooling, he saw that if he had to keep a wary eye in his master's direction, she had to think of her bourgeois clientele. Besides, he was a bachelor, and would remain one. She had to manage her inexpressibly dull, if highly successful, old scissors-and-shears manufacturer, well past 50 and probably as suspicious as he was boring; so intensely, so exhaustingly boring that the only subject about which she could herself nearly become boring was her frequent complaints about his boringness. Once she *was* frightening, when she spat out that she had hated her husband ever since the first night of their marriage. He had taken her—it was odd how long, and how intensely, this memory had rankled—not, as he had promised, to Paris for their honeymoon but to his bloody scissors-and-shears factory in the wet wilds of northern Donegal. ("Just me, dear, ha-ha, to let 'em see, ha-ha, t'other half of me scissors.")

Ferdy had, of course, never asked her why she had married such a cretin; not after sizing up her house, her furniture, her pictures, her clothes, her boutique. Anyway, only another cretin would discourage any pretty woman from grumbling about her husband: (A) because

such grumblings give a man a chance to show what a deeply sympathetic nature he has and (B) because the information incidentally supplied helps one arrange one's assignations in places and at times suitable to all concerned.

Adding it all up (he was a persistent adder-upper), only one problem
had so far defeated him: that he was a foreigner and did not know
what sort of women Irishwomen are. It was not as if he had not done
his systematic best to find out, beginning with a course of reading
through the novels of her country. A vain exercise. With the exception
of the Molly Bloom of James Joyce, the Irish Novel had not only failed
to present him with any fascinating woman but it had presented him
with, in his sense of the word, no woman at all. Irish fiction was a lot of
19th Century *connerie* about half-savage Brueghelesque peasants, or
urban *petits fonctionnaires* who invariably solved their frustrations by
getting drunk on religion, patriotism or undiluted whisky, or by taking
flight to England. Pastoral melodrama (Giono at his worst). Or pastoral humbuggery (Bazin at his most sentimental). Or, at its best, pastoral lyricism (Daudet and rose water). As for Molly Bloom! He enjoyed
the smell of every kissable pore of her voluptuous body without for one
moment believing that she had ever existed. James Joyce in drag.

"But," he had finally implored his best friend in Ailesbury Road,
Hamid Bey, the third secretary of the Turkish embassy, whose amorous
secrets he willingly purchased with his own, "if it is too much to expect
Ireland to produce a bevy of Manons, Mitsous, Gigis, Claudines,
Kareninas, Oteros, Leahs, Sanseverinas, what about those great-thighed,
vast-bottomed creatures dashing around the country on horseback like
Diana followed by all her minions? Are they not interested in love?
And, if so, why aren't there novels about them?"

His friend laughed a gelatinous laugh, like Turkish delight and replied in English in his laziest Noel Coward drawl, all the vowels fron-
tal, as if he were talking through bubble gum, all his Rs either left out
where they should be, as in *deah* or *cleah*, or inserted where they should
not be, as in *India-r* or *Iowa-r*.

"My deah Ferdy, did not your deah fatheh or your deah momma-r
eveh tell you that all Irish hohsewomen are in love with their hohses?
And anyway, it is well known that the favorite pinup gihl of Ahland is
a gelding."

"Naked?" Ferdinand asked coldly, and refused to believe him,
remembering that his beloved had been a hohsewoman and satisfied
that he was not a gelding. Instead, he approached the Italian ambassador at a cocktail party, given by the Indonesian embassy, to whisper to

him about *l'amore irlandese* in his best stage-French manner, eyebrows
lifted above fluttering eyelids, voice as hoarse as, he guessed, his ex-
cellency's mind would be on its creaking way back to memories of
Gabin, Jouvet, Brasseur, Fernandel, Montand. It proved to be another
futile exercise. His ex groaned as operatically as every Italian groans
over such vital, and lethal, matters as the Mafia, food, taxation and
women, threw up his hands, made a face like a more than usually desic-
cated De Sica and sighed, "*Les femmes d'Irlande? Mon pauvre gars!
Elles sont d'une chasteté*"—he paused and roared the adjective—"*FOR-
MIDABLE!*"

Ferdinand had heard this yarn about feminine chastity in other countries and (with those two or three exceptions already mentioned) found
it true only until one had established the precise local variation of the
meaning of chastity. But how was he to discover the Irish variation? In
the end, it was Celia herself who, unwittingly, revealed it to him and,
in doing so, dispelled his last doubts about her susceptibility, inflam-
mability and volatility—despite the very proper sisters of the Spanish
Steps.

The revelation occurred one night in early May—her Meehawl being
away in the west, presumably checking what she contemptuously called
his Gaelic-squeaking scissors. Ferdy had driven her back to his flat for a
nightcap after witnessing the prolonged death of Mimi in *La Bohème*.
She happened to quote to him Oscar Wilde's remark about the death
of Little Nell that only a man with a heart of stone could fail to laugh
at it; and in this vein they had continued for a while over the rolling
brandy, seated side by side on his settee, his hand on her bare shoulder
leading him to hope more and more fondly that this might be his horizon night, until, suddenly, she asked him a coldly probing question.

"Ferdy! Tell me exactly why we did not believe in the reality of
Mimi's death."

His palm oscillated gently between her clavicle and her scapula.

"Because, my little cabbage, we were not expected to. Singing away
like a lark? With her last breath? And no lungs? I am a Frenchman. I
understand the nature of reality and can instruct you about it. Art, my
dear Celia, is art because it is not reality. It does not copy or represent
nature. It improves upon it. It embellishes it. This is the kernel of the
classical French attitude to life. And," he beamed at her, "to love. We
make of our wildest feelings of passion the gentle art of love."

He suddenly stopped fondling her shoulder and surveyed her with
feelings of chagrin and admiration. The sight of her belied his words.
Apart from dressing with taste and, he felt certain, undressing with

even greater taste, she used no art at all. She was as innocent of make-up as a peasant girl of the Vosges. Had he completely misread her? Was she that miracle, a fully ripe peach brought into the center of the city some 20 years ago from a walled garden in the heart of the country, still warm from the sun, still glowing, downy, pristine, innocent as the dew? He felt her juice dribbling down the corner of his mouth. Was this the missing piece of her jigsaw? An ensealed innocence? If so, he had wasted six whole weeks. This siege could last six years.

"No, Ferdy!" she said crossly. "You have it all wrong. I'm talking about life, not about art. The first and last thought of any real Catholic girl on her deathbed would be to ask for a priest. She was facing her God."

Who at once pointed a finger at him through the chandelier? Within seconds they were discussing love among the English, Irish, French, Indians, Moslems, Italians, naturally the Papacy, Alexander the Sixth and incest, Savonarola and dirty pictures, Joan of Arc and martyrdom, death, sin, hell-fire, Cesare Borgia, who, she insisted, screamed for a priest to pray for him at the end.

"A lie," he snarled, "that some beastly priest told you in a sermon when you were a schoolgirl. Pray? I suppose," he challenged furiously, "you pray even against me."

Abashed, she shook her autumn-gold head at him, threw a kipper-eyed glance up to the chandelier, gave him a ravishingly penitential smile and sighed like an unmasked sinner.

"Ah, Ferdy! Ferdy! If you only knew the real truth about me! Me pray against you? I don't pray at all. You remember Mimi's song at the end of the first act? 'I do not always go to Mass, but I pray quite a bit to the good Lord.' Now, I hedge my bets in a very different way. I will not pray, because I refuse to go on my knees to anybody. Yet, there I go meekly trotting off to Mass every Sunday and holyday. And why? Because I am afraid not to, because it would be a mortal sin not to." She gripped his tensed hand, trilling her Rs over the threshold of her lower lip and tenderly umlauting her vowels. Dürling. Cöward. Li-er. "Amn't I the weak cöward, dürling? Amn't I the awful li-er? A crook en-tirrrely?"

Only a thin glint of streetlight peeping between his curtains witnessed the wild embrace of a man illuminated by an avowal so patently bogus as to be the transparent truth.

"You a liar?" he gasped, choking with laughter. "You a shivering coward? A double-faced hedger of bets? A deceiving crook? A wicked sinner? For the last five minutes you have been every single one of them by pretending to be them. What you really are is a woman full of cool, hardheaded discretion, which you would like to sell to me as a charming weakness. Full of dreams that you would like to disguise as wicked lies. Of common sense that it suits you to pass off as crookedness. Of worldly wisdom still moist from your mother's nipple that, if you thought you would get away with the deception, you would stoop to call a sin. My dearest Celia, your yashmak reveals by pretending to conceal. Your trick is to be perfection masquerading as villainy. I think it is enchanting."

For the first time, he saw her in a rage.

"But it is *all* true. I *am* a liar. I *do* go to Mass every Sunday. I do *not* pray. I *am* afraid of damnation. I——"

He silenced her with three fingers laid momentarily on her lips.

"Of course you go to Mass every Sunday. My father, a master tailor of Nancy, used to go to Mass every Sunday, not once but three times, and always as conspicuously as possible. Why? Because he was a tailor. Just as you do because you run a boutique. You don't pray? Sensible woman. Why should you bother your *Bon Dieu*, if there is a *Bon Dieu*, with your pretty prattle about things that He knew all about a thousand million years before you were a twinkle in your mother's eye? My dearest and most perfect love, you have told me everything about Irishwomen that I need to know. None of you says what you think. Every one of you means what you don't say. None of you thinks about what she is going to do. But every one of you knows it to the last dot. You dream like opium eaters and your eyes are as calm as resting snow. You are all of you realists to your bare backsides. Yes, yes, yes, yes, yes, you will say this is true of all women, but it is not. It is not even true of Frenchwomen. They may be realists in lots of things. But in love, they are just as stupid as all the rest of us. But not Irishwomen! Or not, I swear it, if they are all like you. I'll prove it to you with a single question. Would you, like Mimi, live for the sake of love in a Paris garret?"

She gravely considered a proposition that sounded delightfully like a proposal.

"How warm would the garret be? Would I have to die of consumption? You remember how the poor bohemian poet had to burn his play to keep them all from being famished with the cold."

"Yes!" Ferdy laughed. "And as the fire died away, he said, 'I always knew that first act was too damned short.' But you are dodging my question."

"I suppose, dürling, any woman's answer to your question would

depend on how much she was in love with whoever he was. Or
wouldn't it?"

Between delight and fury he dragged her into his arms.

"You know perfectly well, you sweet slut, that what I am asking you
is, Do you love me a lot or a little? A garretful or a palaceful? Which is
it?"

Chuckling, she slid down low in the settee and smiled up at him between sleepy-cat eyelashes.

"And you, Ferdy, must know perfectly well that it is pointless to ask
any woman silly questions like that. If some man I loved very much
were to ask me, 'Do you love me, Celia?' I would naturally answer,
'No!' in order to make him love me more. And if it was some man I did
not like at all, I would naturally say, 'Yes, I love you so much I think
we ought to get married,' in order to cool him off. Which, Ferdy, do
you want me to say to you?"

"Say," he whispered adoringly, "that you hate me beyond the ninth
circle of Dante's hell."

She made a grave face.

"I'm afraid, Ferdy, the fact is I don't like you at all. Not at all! Not
one least little bit at all, at all."

At which lying, laughing, enlacing and unlacing moment they kissed
pneumatically and he knew that if all Irishwomen were Celias, then the
rest of mankind were mad ever to have admired women of any other
race.

Their lovemaking was not as he had foredreamed it. She hurled her
clothes to the four corners of the room, crying out, "And about time,
too! Ferdy, what the hell have you been footling around for during the
last six weeks?" Within five minutes she smashed him into bits. In her
passion she was more like a lion than a lioness. There was nothing
about her either titillating or erotic, indolent or indulgent, she was as
wild, as animal, as unrestrained as a forest fire. When, panting beside
her, he recovered enough breath to speak, he expressed his surprise that
one so cool, so ladylike in public could be so different in private. She
grunted peacefully and said in her muted brogue, "Ah, shure, dürling,
everything changes in the beddaroom."

He woke at 3:25 in the morning with that clear bang so familiar to
everybody who drinks too much after the chimes at midnight, rose to
drink a pint of cold water, lightly opened his curtains to survey the
predawn May sky and, turning toward the bed, saw the pallid street
lamp's light fall across her sleeping face, as calm, as soothed, as innocently sated as a baby filled with its mother's milk. He sat on the side

of the bed looking down at her for a long time, overcome by the terrifying knowledge that he had, for the first time in his life, fallen in love.

The eastern clouds were growing as pink as petals while they drank the coffee he had quietly prepared. Over it he arranged in unnecessarily gasping whispers for their next meeting the following afternoon—"*This* afternoon!" he said joyously—at 3:25 o'clock, henceforth his Mystic Hour for Love, but only on the strict proviso that he would not count on her unless she had set three red geraniums in a row on the window sill of her boutique before three o'clock and that she, for her part, must divine a tragedy if the curtains of his flat were not looped high when she approached at 3:20 o'clock. He could, she knew, have more easily checked with her by telephone, but also knowing how romantically, voluptuously, erotically minded he was, she accepted with an indulgent amusement what he obviously considered ingenious devices for increasing the voltage of passion by the trappings of conspiracy. To herself she thought, "Poor boy! He's been reading too many books."

Between two P.M. and three P.M. that afternoon, she was entertained to see him pass her boutique three times in dark glasses. She cruelly made him pass a fourth time before, precisely at three o'clock, she gave him the pleasure of seeing two white hands with pink fingernails—not, wickedly, her own: her assistant's—emerge from under the net curtains of her window to arrange three small scarlet geraniums on the sill. He must have hastened perfervidly to the nearest florist to purchase the pink roses whose petals, when she rang his bell five cruel moments after his Mystic Hour, she found tessellating the silk sheets of his bed. His gramophone, muted by a bath towel, was murmuring Wagner. A joss stick in a brass bowl stank cloyingly. He had cast a pink-silk head scarf over the bedside lamp. His dressing-table mirror had been tilted so that from where they lay they could see themselves. Within five minutes he did not see, hear nor smell anything, tumbling, falling, hurling headlong to consciousness of her wild laughter at the image of her bottom mottled all over by his clinging rose petals. It cost him a brutal effort to laugh with her, at himself.

All that afternoon he talked only of flight, divorce and remarriage. To cool him, she encouraged him. He talked of it again and again every time they met. Loving him, she humored him. On the Wednesday of their third week as lovers, they met briefly and chastely, because her Meehawl was throwing a dinner at their house that evening for a few of his business colleagues previous to flying out to Manchester for a two-day convention of cutlers. Ferdy at once promised her to lay in a store of champagne, caviar, *pâté de foie* and brioches, so that they need not stir from their bed for the whole of those two days.

"Not even once?" she asked coarsely, and he made a *moue* of disapproval.

"You do not need to be all that realistic, Celia!"

Already by 3:15 that Thursday afternoon, he was shuffling nervously from window to window. By 3:25 he was muttering, "I hope she's not going to be late." He kept feeling the champagne to be sure it was not getting too cold. At 3:35 he moaned, "She *is* late!" At 3:40 he cried out in a jealous fury, glaring up and down the street, "The slut is betraying me!" At a quarter to four his bell rang, he leaped to the door. She faced him as coldly as a newly carved statue of Carrara marble. She repulsed his arms. She would not stir beyond his door mat. Her eyes were dilated.

"It is Meehawl!" she whispered.

"He has found us out?"

"It's the judgment of God on us both!"

The word smacked his face.

"He is dead?" he cried, hopefully brushing aside his fear and despair.

"A stroke."

She made a violent, downward swish with the side of her open palm.

"*Une attaque? De paralysie?*"

"He called at the boutique on his way to the plane. He said goodbye to me. He walked out to the taxi. I went into my office to prepare my vanity case and do peepee before I met you. The taxi driver ran in, shouting that he had fallen in a fit on the pavement. We drove him to ninety-six. That's Saint Vincent's. The hospital near the corner of the green. He is conscious. But he cannot speak. One side of him is paralyzed. He may not live."

She turned and went galloping down the stairs.

His immediate rebound was to roar curses on all the gods that never were. Why couldn't the old fool have his attack next week? His second thought was glorious. "He will die, we will get married." His third made him weep, "Poor little cabbage!" His fourth thought was, "The brioches I throw out, the rest into the fridge." His fifth, sixth and seventh were three Scotches while he rationally considered all her possible reactions to the brush of the dark angel's wing. Only time, he decided, would tell.

But when liars become the slaves of time, what can time do but lie like them? A vat, solid-looking enough for old wine; it leaks at every stave. A ship rigged for the wildest seas; it is rust-bound to its bollards on the quay. She said firmly that nothing between them could change. He refuted her. Everything had changed, for the better. He rejoiced when the doctors said their patient was doomed. After two more weeks, she reported that the doctors were impressed by her husband's remarkable tenacity. He spoke of flight. She spoke of time. One night as she lay hot in his arms in his bed, he shouted triumphantly to the chandelier that when husbands are imprisoned, lovers are free. She demurred, saying that she could never spend a night with him in her own bed; not with a resident housekeeper upstairs. He tossed it aside. What matter where they slept? He would be happy sleeping with her in the Phoenix Park. She was furious. She pointed out that it was raining. "Am I a seal?" He proffered her champagne. She confessed the awful truth. This night was the last night they could be together.

"While he was dying, a few of his business pals used to call on him at the nursing home—the place all Dublin knows as ninety-six. Now that the old devil is refusing to die, they refuse to call on him anymore. I am his only faithful visitor. He so bores everybody. And with his paralyzed mouth, they don't know what the hell he is saying. Do you realize, Ferdy, what this means? He is riding me like a nightmare. He rang me four times the day before yesterday at the boutique. He rang again while I was here with you having a drink. He said whenever I go out I must leave a number where he can call me. The night before last, he rang me at three o'clock in the morning. Thank God I was back in my own bed and not here with you. He said he was lonely. Has terrible dreams. The nights are long. He is frightened. That if he gets another stroke, he will die. Dürling! I cannot spend a whole night with you again!"

Ferdy became Napoleon. He took command of the campaign. He accompanied her on her next visit to 96. This, he discovered, was a luxury (i.e., Victorian) nursing home in Lower Leeson Lane, where only cardinals died, only coal fires were in order, where everybody was presented with a menu from which to choose his lunch and dinner. The carpets were an inch thick. The only internal sound heard was the Mass bell tinkling along the corridors early every morning as the priest went from room to room with the Eucharist for the dying faithful. The Irish, Ferdy decided, know how to die. He, knowing no better, bore with him copies of *Le Canard Enchaîné* and *La Vie Parisienne*. Celia deftly impounded them. "Do you want him to die of high blood pressure? Do you want the nuns to think he's a queer? A fellow who prefers women to drink?" Seated at one side of the bed, facing her seated at the other, he watched her, with her delicate lace-edged handkerchief (so disturb-

ingly reminiscent of her lace-edged panties), wiping the unshaven chin
of the dribbling half-idiot on the pillow. In an unconsumed rage, he
lifted his eyebrows into his hair, surveyed the moving mass of clouds
above Georgian Dublin, smoothed his already blackboard-smooth
hair, gently touched the white carnation in his lapel, forced himself to
listen calmly to the all-but-unintelligible sounds dribbling from the
dribbling corner of the twisted mouth, and agonizingly asked himself
by what unimaginably devious machinery, and for what indivinable purpose, the universe had been so arranged since the beginning of time
that this bronze-capped, pastel-eyed, rosy-breasted, round-buttocked, exquisite flower of paradise sitting opposite him should, in the first place,
have matched and mated with this slob between them, and then, or
rather *and then*, or rather AND THEN make it so happen that he, Ferdinand Louis Jean-Honoré Clichy, of 9 *bis* Rue des Dominicains,
Nancy, in the Department of Meurthe et Moselle, population 123,428,
altitude 212 meters, should happen to discover her in remote Dublin
and fall so utterly into her power that if he were required at that particular second to choose between becoming ambassador to the Court of
Saint James for life and one night alone in bed with her, he would have
at once replied, "Even for one hour!"

He gathered that the object on the pillow was addressing him.

"Oh, mosheer! Thacks be to the evercliving and cloving Gog I khav
mosht devote clittle wife in all Khlistendom. . . . I'd be chlost without
her. . . . Ah, mosheer! If you ever dehide to marry, marry an Irihk-
woman. . . . Mosht fafeful cleatures in all exhishtench. . . . Would
any Frenchwoman attend shoopid ole man chlike me the way Chelia
doesh?"

Ferdy closed his eyes. She was tenderly dabbing the spittled corners
of the distorted mouth. What happened next was that a sister took
Celia out to the corridor for a few private words and that Ferdy at once
leaned forward and whispered to the apparently immortal O'Sullivan,
"Monsieur O'Sullivan, your wife does not look at all well. I fear she is
wilting under the strain of your illness."

"Chlstrain!" the idiot said in astonishment. "What chlstrain? I
khlsee no khlsignch of any chlstrain!"

Ferdy whispered with a gentle fierceness that when one is gravely ill,
one may sometimes fail to observe the grave illness of others.

"We have to remember, monsieur, that if your clittle wife were to
collapse under the chlstr . . . under the *strain* of your illness, it would
be very serious, for *you!*"

After that day, the only reason he agreed to accompany his love on these painful and piteous visits to 96 was that they always ended with O'Sullivan's begging him to take his poor clittle, cloving clittle, devote clittle pet of a wife to a movie for a relaxation and a rest, or for a drink in the Russell, or to the evening races in the park; whereupon they would both hasten, panting, to Ferdy's flat to make love swiftly, wildly and vindictively—swiftly because their time was limited, wildly because her Irish storms had by now become Oriental typhoons of rage, and he had simultaneously become cured of rose petals, Wagner, dim lights and pink champagne, and vindictively in order to declare and crush their humiliation at being subject to another man in another bed.

Inevitably, the afternoon came—it was now July—when Ferdy's pride and nerves cracked. He decided that enough was enough. They must escape to freedom. At once.

"Celia! If we have to fly to the end of the world! It won't really ruin my career. My master is most sympathetic. In fact, since I hinted to him that I am in love with a *belle mariée*, he does nothing but complain about his wife to me. And he can't leave her, his career depends on her, she is the daughter of a secretary of state for foreign affairs—and rich. He tells me that at worst I would be moved off to some place like Los Angeles or Reykjavík. Celia! My beloved flower! We could be as happy as two puppies in a basket in Iceland."

She permitted a measure of Icelandic silence to create itself and then asked reflectively if it is ever warm in Iceland, at which he pounced with a loud "What do you mean? What are you asking? What is really in your mind?"

She said, "Nothing, dürling," for how could she dare say that whereas he could carry his job with him wherever he went, she, to be with him, would have to give up her lovely old, friendly old, silly old boutique on the green where her friends came to chat over morning coffee, where she met every rich tourist who visited Dublin, where she made nice money of her own, where she felt independent and free; just as she could never hope to make him understand why she simply could not just up and out and desert her husband.

"But there's nothing to hold you here! In his condition, you'd be sure to get custody of the children. Apart from the holidays, they could remain in school here the year round."

So he had been thinking it all out. She stroked his hairy chest.

"I know."

"The man, even at his best, you've acknowledged it yourself, over and over, is a fool. He is a muzhik. He is a bore."

"I know!" she groaned. "Who should better know what a crasher he is? He is a child. He hasn't had a new idea in his head for thirty years. There have been times when I've hated the smell of him. He reminds me of a hotel ashtray. Times when I've wished to God that a thief would break into the house some night and kill him. And," at which point she began to weep on his tummy, "I know now that there is only one thief who will come for him and he is so busy elsewhere that it will be years before he catches up with him. And then I think of the poor bastard in his hospital bed, unable to stir, scarcely able to talk, looking up at his ceiling, incontinent, practically a wet-and-dirty case, with no scissors, no golf, no friends, no nothing, except me. How can I desert him?"

Ferdy clasped his hands behind his head, stared up at heaven's pure ceiling and heard her weeping like the summer rain licking his window-pane. He created a long Irish silence. He heard the city whispering. Far away. Farther away. And then not at all.

"And to think," he said at last, "that I once called you a realist!"

She considered this. She, too, no longer heard the muttering of the city's traffic.

"This is how the world is made," she decided.

"I presume," he said briskly, "that you do realize that all Dublin knows that you are meanwhile betraying your beloved Meehawl with me?"

"I know that there's not one of those bitches who wouldn't give her left breast to be where I am at this moment."

They got out of bed and began to dress.

"And, also meanwhile, I presume you do *not* know that they have a snotty name for you?"

"What name?"—and she turned her bare back for the knife.

"They call you The Diplomatic Hack."

For five minutes, neither of them spoke.

While he was stuffing his shirt into his trousers and she, dressed fully except for her frock, was patting her penny-brown hair into place before his mirror, he said to her, "Furthermore, I suppose you do realize that whether I like it or not, I shall one day be shifted to some other city in some other country. What would you do then? For once in your life, tell me the plain truth! Just to bring you to the crunch. What would you do then?"

She turned, comb in hand, leaned her behind against his dressing table and looked him straight in the fly, which he was still zipping.

"Die," she said flatly.

"That," he said coldly, "is a manner of speech. Even so, would you

consider it an adequate conclusion to a love that we have so often said
is forever?"

They were now side by side in the mirror, she tending her brown
hair, he his black, like any long-married couple. She smiled a little
sadly.

"Forever? Dürling, does love know that lovely word? You love me. I
know it. I love you. You know it. We will always know it. People die,
but if you have ever loved them, they are never gone. Apples fall from
the tree, but the tree never forgets its blossoms. But marriage is
different. You remember the day he advised you that if you ever
marry, you should marry an Irishwoman. Don't, Ferdy! If you do, she
will stick to you forever. And you wouldn't really want that." She lifted
her frock from the back of a chair and stepped into it. "Zip me up,
dürling, will you? Even my awful husband. There must have been a
time when I thought him attractive. We used to sail together. Play tennis together. He was very good at it. After all, I gave him two children.
What's the date? They'll be home for the holidays soon. All I have left
for him now is contempt and compassion. It is our bond."

Bewildered, he went to the window, buttoning his flowered waistcoat.
He remembered from his café days as a student a ruffle of aphorisms
about love and marriage. Marriage begins only when love ends. Love
opens the door to marriage and quietly steals away. *Il faut toujours s'ap-
puyer sur les principes de l'amour—ils finissent par en céder.* What
would she say to that? Lean heavily on the principles of love—they will
always crumple in the end. Marriage bestows on love the tenderness
due to a parting guest. Every *affaire de coeur* ends as a *mariage de con-
venance.* He turned to her, arranging his jacket, looking for his keys and
his hat. She was peeking into her handbag, checking her purse for her
keys and her lace handkerchief, gathering her gloves, giving a last
glance at her hat. One of the things he liked about her was that she always wore a hat.

"You are not telling me the truth, Celia," he said, quietly. "Oh, I
don't mean about loving me. I have no doubt about you on that score.
But when you persuade yourself that you can't leave him because you
feel compassion for him, that is just your self-excuse for continuing a
marriage that has its evident advantages."

She smiled lovingly at him.

"Will you ring me tomorrow, dürling?"

"Of course."

"I love you very much, dürling."

"And I love you, too. Until tomorrow, then."

"Until tomorrow, dürling."

As usual, he let her go first.

That afternoon was some two years ago. Nine months after it, he was transferred to Brussels. As often as he could wangle special leave of absence, and she could get a relative to stay for a week with her bedridden husband, now back in his own house, they would fly to Paris or London to be together again. He would always ask solicitously after her husband's health, and she would always sigh and say his doctors had assured her that "he will live forever." Once, in Paris, passing a church, he, for some reason, asked her if she ever went to confession. She waved the question away with a laugh, but later that afternoon he returned to it pertinaciously.

"Yes. Once a year."

"Do you tell your priest about us?"

"I tell him that my husband is bedridden. That I am in love with another man. That we make love. And that I cannot give you up. As I can't, dürling."

"And what does he say to that?"

"They all say the same. That it is an impasse. Only one dear old Jesuit gave me a grain of hope. He said that if I liked, I could pray to God that my husband might die."

"And have you so prayed?"

"Dürling, why should I?" she asked gaily, as she stroked the curly hair between his two pink buttons. "As you once pointed out to me yourself, all this was foreknown millions of years ago."

He gazed at the ceiling. In her place, unbeliever though he was, he would, for love's sake, have prayed with passion. Not that she had said directly that she had not. Maybe she had. Two evasions in one sentence! It was all more than flesh and blood could bear. It was the Irish variation all over again: Never let your left ass know what your right ass is doing. He decided to give her one more twirl. When he got home, he wrote tenderly to her, "You are the love of my life!"

He could hear her passionate avowal, "And me, too, dürling!"

What she actually replied was, "Don't I know it?"

Six months later, he had maneuvered himself into the consular service and out of Europe, to Los Angeles. He there consoled his broken heart with a handsome creature named Rosie O'Connor. Quizzed about his partiality for the Irish, he could only flap his hands and say, "I don't know. They are awful liars. There isn't a grain of romance in them. And they are such faithless creatures."

Her Son

by ISAAC BASHEVIS SINGER

One day when I had been in New York only a short time, a poet invited me out to Sholum's Café for lunch. He had a reputation among the Yiddish writers as a dandy, a cynic, a womanizer. He had a wife so fat that she could hardly get through a door—or so someone had told me. She ate out of anguish over her husband's love affairs. Although he was close to seventy, his hair was still a golden blond. He had blue eyes, a high forehead, and a nose and chin that gave the impression of being worldly-wise. He wore an English suit and smoked a Havana cigar. His shirt was striped red and gray, his tie embroidered with gold. He had a diamond ring and monogrammed links in his cuffs. It struck me that he resembled Oscar Wilde. He wrote like Wilde too—with paradoxes and aphorisms. I was twenty-nine, newly arrived from Warsaw, and he spoke to me like an older writer to a beginner, offering advice. He said, "You look like a yeshiva boy, but I can tell from your writing that you know about women."

The door of the café opened to admit a man in a crushed hat. His face was pale, unshaven; his eyes looked bloodshot, sleepy, and full of the gloom of the depressed. He came directly to our table. Without a word, my host—I'll call him Max Blender—reached into his pocket, took out a check, and handed it over. "Well, Bill, are you seeing your way clear yet?" he asked.

"Things just keep getting worse," the man grumbled.

"The loan didn't help?"

"Nothing will help me any more." He spoke Yiddish with an American accent. Although his voice was low, it had the quality of a muffled shriek. Bitterness hovered about his lips. One shoulder was higher than the other. The cheap tie he was wearing had twisted to the side. A button was missing from his coat. From a distance, he had appeared to be in his fifties, but up close I saw that he was much younger. "Well, I'll be going," he said.

"Maybe you'll have a glass of coffee with us? This young man is—"

"I have to go!"

"Where?"

"To kiss somebody's behind so I can borrow a hundred dollars to pay on the mortgage. If I can't get it, I'll lose the house and end up in the street with my family."

Max Blender bit down on his lower lip. "Wait. I'll give you the hundred dollars, and you won't have to kiss anyone's behind."

"It's all the same to me."

Max Blender opened his wallet and counted out a hundred dollars. He shook his head and winked at me. Bill scooped up the money, mumbled something that might have been goodbye, and left. He didn't glance at me.

"A relative, eh?" I said.

Max Blender smiled, showing a mouthful of false teeth. "A son, though not mine. He adopted me for a father, and he had the right to do it. But how did he know that he had this right? I'll tell you the story, if you like. I swear on Asmodeus's beard that I've never told it before. I wanted to write about it myself, but I'm a poet, not a prose writer. Wait—I'll order another plate of blintzes. Let's spend the day together."

"My pleasure."

"Just let me light up." He took out a cigar and rolled it between his fingers.

"I'll make it as brief as I can," he said. "I had a mistress forty years ago who was the greatest love of my life. She has been dead for thirty-seven years, but a day doesn't go by that I don't think about her. You might say, not an hour. I've had other big affairs. Even at my age I'm into this foolishness right up to here—" he held his finger to his throat —"but no one compares to what she was to me and no one ever will.

She had a husband—what else? And not only a husband but a husband who loved her with a savage passion. And she hated him as intensely as he loved her. Her name was Sonia—the most common name a girl from Russia can have. And there was nothing extraordinary about her appearance—the usual dark eyes, the black braids, the whole claptrap that's described in Yiddish novels. But when I met her at the Szydlaw Society—my mother's people came from Szydlaw—and talked with her a few minutes, I fell desperately in love and, believe me, in this case 'desperately' isn't an exaggeration. I felt a burning in all my limbs, and what's more, I realized that she was going through the very same thing. We grew deathly afraid of each other and of what we were starting. Her husband was sitting up there on the dais—he was president of the society—pounding the gavel to keep the crowd quiet. I forgot to tell you the main thing—she was twelve years older than I and had four children. All girls. They lived on Avenue C, downtown, and he was— thank God for that—a traveling salesman. He sold textiles, and he often went to Fall River, Massachusetts, which is the Lodz of America. Chaskell Wallach was his name.

"Sonia was something of an intellectual. She had read Artsybashev's *Sanin* and could recite several pages out of *Eugene Onegin*. She had tried to write poems in Yiddish. She attended the opera when her husband was on the road. She read Socialist pamphlets. Chaskell Wallach both hated and admired her gentility. He had a huge nose, the bulging eyes of a golem, and the voice of an ox. He couldn't speak—only shout. Sonia told me that even when he was in bed with her he shouted. He had had the silly ambition to be head of the Szydlaw Society. At the society's meetings, they talked about only one thing—the cemetery. He attended the funeral of every member who died. To this boor, death had been the means for becoming president, for gorging himself on knishes and drinking liquor at the society's expense.

"He knew as much about sex and love as a eunuch. In time, Sonia told me that during all the years they had been together he had never satisfied her. She began to dream about a lover right after their wedding, but she was essentially a small-town, modest woman, although in moments of passion she could utter words that might surprise the Marquis de Sade.

"Our affair began at our very first meeting. Sonia said that she felt warm, and I took her to Houston Street for ice cream. Going down the stairs, we began to kiss and bite each other like two lunatics, and by the time we reached the ice-cream parlor we had made plans to run away together to California or Europe.

"There are fires that start spontaneously. Maybe you've heard of the Triangle Building fire? In a few minutes, tens or maybe hundreds of factory girls were burned to death there. A fatality doesn't need any kindling.

"I'm not a scientist, but I've read some science. I know the theories and all the babble about evolution. It's a big lie. The universe happened in one second. God alone, if He exists, simply became. There was nothing. Suddenly it was all there—God, the world, life, love, death. Oh, here are our blintzes."

"The blintzes didn't come all of a sudden," I remarked.

"Eh? Not at Sholum's Café. If this cook were God, we would still be in Genesis."

We ate the blintzes, and Max Blender went on. "All the talk about running away came to nothing. A mother of four doesn't run away. The old game of deception began. When Chaskell was on the road, there was nothing to stop us. She met me at a hotel or at a furnished room that I rented. I was married by then, but my wife and I had no children. When he stayed in town, that's when the trouble began. He didn't leave her side for a moment. He couldn't write or figure, and she served as his secretary. Besides, he insisted that she prepare his favorite dishes—stuffed derma, fat soups, and the devil knows what. She would sneak out for an hour and we would fall on each other with a terrible hunger. She told baffling stories. She had the most fantastic dreams and visions—or how should I call them—while awake. As for me, near her I became a veritable giant. The usual love affair cools off in time, but ours grew stronger with the years, and such affairs have no good end.

"My wife found out that I loved somebody else—she had learned to accept my minor affairs—and she used every means that a wife can employ to get me away from Sonia. She took her sister's daughter into our house—a young girl of nineteen—and tried to seduce her in my behalf. If I hadn't experienced such a thing, I wouldn't believe the lengths a jealous woman will go to. She threatened to be unfaithful to me, but those who betray don't threaten. She was one of those women who can have only one man. Whether this is biological or a kind of self-hypnosis, I don't know. Hypnosis is itself biological. The whole human history is a history of hypnosis.

"Why drag it on? Sonia's husband found out about us. When I learned that he knew, I was scared to death. He could kill me with one blow. He had a pair of paws like a coachman. I'm no hero, and it never was my ideal to die for romance. I was so scared I left town for a while.

"Sonia called to tell me what grief he was causing her. He broke all the dishes in the house. He beat her. He terrorized the children. He told the members of the society about us. But for some reason that I still don't understand, he never tried to take revenge against me. He didn't even telephone my wife, which is the least you'd expect. Perhaps he considered all writers charlatans, beneath him to bother with. Anyway, you can't tell what goes on in someone else's brain. A person who has gone through as much as I have knows that psychology is not a science and never will be.

"He used another method—he made Sonia pregnant, so that she wouldn't have time for an affair. After the birth of their fourth daughter, they had exercised a kind of birth control. But now he insisted that she have another child. Sonia was in her forties and didn't believe that she could still get pregnant, but she did, and she gave birth to that fellow you just saw here. He's her son. I know what you're thinking. No, he isn't mine. He looks like his father, although his father was a bruiser and this one is a weakling. As a matter of fact, I suspect that I'm sterile. Anyway, Sonia became pregnant, and it was the hardest pregnancy I have ever seen. When she was in her fifth month, she looked like a woman in her ninth. She became yellow, as if she had jaundice. He had raped her physically and spiritually. We were both sure that she would die in labor. The few times that we managed to meet, she spoke only about death. She made me promise that when my time came I'd be buried beside her. Unfortunately, there's no way I can manage this. Chaskell is already lying there, next to her. The cemetery is so full of the *landsleit* from Szydlaw that I'll have to be buried somewhere else.

"No, she didn't die in labor. She lived nearly two years more, but it was a slow death. Her husband got her pregnant again, and this time she miscarried. I won't go into details. From the day I learned that she was pregnant, all physical relations between us ceased. We had neither the desire nor the opportunity. I had brought about her death, and the sense of guilt was so strong that it left no room for any other feelings. I also began to fear that my own end was close. I went to visit Sonia at her home when she was on her deathbed and she said to me, 'Don't forget Velvel.' Velvel is what his father had named the boy. Later, Velvel became Bill.

"I never liked this child. First, he had killed Sonia, although it hadn't been his fault. Second, he had something of his father's character, albeit none of his strength. A year following Sonia's death, Chaskell remarried and moved to Brooklyn. After the years of the bitterest guilt had passed, the old fire came back—I could only be with other women if I imagined, or forced myself to imagine, that they were she. In moments of intimacy I called them Sonia. For years I suffered from hallucinations. I saw Sonia walking on the street, riding the subway. Once I saw her in Central Park. I had forgotten that she was dead and I began to talk to her, but she disappeared before my very eyes. Sonia had willed me a whole packet of her poems that were written to me. I needn't tell you that they weren't poetry in the usual sense of the word, but they were full of sincerity and therefore had genuine power. Total sincerity is bound to all the forces of nature.

"I read these poems to this day. I know them by heart. A number are about this Velvel that she called Benjamin and Benoni, after Mother Rachel's son. Sonia loved the Scriptures. She had a translation of the Bible in Yiddish that was published by the Christian missionaries. In her poems, she calls him 'your son,' because I was the reason for his coming into the world. It's a kind of spiritual fatherhood.

"Years went by, and I never got in touch with Sonia's children. When she was alive, she told me that the girls—at least the two oldest —cursed my name. Chaskell had confided in his children and had planted a hatred toward me in them. It was because of me that they had a stepmother. Those romantic loves that the poets laud with such lofty phrases actually ruin lives. Our pious grandparents considered what we call love a crime, and that's what it is. If this kind of love were truly virtue, modern man wouldn't deify it so. It is the very opposite of free will—the most extreme form of hypnosis and fatalism. Our God-fearing mothers and fathers lived a decent life without this slavery, and believe me, they were more ready to do things for each other than the people who are involved in love affairs, and this includes myself. Much of the love of our time is sheer betrayal. It is often hatred, too.

"Yes, the years went by and I knew nothing of Chaskell. He was some twenty years older than I. Then I learned that he had died—most probably from overeating. One day the phone rang. It was his son. He said, 'My name is Bill—Velvel. I'm Sonia's son.'

"I didn't care for his voice. Even then I could hear a reproach in it. Nevertheless, I arranged to meet him. He told me that three of his sisters were married. The youngest had gone to England. After Chaskell's death, the family had drifted apart, as families will. Bill recited to me a whole parcel of woes. His father had persecuted him. His sisters both pampered and hated him. He hadn't finished high school. He had had many jobs, but he had been swindled out of each one. He needed money. He looked at me as a son looks at a father who has grown estranged from him. He didn't ask but demanded. Everything about him irked me and I wanted to tell him, 'I don't owe you a thing—get going!' Instead, I gave him everything I had. He took it and didn't even thank me. After he left, I swore not to see that miserable creature again. But I knew that I was helpless against him. I owed him a debt that I could never repay."

Max Blender stopped a moment to order more coffee. "I've seen lots of good-for-nothings in my life," he continued, "but there isn't another schlemiel like this Bill in the world. He did everything upside down. He wouldn't study, he wouldn't train for a profession, he wasn't suited for any business. He failed at whatever he tried. How does the saying go? 'If he was dealing in shrouds, no one would die.' Sometimes a man like that makes a good marriage and gets an energetic wife who helps him. But he married a lazy girl—some lump—and she started right off to spray with children. Five girls. Children get sick and grownups do, too, but his house was like a hospital. Half the income he had went for doctors and medicines. He had other misfortunes, too. Once, there was a fire. Another time, a leak in the plumbing and a ceiling collapsed. With every disaster, he came running to me in a sweat, and I did as much as I could.

"You may not know this, but for years I had a printing shop—my own books earned me next to nothing. I never figured up how much this Bill cost me, but it came to thousands of dollars. I helped him buy that house we spoke about just now. Naturally, he knew he had to make the mortgage payments, but each time one was due he came running to me—always on the last day. One thing I do regret—that I didn't write down all these mishaps of his and catastrophes. A book might have been put together out of them that would have been both tragic and funny.

"There were times when I wanted to rebel. After all, he wasn't my flesh and blood. If I could be sure that there is a hereafter and that Sonia—wherever she is—knows what I'm doing for her darling, then I would move Heaven and earth to take care of him. But if there is nothing on high and Sonia is only a heap of dust, for whom am I sacrificing? It has never even occurred to him to bring me some trifle for Hanukkah or for a birthday. When my books came out, my colleagues occasionally honored me with a banquet. I always asked that an invitation be sent him. He never showed up. You saw how he grabbed what I gave him without so much as a thank you. That's how he has been for years.

"This pipsqueak is my enemy because he somehow knows—call it subconsciousness or simply instinct—that I'm responsible for his being in this world. He carries a grudge against me. He seems to believe that his failures are also somehow connected to me. A cabalist told me that when a man rapes a woman or gives her a child against her will, he drags down from the Throne of Glory a soul that shouldn't be on earth and such a soul strays about as if in the World of Chaos. In the few conversations that I have had with this Bill, he has always said the same thing: that he wouldn't live for long. But this didn't stop him from hinting that I should remember him in my will. He is made up of contradictions. It may be that the whole universe is one big contradiction. God contradicted Himself, and from this the world evolved. How does that philosophy strike you?

"Now listen to this. I told you Bill has five girls—each one brighter than the next. With children, of all things, he did succeed. He didn't have the money to send them to school, but three of them worked their way through college. They got scholarships, too. I was interested in his daughters. I often asked him to let me meet them, but he kept me at a distance. You wouldn't believe this, but I was never invited to this house that I helped him buy. I assumed that he would name one of the girls after his mother, but he gave them all Gentile names: Jean and Beatrice and Nancy and the like. He doesn't want to know any Jewishness. He buys a tree on Christmas. That's actually what caused the fire at his house.

"I've made peace with the fact that as long as I live I'll owe him a debt, but I won't leave him a penny. Besides, I have little to leave. I liquidated my print shop years ago.

"Now comes the real stuff. A couple of months ago, my book *The Amber Idol* came out. Don't look so surprised. I like unusual names. Somewhere inside me I'm a Dadaist, a futurist—give it what name you like. Since there were idols of gold, silver, and stone, why couldn't there have been one of amber? And even if there weren't one in reality, why shouldn't there be one in poetry? You know better than I do that the cabala is based on combinations of letters. When you combine two things that never existed together before, they begin a new existence and perhaps the spheres become enriched from this.

"In brief, my good colleagues arranged an evening for me. They asked whom to invite, and I gave them the list of names and addresses my wife uses to send out New Year's greetings and such. We all ate dinner and we maligned other writers, the way these things go. As I sat there struggling with a quarter of a tough rooster, *Sonia* came to the table. Yes, Bill's daughter. Her name was Nancy, but it was Sonia as she might have looked at eighteen. I sat there speechless. She said to me, 'You don't know me, but I know you. On account of you I studied Yiddish, so that I could read your poems. I'm Sonia's granddaughter!' And she smiled as if the whole thing were a joke.

"I could hardly keep from crying. I said, 'You look exactly like your grandmother.' Just as if she were afraid to shatter my illusions, she told me right then and there that she was going out with a young man and that they were ready to marry. He was a student at Princeton University, and he came from somewhere in Arizona or thereabouts. She told me more: that her future husband—and probably her current lover— had taken an interest in my work too, and wanted to learn Yiddish. He was studying literature.

"I barely heard what she was saying. The pious speak of resurrection, and here was resurrection in front of me. Well, but Sonia was Sonia and this was Nancy. She lacked her grandmother's intensity. I asked her to sit down next to me. Little time remained before the speeches would begin. I heard her say, 'Why don't you ever come to visit us? We all consider you our grandfather. Now that we have a house in the country, you could rest up there or write. We have a guest room.'

" 'A house in the country?' I asked, and she said, 'My father didn't tell you? Imagine it. He can hardly pay off the mortgage on the old house, and here he buys a new house with new debts. My father has to have things to worry about and to rack his brain over. The old house is almost paid for, and we girls are already earning money. We could soon be independent. So he buys a summer house and now there'll be new crises. That's my daddy.'

"The whole thing upset me so that I didn't hear the speeches, and when it came my turn to respond I didn't know what I was saying. I'm considered a good speaker. On that evening I ruined my reputation.

"That night, I didn't sleep a wink. I swore the most solemn oath that when Bill showed up the next time I'd grab him by the collar and say, 'Get to hell out of here.' I called myself 'ox,' 'horse,' 'dumbhead.' A week didn't go by and there he stood before me again, with the twisted buttons, the ragged clothes, the pale face, the gloom in his eyes—an image of despair. He looked at me as the victim looks at the murderer and said, 'Only one way out for me—to hang myself.'

"I wanted to shout, 'Sell your summer house, you faker! You parasite. You lousy schnorrer!' But at the same time I thought, Why shouldn't he be allowed to have a summer house? Why shouldn't he have a place where he can go and rest up? And what if he kept his word and really

hanged himself? I had seen idiots jump out of windows during the
Wall Street crash of 1929 when their stocks fell. The rest you know already I pay like a father. You were just a witness. What do you say to
all this?"

"Spinoza maintains that everything can become a passion. 'Everything' includes all possible emotions," I said.

"Pity, too?"

"Pity, too."

"What about love?" he asked.

"Spinoza compares those in love to the insane," I said.

"Really? Well, he's absolutely right. But after all these years it's too
late for me to become sane."

Translated by Joseph Singer

The Admiralty Spire

by VLADIMIR NABOKOV

You will please pardon me, dear madam, but I am a rude and straight-forward person, so I'll come right out with it: Do not labor under any delusion; this is far from being a fan letter. On the contrary, as you will realize yourself in a minute, it is a rather odd little epistle that—who knows?—might serve as a lesson of sorts not only for you but for other impetuous lady novelists as well. I hasten, first of all, to introduce myself, so that my visual image may show through like a watermark; this is much more honest than to encourage by silence the incorrect conclusions that the eye involuntarily draws from the calligraphy of penned lines. No, in spite of my slender handwriting and the youthful flourish of my commas, I am stout and middle-aged; true, my corpulence is not flabby but has piquancy, zest, waspishness. It is far removed, madam, from the turndown collars of the poet Apukhtin, the fat pet of ladies. But that will do. You, as a writer, have already collected these clues to fill in the rest of me. *Bonjour, madame*. And now let's get down to business.

The other day at a Russian library, relegated by illiterate fate to a murky Berlin alleyway, I took out three or four new items, and among them your novel *The Admiralty Spire*. Neat title, if for no other reason than that it is—isn't it?—an iambic tetrameter, *admiralteyskaya igla*, and a famous Pushkin line to boot. But it was the very neatness of that title that bode no good. Besides, I am generally wary of books published in the backwoods of our expatriation, such as Riga or Reval. Nevertheless, as I was saying, I did take your novel.

Ah, my dear madam; ah, "Mr." Serge Solntsev, how easy it is to guess that the author's name is a pseudonym, that the author is not a man! Every sentence of yours buttons to the left. Your predilection for such expressions as "time passed" or "cuddled up *frileusement* in Mother's shawl," the inevitable appearance of an episodic ensign (straight from imitations of *War and Peace*) who pronounces the letter R as a hard G, and, finally, footnotes with translations of French clichés, afford sufficient indication of your literary skill. But all this is only half the trouble.

Imagine the following: Suppose I once took a walk through a marvelous landscape, where turbulent waters tumble and bindweed chokes the columns of desolate ruins, and then, many years later, in a stranger's house, I come across a snapshot showing me in a swaggering pose in front of what is obviously a pasteboard pillar; in the background there is the whitish smear of a daubed-in cascade, and somebody has inked a mustache on me. Where did the thing come from? Take away this horror! The dinning waters I remember were real and, what is more, no one took a picture of me there.

Shall I interpret the parable for you? Shall I tell you that I had the same feeling, only nastier and sillier, on reading your nimble handiwork, your terrible *Spire*? As my index finger burst the uncut pages open and my eyes raced along the lines, I could only blink from the bewildering shock.

Do you wish to know what happened? Glad to oblige. As you lay massively in your hammock and recklessly allowed your pen to flow like a fountain (a near pun), you, madam, wrote the story of my first love. Yes, a bewildering shock, and, as I, too, am a massive person, bewilderment is accompanied by shortness of breath. By now you and I are both puffing, for, doubtless, you are also dumfounded by the sudden appearance of the hero whom you invented. No, that was a slip—the trimmings are yours, I'll concede, and so are the stuffing and the sauce, but the game (another near pun), the game, madam, is not yours but mine, with my buckshot in its wing. I am amazed—where and how could a lady unknown to me have kidnaped my past? Must I admit the possibility that you are acquainted with Katya—that you are close friends, even—and that she blabbed the whole business, as she whiled away summer crepuscles under the Baltic pines with you, the voracious novelist? But how did you dare, where did you find the gall not only to use Katya's narrative but, on top of that, to distort it so irreparably?

Since the day of our last meeting, there has been a lapse of 16 years—the age of a young bride, an old dog or the Soviet republic. Incidentally, let us note the first, but not the worst by far, of your innumerable and sloppy mistakes: Katya and I are not coevals. I was going on 18 and she on 20. Relying on a tried-and-true method, you have your heroine strip before a full-length mirror, whereupon you proceed to describe her loose hair, ash-blonde, of course, and her young curves. According to you, her cornflower eyes would turn violet in pensive moments—a botanical miracle! You shaded them with the black fringe of lashes, which, if I may make a contribution of my own, seemed longer toward the outer corners, giving her eyes a very special, though illusory slant. Katya's figure was graceful, but she cultivated a slight stoop and would lift her shoulders as she entered a room. You make her a stately maiden with contralto tones in her voice.

Sheer torture. I had a mind to copy out your images, all of which ring false, and scathingly juxtapose my infallible observations, but the result would have been "nightmarish nonsense," as the real Katya would have said, for the Logos allotted me does not possess sufficient precision or power to get disentangled from you. On the contrary, I myself get bogged down in the sticky snares of your conventional descriptions and have no strength left to liberate Katya from your pen. Nevertheless, like Hamlet, I will argue and, in the end, will outargue you.

The theme of your concoction is love: a slightly decadent love with the February Revolution for backdrop, but still, love. Katya has been renamed Olga by you and I have become Leonid. Well and good. Our first encounter, at the house of friends on Christmas Eve; our meetings at the Yusupov Skating Rink; her room, its indigo wallpaper, its mahogany furniture and its only ornament, a porcelain ballerina with lifted leg—this is all right, this is all true. Except that you managed to give it all a taint of pretentious fabrication. As he takes his seat at the Parisiana Cinema on Nevsky Prospekt, Leonid, a student of the Imperial Lyceum, puts his gloves in his three-cornered hat, while a couple of pages later he is already wearing civilian clothes: He doffs his bowler and the reader is faced by an elegant young man, with his hair parted *à l'anglaise* exactly in the middle of his small, lacquered-looking head, and a purple handkerchief drooping out of his breast pocket. I do, in fact, remember dressing like the film actor Max Linder, and recall the generous spurts of *Vezhetal* lotion cooling my scalp, and Monsieur

Pierre taking aim with his comb and flipping my hair over with a lino-type swing, and then, as he yanked off the sheet, yelling to a middle-aged, mustachioed fellow, "Boy! Bross off the 'air!" Today my memory reacts with irony to the breast-pocket handkerchief and white spats of those days but, on the other hand, can in no way reconcile the remem-bered torments of adolescent shaving with your Leonid's "smooth opaque pallor." And I shall leave on your conscience his Lermontovian lusterless eyes and aristocratic profile, as it is impossible to discern much today because of an unexpected increase in fleshiness.

Good Lord, keep me from bogging down in the prose of this lady writer, whom I do not know and do not wish to know, but who has encroached with astonishing insolence on another person's past! How dare you write, "The pretty Christmas tree with its chatoyant lights seemed to augur to them joy jubilant"? You have extinguished the whole tree with your breath, for one adjective placed after the noun for the sake of elegance is enough to kill the best of recollections. Before the disaster—i.e., before your book—one such recollection of mine was the rippling, fragmentary light in Katya's eyes and the cherry reflection on her cheek from the glossy little dollhouse of plasmic paper hanging on a branch as, brushing aside the bristly foliage, she stretched to pinch out the flame of a candle that had gone berserk. What do I have left of all this? Nothing—just a nauseating whiff of literary combustion.

Your version gives the impression that Katya and I inhabited a kind of exquisitely cultured beau monde. You have your parallax wrong, dear lady. That upperclass milieu—the fashionable set, if you will—to which Katya belonged had backward tastes, to put it mildly. Chekhov was considered an "impressionist," the society rhymester Grand Duke Con-stantine, a major poet, and the arch-Christian Aleksandr Blok, a wicked Jew who wrote futuristic sonnets about dying swans and lilac liqueurs. Handwritten copies of album verse, French and English, made the rounds, and were recopied in turn, not without distortions, while the author's name imperceptibly vanished, so that those outpourings quite accidentally assumed a glamorous anonymity; and, generally speaking, it is amusing to juxtapose their meanderings with the clandestine copying of seditious jingles practiced in lower circles. A good indication of how undeservedly these male and female monologs about love were consid-ered most modern examples of foreign lyricism is the fact that the dar-ling among them was a piece by poor Louis Bouilhet, who wrote in the middle of the last century. Reveling in the rolling cadences, Katya would declaim his Alexandrines and scold me for finding fault with a certain highly sonorous strophe in which, after having referred to his passion as a violin bow, the author compares his mistress to a guitar.

Apropos of guitars, madam, you write that "in the evening the young people would gather and Olga would sit at a table and sing in a rich contralto." Oh, well—one more death, one more victim of your sumptuous prose. Yet how I cherished the echoes of modish *tziganshchina* that inclined Katya to singing and me to composing verse! Well do I know that this was no longer authentic gypsy art such as that which enchanted Pushkin and, later, Apollon Grigoriev, but a barely breathing, jaded and doomed muse; everything contributed to her ruin: the gramophone, the war and various so-called *tzigane* songs. It was for good reason that Blok, in one of his customary spells of providence, wrote down whatever words he remembered from gypsy lyrics, as if hastening to save at least this before it was too late.

Should I tell you what those husky murmurs and plaints meant to us? Should I reveal to you the image of a distant, strange world where:

> *Pendulous willow boughs slumber*
> *Drooping low over the pond,*

where, deep in the lilac bushes,

> *The nightingale sobs out her passion,*

and where all the senses are dominated by the memory of lost love, that wicked ruler of pseudo-gypsy romanticism? Katya and I also would have liked to reminisce, but, since we had nothing yet to reminisce about, we would counterfeit the remoteness of time and push back into it our immediate happiness. We transformed everything we saw into monuments to our still inexistent past by trying to look at a garden path, at the moon, at the weeping willows with the same eyes with which *now*—when fully conscious of irreparable losses—we might have looked at that old, waterlogged raft on the pond, at that moon above the black cowshed. I even suppose that, thanks to a vague inspiration, we were preparing in advance for certain things, training ourselves to remember, imagining a distant past and practicing nostalgia, so that subsequently, when that past really existed for us, we would know how to cope with it and not perish under its burden.

But what do you care about all this? When you describe my summer sojourn at the ancestral estate you dub "Glinskoye," you chase me into the woods and there compel me to write verse "redolent of youth and faith in life." This was all not quite so. While the others played tennis (using a single red ball and some Doherty rackets, heavy and saggy, found in the attic) or croquet on a ridiculously overgrown lawn with a dandelion in front of every hoop, Katya and I would make for the kitchen garden and, squatting there, gorge ourselves on two species of strawberry—the bright-crimson Victoria (*sadovaya zemlyanika*) and the Russian *hautbois* (*klubnika*), purplish berries often slimed by frogs; and there was also our favorite *Ananas* variety, unripe-looking yet wonderfully sweet. Without straightening our backs, we moved, grunting, along the furrows, and the tendons behind our knees ached, and our insides filled with a rubious weight. The hot sun bore down, and that sun, and the strawberries, and Katya's frock of tussore silk with darkening blotches under the arms, and the patina of tan on the back of her neck —all of it blended into a sense of oppressive delight; and what bliss it was, without rising, still picking berries, to clasp Katya's warm shoulder and hear her soft laughter and little grunts of greed and the crunch of her joints as she rummaged under the leaves. Forgive me if I pass directly from that orchard, floating by with the blinding gleam of its hothouses and the swaying of hairy poppies along its avenues, to the water closet, where, in the pose of Rodin's *Thinker*, my head still hot from the sun, I composed my verse. It was dismal in all senses of the word, that verse; it contained the trills of nightingales from *tzigane* songs and bits of Blok, and helpless echoes of Verlaine: *Souvenir, souvenir, que me veux-tu? L'automne*—even though autumn was still far off, and my happiness shouted with its marvelous voice nearby, probably over there, by the bowling alley, behind the old lilac bushes under which lay piles of kitchen refuse, and hens walked about. In the evenings, on the veranda, the gramophone's gaping mouth, as red as the lining of a Russian general's coat, would pour forth uncontrollable gypsy passion; or, to the tune of *Under a Cloud the Moon's Hidden*, a menacing voice would mimic the Kaiser: "Give me a nib and a holder, to write ultimatums it's time." And on the garden terrace a game of *Gorodki* (townlets) was going on: Katya's father, his collar unbuttoned, one foot advanced in its soft house boot, would take aim with a cudgel as if he were firing a rifle and then hurl it with force (but wide of the mark) at the "townlet" of skittles while the setting sun, with the tip of its final ray, brushed across the palisade of pine trunks, leaving on each a fiery band. And when night finally fell, and the house was asleep, Katya and I would look at the dark house from the park where we kept huddled on a hard, cold, invisible bench until our bones ached, and it all seemed to us like something that had already once happened long ago: the outline of the house against the pale-green sky, the sleepy movements of the foliage, our prolonged, blind kisses.

In your elegant description, with profuse dots, of that summer, you naturally do not forget for a minute—as we used to forget—that since February of that year the nation was "under the rule of the Provisional Government," and you oblige Katya and me to follow revolutionary events with keen concern; that is, to conduct (for dozens of pages) political and mystical conversations that—I assure you—we never had. In the first place, I would have been embarrassed to speak, with the righteous pathos you lend me, of Russia's destiny and, in the second place, Katya and I were too absorbed in each other to pay much attention to the Revolution. I need but say that my most vivid impression in that respect was a mere trifle: One day, on Million Street in St. Petersburg, a truck packed with jolly rioters made a clumsy but accurate swerve so as to deliberately squash a passing cat, which remained lying there, as a perfectly flat, neatly ironed, black rag (only the tail still belonged to a cat—it stood upright, and the tip, I think, still moved). At the time, this struck me with some deep occult meaning, but I have since had occasion to see a bus, in a bucolic Spanish village, flatten by exactly the same method an exactly similar cat, so I have become disenchanted with hidden meanings. You, on the other hand, have not only exaggerated my poetic talent beyond recognition but have made me a prophet besides, for only a prophet could have talked, in the fall of 1917, about the green pulp of Lenin's deceased brain or the "inner" emigration of intellectuals in Soviet Russia.

No, that fall and that winter we talked of other matters. I was in anguish. The most awful things were happening to our romance. You give a simple explanation: "Olga began to understand that she was sensual rather than passionate, while for Leonid it was the opposite. Their risky caresses understandably inebriated her, but deep inside there always remained a little unmelted piece"—and so on, in the same vulgar, pretentious spirit. What do you understand of our love? So far, I have deliberately avoided direct discussion of it; but now, if I were not afraid of contagion by your style, I would describe in greater detail both its fire and its underlying melancholy. Yes, there was the summer, and the foliage's omnipresent rustle, and the headlong pedaling along all of the park's winding paths, to see who would be the first to race from different directions to the *rond-point*, where the red sand was covered by the writhing serpentine tracks of our rock-hard tires, and each live, everyday detail of that final Russian summer screamed at us in desperation, "I am real! I am now!" As long as all of this sunny euphoria man-

aged to stay on the surface, the innate sadness of our love went no further than the devotion to a nonexistent past. But when Katya and I
once again found ourselves in Petersburg, and it had already snowed
more than once, and the wooden paving blocks were already filmed
with that yellowish layer—a mixture of snow and horse dung—without
which I cannot picture a Russian city, the flaw emerged and we were
left with nothing but torment.

I can see her now, in her black sealskin coat, with a big, flat muff and
gray fur-trimmed boots, walking on her slender legs, as if on stilts, along
a very slippery sidewalk; or in a dark, high-necked dress, sitting on a
blue divan, her face heavily powdered after much crying. As I walked to
her house in the evenings and returned after midnight, I would recognize amid the granite night, under a frosty sky, dove-gray with starlight,
the imperturbable and immutable landmarks of my itinerary—always
those same huge Petersburg objects, lone edifices of legendary times,
adorning the nocturnal wastes and half turning away from the traveler
as all beauty does: It sees you not, it is pensive and listless, its mind is
elsewhere. I would talk to myself, exhorting fate, Katya, the stars, the
columns of a huge, mute, abstracted cathedral; and when a desultory exchange of fire began in the dark streets, it would occur to me casually,
and not without a sense of pleasure, that I might be picked off by a
stray bullet and die right there, reclining on dim snow, in my elegant
fur coat, my bowler askew, among scattered white paperbacks of
Gumilyov's or Mandelshtam's new collections of verse that I had
dropped and that were barely visible against the snow. Or else, sobbing
and moaning as I walked, I would try to persuade myself that it was I
who had stopped loving Katya, as I hastened to gather up all I could recall of her mendacity, her presumption, her vacuity, the pretty patch
masking a pimple, the artificial *grasseyement* that would appear in her
speech when she needlessly switched to French, her invulnerable weakness for titled poetasters and the ill-tempered, dull expression of her eyes
when, for the 100th time, I tried to make her tell me with whom she
had spent the previous evening. And when it was all gathered and
weighed in the balance, I would perceive with anguish that my love,
burdened as it was with all that trash, had settled and lodged only
deeper, and that not even draft horses with iron muscles could haul it
out of the morass. And the following evening again, I would make my
way through the sailor-manned identity checks on the street corners
(documents were demanded that allowed me access at least to the
threshold of Katya's soul and were invalid beyond that point); I would
once again go to gaze at Katya, who, at the first pitiful word of mine,

would turn into a large, rigid doll who would lower her convex eyelids and respond in china-doll language. When, one memorable night, I demanded that she give me a final, supertruthful reply, Katya simply said nothing and, instead, remained lying motionless on the couch, her mirrorlike eyes reflecting the flame of the candle that on that night of historical turbulence substituted for electric light, and after hearing her silence through to the end, I got up and left. Three days later, I had my valet take a note to her, in which I wrote that I would commit suicide if I could not see her just once more. So one glorious morning, with a rosy round sun and creaking snow, we met on Post Office Street; I silently kissed her hand and for a quarter of an hour, without a single word interrupting our silence, we strolled to and fro, while nearby, on the corner of the Horse Guards Boulevard, stood smoking, with feigned nonchalance, a perfectly respectable-looking man in an astrakhan cap. As she and I silently walked to and fro, a little boy passed, pulling by its string a baized hand sled with a tattered fringe, and a drainpipe suddenly gave a rattle and disgorged a chunk of ice, while the man on the corner kept smoking; then, at precisely the same spot where we had met, I just as silently kissed her hand, which slipped back into its muff forever.

> *Farewell, my anguish and my ardor,*
> *Farewell, my dream, farewell, my pain!*
> *Along the paths of the old garden*
> *We two shall never pass again.*

Yes, yes: Farewell, as the *tzigane* song has it. In spite of everything, you were beautiful, impenetrably beautiful, and so adorable that I could cry, ignoring your myopic soul, and the triviality of your opinions, and a thousand minor betrayals; while I, with my overambitious verse, the heavy and hazy array of my feelings and my breathless, stuttering speech, in spite of all my love for you, must have been contemptible and repulsive. And there is no need for me to tell you what torments I went through afterward, how I looked and looked at the snapshot in which, with a gleam on your lip and a glint in your hair, you are looking past me. Katya, why have you made such a mess of it now?

Come, let us have a calm, heart-to-heart talk. With a lugubrious hiss the air has now been let out of the arrogant rubber fatman who, tightly inflated, clowned around at the beginning of this letter; and you, my dear, are really not a corpulent lady novelist in her novelistic hammock but the same old Katya, with Katya's calculated dash of demeanor, Katya of the narrow shoulders, a comely, discreetly made-up lady who, out of silly coquetry, has concocted a worthless book. To think that you did not even spare our parting! Leonid's letter, in which he threatens to shoot Olga, and which she discusses with her future husband; that future husband, in the role of undercover agent, standing on a street corner, ready to rush to the rescue if Leonid should draw the revolver that he is clutching in his coat pocket, as he passionately entreats Olga not to go, and keeps interrupting with his sobs her levelheaded words: What a disgusting, senseless fabrication! And at the end of the book, you have me join the White Army and get caught by the Reds during a reconnaissance and, with the names of two traitresses—Russia, Olga— on my lips, die valiantly, felled by the bullet of a "Hebrew-dark" commissar. How intensely I must have loved you if I still see you are you were 16 years ago, make agonizing efforts to free our past from its humiliating captivity and save your image from the rack and disgrace of your own pen! I honestly do not know, though, if I am succeeding. My letter smacks strangely of those rhymed epistles that you would rattle off by heart—remember?

The sight of my handwriting may surprise you

but I shall refrain from closing, as Apukhtin does, with the invitation:

The sea awaits you here, as vast as love
And love, vast as the sea!

I shall refrain, because, in the first place, there is no sea here and, in the second, I have not the least desire to see you. For, after your book, Katya, I am afraid of you. Truly there was no point in rejoicing and suffering as we rejoiced and suffered only to find one's past besmirched in a lady's novel. Listen—stop writing books! At least let this flop serve as a lesson. "At least," for I have the right to wish that you will be stunned by horror upon realizing what you have perpetrated. And do you know what else I long for? Perhaps, perhaps (this is a very small and sickly "perhaps," but I grasp at it and hence do not sign this letter), perhaps, after all, Katya, in spite of everything, a rare coincidence has occurred, and it is not you who wrote this tripe, and your equivocal but enchanting image has not been mutilated. In that case, please forgive me, colleague Solntsev.

Tarzan's First Love

by EDGAR RICE BURROUGHS

Teeka, stretched at luxurious ease in the shade of the tropical forest, presented, unquestionably, a most alluring picture of young, feminine loveliness. Or at least so thought Tarzan of the Apes, who squatted upon a low-swinging branch in a near-by tree and looked down upon her.

Just to have seen him there, lolling upon the swaying bough of the jungle-forest giant, his brown skin mottled by the brilliant equatorial sunlight which percolated through the leafy canopy of green above him, his clean-limbed body relaxed in graceful ease, his shapely head partly turned in contemplative absorption and his intelligent, gray eyes dreamily devouring the object of their devotion, you would have thought him the reincarnation of some demigod of old.

You would not have guessed that in infancy he had suckled at the breast of a hideous, hairy she-ape, nor that in all his conscious past since his parents had passed away in the little cabin by the landlocked harbor at the jungle's verge, he had known no other associates than the sullen bulls and the snarling cows of the tribe of Kerchak, the great ape.

Nor, could you have read the thoughts which passed through that active, healthy brain, the longings and desires and aspirations which the sight of Teeka inspired, would you have been any more inclined to give credence to the reality of the origin of the ape-man. For, from his thoughts alone, you could never have gleaned the truth—that he had been born to a gentle English lady or that his sire had been an English nobleman of time-honored lineage.

Lost to Tarzan of the Apes was the truth of his origin. That he was John Clayton, Lord Greystoke, with a seat in the House of Lords, he did not know, nor, knowing, would have understood.

Yes, Teeka was indeed beautiful!

Of course Kala had been beautiful—one's mother is always that—but Teeka was beautiful in a way all her own, an indescribable sort of way which Tarzan was just beginning to sense in a rather vague and hazy manner.

For years had Tarzan and Teeka been play-fellows, and Teeka still continued to be playful while the young bulls of her own age were rapidly becoming surly and morose. Tarzan, if he gave the matter much thought at all, probably reasoned that his growing attachment for the young female could be easily accounted for by the fact that of the former playmates she and he alone retained any desire to frolic as of old.

But today, as he sat gazing upon her, he found himself noting the beauties of Teeka's form and features—something he never had done before, since none of them had aught to do with Teeka's ability to race nimbly through the lower terraces of the forest in the primitive games of tag and hide-and-go-seek which Tarzan's fertile brain evolved.

Tarzan scratched his head, running his fingers deep into the shock of black hair which framed his shapely, boyish face—he scratched his head and sighed. Teeka's new-found beauty became as suddenly his despair. He envied her the handsome coat of hair which covered her body. His own smooth, brown hide he hated with a hatred born of disgust and contempt. Years back he had harbored a hope that some day he, too, would be clothed in hair as were all his brothers and sisters; but of late he had been forced to abandon the delectable dream.

Then there were Teeka's great teeth, not so large as the males, of course, but still mighty, handsome things by comparison with Tarzan's feeble white ones. And her beetling brows, and broad, flat nose, and her mouth! Tarzan had often practiced making his mouth into a little round circle and then puffing out his cheeks while he winked his eyes rapidly; but he felt that he could never do it in the same cute and irresistible way in which Teeka did it.

And as he watched her that afternoon, and wondered, a young bull ape who had been lazily foraging for food beneath the damp, matted carpet of decaying vegetation at the roots of a near-by tree lumbered awkwardly in Teeka's direction. The other apes of the tribe of Kerchak moved listlessly about or lolled restfully in the midday heat of the equatorial jungle. From time to time one or another of them had passed close to Teeka, and Tarzan had been uninterested. Why was it then that his brows contracted and his muscles tensed as he saw Taug pause beside the young she and then squat down close to her?

Tarzan always had liked Taug. Since childhood they had romped together. Side by side they had squatted near the water, their quick, strong fingers ready to leap forth and seize Pisah, the fish, should that wary denizen of the cool depths dart surfaceward to the lure of the insects Tarzan tossed upon the face of the pool.

Together they had baited Tublat and teased Numa, the lion. Why, then, should Tarzan feel the rise of the short hairs at the nape of his neck merely because Taug sat close to Teeka?

It is true that Taug was no longer the frolicsome ape of yesterday. When his snarling-muscles bared his giant fangs no one could longer imagine that Taug was in as playful a mood as when he and Tarzan had rolled upon the turf in mimic battle. The Taug of today was a huge, sullen bull ape, somber and forbidding. Yet he and Tarzan never had quarreled.

For a few minutes the young ape-man watched Taug press closer to Teeka. He saw the rough caress of the huge paw as it stroked the sleek shoulder of the she, and then Tarzan of the Apes slipped catlike to the ground and approached the two.

As he came his upper lip curled into a snarl, exposing his fighting fangs, and a deep growl rumbled from his cavernous chest. Taug looked up, batting his blood-shot eyes. Teeka half raised herself and looked at Tarzan. Did she guess the cause of his perturbation? Who may say? At any rate, she was feminine, and so she reached up and scratched Taug behind one of his small, flat ears.

Tarzan saw, and in the instant that he saw, Teeka was no longer the little playmate of an hour ago; instead she was a wondrous thing—the most wondrous in the world—and a possession for which Tarzan would fight to the death against Taug or any other who dared question his right of proprietorship.

Stooped, his muscles rigid and one great shoulder turned toward the young bull, Tarzan of the Apes sidled nearer and nearer. His face was partly averted, but his keen gray eyes never left those of Taug, and as he came, his growls increased in depth and volume.

Taug rose upon his short legs, bristling. His fighting fangs were bared. He, too, sidled, stiff-legged, and growled.

"Teeka is Tarzan's," said the ape-man, in the low gutturals of the great anthropoids.

"Teeka is Taug's," replied the bull ape.

Thaka and Numgo and Gunto, disturbed by the growlings of the two young bulls, looked up half apathetic, half interested. They were sleepy, but they sensed a fight. It would break the monotony of the humdrum jungle life they led.

Coiled about his shoulders was Tarzan's long grass rope, in his hand was the hunting knife of the long-dead father he had never known. In Taug's little brain lay a great respect for the shiny bit of sharp metal which the ape-boy knew so well how to use. With it had he slain Tublat, his fierce foster father, and Bolgani, the gorilla. Taug knew these things, and so he came warily, circling about Tarzan in search of an opening. The latter, made cautious because of his lesser bulk and the inferiority of his natural armament, followed similar tactics.

For a time it seemed that the altercation would follow the way of the majority of such differences between members of the tribe and that one of them would finally lose interest and wander off to prosecute some other line of endeavor. Such might have been the end of it had the *casus belli* been other than it was; but Teeka was flattered at the attention that was being drawn to her and by the fact that these two young bulls were contemplating battle on her account. Such a thing never before had occurred in Teeka's brief life. She had seen other bulls battling for other and older shes, and in the depth of her wild little heart she had longed for the day when the jungle grasses would be reddened with the blood of mortal combat for her fair sake.

So now she squatted upon her haunches and insulted both her admirers impartially. She hurled taunts at them for their cowardice, and called them vile names, such as Histah, the snake, and Dango, the hyena. She threatened to call Mumga to chastise them with a stick— Mumga, who was so old that she could no longer climb and so toothless that she was forced to confine her diet almost exclusively to bananas and grubworms.

The apes who were watching heard and laughed. Taug was infuriated. He made a sudden lunge for Tarzan, but the ape-boy leaped nimbly to one side, eluding him, and with the quickness of a cat wheeled and leaped back again to close quarters. His hunting knife was raised above his head as he came in, and he aimed a vicious blow at

Taug's neck. The ape wheeled to dodge the weapon so that the keen blade struck him but a glancing blow upon the shoulder.

The spurt of red blood brought a shrill cry of delight from Teeka. Ah, but this was something worth while! She glanced about to see if others had witnessed this evidence of her popularity. Helen of Troy was never one whit more proud than was Teeka at that moment.

If Teeka had not been so absorbed in her own vaingloriousness she might have noted the rustling of leaves in the tree above her—a rustling which was not caused by any movement of the wind, since there was no wind. And had she looked up she might have seen a sleek body crouching almost directly over her and wicked yellow eyes glaring hungrily down upon her, but Teeka did not look up.

With his wound Taug had backed off growling horribly. Tarzan had followed him, screaming insults at him, and menacing him with his brandishing blade. Teeka moved from beneath the tree in an effort to keep close to the duelists.

The branch above Teeka bent and swayed a trifle with the movement of the body of the watcher stretched along it. Taug had halted now and was preparing to make a new stand. His lips were flecked with foam, and saliva drooled from his jowls. He stood with head lowered and arms outstretched, preparing for a sudden charge to close quarters. Could he but lay his mighty hands upon that soft, brown skin the battle would be his. Taug considered Tarzan's manner of fighting unfair. He would not close. Instead, he leaped nimbly just beyond the reach of Taug's muscular fingers.

The ape-boy had as yet never come to a real trial of strength with a bull ape, other than in play, and so he was not at all sure that it would be safe to put his muscles to the test in a life and death struggle. Not that he was afraid, for Tarzan knew nothing of fear. The instinct of self-preservation gave him caution—that was all. He took risks only when it seemed necessary, and then he would hesitate at nothing.

His own method of fighting seemed best fitted to his build and to his armament. His teeth, while strong and sharp, were, as weapons of offense, pitifully inadequate by comparison with the mighty fighting fangs of the anthropoids. By dancing about, just out of reach of an antagonist, Tarzan could do infinite injury with his long, sharp hunting knife, and at the same time escape many of the painful and dangerous wounds which would be sure to follow his falling into the clutches of a bull ape.

And so Taug charged and bellowed like a bull, and Tarzan of the

Apes danced lightly to this side and that, hurling jungle billingsgate at his foe, the while he nicked him now and again with his knife.

There were lulls in the fighting when the two would stand panting for breath, facing each other, mustering their wits and their forces for a new onslaught. It was during a pause such as this that Taug chanced to let his eyes rove beyond his foeman. Instantly the entire aspect of the ape altered. Rage left his countenance to be supplanted by an expression of fear.

With a cry that every ape there recognized, Taug turned and fled. No need to question him—his warning proclaimed the near presence of their ancient enemy.

Tarzan started to seek safety, as did the other members of the tribe, and as he did so he heard a panther's scream mingled with the frightened cry of a she-ape. Taug heard, too; but he did not pause in his flight.

With the ape-boy, however, it was different. He looked back to see if any member of the tribe was close pressed by the beast of prey, and the sight that met his eye filled them with an expression of horror.

Teeka it was who cried out in terror as she fled across a little clearing toward the trees upon the opposite side, for after her leaped Sheeta, the panther, in easy, graceful bounds. Sheeta appeared to be in no hurry. His meat was assured, since even though the ape reached the trees ahead of him she could not climb beyond his clutches before he could be upon her.

Tarzan saw that Teeka must die. He cried to Taug and the other bulls to hasten to Teeka's assistance, and at the same time he ran toward the pursuing beast, taking down his rope as he came. Tarzan knew that once the great bulls were aroused none of the jungle, not even Numa, the lion, was anxious to measure fangs with them, and that if all those of the tribe who chanced to be present today would charge, Sheeta, the great cat, would doubtless turn tail and run for his life.

Taug heard, as did the others, but no one came to Tarzan's assistance or Teeka's rescue, and Sheeta was rapidly closing up the distance between himself and his prey.

The ape-boy, leaping after the panther, cried aloud to the beast in an effort to turn it from Teeka or otherwise distract its attention until the she-ape could gain the safety of the higher branches where Sheeta dared not go. He called the panther every opprobrious name that fell to his tongue. He dared him to stop and do battle with him; but Sheeta only loped on after the luscious titbit now almost within his reach.

Tarzan was not far behind and he was gaining, but the distance was so short that he scarce hoped to overhaul the carnivore before it had felled Teeka. In his right hand the boy swung his grass rope above his head as he ran. He hated to chance a miss, for the distance was much greater than he ever had cast before except in practice. It was the full length of his grass rope which separated him from Sheeta, and yet there was no other thing to do. He could not reach the brute's side before it overhauled Teeka. He must chance a throw.

And just as Teeka sprang for the lower limb of a great tree, and Sheeta rose behind her in a long, sinuous leap, the coils of the ape-boy's grass rope shot swiftly through the air, straightening into a long thin line as the open noose hovered for an instant above the savage head and the snarling jaws. Then it settled—clean and true about the tawny neck it settled, and Tarzan, with a quick twist of his rope-hand, drew the noose taut, bracing himself for the shock when Sheeta should have taken up the slack.

Just short of Teeka's glossy rump the cruel talons raked the air as the rope tightened and Sheeta was brought to a sudden stop—a stop that snapped the big beast over upon his back. Instantly Sheeta was up—with glaring eyes, and lashing tail, and gaping jaws, from which issued hideous cries of rage and disappointment.

He saw the ape-boy, the cause of his discomfiture, scarce forty feet before him, and Sheeta charged.

Teeka was safe now; Tarzan saw to that by a quick glance into the tree whose safety she had gained not an instant too soon, and Sheeta was charging. It was useless to risk his life in idle and unequal combat from which no good could come; but could he escape a battle with the enraged cat? And if he was forced to fight, what chance had he to survive? Tarzan was constrained to admit that his position was aught but a desirable one. The trees were too far to hope to reach in time to elude the cat. Tarzan could but stand facing that hideous charge. In his right hand he grasped his hunting knife—a puny, futile thing indeed by comparison with the great rows of mighty teeth which lined Sheeta's powerful jaws, and the sharp talons encased within his padded paws; yet the young Lord Greystoke faced it with the same courageous resignation with which some fearless ancestor went down to defeat and death on Senlac Hill by Hastings.

From safety points in the trees the great apes watched, screaming hatred at Sheeta and advice at Tarzan, for the progenitors of man have, naturally, many human traits. Teeka was frightened. She screamed at the bulls to hasten to Tarzan's assistance; but the bulls were otherwise engaged—principally in giving advice and making faces. Anyway, Tarzan was not a real Mangani, so why should they risk their lives in an effort to protect him?

And now Sheeta was almost upon the lithe, naked body, and—the body was not there. Quick as was the great cat, the ape-boy was quicker. He leaped to one side almost as the panther's talons were closing upon him, and as Sheeta went hurtling to the ground beyond, Tarzan was racing for the safety of the nearest tree.

The panther recovered himself almost immediately and, wheeling, tore after his prey, the ape-boy's rope dragging along the ground behind him. In doubling back after Tarzan, Sheeta had passed around a low bush. It was a mere nothing in the path of any jungle creature of the size and weight of Sheeta—provided it had no trailing rope dangling behind. But Sheeta was handicapped by such a rope, and as he leaped once again after Tarzan of the Apes the rope encircled the small bush, became tangled in it and brought the panther to a sudden stop. An instant later Tarzan was safe among the higher branches of a small tree into which Sheeta could not follow him.

Here he perched, hurling twigs and epithets at the raging feline beneath him. The other members of the tribe now took up the bombardment, using such hard-shelled fruits and dead branches as came within their reach, until Sheeta, goaded to frenzy and snapping at the grass rope, finally succeeded in severing its strands. For a moment the panther stood glaring first at one of his tormentors and then at another, until, with a final scream of rage, he turned and slunk off into the tangled mazes of the jungle.

A half hour later the tribe was again upon the ground, feeding as though naught had occurred to interrupt the somber dullness of their lives. Tarzan had recovered the greater part of his rope and was busy fashioning a new noose, while Teeka squatted close beside him, in evident token that her choice was made.

Taug eyed them sullenly. Once when he came close, Teeka bared her fangs and growled at him, and Tarzan showed his canines in an ugly snarl; but Taug did not provoke a quarrel. He seemed to accept after the manner of his kind the decision of the she as an indication that he had been vanquished in his battle for her favors.

Later in the day, his rope repaired, Tarzan took to the trees in search of game. More than his fellows he required meat, and so, while they were satisfied with fruits and herbs and beetles, which could be discovered without much effort upon their part, Tarzan spent considerable time hunting the game animals whose flesh alone satisfied the cravings of his stomach and furnished sustenance and strength to the mighty thews which, day by day, were building beneath the soft, smooth texture of his brown hide.

Taug saw him depart, and then, quite casually, the big beast hunted closer and closer to Teeka in his search for food. At last he was within a few feet of her, and when he shot a covert glance at her he saw that she was appraising him and that there was no evidence of anger upon her face.

Taug expanded his great chest and rolled about on his short legs, making strange growlings in his throat. He raised his lips, baring his fangs. My, but what great, beautiful fangs he had! Teeka could not but notice them. She also let her eyes rest in admiration upon Taug's beetling brows and his short, powerful neck. What a beautiful creature he was indeed!

Taug, flattered by the unconcealed admiration in her eyes, strutted about, as proud and as vain as a peacock. Presently he began to inventory his assets, mentally, and shortly he found himself comparing them with those of his rival.

Taug grunted, for there was no comparison. How could one compare his beautiful coat with the smooth and naked hideousness of Tarzan's bare hide? Who could see beauty in the stingy nose of the Tarmangani after looking at Taug's broad nostrils? And Tarzan's eyes! Hideous things, showing white about them, and entirely unrimmed with red. Taug knew that his own blood-shot eyes were beautiful, for he had seen them reflected in the glassy surface of many a drinking pool.

The bull drew nearer to Teeka, finally squatting close against her. When Tarzan returned from his hunting a short time later it was to see Teeka contentedly scratching the back of his rival.

Tarzan was disgusted. Neither Taug nor Teeka saw him as he swung through the trees into the glade. He paused a moment, looking at them; then, with a sorrowful grimace, he turned and faded away into the labyrinth of leafy boughs and festooned moss out of which he had come.

Tarzan wished to be as far away from the cause of his heartache as he could. He was suffering the first pangs of blighted love, and he didn't quite know what was the matter with him. He thought that he was angry with Taug, and so he couldn't understand why it was that he had run away instead of rushing into mortal combat with the destroyer of his happiness.

He also thought that he was angry with Teeka, yet a vision of her many beauties persisted in haunting him, so that he could only see her in the light of love as the most desirable thing in the world.

The ape-boy craved affection. From babyhood until the time of her death, when the poisoned arrow of Kulonga had pierced her savage heart, Kala had represented to the English boy the sole object of love which he had known.

In her wild, fierce way Kala had loved her adopted son, and Tarzan had returned that love, though the outward demonstrations of it were no greater than might have been expected from any other beast of the jungle. It was not until he was bereft of her that the boy realized how deep had been his attachment for his mother, for as such he looked upon her.

In Teeka he had seen within the past few hours a substitute for Kala —someone to fight for and to hunt for—someone to caress; but now his dream was shattered. Something hurt within his breast. He placed his hand over his heart and wondered what had happened to him. Vaguely he attributed his pain to Teeka. The more he thought of Teeka as he had last seen her, caressing Taug, the more the thing within his breast hurt him.

Tarzan shook his head and growled; then on and on through the jungle he swung, and the farther he traveled and the more he thought upon his wrongs, the nearer he approached becoming an irreclaimable misogynist.

Two days later he was still hunting alone—very morose and very unhappy; but he was determined never to return to the tribe. He could not bear the thought of seeing Taug and Teeka always together. As he swung upon a great limb Numa, the lion, and Sabor, the lioness, passed beneath him, side by side, and Sabor leaned against the lion and bit playfully at his cheek. It was a half-caress. Tarzan sighed and hurled a nut at them.

Later he came upon several of Mbonga's black warriors. He was upon the point of dropping his noose about the neck of one of them, who was a little distance from his companions, when he became interested in the thing which occupied the savages. They were building a cage in the trail and covering it with leafy branches. When they had completed their work the structure was scarcely visible.

Tarzan wondered what the purpose of the thing might be, and why, when they had built it, they turned away and started back along the trail in the direction of their village.

It had been some time since Tarzan had visited the blacks and looked down from the shelter of the great trees which overhung their palisade upon the activities of his enemies, from among whom had come the slayer of Kala.

Although he hated them, Tarzan derived considerable entertainment in watching them at their daily life within the village, and especially at their dances, when the fires glared against their naked bodies as they leaped and turned and twisted in mimic warfare. It was rather in the hope of witnessing something of the kind that he now followed the warriors back toward their village, but in this he was disappointed, for there was no dance that night.

Instead, from the safe concealment of his tree, Tarzan saw little groups seated about tiny fires discussing the events of the day, and in the darker corners of the village he descried isolated couples talking and laughing together, and always one of each couple was a young man and the other a young woman.

Tarzan cocked his head upon one side and thought, and before he went to sleep that night, curled in the crotch of the great tree above the village, Teeka filled his mind, and afterward she filled his dreams—she and the young black men laughing and talking with the young black women.

Taug, hunting alone, had wandered some distance from the balance of the tribe. He was making his way slowly along an elephant path when he discovered that it was blocked with undergrowth. Now Taug, come into maturity, was an evil-natured brute of an exceeding short temper. When something thwarted him, his sole idea was to overcome it by brute strength and ferocity, and so now when he found his way blocked, he tore angrily into the leafy screen and an instant later found himself within a strange lair, his progress effectually blocked, notwithstanding his most violent efforts to forge ahead.

Biting and striking at the barrier, Taug finally worked himself into a frightful rage, but all to no avail; and at last he became convinced that he must turn back. But when he would have done so, what was his chagrin to discover that another barrier had dropped behind him while he fought to break down the one before him! Taug was trapped. Until exhaustion overcame him he fought frantically for his freedom; but all for naught.

In the morning a party of blacks set out from the village of Mbonga in the direction of the trap they had constructed the previous day, while among the branches of the trees above them hovered a naked young giant filled with the curiosity of the wild things. Manu, the monkey, chattered and scolded as Tarzan passed, and though he was not afraid of the familiar figure of the ape-boy, he hugged closer to him the little brown body of his life's companion. Tarzan laughed as he saw it; but the laugh was followed by a sudden clouding of his face and a deep sigh.

A little farther on, a gaily feathered bird strutted about before the admiring eyes of his somber-hued mate. It seemed to Tarzan that everything in the jungle was combining to remind him that he had lost Teeka; yet every day of his life he had seen these same things and thought nothing of them.

When the blacks reached the trap, Taug set up a great commotion. Seizing the bars of his prison, he shook them frantically, and all the while he roared and growled terrifically. The blacks were elated, for while they had not built their trap for this hairy tree man, they were delighted with their catch.

Tarzan pricked up his ears when he heard the voice of a great ape and, circling quickly until he was down wind from the trap, he sniffed at the air in search of the scent spoor of the prisoner. Nor was it long before there came to those delicate nostrils the familiar odor that told Tarzan the identity of the captive as unerringly as though he had looked upon Taug with his eyes. Yes, it was Taug, and he was alone.

Tarzan grinned as he approached to discover what the blacks would do to their prisoner. Doubtless they would slay him at once. Again Tarzan grinned. Now he could have Teeka for his own, with none to dispute his right to her. As he watched, he saw the black warriors strip the screen from about the cage, fasten ropes to it and drag it away along the trail in the direction of their village.

Tarzan watched until his rival passed out of sight, still beating upon the bars of his prison and growling out his anger and his threats. Then the ape-boy turned and swung rapidly off in search of the tribe, and Teeka.

Once, upon the journey, he surprised Sheeta and his family in a little overgrown clearing. The great cat lay stretched upon the ground, while his mate, one paw across her lord's savage face, licked at the soft white fur at his throat.

Tarzan increased his speed then until he fairly flew through the forest, nor was it long before he came upon the tribe. He saw them before they saw him, for of all the jungle creatures, none passed more quietly than Tarzan of the Apes. He saw Kamma and her mate feeding side by side, their hairy bodies rubbing against each other. And he saw Teeka feeding by herself. Not for long would she feed thus in loneliness, thought Tarzan, as with a bound he landed amongst them.

There was a startled rush and a chorus of angry and frightened snarls, for Tarzan had surprised them; but there was more, too, than mere nervous shock to account for the bristling neck hair which remained standing long after the apes had discovered the identity of the new-comer.

Tarzan noticed this as he had noticed it many times in the past—that always his sudden coming among them left them nervous and unstrung for a considerable time, and that they one and all found it necessary to satisfy themselves that he was indeed Tarzan by smelling about him a half dozen or more times before they calmed down.

Pushing through them, he made his way toward Teeka; but as he approached her the ape drew away.

"Teeka," he said, "it is Tarzan. You belong to Tarzan. I have come for you."

The ape drew closer, looking him over carefully. Finally she sniffed at him, as though to make assurance doubly sure.

"Where is Taug?" she asked.

"The Gomangani have him," replied Tarzan. "They will kill him."

In the eyes of the she, Tarzan saw a wistful expression and a troubled look of sorrow as he told her of Taug's fate; but she came quite close and snuggled against him, and Tarzan, Lord Greystoke, put his arm about her.

As he did so he noticed, with a start, the strange incongruity of that smooth, brown arm against the black and hairy coat of his lady-love. He recalled the paw of Sheeta's mate across Sheeta's face—no incongruity there. He thought of little Manu hugging his she, and how the one seemed to belong to the other. Even the proud male bird, with his gay plumage, bore a close resemblance to his quieter spouse, while Numa, but for his shaggy mane, was almost a counterpart of Sabor, the lioness. The males and the females differed, it was true; but not with such differences as existed between Tarzan and Teeka.

Tarzan was puzzled. There was something wrong. His arm dropped from the shoulder of Teeka. Very slowly he drew away from her. She looked at him with her head cocked upon one side. Tarzan rose to his full height and beat upon his breast with his fists. He raised his head toward the heavens and opened his mouth. From the depths of his lungs rose the fierce, weird challenge of the victorious bull ape. The tribe turned curiously to eye him. He had killed nothing, nor was there any antagonist to be goaded to madness by the savage scream. No, there was no excuse for it, and they turned back to their feeding, but with an eye upon the ape-man lest he be preparing to suddenly run amuck.

As they watched him they saw him swing into a near-by tree and disappear from sight. Then they forgot him, even Teeka.

Mbonga's black warriors, sweating beneath their strenuous task, and resting often, made slow progress toward their village. Always the savage beast in the primitive cage growled and roared when they moved him. He beat upon the bars and slavered at the mouth. His noise was hideous.

They had almost completed their journey and were making their final rest before forging ahead to gain the clearing in which lay their village. A few more minutes would have taken them out of the forest, and then, doubtless, the thing would not have happened which did happen.

A silent figure moved through the trees above them. Keen eyes inspected the cage and counted the number of warriors. An alert and daring brain figured upon the chances of success when a certain plan should be put to the test.

Tarzan watched the blacks lolling in the shade. They were exhausted. Already several of them slept. He crept closer, pausing just above them. Not a leaf rustled before his stealthy advance. He waited in the infinite patience of the beast of prey. Presently but two of the warriors remained awake, and one of these was dozing.

Tarzan of the Apes gathered himself, and as he did so the black who did not sleep arose and passed around to the rear of the cage. The ape-boy followed just above his head. Taug was eyeing the warrior and emitting low growls. Tarzan feared that the anthropoid would awaken the sleepers.

In a whisper which was inaudible to the ears of the Negro, Tarzan whispered Taug's name, cautioning the ape to silence, and Taug's growling ceased.

The black approached the rear of the cage and examined the fastenings of the door, and as he stood there the beast above him launched itself from the tree full upon his back. Steel fingers circled his throat, choking the cry which sprang to the lips of the terrified man. Strong teeth fastened themselves in his shoulder, and powerful legs wound themselves about his torso.

The black in a frenzy of terror tried to dislodge the silent thing which clung to him. He threw himself to the ground and rolled about; but still those mighty fingers closed more and more tightly their deadly grip.

The man's mouth gaped wide, his swollen tongue protruded, his eyes started from their sockets; but the relentless fingers only increased their pressure.

Taug was a silent witness of the struggle. In his fierce little brain he doubtless wondered what purpose prompted Tarzan to attack the black.

Taug had not forgotten his recent battle with the ape-boy, nor the cause of it. Now he saw the form of the Gomangani suddenly go limp. There was a convulsive shiver and the man lay still.

Tarzan sprang from his prey and ran to the door of the cage. With nimble fingers he worked rapidly at the thongs which held the door in place. Taug could only watch—he could not help. Presently Tarzan pushed the thing up a couple of feet and Taug crawled out. The ape would have turned upon the sleeping blacks that he might wreak his pent vengeance; but Tarzan would not permit it.

Instead, the ape-boy dragged the body of the black within the cage and propped it against the side bars. Then he lowered the door and made fast the thongs as they had been before.

A happy smile lighted his features as he worked, for one of his principal diversions was the baiting of the blacks of Mbonga's village. He could imagine their terror when they awoke and found the dead body of their comrade fast in the cage where they had left the great ape safely secured but a few minutes before.

Tarzan and Taug took to the trees together, the shaggy coat of the fierce ape brushing the sleek skin of the English lordling as they passed through the primeval jungle side by side.

"Go back to Teeka," said Tarzan. "She is yours. Tarzan does not want her."

"Tarzan has found another she?" asked Taug.

The ape-boy shrugged.

"For the Gomangani there is another Gomangani," he said; "for Numa, the lion, there is Sabor, the lioness; for Sheeta there is a she of his own kind; for Bara, the deer; for Manu, the monkey; for all the beasts and the birds of the jungle is there a mate. Only for Tarzan of the Apes is there none. Taug is an ape. Teeka is an ape. Go back to Teeka. Tarzan is a man. He will go alone."

Coming, Aphrodite!

by WILLA CATHER

I

Don Hedger had lived for four years on the top floor of an old house on the south side of Washington Square, and nobody had ever disturbed him. He occupied one big room with no outside exposure except on the north, where he had built in a many-paned studio window that looked upon a court and upon the roofs and walls of other buildings. His room was very cheerless, since he never got a ray of direct sunlight; the south corners were always in shadow. In one of the corners was a clothes closet, built against the partition, in another a wide divan, serving as a seat by day and a bed by night. In the front corner, the one farther from the window, was a sink, and a table with two gas burners where he sometimes cooked his food. There, too, in the perpetual dusk, was the dog's bed, and often a bone or two for his comfort.

The dog was a Boston bull terrier, and Hedger explained his surly disposition by the fact that he had been bred to the point where it told on his nerves. His name was Caesar III, and he had taken prizes at very exclusive dog shows. When he and his master went out to prowl about University Place or to promenade along West Street, Caesar III was invariably fresh and shining. His pink skin showed through his mottled coat, which glistened as if it had just been rubbed with olive oil, and he wore a brass-studded collar, bought at the smartest saddler's. Hedger, as often as not, was hunched up in an old striped blanket coat, with a shapeless felt hat pulled over his bushy hair, wearing black shoes that had become grey, or brown ones that had become black, and he never put on gloves unless the day was biting cold.

Early in May, Hedger learned that he was to have a new neighbour in the rear apartment—two rooms, one large and one small, that faced the west. His studio was shut off from the larger of these rooms by double doors, which, though they were fairly tight, left him a good deal at the mercy of the occupant. The rooms had been leased, long before he came there, by a trained nurse who considered herself knowing in old furniture. She went to auction sales and bought up mahogany and dirty brass and stored it away here, where she meant to live when she retired from nursing. Meanwhile, she sub-let her rooms, with their precious furniture, to young people who came to New York to "write" or to "paint"—who proposed to live by the sweat of the brow rather than of the hand, and who desired artistic surroundings. When Hedger first moved in, these rooms were occupied by a young man who tried to write plays,—and who kept on trying until a week ago, when the nurse had put him out for unpaid rent.

A few days after the playwright left, Hedger heard an ominous murmur of voices through the bolted double doors: the lady-like intonation of the nurse—doubtless exhibiting her treasures—and another voice, also a woman's, but very different; young, fresh, unguarded, confident. All the same, it would be very annoying to have a woman in there. The only bath-room on the floor was at the top of the stairs in the front hall, and he would always be running into her as he came or went from his bath. He would have to be more careful to see that Caesar didn't leave bones about the hall, too; and she might object when he cooked steak and onions on his gas burner.

As soon as the talking ceased and the women left, he forgot them. He was absorbed in a study of paradise fish at the Aquarium, staring out at people through the glass and green water of their tank. It was a highly gratifying idea; the incommunicability of one stratum of animal life with another,—though Hedger pretended it was only an experiment in unusual lighting. When he heard trunks knocking against the sides of the narrow hall, then he realized that she was moving in at once. Toward noon, groans and deep gasps and the creaking of ropes, made him aware that a piano was arriving. After the tramp of the movers died away down the stairs, somebody touched off a few scales and chords on the instrument, and then there was peace. Presently he heard her lock her door and go down the hall humming something; going out to lunch, probably. He stuck his brushes in a can of turpentine and put on his hat, not stopping to wash his hands. Caesar was smelling along the crack under the bolted doors; his bony tail stuck out hard as a hickory withe, and the hair was standing up about his elegant collar.

Hedger encouraged him. "Come along, Caesar. You'll soon get used to a new smell."

In the hall stood an enormous trunk, behind the ladder that led to the roof, just opposite Hedger's door. The dog flew at it with a growl of hurt amazement. They went down three flights of stairs and out into the brilliant May afternoon.

Behind the Square, Hedger and his dog descended into a basement oyster house where there were no tablecloths on the tables and no handles on the coffee cups, and the floor was covered with sawdust, and Caesar was always welcome,—not that he needed any such precautionary flooring. All the carpets of Persia would have been safe for him. Hedger ordered steak and onions absentmindedly, not realizing why he had an apprehension that this dish might be less readily at hand hereafter. While he ate, Caesar sat beside his chair, gravely disturbing the sawdust with his tail.

After lunch Hedger strolled about the Square for the dog's health and watched the stages pull out;—that was almost the very last summer of the old horse stages on Fifth Avenue. The fountain had but lately begun operations for the season and was throwing up a mist of rainbow water which now and then blew south and sprayed a bunch of Italian babies that were being supported on the outer rim by older, very little older, brothers and sisters. Plump robins were hopping about on the soil; the grass was newly cut and blindingly green. Looking up the Avenue through the Arch, one could see the young poplars with their bright, sticky leaves, and the Brevoort glistening in its spring coat of paint, and shining horses and carriages,—occasionally an automobile, mis-shapen and sullen, like an ugly threat in a stream of things that were bright and beautiful and alive.

While Caesar and his master were standing by the fountain, a girl approached them, crossing the Square. Hedger noticed her because she wore a lavender cloth suit and carried in her arms a big bunch of fresh lilacs. He saw that she was young and handsome,—beautiful, in fact, with a splendid figure and good action. She, too, paused by the fountain and looked back through the Arch up the Avenue. She smiled rather patronizingly as she looked, and at the same time seemed delighted. Her slowly curving upper lip and half-closed eyes seemed to say: "You're gay, you're exciting, you are quite the right sort of thing; but you're none too fine for me!"

In the moment she tarried, Caesar stealthily approached her and sniffed at the hem of her lavender skirt, then, when she went south like an arrow, he ran back to his master and lifted a face full of emotion and alarm, his lower lip twitching under his sharp white teeth and his hazel eyes pointed with a very definite discovery. He stood thus, motionless, while Hedger watched the lavender girl go up the steps and through the door of the house in which he lived.

"You're right, my boy, it's she! She might be worse looking, you know."

When they mounted to the studio, the new lodger's door, at the back of the hall, was a little ajar, and Hedger caught the warm perfume of lilacs just brought in out of the sun. He was used to the musty smell of the old hall carpet. (The nurse-lessee had once knocked at his studio door and complained that Caesar must be somewhat responsible for the particular flavour of that mustiness, and Hedger had never spoken to her since.) He was used to the old smell, and he preferred it to that of the lilacs, and so did his companion, whose nose was so much more discriminating. Hedger shut his door vehemently, and fell to work.

Most young men who dwell in obscure studios in New York have had a beginning, come out of something, have somewhere a home town, a family, a paternal roof. But Don Hedger had no such background. He was a foundling, and had grown up in a school for homeless boys, where book-learning was a negligible part of the curriculum. When he was sixteen, a Catholic priest took him to Greensburg, Pennsylvania, to keep house for him. The priest did something to fill in the large gaps in the boy's education,—taught him to like "Don Quixote" and "The Golden Legend," and encouraged him to mess with paints and crayons in his room up under the slope of the mansard. When Don wanted to go to New York to study at the Art League, the priest got him a night job as packer in one of the big department stores. Since then, Hedger had taken care of himself; that was his only responsibility. He was singularly unencumbered; had no family duties, no social ties, no obligations toward any one but his landlord. Since he travelled light, he had travelled rather far. He had got over a good deal of the earth's surface, in spite of the fact that he never in his life had more than three hundred dollars ahead at any one time, and he had already outlived a succession of convictions and revelations about his art.

Though he was not but twenty-six years old, he had twice been on the verge of becoming a marketable product; once through some studies of New York streets he did for a magazine, and once through a collection of pastels he brought home from New Mexico, which Remington, then at the height of his popularity, happened to see, and generously tried to push. But on both occasions Hedger decided that this was something he didn't wish to carry further,—simply the old thing over again and got nowhere,—so he took enquiring dealers experiments in a "later manner," that made them put him out of the shop. When he ran short of money, he could always get any amount of commercial work; he was an expert draughtsman and worked with lightning speed. The rest of his time he spent in groping his way from one kind of painting into another, or travelling about without luggage, like a tramp, and he was chiefly occupied with getting rid of ideas he had once thought very fine.

Hedger's circumstances, since he had moved to Washington Square, were affluent compared to anything he had ever known before. He was now able to pay advance rent and turn the key on his studio when he went away for four months at a stretch. It didn't occur to him to wish to be richer than this. To be sure, he did without a great many things other people think necessary, but he didn't miss them, because he had never had them. He belonged to no clubs, visited no houses, had no studio friends, and he ate his dinner alone in some decent little restaurant, even on Christmas and New Year's. For days together he talked to nobody but his dog and the janitress and the lame oysterman.

After he shut the door and settled down to his paradise fish on that first Tuesday in May, Hedger forgot all about his new neighbour. When the light failed, he took Caesar out for a walk. On the way home he did his marketing on West Houston Street, with a one-eyed Italian woman who always cheated him. After he had cooked his beans and scallopini, and drunk half a bottle of Chianti, he put his dishes in the sink and went up on the roof to smoke. He was the only person in the house who ever went to the roof, and he had a secret understanding with the janitress about it. He was to have "the privilege of the roof," as she said, if he opened the heavy trapdoor on sunny days to air out the upper hall, and was watchful to close it when rain threatened. Mrs. Foley was fat and dirty and hated to climb stairs,—besides, the roof was reached by a perpendicular iron ladder, definitely inaccessible to a woman of her bulk, and the iron door at the top of it was too heavy for any but Hedger's strong arm to lift. Hedger was not above medium height, but he practised with weights and dumb-bells, and in the shoulders he was as strong as a gorilla.

So Hedger had the roof to himself. He and Caesar often slept up there on hot nights, rolled in blankets he had brought home from Arizona. He mounted with Caesar under his left arm. The dog had never learned to climb a perpendicular ladder, and never did he feel so much his master's greatness and his own dependence upon him, as when he crept under his arm for this perilous ascent. Up there was even gravel to scratch in, and a dog could do whatever he liked, so long as he did not bark. It was a kind of Heaven, which no one was strong enough to reach but his great, paint-smelling master.

On this blue May night there was a slender, girlish looking young moon in the west, playing with a whole company of silver stars. Now and then one of them darted away from the group and shot off into the gauzy blue with a soft little trail of light, like laughter. Hedger and his dog were delighted when a star did this. They were quite lost in watching the glittering game, when they were suddenly diverted by a sound,—not from the stars, though it was music. It was not the Prologue to Pagliacci, which rose ever and anon on hot evenings from an Italian tenement on Thompson Street, with the gasps of the corpulent baritone who got behind it; nor was it the hurdy-gurdy man, who often played at the corner in the balmy twilight. No, this was a woman's voice, singing the tempestuous, over-lapping phrases of Signor Puccini, then comparatively new in the world, but already so popular that even Hedger recognized his unmistakable gusts of breath. He looked about over the roofs; all was blue and still, with the well-built chimneys that were never used now standing up dark and mournful. He moved softly toward the yellow quadrangle where the gas from the hall shone up through the half-lifted trapdoor. Oh yes! It came up through the hole like a strong draught, a big, beautiful voice, and it sounded rather like a professional's. A piano had arrived in the morning, Hedger remembered. This might be a very great nuisance. It would be pleasant enough to listen to, if you could turn it on and off as you wished; but you couldn't. Caesar, with the gas light shining on his collar and his ugly but sensitive face, panted and looked up for information. Hedger put down a reassuring hand.

"I don't know. We can't tell yet. It may not be so bad."

He stayed on the roof until all was still below, and finally descended, with quite a new feeling about his neighbour. Her voice, like her figure, inspired respect,—if one did not choose to call it admiration. Her door was shut, the transom was dark; nothing remained of her but the obtrusive trunk, unrightfully taking up room in the narrow hall.

II

For two days Hedger didn't see her. He was painting eight hours a day just then, and only went out to hunt for food. He noticed that she practised scales and exercises for about an hour in the morning; then she locked her door, went humming down the hall, and left him in peace. He heard her getting her coffee ready at about the same time he got his. Earlier still, she passed his room on her way to her bath. In the evening she sometimes sang, but on the whole she didn't bother him. When he was working well he did not notice anything much. The morning paper lay before his door until he reached out for his milk bottle, then he kicked the sheet inside and it lay on the floor until evening. Sometimes he read it and sometimes he did not. He forgot there was anything of importance going on in the world outside of his third floor studio. Nobody had ever taught him that he ought to be interested in other people; in the Pittsburgh steel strike, in the Fresh Air Fund, in the scandal about the Babies' Hospital. A grey wolf, living in a Wyoming canyon, would hardly have been less concerned about these things than was Don Hedger.

One morning he was coming out of the bath-room at the front end of the hall, having just given Caesar his bath and rubbed him into a glow with a heavy towel. Before the door, lying in wait for him, as it were, stood a tall figure in a flowing blue silk dressing gown that fell away from her marble arms. In her hands she carried various accessories of the bath.

"I wish," she said distinctly, standing in his way, "I wish you wouldn't wash your dog in the tub. I never heard of such a thing! I've found his hair in the tub, and I've smelled a doggy smell, and now I've caught you at it. It's an outrage!"

Hedger was badly frightened. She was so tall and positive, and was fairly blazing with beauty and anger. He stood blinking, holding on to his sponge and dog-soap, feeling that he ought to bow very low to her. But what he actually said was:

"Nobody has ever objected before. I always wash the tub,—and, anyhow, he's cleaner than most people."

"Cleaner than me?" her eyebrows went up, her white arms and neck and her fragrant person seemed to scream at him like a band of outraged nymphs. Something flashed through his mind about a man who was turned into a dog, or was pursued by dogs, because he unwittingly intruded upon the bath of beauty.

"No, I didn't mean that," he muttered, turning scarlet under the bluish stubble of his muscular jaws. "But I know he's cleaner than I am."

"That I don't doubt!" Her voice sounded like a soft shivering of crystal, and with a smile of pity she drew the folds of her voluminous blue robe close about her and allowed the wretched man to pass. Even Caesar was frightened; he darted like a streak down the hall, through the door and to his own bed in the corner among the bones.

Hedger stood still in the doorway, listening to indignant sniffs and coughs and a great swishing of water about the sides of the tub. He had washed it; but as he had washed it with Caesar's sponge, it was quite possible that a few bristles remained; the dog was shedding now. The playwright had never objected, nor had the jovial illustrator who occupied the front apartment,—but he, as he admitted, "was usually pie-eyed, when he wasn't in Buffalo." He went home to Buffalo sometimes to rest his nerves.

It had never occurred to Hedger that any one would mind using the tub after Caesar;—but then, he had never seen a beautiful girl caparisoned for the bath before. As soon as he beheld her standing there, he realized the unfitness of it. For that matter, she ought not to step into a tub that any other mortal had bathed in; the illustrator was sloppy and left cigarette ends on the moulding.

All morning as he worked he was gnawed by a spiteful desire to get back at her. It rankled that he had been so vanquished by her disdain. When he heard her locking her door to go out for lunch, he stepped quickly into the hall in his messy painting coat, and addressed her.

"I don't wish to be exigent, Miss,"—he had certain grand words that he used upon occasion—"but if this is your trunk, it's rather in the way here."

"Oh, very well!" she exclaimed carelessly, dropping her keys into her handbag. "I'll have it moved when I can get a man to do it," and she went down the hall with her free, roving stride.

Her name, Hedger discovered from her letters, which the postman left on the table in the lower hall, was Eden Bower.

III

In the closet that was built against the partition separating his room from Miss Bower's, Hedger kept all his wearing apparel, some of it on hooks and hangers, some of it on the floor. When he opened his closet door now-a-days, little dust-coloured insects flew out on downy wing, and he suspected that a brood of moths were hatching in his winter overcoat. Mrs. Foley, the janitress, told him to bring down all his heavy clothes and she would give them a beating and hang them in the court. The closet was in such disorder that he shunned the encounter, but one hot afternoon he set himself to the task. First he threw out a pile of forgotten laundry and tied it up in a sheet. The bundle stood as high as his middle when he had knotted the corners. Then he got his shoes and overshoes together. When he took his overcoat from its place against the partition, a long ray of yellow light shot across the dark enclosure,— a knot hole, evidently, in the high wainscoting of the west room. He had never noticed it before, and without realizing what he was doing, he stooped and squinted through it.

Yonder, in a pool of sunlight, stood his new neighbour, wholly unclad, doing exercises of some sort before a long gilt mirror. Hedger did not happen to think how unpardonable it was of him to watch her. Nudity was not improper to any one who had worked so much from the figure, and he continued to look, simply because he had never seen a woman's body so beautiful as this one,—positively glorious in action. As she swung her arms and changed from one pivot of motion to another, muscular energy seemed to flow through her from her toes to her finger-tips. The soft flush of exercise and the gold of afternoon sun played over her flesh together, enveloped her in a luminous mist which, as she turned and twisted, made now an arm, now a shoulder, now a thigh, dissolve in pure light and instantly recover its outline with the next gesture. Hedger's fingers curved as if he were holding a crayon; mentally he was doing the whole figure in a single running line, and the charcoal seemed to explode in his hand at the point where the energy of each gesture was discharged into the whirling disc of light, from a foot or shoulder, from the up-thrust chin or the lifted breasts.

He could not have told whether he watched her for six minutes or sixteen. When her gymnastics were over, she paused to catch up a lock of hair that had come down, and examined with solicitude a little reddish mole that grew under her left arm-pit. Then, with her hand on her hip, she walked unconcernedly across the room and disappeared through the door into her bedchamber.

Disappeared—Don Hedger was crouching on his knees, staring at the golden shower which poured in through the west windows, at the lake of gold sleeping on the faded Turkish carpet. The spot was enchanted;

a vision out of Alexandria, out of the remote pagan past, had bathed itself there in Helianthine fire.

When he crawled out of his closet, he stood blinking at the grey sheet stuffed with laundry, not knowing what had happened to him. He felt a little sick as he contemplated the bundle. Everything here was different; he hated the disorder of the place, the grey prison light, his old shoes and himself and all his slovenly habits. The black calico curtains that ran on wires over his big window were white with dust. There were three greasy frying pans in the sink, and the sink itself—He felt desperate. He couldn't stand this another minute. He took up an armful of winter clothes and ran down four flights into the basement.

"Mrs. Foley," he began, "I want my room cleaned this afternoon, thoroughly cleaned. Can you get a woman for me right away?"

"Is it company you're having?" the fat, dirty janitress enquired. Mrs. Foley was the widow of a useful Tammany man, and she owned real estate in Flatbush. She was huge and soft as a feather bed. Her face and arms were permanently coated with dust, grained like wood where the sweat had trickled.

"Yes, company. That's it."

"Well, this is a queer time of the day to be asking for a cleaning woman. It's likely I can get you old Lizzie, if she's not drunk. I'll send Willy round to see."

Willy, the son of fourteen, roused from the stupor and stain of his fifth box of cigarettes by the gleam of a quarter, went out. In five minutes he returned with old Lizzie,—she smelling strong of spirits and wearing several jackets which she had put on one over the other, and a number of skirts, long and short, which made her resemble an animated dish-clout. She had, of course, to borrow her equipment from Mrs. Foley, and toiled up the long flights, dragging mop and pail and broom. She told Hedger to be of good cheer, for he had got the right woman for the job, and showed him a great leather strap she wore about her wrist to prevent dislocation of tendons. She swished about the place, scattering dust and splashing soapsuds, while he watched her in nervous despair. He stood over Lizzie and made her scour the sink, directing her roughly, then paid her and got rid of her. Shutting the door on his failure, he hurried off with his dog to lose himself among the stevedores and dock labourers on West Street.

A strange chapter began for Don Hedger. Day after day, at that hour in the afternoon, the hour before his neighbour dressed for dinner, he crouched down in his closet to watch her go through her mysterious exercises. It did not occur to him that his conduct was detestable; there was nothing shy or retreating about this unclad girl,—a bold body, studying itself quite coolly and evidently well pleased with itself, doing all this for a purpose. Hedger scarcely regarded his action as conduct at all; it was something that had happened to him. More than once he went out and tried to stay away for the whole afternoon, but at about five o'clock he was sure to find himself among his old shoes in the dark. The pull of that aperture was stronger than his will,—and he had always considered his will the strongest thing about him. When she threw herself upon the divan and lay resting, he still stared, holding his breath. His nerves were so on edge that a sudden noise made him start and brought out the sweat on his forehead. The dog would come and tug at his sleeve, knowing that something was wrong with his master. If he attempted a mournful whine, those strong hands closed about his throat.

When Hedger came slinking out of his closet, he sat down on the edge of the couch, sat for hours without moving. He was not painting at all now. This thing, whatever it was, drank him up as ideas had sometimes done, and he sank into a stupor of idleness as deep and dark as the stupor of work. He could not understand it; he was no boy, he had worked from models for years, and a woman's body was no mystery to him. Yet now he did nothing but sit and think about one. He slept very little, and with the first light of morning he awoke as completely possessed by this woman as if he had been with her all the night before. The unconscious operations of life went on in him only to perpetuate this excitement. His brain held but one image now—vibrated, burned with it. It was a heathenish feeling; without friendliness, almost without tenderness.

Women had come and gone in Hedger's life. Not having had a mother to begin with, his relations with them, whether amorous or friendly, had been casual. He got on well with janitresses and washwomen, with Indians and with the peasant women of foreign countries. He had friends among the silk-skirt factory girls who came to eat their lunch in Washington Square, and he sometimes took a model for a day in the country. He felt an unreasoning antipathy toward the well-dressed women he saw coming out of big shops, or driving in the Park. If, on his way to the Art Museum, he noticed a pretty girl standing on the steps of one of the houses on upper Fifth Avenue, he frowned at her and went by with his shoulders hunched up as if he were cold. He had never known such girls, or heard them talk, or seen the inside of the houses in which they lived; but he believed them all to be artificial and, in an aesthetic sense, perverted. He saw them enslaved by desire of merchandise and manufactured articles, effective only in making life complicated and insincere and in embroidering it with ugly and meaningless trivialities. They were enough, he thought, to make one almost forget woman as she existed in art, in thought, and in the universe.

He had no desire to know the woman who had, for the time at least, so broken up his life,—no curiosity about her every-day personality. He shunned any revelation of it, and he listened for Miss Bower's coming and going, not to encounter, but to avoid her. He wished that the girl who wore shirt-waists and got letters from Chicago would keep out of his way, that she did not exist. With her he had naught to make. But in a room full of sun, before an old mirror, on a little enchanted rug of sleeping colours, he had seen a woman who emerged naked through a door, and disappeared naked. He thought of that body as never having been clad, or as having worn the stuffs and dyes of all the centuries but his own. And for him she had no geographical associations; unless with Crete, or Alexandria, or Veronese's Venice. She was the immortal conception, the perennial theme.

The first break in Hedger's lethargy occurred one afternoon when two young men came to take Eden Bower out to dine. They went into her music room, laughed and talked for a few minutes, and then took her away with them. They were gone a long while, but he did not go out for food himself; he waited for them to come back. At last he heard them coming down the hall, gayer and more talkative than when they left. One of them sat down at the piano, and they all began to sing. This Hedger found absolutely unendurable. He snatched up his hat and went running down the stairs. Caesar leaped beside him, hoping that old times were coming back. They had supper in the oysterman's basement and then sat down in front of their own doorway. The moon stood full over the Square, a thing of regal glory; but Hedger did not see the moon; he was looking, murderously, for men. Presently two, wearing straw hats and white trousers and carrying canes, came down the steps from his house. He rose and dogged them across the Square. They were laughing and seemed very much elated about something. As one stopped to light a cigarette, Hedger caught from the other:

"Don't you think she has a beautiful talent?"

His companion threw away his match. "She has a beautiful figure." They both ran to catch the stage.

Hedger went back to his studio. The light was shining from her transom. For the first time he violated her privacy at night, and peered through that fatal aperture. She was sitting, fully dressed, in the window, smoking a cigarette and looking out over the housetops. He watched her until she rose, looked about her with a disdainful, crafty smile, and turned out the light.

The next morning, when Miss Bower went out, Hedger followed her. Her white skirt gleamed ahead of him as she sauntered about the Square. She sat down behind the Garibaldi statue and opened a music book she carried. She turned the leaves carelessly, and several times glanced in his direction. He was on the point of going over to her, when she rose quickly and looked up at the sky. A flock of pigeons had risen from somewhere in the crowded Italian quarter to the south, and were wheeling rapidly up through the morning air, soaring and dropping, scattering and coming together, now grey, now white as silver, as they caught or intercepted the sunlight. She put up her hand to shade her eyes and followed them with a kind of defiant delight in her face.

Hedger came and stood beside her. "You've surely seen them before?"

"Oh, yes," she replied, still looking up. "I see them every day from my windows. They always come home about five o'clock. Where do they live?"

"I don't know. Probably some Italian raises them for the market. They were here long before I came, and I've been here four years."

"In that same gloomy room? Why didn't you take mine when it was vacant?"

"It isn't gloomy. That's the best light for painting."

"Oh, is it? I don't know anything about painting. I'd like to see your pictures sometime. You have such a lot in there. Don't they get dusty, piled up against the wall like that?"

"Not very. I'd be glad to show them to you. Is your name really Eden Bower? I've seen your letters on the table."

"Well, it's the name I'm going to sing under. My father's name is Bowers, but my friend Mr. Jones, a Chicago newspaper man who writes about music, told me to drop the 's.' He's crazy about my voice."

Miss Bower didn't usually tell the whole story,—about anything. Her first name, when she lived in Huntington, Illinois, was Edna, but Mr. Jones had persuaded her to change it to one which he felt would be worthy of her future. She was quick to take suggestions, though she told him she "didn't see what was the matter with 'Edna.' "

She explained to Hedger that she was going to Paris to study. She was waiting in New York for Chicago friends who were to take her over, but who had been detained. "Did you study in Paris?" she asked.

"No, I've never been in Paris. But I was in the south of France all last summer, studying with C——. He's the biggest man among the moderns,—at least I think so."

Miss Bower sat down and made room for him on the bench. "Do tell me about it. I expected to be there by this time, and I can't wait to find out what it's like."

Hedger began to relate how he had seen some of this Frenchman's work in an exhibition, and deciding at once that this was the man for him, he had taken a boat for Marseilles the next week, going over steerage. He proceeded at once to the little town on the coast where his painter lived, and presented himself. The man never took pupils, but because Hedger had come so far, he let him stay. Hedger lived at the master's house and every day they went out together to paint, sometimes on the blazing rocks down by the sea. They wrapped themselves in light woollen blankets and didn't feel the heat. Being there and working with C—— was being in Paradise, Hedger concluded; he learned more in three months than in all his life before.

Eden Bower laughed. "You're a funny fellow. Didn't you do anything but work? Are the women very beautiful? Did you have awfully good things to eat and drink?"

Hedger said some of the women were fine looking, especially one girl who went about selling fish and lobsters. About the food there was nothing remarkable,—except the ripe figs, he liked those. They drank sour wine, and used goat-butter, which was strong and full of hair, as it was churned in a goat skin.

"But don't they have parties or banquets? Aren't there any fine hotels down there?"

"Yes, but they are all closed in summer, and the country people are poor. It's a beautiful country, though."

"How, beautiful?" she persisted.

"If you want to go in, I'll show you some sketches, and you'll see."

Miss Bower rose. "All right. I won't go to my fencing lesson this morning. Do you fence? Here comes your dog. You can't move but he's after you. He always makes a face at me when I meet him in the hall, and shows his nasty little teeth as if he wanted to bite me."

In the studio Hedger got out his sketches, but to Miss Bower, whose favourite pictures were Christ Before Pilate and a redhaired Magdalen of Henner, these landscapes were not at all beautiful, and they gave her no idea of any country whatsoever. She was careful not to commit herself, however. Her vocal teacher had already convinced her that she had a great deal to learn about many things.

"Why don't we go out to lunch somewhere?" Hedger asked, and

began to dust his fingers with a handkerchief—which he got out of sight as swiftly as possible.

"All right, the Brevoort," she said carelessly. "I think that's a good place, and they have good wine. I don't care for cocktails."

Hedger felt his chin uneasily. "I'm afraid I haven't shaved this morning. If you could wait for me in the Square? It won't take me ten minutes."

Left alone, he found a clean collar and handkerchief, brushed his coat and blacked his shoes, and last of all dug up ten dollars from the bottom of an old copper kettle he had brought from Spain. His winter hat was of such a complexion that the Brevoort hall boy winked at the porter as he took it and placed it on the rack in a row of fresh straw ones.

IV

That afternoon Eden Bower was lying on the couch in her music room, her face turned to the window, watching the pigeons. Reclining thus she could see none of the neighbouring roofs, only the sky itself and the birds that crossed and recrossed her field of vision, white as scraps of paper blowing in the wind. She was thinking that she was young and handsome and had had a good lunch, that a very easy-going, light-hearted city lay in the streets below her; and she was wondering why she found this queer painter chap, with his lean, bluish cheeks and heavy black eyebrows, more interesting than the smart young men she met at her teacher's studio.

Eden Bower was, at twenty, very much the same person that we all know her to be at forty, except that she knew a great deal less. But one thing she knew: that she was to be Eden Bower. She was like some one standing before a great show window full of beautiful and costly things, deciding which she will order. She understands that they will not all be delivered immediately, but one by one they will arrive at her door. She already knew some of the many things that were to happen to her; for instance, that the Chicago millionaire who was going to take her abroad with his sister as chaperone, would eventually press his claim in quite another manner. He was the most circumspect of bachelors, afraid of everything obvious, even of women who were too flagrantly handsome. He was a nervous collector of pictures and furniture, a nervous patron of music, and a nervous host; very cautious about his health, and about any course of conduct that might make him ridiculous. But she knew that he would at last throw all his precautions to the winds.

People like Eden Bower are inexplicable. Her father sold farming machinery in Huntington, Illinois, and she had grown up with no acquaintances or experiences outside of that prairie town. Yet from her earliest childhood she had not one conviction or opinion in common with the people about her,—the only people she knew. Before she was out of short dresses she had made up her mind that she was going to be an actress, that she would live far away in great cities, that she would be much admired by men and would have everything she wanted. When she was thirteen, and was already singing and reciting for church entertainments, she read in some illustrated magazine a long article about the late Czar of Russia, then just come to the throne or about to come to it. After that, lying in the hammock on the front porch on summer evenings, or sitting through a long sermon in the family pew, she amused herself by trying to make up her mind whether she would or would not be the Czar's mistress when she played in his Capital. Now Eden had met this fascinating world only in the novels of Ouida,—her hard-worked little mother kept a long row of them in the upstairs storeroom, behind the linen chest. In Huntington, women who bore that relation to men were called by a very different name, and their lot was not an enviable one; of all the shabby and poor, they were the shabbiest. But then, Eden had never lived in Huntington, not even before she began to find books like "Sappho" and "Mademoiselle de Maupin," secretly sold in paper covers throughout Illinois. It was as if she had come into Huntington, into the Bowers family, on one of the trains that puffed over the marshes behind their back fence all day long, and was waiting for another train to take her out.

As she grew older and handsomer, she had many beaux, but these small-town boys didn't interest her. If a lad kissed her when he brought her home from a dance, she was indulgent and she rather liked it. But if he pressed her further, she slipped away from him laughing. After she began to sing in Chicago, she was consistently discreet. She stayed as a guest in rich people's houses, and she knew that she was being watched like a rabbit in a laboratory. Covered up in bed, with the lights out, she thought her own thoughts, and laughed.

This summer in New York was her first taste of freedom. The Chicago capitalist, after all his arrangements were made for sailing, had been compelled to go to Mexico to look after oil interests. His sister knew an excellent singing master in New York. Why should not a discreet, well-balanced girl like Miss Bower spend the summer there, studying quietly? The capitalist suggested that his sister might enjoy a summer on Long Island; he would rent the Griffith's place for her, with all the servants, and Eden could stay there. But his sister met this proposal with a cold stare. So it fell out, that between selfishness and greed, Eden got a summer all her own,—which really did a great deal toward making her an artist and whatever else she was afterward to become. She had time to look about, to watch without being watched; to select diamonds in one window and furs in another, to select shoulders and moustaches in the big hotels where she went to lunch. She had the easy freedom of obscurity and the consciousness of power. She enjoyed both. She was in no hurry.

While Eden Bower watched the pigeons, Don Hedger sat on the other side of the bolted doors, looking into a pool of dark turpentine, at his idle brushes, wondering why a woman could do this to him. He, too, was sure of his future and knew that he was a chosen man. He could not know, of course, that he was merely the first to fall under a fascination which was to be disastrous to a few men and pleasantly stimulating to many thousands. Each of these two young people sensed the future, but not completely. Don Hedger knew that nothing much would ever happen to him. Eden Bower understood that to her a great deal would happen. But she did not guess that her neighbour would have more tempestuous adventures sitting in his dark studio than she would find in all the capitals of Europe, or in all the latitude of conduct she was prepared to permit herself.

V

One Sunday morning Eden was crossing the Square with a spruce young man in a white flannel suit and a panama hat. They had been breakfasting at the Brevoort and he was coaxing her to let him come up to her rooms and sing for an hour.

"No, I've got to write letters. You must run along now. I see a friend of mine over there, and I want to ask him about something before I go up."

"That fellow with the dog? Where did you pick him up?" the young man glanced toward the seat under a sycamore where Hedger was reading the morning paper.

"Oh, he's an old friend from the West," said Eden easily. "I won't introduce you, because he doesn't like people. He's a recluse. Good-bye. I can't be sure about Tuesday. I'll go with you if I have time after my lesson." She nodded, left him, and went over to the seat littered with newspapers. The young man went up the Avenue without looking back.

"Well, what are you going to do today? Shampoo this animal all morning?" Eden enquired teasingly.

Hedger made room for her on the seat. "No, at twelve o'clock I'm going out to Coney Island. One of my models is going up in a balloon this afternoon. I've often promised to go and see her, and now I'm going."

Eden asked if models usually did such stunts. No, Hedger told her, but Molly Welch added to her earnings in that way. "I believe," he added, "she likes the excitement of it. She's got a good deal of spirit. That's why I like to paint her. So many models have flaccid bodies."

"And she hasn't, eh? Is she the one who comes to see you? I can't help hearing her, she talks so loud."

"Yes, she has a rough voice, but she's a fine girl. I don't suppose you'd be interested in going?"

"I don't know," Eden sat tracing patterns on the asphalt with the end of her parasol. "Is it any fun? I got up feeling I'd like to do something different today. It's the first Sunday I've not had to sing in church. I had that engagement for breakfast at the Brevoort, but it wasn't very exciting. That chap can't talk about anything but himself."

Hedger warmed a little. "If you've never been to Coney Island, you ought to go. It's nice to see all the people; tailors and bar-tenders and prize-fighters with their best girls, and all sorts of folks taking a holiday."

Eden looked sidewise at him. So one ought to be interested in people of that kind, ought one? He was certainly a funny fellow. Yet he was never, somehow, tiresome. She had seen a good deal of him lately, but she kept wanting to know him better, to find out what made him different from men like the one she had just left—whether he really was as different as he seemed. "I'll go with you," she said at last, "if you'll leave that at home." She pointed to Caesar's flickering ears with her sunshade.

"But he's half the fun. You'd like to hear him bark at the waves when they come in."

"No, I wouldn't. He's jealous and disagreeable if he sees you talking to any one else. Look at him now."

"Of course, if you make a face at him. He knows what that means, and he makes a worse face. He likes Molly Welch, and she'll be disappointed if I don't bring him."

Eden said decidedly that he couldn't take both of them. So at twelve o'clock when she and Hedger got on the boat at Desbrosses Street, Caesar was lying on his pallet, with a bone.

Eden enjoyed the boat-ride. It was the first time she had been on the water, and she felt as if she were embarking for France. The light warm breeze and the plunge of the waves made her very wide awake, and she liked crowds of any kind. They went to the balcony of a big, noisy restaurant and had a shore dinner, with tall steins of beer. Hedger had got a big advance from his advertising firm since he first lunched with Miss Bower ten days ago, and he was ready for anything.

After dinner they went to the tent behind the bathing beach, where the tops of two balloons bulged out over the canvas. A red-faced man in a linen suit stood in front of the tent, shouting in a hoarse voice and telling the people that if the crowd was good for five dollars more, a beautiful young woman would risk her life for their entertainment. Four little boys in dirty red uniforms ran about taking contributions in their pill-box hats. One of the balloons was bobbing up and down in its tether and people were shoving forward to get nearer the tent.

"Is it dangerous, as he pretends?" Eden asked.

"Molly says it's simple enough if nothing goes wrong with the balloon. Then it would be all over, I suppose."

"Wouldn't you like to go up with her?"

"I? Of course not. I'm not fond of taking foolish risks."

Eden sniffed. "I shouldn't think sensible risks would be very much fun."

Hedger did not answer, for just then every one began to shove the other way and shout, "Look out. There she goes!" and a band of six pieces commenced playing furiously.

As the balloon rose from its tent enclosure, they saw a girl in green tights standing in the basket, holding carelessly to one of the ropes with one hand and with the other waving to the spectators. A long rope trailed behind to keep the balloon from blowing out to sea.

As it soared, the figure in green tights in the basket diminished to a mere spot, and the balloon itself, in the brilliant light, looked like a big silver-grey bat, with its wings folded. When it began to sink, the girl stepped through the hole in the basket to a trapeze that hung below, and gracefully descended through the air, holding to the rod with both hands, keeping her body taut and her feet close together. The crowd, which had grown very large by this time, cheered vociferously. The men took off their hats and waved, little boys shouted, and fat old women, shining with the heat and a beer lunch, murmured admiring comments upon the balloonist's figure. "Beautiful legs, she has!"

Coming, Aphrodite!

"That's so," Hedger whispered. "Not many girls would look well in that position." Then, for some reason, he blushed a slow, dark, painful crimson.

The balloon descended slowly, a little way from the tent, and the red-faced man in the linen suit caught Molly Welch before her feet touched the ground, and pulled her to one side. The band struck up "Blue Bell" by way of welcome, and one of the sweaty pages ran forward and presented the balloonist with a large bouquet of artificial flowers. She smiled and thanked him, and ran back across the sand to the tent.

"Can't we go inside and see her?" Eden asked. "You can explain to the door man. I want to meet her." Edging forward, she herself addressed the man in the linen suit and slipped something from her purse into his hand.

They found Molly seated before a trunk that had a mirror in the lid and a "make-up" outfit spread upon the tray. She was wiping the cold cream and powder from her neck with a discarded chemise.

"Hello, Don," she said cordially. "Brought a friend?"

Eden liked her. She had an easy, friendly manner, and there was something boyish and devil-may-care about her.

"Yes, it's fun. I'm mad about it," she said in reply to Eden's questions. "I always want to let go, when I come down on the bar. You don't feel your weight at all, as you would on a stationary trapeze."

The big drum boomed outside, and the publicity man began shouting to newly arrived boatloads. Miss Welch took a last pull at her cigarette. "Now you'll have to get out, Don. I change for the next act. This time I go up in a black evening dress, and lose the skirt in the basket before I start down."

"Yes, go along," said Eden. "Wait for me outside the door. I'll stay and help her dress."

Hedger waited and waited, while women of every build bumped into him and begged his pardon, and the red pages ran about holding out their caps for coins, and the people ate and perspired and shifted parasols against the sun. When the band began to play a two-step, all the bathers ran up out of the surf to watch the ascent. The second balloon bumped and rose, and the crowd began shouting to the girl in a black evening dress who stood leaning against the ropes and smiling. "It's a new girl," they called. "It ain't the Countess this time. You're a peach, girlie!"

The balloonist acknowledged these compliments, bowing and looking down over the sea of upturned faces,—but Hedger was determined she should not see him, and he darted behind the tent-fly. He was suddenly dripping with cold sweat, his mouth was full of the bitter taste of anger and his tongue felt stiff behind his teeth. Molly Welch, in a shirt-waist and a white tam-o'-shanter cap, slipped out from the tent under his arm and laughed up in his face. "She's a crazy one you brought along. She'll get what she wants!"

"Oh, I'll settle with you, all right!" Hedger brought out with difficulty.

"It's not my fault, Donnie. I couldn't do anything with her. She bought me off. What's the matter with you? Are you soft on her? She's safe enough. It's as easy as rolling off a log, if you keep cool." Molly Welch was rather excited herself, and she was chewing gum at a high speed as she stood beside him, looking up at the floating silver cone. "Now watch," she exclaimed suddenly. "She's coming down on the bar. I advised her to cut that out, but you see she does it first-rate. And she got rid of the skirt, too. Those black tights show off her legs very well. She keeps her feet together like I told her, and makes a good line along the back. See the light on those silver slippers,—that was a good idea I had. Come along to meet her. Don't be a grouch; she's done it fine!"

Molly tweaked his elbow, and then left him standing like a stump, while she ran down the beach with the crowd.

Though Hedger was sulking, his eye could not help seeing the low blue welter of the sea, the arrested bathers, standing in the surf, their arms and legs stained red by the dropping sun, all shading their eyes and gazing upward at the slowly falling silver star.

Molly Welch and the manager caught Eden under the arms and lifted her aside, a red page dashed up with a bouquet, and the band struck up "Blue Bell." Eden laughed and bowed, took Molly's arm, and ran up the sand in her black tights and silver slippers, dodging the friendly old women, and the gallant sports who wanted to offer their homage on the spot.

When she emerged from the tent, dressed in her own clothes, that part of the beach was almost deserted. She stepped to her companion's side and said carelessly: "Hadn't we better try to catch this boat? I hope you're not sore at me. Really, it was lots of fun."

Hedger looked at his watch. "Yes, we have fifteen minutes to get to the boat," he said politely.

As they walked toward the pier, one of the pages ran up panting. "Lady, you're carrying off the bouquet," he said, aggrievedly.

Eden stopped and looked at the bunch of spotty cotton roses in her hand. "Of course. I want them for a souvenir. You gave them to me yourself."

"I give 'em to you for looks, but you can't take 'em away. They belong to the show."

"Oh, you always use the same bunch?"

"Sure we do. There ain't too much money in this business."

She laughed and tossed them back to him. "Why are you angry?" she asked Hedger. "I wouldn't have done it if I'd been with some fellows, but I thought you were the sort who wouldn't mind. Molly didn't for a minute think you would."

"What possessed you to do such a fool thing?" he asked roughly.

"I don't know. When I saw her coming down, I wanted to try it. It looked exciting. Didn't I hold myself as well as she did?"

Hedger shrugged his shoulders, but in his heart he forgave her.

The return boat was not crowded, though the boats that passed them, going out, were packed to the rails. The sun was setting. Boys and girls sat on the long benches with their arms about each other, singing. Eden felt a strong wish to propitiate her companion, to be alone with him. She had been curiously wrought up by her balloon trip; it was a lark, but not very satisfying unless one came back to something after the flight. She wanted to be admired and adored. Though Eden said nothing, and sat with her arms limp on the rail in front of her, looking languidly at the rising silhouette of the city and the bright path of the sun, Hedger felt a strange drawing near to her. If he but brushed her white skirt with his knee, there was an instant communication between them, such as there had never been before. They did not talk at all, but when they went over the gangplank she took his arm and kept her shoulder close to his. He felt as if they were enveloped in a highly charged atmosphere, an invisible network of subtle, almost painful sensibility. They had somehow taken hold of each other.

An hour later, they were dining in the back garden of a little French hotel on Ninth Street, long since passed away. It was cool and leafy there, and the mosquitoes were not very numerous. A party of South Americans at another table were drinking champagne, and Eden murmured that she thought she would like some, if it were not too expensive. "Perhaps it will make me think I am in the balloon again. That was a very nice feeling. You've forgiven me, haven't you?"

Hedger gave her a quick straight look from under his black eyebrows, and something went over her that was like a chill, except that it was warm and feathery. She drank most of the wine; her companion was indifferent to it. He was talking more to her tonight than he had ever done before. She asked him about a new picture she had seen in his room; a queer thing full of stiff, supplicating female figures. "It's Indian, isn't it?"

"Yes. I call it Rain Spirits, or maybe, Indian Rain. In the Southwest, where I've been a good deal, the Indian traditions make women have to do with the rain-fall. They were supposed to control it, somehow, and to be able to find springs, and make moisture come out of the earth. You see I'm trying to learn to paint what people think and feel; to get away from all that photographic stuff. When I look at you, I don't see what a camera would see, do I?"

"How can I tell?"

"Well, if I should paint you, I could make you understand what I see." For the second time that day Hedger crimsoned unexpectedly, and his eyes fell and steadily contemplated a dish of little radishes. "That particular picture I got from a story a Mexican priest told me; he said he found it in an old manuscript book in a monastery down there, written by some Spanish Missionary, who got his stories from the Aztecs. This one he called 'The Forty Lovers of the Queen,' and it was more or less about rain-making."

"Aren't you going to tell it to me?" Eden asked.

Hedger fumbled among the radishes. "I don't know if it's the proper kind of story to tell a girl."

She smiled; "Oh, forget about that! I've been balloon riding today. I like to hear you talk."

Her low voice was flattering. She had seemed like clay in his hands ever since they got on the boat to come home. He leaned back in his chair, forgot his food, and, looking at her intently, began to tell his story, the theme of which he somehow felt was dangerous tonight.

The tale began, he said, somewhere in Ancient Mexico, and concerned the daughter of a king. The birth of this Princess was preceded by unusual portents. Three times her mother dreamed that she was delivered of serpents, which betokened that the child she carried would have power with the rain gods. The serpent was the symbol of water. The Princess grew up dedicated to the gods, and wise men taught her the rain-making mysteries. She was with difficulty restrained from men and was guarded at all times, for it was the law of the Thunder that she be maiden until her marriage. In the years of her adolescence, rain was abundant with her people. The oldest man could not remember such fertility. When the Princess had counted eighteen summers, her father went to drive out a war party that harried his borders on the north and troubled his prosperity. The King destroyed the invaders and brought home many prisoners. Among the prisoners was a young chief, taller than any of his captors, of such strength and ferocity that the King's people came a day's journey to look at him. When the Princess beheld his great stature, and saw that his arms and breast were covered with the figures of wild animals, bitten into the skin and coloured, she begged his life from her father. She desired that he should practise his art upon her, and prick upon her skin the signs of Rain and Lightning and Thunder, and stain the wounds with herb-juices, as they were upon his own body. For many days, upon the roof of the King's house, the Princess submitted herself to the bone needle, and the women with her marvelled at her fortitude. But the Princess was without shame before the Captive, and it came about that he threw from him his needles and his stains, and fell upon the Princess to violate her honour; and her women ran down from the roof screaming, to call the guard which stood at the gateway of the King's house, and none stayed to protect their mistress. When the guard came, the Captive was thrown into bonds, and he was gelded, and his tongue was torn out, and he was given for a slave to the Rain Princess.

The country of the Aztecs to the east was tormented by thirst, and their King, hearing much of the rain-making arts of the Princess, sent an embassy to her father, with presents and an offer of marriage. So the Princess went from her father to be the Queen of the Aztecs, and she took with her the Captive, who served her in everything with entire fidelity and slept upon a mat before her door.

The King gave his bride a fortress on the outskirts of the city, whither she retired to entreat the rain gods. This fortress was called the Queen's House, and on the night of the new moon the Queen came to it from the palace. But when the moon waxed and grew toward the round, because the god of Thunder had had his will of her, then the Queen returned to the King. Drought abated in the country and rain fell abundantly by reason of the Queen's power with the stars.

When the Queen went to her own house she took with her no servant but the Captive, and he slept outside her door and brought her food after she had fasted. The Queen had a jewel of great value, a turquoise that had fallen from the sun, and had the image of the sun upon it. And when she desired a young man whom she had seen in the army or among the slaves, she sent the Captive to him with the jewel, for a sign that he should come to her secretly at the Queen's House upon business concerning the welfare of all. And some, after she had talked with them, she sent away with rewards; and some she took into her chamber and kept them by her for one night or two. Afterward she called the Captive and bade him conduct the youth by the secret way he had come, underneath the chambers of the fortress. But for the going away of the Queen's lovers the Captive took out the bar that was beneath a stone in the floor of the passage, and put in its stead a rush-reed, and the youth stepped upon it and fell through into a cavern that was the bed of an underground river, and whatever was thrown into it was not seen again. In this service nor in any other did the Captive fail the Queen.

But when the Queen sent for the Captain of the Archers, she detained him four days in her chamber, calling often for food and wine, and was greatly content with him. On the fourth day she went to the Captive outside her door and said: "Tomorrow take this man up by the sure way, by which the King comes, and let him live."

In the Queen's door were arrows, purple and white. When she desired the King to come to her publicly, with his guard, she sent him a white arrow; but when she sent the purple, he came secretly, and covered himself with his mantle to be hidden from the stone gods at the gate. On the fifth night that the Queen was with her lover, the Captive took a purple arrow to the King, and the King came secretly and found them together. He killed the Captain with his own hand, but the Queen he brought to public trial. The Captive, when he was put to the question, told on his fingers forty men that he had let through the underground passage into the river. The Captive and the Queen were put to death by fire, both on the same day, and afterward there was scarcity of rain.

Eden Bower sat shivering a little as she listened. Hedger was not trying to please her, she thought, but to antagonize and frighten her by his brutal story. She had often told herself that his lean, big-boned lower jaw was like his bull-dog's, but tonight his face made Caesar's most savage and determined expression seem an affectation. Now she was looking at the man he really was. Nobody's eyes had ever defied her like this. They were searching her and seeing everything; all she had concealed from Livingston, and from the millionaire and his friends, and from the newspaper men. He was testing her, trying her out, and she was more ill at ease than she wished to show.

"That's quite a thrilling story," she said at last, rising and winding her scarf about her throat. "It must be getting late. Almost every one has gone."

They walked down the Avenue like people who have quarrelled, or who wish to get rid of each other. Hedger did not take her arm at the street crossings, and they did not linger in the Square. At her door he tried none of the old devices of the Livingston boys. He stood like a post, having forgotten to take off his hat, gave her a harsh, threatening glance, muttered "goodnight," and shut his own door noisily.

There was no question of sleep for Eden Bower. Her brain was working like a machine that would never stop. After she undressed, she tried to calm her nerves by smoking a cigarette, lying on the divan by the open window. But she grew wider and wider awake, combating the challenge that had flamed all evening in Hedger's eyes. The balloon had been one kind of excitement, the wine another; but the thing that had roused her, as a blow rouses a proud man, was the doubt, the contempt, the sneering hostility with which the painter had looked at her when he told his savage story. Crowds and balloons were all very well, she reflected, but woman's chief adventure is man. With a mind over active and a sense of life over strong, she wanted to walk across the roofs in the starlight, to sail over the sea and face at once a world of which she had never been afraid.

Hedger must be asleep; his dog had stopped sniffing under the double doors. Eden put on her wrapper and slippers and stole softly down the hall over the old carpet; one loose board creaked just as she reached the ladder. The trapdoor was open, as always on hot nights. When she stepped out on the roof she drew a long breath and walked across it, looking up at the sky. Her foot touched something soft; she heard a low growl, and on the instant Caesar's sharp little teeth caught her ankle and waited. His breath was like steam on her leg. Nobody had ever intruded upon his roof before, and he panted for the movement or the word that would let him spring his jaw. Instead, Hedger's hand seized his throat.

"Wait a minute. I'll settle with him," he said grimly. He dragged the dog toward the manhole and disappeared. When he came back, he found Eden standing over by the dark chimney, looking away in an offended attitude.

"I caned him unmercifully," he panted. "Of course you didn't hear anything; he never whines when I beat him. He didn't nip you, did he?"

"I don't know whether he broke the skin or not," she answered aggrievedly, still looking off into the west.

"If I were one of your friends in white pants, I'd strike a match to find whether you were hurt, though I know you are not, and then I'd see your ankle, wouldn't I?"

"I suppose so."

He shook his head and stood with his hands in the pockets of his old painting jacket. "I'm not up to such boy-tricks. If you want the place to yourself, I'll clear out. There are plenty of places where I can spend the night, what's left of it. But if you stay here and I stay here—" He shrugged his shoulders.

Eden did not stir, and she made no reply. Her head drooped slightly, as if she were considering. But the moment he put his arms about her they began to talk, both at once, as people do in an opera. The instant avowal brought out a flood of trivial admissions. Hedger confessed his crime, was reproached and forgiven, and now Eden knew what it was in his look that she had found so disturbing of late.

Standing against the black chimney, with the sky behind and blue shadows before, they looked like one of Hedger's own paintings of that period; two figures, one white and one dark, and nothing whatever distinguishable about them but that they were male and female. The faces were lost, the contours blurred in shadow, but the figures were a man and a woman, and that was their whole concern and their mysterious beauty,—it was the rhythm in which they moved, at last, along the roof and down into the dark hole; he first, drawing her gently after him. She came down very slowly. The excitement and bravado and uncertainty of that long day and night seemed all at once to tell upon her. When his feet were on the carpet and he reached up to lift her down, she twined her arms about his neck as after a long separation, and turned her face to him, and her lips, with their perfume of youth and passion.

One Saturday afternoon Hedger was sitting in the window of Eden's music room. They had been watching the pigeons come wheeling over the roofs from their unknown feeding grounds.

"Why," said Eden suddenly, "don't we fix those big doors into your studio so they will open? Then, if I want you, I won't have to go through the hall. That illustrator is loafing about a good deal of late."

"I'll open them, if you wish. The bolt is on your side."

"Isn't there one on yours, too?"

"No. I believe a man lived there for years before I came in, and the nurse used to have these rooms herself. Naturally, the lock was on the lady's side."

Eden laughed and began to examine the bolt. "It's all stuck up with paint." Looking about, her eye lighted upon a bronze Buddha which was one of the nurse's treasures. Taking him by his head, she struck the bolt a blow with his squatting posteriors. The two doors creaked, sagged, and swung weakly inward a little way, as if they were too old for such escapades. Eden tossed the heavy idol into a stuffed chair. "That's better," she exclaimed exultantly. "So the bolts are always on the lady's side? What a lot society takes for granted!"

Hedger laughed, sprang up and caught her arms roughly. "Whoever takes you for granted— Did anybody, ever?"

"Everybody does. That's why I'm here. You are the only one who knows anything about me. Now I'll have to dress if we're going out for dinner."

He lingered, keeping his hold on her. "But I won't always be the only one, Eden Bower. I won't be the last."

"No, I suppose not," she said carelessly. "But what does that matter? You are the first."

As a long, despairing whine broke in the warm stillness, they drew apart. Caesar, lying on his bed in the dark corner, had lifted his head at this invasion of sunlight, and realized that the side of his room was broken open, and his whole world shattered by change. There stood his master and this woman, laughing at him! The woman was pulling the long black hair of this mightiest of men, who bowed his head and permitted it.

VI

In time they quarrelled, of course, and about an abstraction,—as young people often do, as mature people almost never do. Eden came in late one afternoon. She had been with some of her musical friends to lunch at Burton Ives' studio, and she began telling Hedger about its splendours. He listened a moment and then threw down his brushes. "I know exactly what it's like," he said impatiently. "A very good department-store conception of a studio. It's one of the show places."

"Well, it's gorgeous, and he said I could bring you to see him. The boys tell me he's awfully kind about giving people a lift, and you might get something out of it."

Hedger started up and pushed his canvas out of the way. "What could I possibly get from Burton Ives? He's almost the worst painter in the world; the stupidest, I mean."

Eden was annoyed. Burton Ives had been very nice to her and had begged her to sit for him. "You must admit that he's a very successful one," she said coldly.

"Of course he is! Anybody can be successful who will do that sort of thing. I wouldn't paint his pictures for all the money in New York."

"Well, I saw a lot of them, and I think they are beautiful."

Hedger bowed stiffly.

"What's the use of being a great painter if nobody knows about you?" Eden went on persuasively. "Why don't you paint the kind of pictures people can understand, and then, after you're successful, do whatever you like?"

"As I look at it," said Hedger brusquely, "I am successful."

Eden glanced about. "Well, I don't see any evidences of it," she said, biting her lip. "He has a Japanese servant and a wine cellar, and keeps a riding horse."

Hedger melted a little. "My dear, I have the most expensive luxury in the world, and I am much more extravagant than Burton Ives, for I work to please nobody but myself."

"You mean you could make money and don't? That you don't try to get a public?"

"Exactly. A public only wants what has been done over and over. I'm painting for painters,—who haven't been born."

"What would you do if I brought Mr. Ives down here to see your things?"

"Well, for God's sake, don't! Before he left I'd probably tell him what I thought of him."

Eden rose. "I give you up. You know very well there's only one kind of success that's real."

"Yes, but it's not the kind you mean. So you've been thinking me a scrub painter, who needs a helping hand from some fashionable studio man? What the devil have you had anything to do with me for, then?"

"There's no use talking to you," said Eden walking slowly toward the door. "I've been trying to pull wires for you all afternoon, and this is what it comes to." She had expected that the tidings of a prospective call from the great man would be received very differently, and had been thinking as she came home in the stage how, as with a magic wand, she might gild Hedger's future, float him out of his dark hole on a tide of prosperity, see his name in the papers and his pictures in the windows on Fifth Avenue.

Hedger mechanically snapped the midsummer leash on Caesar's collar and they ran downstairs and hurried through Sullivan Street off toward the river. He wanted to be among rough, honest people, to get down where the big drays bumped over stone paving blocks and the men wore corduroy trowsers and kept their shirts open at the neck. He stopped for a drink in one of the sagging bar-rooms on the water front. He had never in his life been so deeply wounded; he did not know he could be so hurt. He had told this girl all his secrets. On the roof, in these warm, heavy summer nights, with her hands locked in his, he had been able to explain all his misty ideas about an unborn art the world was waiting for; had been able to explain them better than he had ever done to himself. And she had looked away to the chattels of this up-town studio and coveted them for him! To her he was only an unsuccessful Burton Ives.

Then why, as he had put it to her, did she take up with him? Young, beautiful, talented as she was, why had she wasted herself on a scrub? Pity? Hardly; she wasn't sentimental. There was no explaining her. But in this passion that had seemed so fearless and so fated to be, his own position now looked to him ridiculous; a poor dauber without money or fame,—it was her caprice to load him with favours. Hedger ground his teeth so loud that his dog, trotting beside him, heard him and looked up.

While they were having supper at the oysterman's, he planned his escape. Whenever he saw her again, everything he had told her, that he should never have told any one, would come back to him; ideas he had never whispered even to the painter whom he worshipped and had gone all the way to France to see. To her they must seem his apology for not having horses and a valet, or merely the puerile boastfulness of a weak man. Yet if she slipped the bolt tonight and came through the doors and said, "Oh, weak man, I belong to you!" what could he do? That was the danger. He would catch the train out to Long Beach tonight, and tomorrow he would go on to the north end of Long Island, where an old friend of his had a summer studio among the sand dunes. He would stay until things came right in his mind. And she could find a smart painter, or take her punishment.

When he went home, Eden's room was dark; she was dining out somewhere. He threw his things into a hold-all he had carried about the world with him, strapped up some colours and canvases, and ran downstairs.

VII

Five days later Hedger was a restless passenger on a dirty, crowded Sunday train, coming back to town. Of course he saw now how unreasonable he had been in expecting a Huntington girl to know anything about pictures; here was a whole continent full of people who knew nothing about pictures and he didn't hold it against them. What had such things to do with him and Eden Bower? When he lay out on the dunes, watching the moon come up out of the sea, it had seemed to him that there was no wonder in the world like the wonder of Eden Bower. He was going back to her because she was older than art, because she was the most overwhelming thing that had ever come into his life.

He had written her yesterday, begging her to be at home this evening, telling her that he was contrite, and wretched enough.

Now that he was on his way to her, his stronger feeling unaccountably changed to a mood that was playful and tender. He wanted to share everything with her, even the most trivial things. He wanted to tell her about the people on the train, coming back tired from their holiday with bunches of wilted flowers and dirty daisies; to tell her that the fishman, to whom she had often sent him for lobsters, was among the passengers, disguised in a silk shirt and a spotted tie, and how his wife looked exactly like a fish, even to her eyes, on which cataracts were forming. He could tell her, too, that he hadn't as much as unstrapped his canvases,—that ought to convince her.

In those days passengers from Long Island came into New York by ferry. Hedger had to be quick about getting his dog out of the express car in order to catch the first boat. The East River, and the bridges, and the city to the west, were burning in the conflagration of the sunset; there was that great home-coming reach of evening in the air.

The car changes from Thirty-fourth Street were too many and too perplexing; for the first time in his life Hedger took a hansom cab for Washington Square. Caesar sat bolt upright on the worn leather cushion beside him, and they jogged off, looking down on the rest of the world.

It was twilight when they drove down lower Fifth Avenue into the Square, and through the Arch behind them were the two long rows of pale violet lights that used to bloom so beautifully against the grey stone and asphalt. Here and yonder about the Square hung globes that shed a radiance not unlike the blue mists of evening, emerging softly when daylight died, as the stars emerged in the thin blue sky. Under them the sharp shadows of the trees fell on the cracked pavement and the sleeping grass. The first stars and the first lights were growing silver against the gradual darkening, when Hedger paid his driver and went into the house,—which, thank God, was still there! On the hall table lay his letter of yesterday, unopened.

He went upstairs with every sort of fear and every sort of hope clutching at his heart; it was as if tigers were tearing him. Why was there no gas burning in the top hall? He found matches and the gas bracket. He knocked, but got no answer; nobody was there. Before his own door were exactly five bottles of milk, standing in a row. The milk-boy had taken spiteful pleasure in thus reminding him that he forgot to stop his order.

Hedger went down to the basement; it, too, was dark. The janitress was taking her evening airing on the basement steps. She sat waving a palm-leaf fan majestically, her dirty calico dress open at the neck. She told him at once that there had been "changes." Miss Bower's room was to let again, and the piano would go tomorrow. Yes, she left yesterday, she sailed for Europe with friends from Chicago. They arrived on Friday, heralded by many telegrams. Very rich people they were said to be, though the man had refused to pay the nurse a month's rent in lieu of notice,—which would have been only right, as the young lady had agreed to take the rooms until October. Mrs. Foley had observed, too, that he didn't overpay her or Willy for their trouble, and a great deal of trouble they had been put to, certainly. Yes, the young lady was very pleasant, but the nurse said there were rings on the mahogany table where she had put tumblers and wine glasses. It was just as well she was gone. The Chicago man was uppish in his ways, but not much to look at. She supposed he had poor health, for there was nothing to him in-side his clothes.

Hedger went slowly up the stairs—never had they seemed so long, or his legs so heavy. The upper floor was emptiness and silence. He unlocked his room, lit the gas, and opened the windows. When he went to put his coat in the closet, he found, hanging among his clothes, a pale, flesh-tinted dressing gown he had liked to see her wear, with a perfume—oh, a perfume that was still Eden Bower! He shut the door behind him and there, in the dark, for a moment he lost his manliness. It was when he held this garment to him that he found a letter in the pocket.

The note was written with a lead pencil, in haste: She was sorry that he was angry, but she still didn't know just what she had done. She had thought Mr. Ives would be useful to him; she guessed he was too proud. She wanted awfully to see him again, but Fate came knocking at her door after he had left her. She believed in Fate. She would never forget him, and she knew he would become the greatest painter in the world. Now she must pack. She hoped he wouldn't mind her leaving the dress-ing gown; somehow, she could never wear it again.

After Hedger read this, standing under the gas, he went back into the closet and knelt down before the wall; the knot hole had been plugged up with a ball of wet paper,—the same blue note-paper on which her letter was written.

He was hard hit. Tonight he had to bear the loneliness of a whole lifetime. Knowing himself so well, he could hardly believe that such a thing had ever happened to him, that such a woman had lain happy and contented in his arms. And now it was over. He turned out the light and sat down on his painter's stool before the big window. Caesar, on the floor beside him, rested his head on his master's knee. We must leave Hedger thus, sitting in his tank with his dog, looking up at the stars.

COMING, APHRODITE! This legend, in electric lights over the Lexington Opera House, had long announced the return of Eden Bower to New York after years of spectacular success in Paris. She came at last, under the management of an American Opera Company, but bringing her own *chef d'orchestre*.

One bright December afternoon Eden Bower was going down Fifth Avenue in her car, on the way to her broker, in Williams Street. Her thoughts were entirely upon stocks,—Cerro de Pasco, and how much she should buy of it,—when she suddenly looked up and realized that she was skirting Washington Square. She had not seen the place since she rolled out of it in an old-fashioned four-wheeler to seek her fortune, eighteen years ago.

"*Arrêtez, Alphonse. Attendez moi,*" she called, and opened the door before he could reach it. The children who were streaking over the asphalt on roller skates saw a lady in a long fur coat, and short, high-heeled shoes, alight from a French car and pace slowly about the Square, holding her muff to her chin. This spot, at least, had changed very little, she reflected; the same trees, the same fountain, the white arch, and over yonder, Garibaldi, drawing the sword for freedom. There, just opposite her, was the old red brick house.

"Yes, that is the place," she was thinking. "I can smell the carpets now, and the dog,—what was his name? That grubby bath-room at the end of the hall, and that dreadful Hedger—still, there was something about him, you know—" She glanced up and blinked against the sun. From somewhere in the crowded quarter south of the Square a flock of pigeons rose, wheeling quickly upward into the brilliant blue sky. She threw back her head, pressed her muff closer to her chin, and watched them with a smile of amazement and delight. So they still rose, out of all that dirt and noise and squalor, fleet and silvery, just as they used to rise that summer when she was twenty and went up in a balloon on Coney Island!

Alphonse opened the door and tucked her robes about her. All the way down town her mind wandered from Cerro de Pasco, and she kept smiling and looking up at the sky.

When she had finished her business with the broker, she asked him to look in the telephone book for the address of M. Gaston Jules, the picture dealer, and slipped the paper on which he wrote it into her glove. It was five o'clock when she reached the French Galleries, as they were called. On entering she gave the attendant her card, asking him to take it to M. Jules. The dealer appeared very promptly and begged her to come into his private office, where he pushed a great chair toward his desk for her and signalled his secretary to leave the room.

"How good your lighting is in here," she observed, glancing about. "I met you at Simon's studio, didn't I? Oh, no! I never forget anybody who interests me." She threw her muff on his writing table and sank into the deep chair. "I have come to you for some information that's not in my line. Do you know anything about an American painter named Hedger?"

He took the seat opposite her. "Don Hedger? But, certainly! There are some very interesting things of his in an exhibition at V——'s. If you would care to—"

She held up her hand. "No, no. I've no time to go to exhibitions. Is he a man of any importance?"

"Certainly. He is one of the first men among the moderns. That is to say, among the very moderns. He is always coming up with something different. He often exhibits in Paris, you must have seen—"

"No, I tell you I don't go to exhibitions. Has he had great success? That is what I want to know."

M. Jules pulled at his short grey moustache. "But, Madame, there are many kinds of success," he began cautiously.

Madame gave a dry laugh. "Yes, so he used to say. We once quarrelled on that issue. And how would you define his particular kind?"

M. Jules grew thoughtful. "He is a great name with all the young men, and he is decidedly an influence in art. But one can't definitely place a man who is original, erratic, and who is changing all the time."

She cut him short. "Is he much talked about at home? In Paris, I mean? Thanks. That's all I want to know." She rose and began buttoning her coat. "One doesn't like to have been an utter fool, even at twenty."

"*Mais, non!*" M. Jules handed her her muff with a quick, sympathetic glance. He followed her out through the carpeted show-room, now closed to the public and draped in cheesecloth, and put her into her car with words appreciative of the honour she had done him in calling.

Leaning back in the cushions, Eden Bower closed her eyes, and her face, as the street lamps flashed their ugly orange light upon it, became hard and settled, like a plaster cast; so a sail, that has been filled by a strong breeze, behaves when the wind suddenly dies. Tomorrow night the wind would blow again, and this mask would be the golden face of Aphrodite. But a "big" career takes its toll, even with the best of luck.

Animal Behavior

by LAURIE COLWIN

Nothing is more easy than to tame an animal and few things are more difficult than to get it to breed freely in confinement, even in the many cases when the male and female unite.

—Charles Darwin, *The Origin of Species*

On the roof of the East Wing of the American Naturalist Museum was a greenhouse, blocked from public view by turrets and façades. The skylights could be opened with a brass pole. Every third pane was a window. In midmorning, and sometimes in the afternoon, Roddy Phelps went up the spiral staircase to the finch room of the greenhouse and took a nap.

It was the middle of March, and Roddy was feeling slightly but constantly chilled. The weather made no sense to his body, although he knew it was supposed to be cold before the beginning of spring. Even on the coldest, rainiest days, the greenhouse was warm and faintly tropic. Birdcages were arranged on rows of pine tables, and on an empty table in the farthest row, by the window, Roddy took his naps. He had stashed a car pillow under a shelf in a paper bag.

The greenhouse was filled with potted ferns, palms, and heather. Ivy hung from crossbeams in mossy wire baskets. Each species of bird had its own room. Drifting off to sleep, Roddy was soothed by the diminutive, random noises the birds made—twitters, clacks, and cheeps, which he thought of as auditory litter. Once in a while, he brought a transistor radio with him and listened to the birds counterpointing Mozart.

The year before, Roddy's wife, Garlin, had left him, taking their child, Sara Justina, and retired to the country. At Thanksgiving, New Year's, and Easter, Roddy drove to Templeton, New Hampshire, and collected Sara Justina, who spent these holidays and a part of the summer with Roddy and his parents in Westchester. The rest of the time, silence was generally maintained between New York and Templeton, except for legal occasions when separation, alimony, divorce, and child-support papers passed between Roddy and Garlin. These entailed long conversations with the lawyers for both sides, and expensive, jagged long-distance calls from New York to New Hampshire.

The last week in March there was a brief hot spell, and Roddy's chill became more acute. Dampness settled in his bones. He began to think that he was suffering from eyestrain and spent dizzy, unfocused, and dislocated days feeling as if he were hung over. The naps in the finch room sometimes helped, but often they made his unfocused condition worse and he staggered off the table while the room went black, yellow, and dazzling gray in front of his eyes.

After Garlin's departure, Roddy had gone into a work spurt that produced two papers on the social behavior of caged finches—one for *Scientific American* and one for *American Birds*. The uncorrected galleys of both had been lying on his desk for several months. Then he started on the breeding and nesting patterns of the African finch in captivity. He had been studying this aspect of the finch since December but had run into trouble, as his finches seemed unwilling to breed in their large Victorian cages and appeared uninterested in building nests out of the pampas grass, string, and clover he provided for them.

Roddy had a corner office on the sixth floor of the museum, which housed the Department of Animal Behavior. He kept two pairs of finches there—Aggie and Bert, Gem and Russell—pets, not experimental birds, who had been left by a colleague departing for the Galápagos. When Roddy arrived in the morning, he let them out of their cage, and in the evening he spent an hour getting them back in.

The finch room was his exclusively. There was a greenhouse caretaker, José Jacinto Flores, whose job it was to clean the cages and feed the birds, but, by friendly edict, in the finch room Roddy took care of this himself. José Jacinto had appropriated a back room where he kept a tank of tropical fish and a pair of lovebirds who warbled tenderly to each other. He was a wiry, squat man, the color of cherry wood, and Roddy often saw him smoking a cheroot with the windows open, speaking softly in Spanish to his birds.

The table Roddy napped on was the last in a series of four. He was blocked by cages of birds and pots of palm and heather that shut him off from view, he thought, since he could never see anything through them.

On the last Thursday in March, Roddy left his office and went up to the greenhouse. He had not slept well the night before, tossing and brooding about his experiments, settling finally into a brief, unrefreshing sleep. A few minutes before in his office, the telephone rang and it was Garlin to tell him that Sara Justina had bronchitis.

"Did you call just to tell me that?" Roddy asked. Garlin almost never called him when Sara Justina was sick.

"Bronchitis isn't a cold," said Garlin.

"What am I supposed to do? Do you want me to come up to Templeton?"

"I thought you should know she's sick, and, by the way, did your lawyer call mine about the final papers?"

"I have to check," said Roddy.

"It's your life," Garlin said.

"What's that supposed to mean?"

"It means that you should have checked a month ago. You have no idea what's serious and what isn't. Your marriage is being disbanded and you haven't even bothered to call your lawyer."

"I've been working very hard, Garlin, and I think this whole thing is unpleasant enough without remarks like that."

"That's why your marriage is being disbanded," said Garlin, and she hung up.

The finches peered from the curtain rod. Aggie, his favorite, flew down and sat on his dictionary. Roddy watched her, feeling tired and worn down, like a statue battered by the weather. In the dove room he noticed it was raining. The sky was silvery, and drops hit the glass on a slant. At the entrance to the finch room, chilled and desperate for his nap, he discovered a girl standing in front of one of the cages. She had some millet seed on the tips of her fingers and was waiting patiently for one of the birds to take it from her.

"What are you doing here?" Roddy said.

The girl didn't move her hand but turned to look at him. She was a small girl in a gray lab coat, whose thick, ashy hair was loosely knotted at her neck. She had an oval, symmetrical face and eyes that were an intense, almost colorless gray. Under the lab coat she was wearing a gray skirt, sweater, and brown stockings.

"I'm sorry," she said. "Are these your birds?"

"Yes, and I'd like to know what you're doing here."

"I'm awfully sorry. I'm down on the fifth floor with Dr. Reddicker, working on song patterns. Until yesterday I didn't even know there was a greenhouse here, so I just came up to see what it was like. Sorry."

"Are you new here?" Roddy said.

"I started a couple of months ago. I'm Dr. Reddicker's assistant, in the doctoral program."

"After you've been here a while, you get hysterical about security."

The first three floors of the museum were open to the public and contained, in addition to cases of stuffed birds in replicas of their natural habitats, a bookstore, a small but rare gem collection, the letters and papers of John James Audubon, and several galleries filled with paintings, drawings, sculpture, and tapestries of birds. It was the largest and best collection of its kind in the world. The rest of the museum was devoted to research and teaching facilities, and rigid security was maintained. All members of the staff, from the ornithologists and researchers to the girls in the bookstore, wore plastic tags bearing their names and color photographs. Roddy stepped closer to the girl. Her tag read "Mary Leibnitz," and the photograph looked as if it had taken her by surprise. Roddy's tag was pinned to his jacket in his office.

"I'm Raiford Phelps," he said.

"This tag embarrasses me," Mary Leibnitz said. "Everyone knows my name before I'm introduced."

"Do you want to be shown around?" Roddy asked. She nodded, and he steered her through the parrot room, the sicklebills, woodpeckers, and hummingbirds. He led her back through the finches, canaries, and doves.

She stopped before a cage of pigeons. "I love the sound they make," she said. "It's kind of a gurgle. I've tried to imitate it, but I can't. Thanks very much for showing me through."

He watched her as she walked toward the stairs. She had a serious kind of grace, as if she alone were responsible for holding herself together. Roddy got his pillow from the shelf, took off his shoes, and lay down on the pine table. He leaned down to turn on his radio, but the thought of music suddenly upset him. The finches chirped him into sleep.

It became colder and less springlike. There were days when Roddy could barely keep his eyes open. He began to take two naps—one in the morning and one in the afternoon. He paced in his office, skimmed his galleys, went to bed early, twisting, brooding, unable to sleep. He made several trips to the fifth floor to look for Mary Leibnitz. He met her once briefly in the hallway and told her that if she came to his office he would show her what he was working on. Walking past her office one day, he saw her sitting diminutively next to Ethel Reddicker, a large red-headed woman, going over a series of charts. A week went by and Mary Leibnitz did not appear at his office.

Every Sunday night, Roddy called Templeton to speak to Sara Justina, with whom he had long baby conversations, followed by terse, practical conversations with Garlin. Mondays he awoke feeling drained. It seemed that on Monday it always rained or was overcast. He began to oversleep in the finch room, and he brought an alarm clock with him.

One Monday he forgot to set it and woke to find Mary Leibnitz standing by a cage looking at him; he blinked to get the blackness out of the room and blinked again because he was horrified. Nothing that fought its way to his voice was appropriate. He merely stared at her.

She looked at him calmly—he might have been one of the birds she waited to feed. Her lab coat hung away from her. She turned and walked out.

"Wait," Roddy said.

Mary Leibnitz stopped next to a cage of green siskins.

He got off the table, stepped into his shoes, and confronted her. "I don't like this," he said. "Being spied on."

"I'm not spying on you," Mary said. "I went to your office, but you weren't there, so I thought I might find you up here."

"I *told* you to come to my office."

"I did, but you weren't there. I'm really awfully sorry, but I don't know why you're making such a fuss."

"I'm not making a fuss," Roddy said. "I just don't like being spied on."

"What you mean is that you take secret naps up here and you don't like being caught out. There's nothing wrong with it. I'd sleep up here too. It smells good."

"That's not why. I don't like my privacy invaded."

"Would it interest you to know I've seen you sleeping before?"

"Well, I don't like it. I don't like it at all. What are you doing, snooping around up here?"

Mary put a cool hand on his arm. "Don't shout," she said. "You're overreacting. I've been here a couple of times to talk to Mr. Flores.

He's Peruvian, and I used to live in Lima when I was little, so I come
up to speak Spanish to him."

"How nice for you."

"No need to be nasty," Mary said. "I really *am* sorry I woke you up.
Goodbye."

"How long were you standing around?"

"You lost ten minutes of privacy," Mary said. "I didn't wake you, because you looked so angelic." She moved as quickly as a cat and was
gone before Roddy had collected himself.

On Saturday afternoon, Roddy was going over galleys in his office at
the museum. He heard a knock and turned to find Mary Leibnitz
standing at the threshold, wearing bluejeans and her lab coat.

"Hello," she said. "Should I go away? I only came by because I
wanted to go upstairs and was checking to see if you were here."

"Why did you ask if you should go away?"

"You said you didn't want your privacy invaded. I don't want to
people your solitude unless you want it peopled."

"People my solitude," Roddy repeated. She looked very fragile in the
doorway. There was a sweetness in her eyes when she looked at him.

"Can I go up and see the finches? I mean, is it all right?" she asked.

Roddy stood looking at Mary for a long time before he spoke.
"You're not like other people," he said.

Mary looked at the floor. "Can I go up?"

"I'll go with you," said Roddy, and he took her arm.

She followed him up the spiral staircase. He was tall and rangy and
hunched his shoulders. Where his hair waved slightly, it was reddish,
but generally it was brown. By a cage of golden finches, Mary studied
him. He had round green eyes, with delicate lines around them that
made him look tired in an exquisite way. His skin was very fine and his
nose was flat. In the light he looked boyish.

"What do you want to see?" he asked.

"I just wanted to be here," Mary said. "I don't think I've ever seen a
room I've liked so much."

"There's a lot I can show you," Roddy said.

"I just wanted to be here," Mary said. She smiled, then she stopped.
"It never occurred to me. I'm really sorry. I probably took you away
from your work, just for an aesthetic thrill. I mean, I didn't want to
come up for any scientific reason. I'm really sorry if I took your time."

"It's all right," said Roddy. "At least you like birds."

When they opened the door of his office, Aggie, Bert, Russell, and Gem started from the curtain rod and flew to the bookshelves. Roddy pulled down the blinds.

"I have to get them into their cage. Stand by the switch, and when I tell you, turn the lights off." He stood in the center of the room, waving his arms. The birds left the bookshelves and flew to the corners. "Now!" he shouted.

Mary turned off the lights and heard the sound of wings threshing the air, then beating furiously against the wall.

"O.K.," Roddy said. "Put them on." He had a towel in his hand and from it poked a tiny white-and-yellow head. "It's Aggie," he said. "Come and see."

Mary watched as he put the towel to the cage door and Aggie hopped out to the back of the cage, looking rumpled and frightened. "Can't you catch them any other way?" she asked.

"No. I go through this every afternoon."

"I can't bear to hear them beating against the wall like that," Mary said.

"There isn't any other way. They have to be in their cage at night."

"Won't they fly onto your hand?"

"Not these. They're friendly but not very trusting."

"Mr. Flores seems to pick them out of the air."

"You stick with Flores," Roddy said. "He's a regular Francis of Assisi."

When Gem, Russell, and Bert had been caught, Mary leaned back against the wall. "That's the most unnatural sound I've ever heard," she said.

"No more unnatural than anything else you have to get used to," said Roddy, covering the cage with a blue cloth.

They walked away from the museum past a line of trees. Damp leaves printed the sidewalks.

"I live quite close by," Mary said. "Would you like to come and have coffee?"

"I don't think so," Roddy said. "I've got lots of work to do."

Mary lived in a brownstone with a wide oak door. Her apartment looked over a garden in whose center a cement Cupid with a broken-off right arm was standing in a pool of watery dead leaves. The pictures on the wall were old-fashioned watercolors of flowers. She had a small prayer rug and a Peruvian wall hanging. Her furniture was plain and comfortable. There was an oak desk, an oak table, a gray sofa, and two blue armchairs.

From the window Roddy could see the spires of the museum and the edge of the park. In the corner of the garden grew a catalpa tree, whose dried pods hung like snakeskins amid green emerging buds.

Mary appeared and put a tray of coffee and cups on the table.

"It's bliss here," Roddy said. "How can you like the finch room so much if you have this?"

"I'm glad you decided to come up after all," Mary said. "Come have coffee."

"Wait a minute," Roddy said. He took her by the shoulders and pointed her into the afternoon light. Her eyes were level and serious. Then she grinned and he kissed her.

"Thank you," she said.

"Thank me?"

"I was hoping you'd kiss me, but I didn't know how I could arrange it. I'm shy."

"You don't seem very shy," said Roddy.

"I am, but not in usual ways," she said. She bent toward the coffeepot, but he caught her arm and kissed her again. They stood at the window with their hands interlocked, and she scanned his face as if she were memorizing it.

"I'm married," he said.

"You shouldn't have kissed me, then."

"I mean, I'm getting a divorce. I'm in the process of it. I'm not telling you that so you'll think I'm available or anything." He let go of her hand and sat down.

"Raiford," Mary said.

"Roddy," said Roddy.

"Roddy. How old are you?"

"Thirty-one."

"You're very silly for thirty-one."

"I don't like this conversation," said Roddy. He drank his coffee and looked out the window. "You have no idea how nice it is here. Why am I silly for thirty-one?"

"Because first of all you kiss me, then you say you're married, then you say you're not married, and then you tell me not to think you're available. How do you know I'm available? How do you know I'm not married?"

"Are you?" Roddy said. "I saw the picture of that guy on your mantelpiece. Is he someone in your life?"

"He used to be my fiancé," Mary said. "We were going to get married last July, but we broke it off. He's in India now, but we write to each other. We're still friends."

"You are?"

"We started out friends," Mary said. "You can stop being lovers, but you can't cancel out friendship. Maybe it's different if you're getting a divorce—harder to know if you and your wife are still friends."

"I don't know what we were," said Roddy. "We had a kid, but it didn't seem to help much."

Mary looked at him sadly. He was sitting in a dark corner of the sofa; his head was lowered, hidden in a shadow. When she turned a lamp on, he looked up and the glow hit him full in the face. She sat on her side of the sofa watching him. The light played over his face like expression, and when he finally turned to her the slight lines around his eyes softened.

"This is the first time I've felt comfortable in months," Roddy said. "You have no idea how nice you are."

On Sunday evening, Roddy sat in his apartment waiting for Mary, who was coming to borrow his copy of *Darwin's Finches.* He was happy and nervous anticipating her, so he thought about her apartment, which to him was like the finch room. He liked the way she watched him, the serious way she reacted. "It's like a movie, being with you," he had said to her. "I feel like a camera being watched by a camera. It's like being in a situation and outside it at the same time. If I look at you, I can watch me being here. I've never seen anything like it, the way you take note."

She arrived on time, wearing a raincoat, a gray skirt, a white sweater. "Don't you ever wear anything that's a color?" Roddy asked.

His apartment was on the ground floor of a dingy brick building near the river. In the living room was an aluminum work table, piled with papers, two cheap chairs, and a matching sofa. It looked as if someone had lived in the two rooms for a brief, uninspired time and had fled abruptly, leaving faded furniture and curtains behind. In the middle of the floor was an air-conditioner turned over on its side. Its parts were strewn in a circle around it.

"I'm in the process of fixing it," Roddy explained.

Behind a partition was his bedroom—a nook big enough for a bed, on top of which were stacks of clean laundry and a small generator. In the kitchen was a Bunsen burner and a pegboard hung with hammers, ratchets, wrenches, and drills. On the Formica sideboard was an acid beaker that functioned as coffeemaker. There were two tin plates and two tin cups that he had gotten as a premium for buying the five bottles of soy sauce that were lined up on a shelf next to some empty orange-juice tins. The icebox emitted a hum, and when Roddy hit it with his forearm the door opened, revealing a container of cottage cheese, a bottle of wine, and a carton of eggs.

"That's my next project, that icebox," Roddy said. "I got the hum out once, but it came back."

He made coffee in the acid beaker. There was powdered milk and sugar he had filched from the museum cafeteria.

"What an odd way to live," Mary said. "You go to all the trouble of making coffee with filter paper and then you don't have any proper milk. These are only temporary quarters to you, aren't they?"

"Proper milk, as you call it, doesn't keep, and since I'm not here all that often, why bother?"

"Then why bother about anything?" Mary said.

"I work most of the time. That's what my time is for."

They drank their coffee side by side on the sofa, holding hands. The icebox began to hum.

"I've got to fix that, but first I have to call Templeton. I've been trying to get Garlin all day. She's never in, or else she's not answering the phone." He dragged the telephone from under the couch and dialed a series of numbers.

"Let me speak to Sara," he said into the receiver. "Is she any better? . . . Hello? S. J., it's Poppa. I hear you got a shot. You didn't cry? Well, I'm very pleased to hear that. I'm sending you a postcard in the mail and I want you to send me one of the pictures you draw at school. O.K.? Ask Mama if she wants to speak to me. . . . Hi. I didn't get the lawyer. I'll call him tomorrow. O.K.? Right." He hung up.

Mary had moved to a corner of the sofa, to keep a distance between herself and the conversation.

"Why are you hiding over there?" Roddy said. "To pay me back for calling my wife? You can call your boyfriend in India if you want."

"Don't tease," said Mary. "How old's your little girl?"

"Four."

"Do you have any pictures of her?"

"I don't have anything around," Roddy said. "Most of my stuff is with my parents in Westchester. I brought a whole bunch of stuff back from New Caledonia once—feathers and nests and bows, carved boats, that sort of thing. After I got married, it was all nicely on display, and

Sara got her baby hands on what hadn't disintegrated and tore it apart."

"It's a spare life," Mary said, smiling.

"You can be my possession. I'd put you in a little nook and lay flowers at your feet."

"Don't tease," said Mary.

"I wish I *were* teasing," Roddy said. "God, how glad I am you're here."

He took the wine from the icebox, opened it with a corkscrew, and poured out two water glasses.

"Celebration," he said.

"Cheers," said Mary. "It's the beginning of April."

They stood in happy silence, drinking wine. The icebox hummed.

"Stand over here," Roddy said. "I'm going to fix that damned thing once and for all."

"Don't fix it, Roddy. Talk to me."

"I've got the time now and I might not tomorrow. Besides, I can do both. Hand me that wrench—the smaller one."

He took the wrench and a screwdriver and, after taking off the bottom plate, lay on his back, looking into the motor of the icebox.

"There's a flashlight in that drawer," he said. "Can you shine it right above my head so I can see into this?"

She held it as she was told, flashing the beam from time to time onto his face.

"This machine is an antique," Roddy said. "Why do you keep flashing that into my eyes?"

"To behold you."

Half an hour later, the hum diminished, Roddy got up from the floor and took the flashlight from Mary.

"I shouldn't be doing this," he said.

"Fixing the icebox?"

"Asking you if you'll stay here tonight."

"You know I will," said Mary.

"Why?"

"Because it's the right thing to do."

"Do you always do things for a reason?" he asked.

"Aren't you doing this for a reason?"

"Your coming up to the finch room was an act of vast good fortune for me," Roddy said. "You're the nicest person I think I've ever met. You're the only person I've ever met who seems to be *prepared* for things. Are you prepared for a lot of pain?"

"I have no idea what you're talking about," said Mary. "I don't think you do, either." She rinsed the glasses, happy to feel the water running over her wrists.

Every day, they left the museum together, took walks through the park, and had dinner. During the week, they spent nights at Roddy's, and on the weekends at Mary's. Often in the middle of dinner or a walk, they would stop and look at each other seraphically.

"I've never been this happy," Roddy said.

"Neither have I," said Mary.

"I love walking through time with you," Roddy said frequently.

They read each other's books, talked for hours, and planned to write a paper together on the function of song patterns in caged and wild finches. Roddy was astonished at how long Mary liked to sit over dinner. They talked, and quarreled, and kept regular hours. Each day the leaves got rounder. The cherry trees in the museum garden blossomed. The grass was lusher—wet and slick in the evenings. They did not arrive at the museum together in the mornings.

In the middle of June, they strolled through the park. The earth gave up a cold mist that collected in fuzzy halos under the street lights. The trees had blossomed late and were just shedding their petals, which fell on the grass like spilled paint. They did not walk hand in hand but held themselves in a close orbit, arm against arm. They stopped by a stone wall and studied each other. He had a way of keeping his face in a state of blankness tinged only by worry. When the tightness broke and he smiled, Mary sometimes found herself close to tears. Often he looked at her with a tenderness so intense that she had to force herself to make him laugh in order to break it.

"You are a blessing I don't deserve," Roddy said.

"Shut up."

"When I think that it's only chance that you work at the museum, that you might not have come up to the greenhouse . . ."

"You think it's chance that we're together," Mary said. She walked under a plane tree, out of the light.

"Why are we, then?"

"I don't know about you," said Mary, almost mumbling. "But some people act out of love."

He caught her by the elbow. "Does that mean you love me?"

"That's not your business," Mary said.

"What do you mean, it's not my business?"

"It isn't information you really want," she said. "Don't go trying to get me to say what you don't want to hear."

The summer seemed reluctant to break. By the middle of July it was still cold and wet, and the stone corridors of the museum were damp. The days spun themselves out in solid grayness. On a rainy Friday in August, Roddy and Mary ambled under an umbrella toward Mary's apartment. People on the streets moved in slow motion against the downpour, and the trees moved like underwater flora. The front door to Mary's apartment was swollen with damp and Roddy had to shove it open.

He sprawled on the couch and shut his eyes. Mary sat on the floor pouring coffee.

"Are you sleepy?" she asked. For a couple of weeks, he had been edgy and occasionally sleepless.

"I'm trying to see what this will look like in memory," Roddy said. "We're not living in real time. This isn't real time at all."

"It's real enough for me," said Mary. She looked up to find him still lying there, his hands folded on his chest, his eyes shut, like a knight on a medieval coffin.

"It isn't real. It's pleasurable suspension. Real time has nothing to do with chance. It's loaded with obligations and countercharges and misfires."

She put her cup down and wound her arms around her knees. "Is something going to make this change?" she said. "Is that why you're so restless?"

He sat beside her on the floor and took the pins out of her hair. "You think life goes in a straight line, Mary. This all seems clear and straightforward to you, because that's what you're like, but it isn't that way for me."

"If you mean that you have to go to Westchester with Sara Justina, I knew that a long time ago."

"Look, Mary. What we have now is a little gift wrapped up in time. It'll never be this way again. There are things I have to do that will cut me off from you eventually, and you'll hate me." He wound her hair around his wrist. Then he let go, and she got up and sat in a hard-backed chair, clutching the cane seating until she could feel it imprint her hand. She had been haunted for a month, expecting some dire interruption between them.

"If what you're saying, Roddy, is that we can't be together any more, say it. Don't be such a chicken."

He kneeled in front of the chair. "I'm used to these lovely free days, and I get sick to think what the world is going to do to them."

"Talk straight," Mary said. She collected the coffee cups, and when she reached for the cream pitcher it slipped out of her hand and smashed on the floor. She sat down abruptly, put her head in her hands, and cried for several minutes.

Roddy put his arms around her. He ran his fingers over the tears on her face and drew a little pattern on her cheekbone. "I want to maintain the time we have," he said. "But, Mary, the earth spins on its axis and everything changes. You can't freeze things, not things as delicate as this, and hope they'll survive a thaw."

"I don't know how to fight you on this," Mary said, "when I don't know what I'm fighting."

"Time," said Roddy. "I've never seen a life arranged like yours. It's organized for a kind of comfort. Mine isn't."

Her eyes were very grave. "You said I was a good arranger," she said. "Time is the easiest thing in the world to arrange."

"I want to be with you," Roddy said into her hair. "But I don't see how. All I see is a messy world nibbling at the corners of this."

"You're not talking about the world. You're talking about yourself. The world is outside us. This is an inside job."

"Look, life has a lot of holes in it. This is going to get worse, not better. That's why all this time was so beautiful—because nothing got in the way of it."

She spoke very slowly. "I didn't want to say this to you, Roddy, but you know I love you. I can't get to the bottom of what's bothering you, but if it's something you have to go through by yourself, I'll stand by you. You go off and take care of Sara Justina, and when that's finished we can sort it out. I don't want to live in unreal time with you."

"You're making this very hard for me," he said.

"I'm trying to make it easy. I'm trying to clear a way for you so you can see us," said Mary. "But don't make me hang too long."

"I'll figure it out," Roddy said wildly. "I'll figure it out."

The first week they were apart, Mary worked on a chart on the song patterns of the thrush. She made tapes of canary songs and wrote them down in musical notation, sitting in her tiny office with a set of headphones clamped to her ears. They blotted out the sound of footsteps, but they did not blot out what she replayed over and over in her mind: Roddy talking to her. When Ethel Reddicker went to lunch or lectures, Mary took off her earphones, locked the door, and wept. She stayed away from Roddy's office, but the thought that he was in the building, walking the corridors, using the elevator, made her feel bonded to him.

At night, she ran their moments together through her mind until, with a sense of loss, she realized that she was thinking in the past tense. There was no one she could talk to—she and Roddy had sealed themselves up, keeping their time to themselves.

Then for a month she kept busy, knowing that he was in Westchester with Sara Justina, but when the month was out she found that she was prone to tears that caught her off guard. She walked through the museum in a glazed and headachy state until she came down with a cold that kept her home for three days, watching the rain clouds low over the spires of the museum.

In the beginning of September, she went to the greenhouse when she was certain Roddy would not be there, to speak to José Jacinto Flores. She found him feeding Roddy's finches. His hand was extended into the cage and the birds perched on his sleeve, picking millet from his palm. He greeted her in soft, courtly Spanish.

"Why are you feeding the finches, Mr. Flores?"

"Because he"—José Jacinto nodded toward the empty table—"went to a conference in Bermuda for two weeks, so I have to take care of them."

This information filled Mary with hope and despair in equal parts: he was back—he had gone away without telling her, but he was away. And how could she hear from him if he was in Bermuda?

Mary knew when he came back—she felt it. Then she saw him in the back of a lecture room as she walked by. He was writing on a blackboard, talking to one of the ornithologists. His shoulders were hunched in the old familiar way. Everything about him was familiar, but she couldn't call to him. She had given him her form of trust, and knew, because he had said so, that he trusted her. If he was waiting, it was for a reason—she had taken him on trust and stood by it. In her memory she heard his soft voice say, "You don't realize that I adore you." She raced to her office in tears.

How they contrived to work in the same building, live in the same neighborhood, and never meet amazed her, but they did. She was not the sort of girl to leave notes in his mailbox or letters taped to his office door. When two months had passed, she realized that he was going to do nothing about her and she was filled with a sense of pain so intense it astonished her.

The last bugs floated lazily on the air currents. The weather was hot and wet, or cold and wet. In Mary's garden, a row of cats sat on the wall, baring their teeth, chattering at the chickadees, making little rattles in the back of their throats.

She had got into the habit of using the public entrance to the museum instead of the staff door. It was the third week of public school, and lines of giggling children patrolled by nervous teachers looped around the stone eagles and spilled down the steps, forming rows on the sidewalk.

One morning before she went to her office, Mary stopped in the gem collection, cutting her way through a sea of beings that reached her waist. She looked down on a mat of bobbing heads. There was a mixed din of shouts and giggles, flattened by the stone walls to a loud hush.

The room was packed; she could hardly walk. Children were standing four deep in front of each glass case and a teacher was reading to them about star sapphires from a printed card.

She fled to one of the galleries. A group of quiet children was standing in front of a bronze stork. At the far end of the gallery was a small tapestry behind a glass shield. A brass plaque announced that it had been woven by the nuns of Belley in the sixteenth century. In a lush green field, full of shells and wild flowers, was a heron—pure white and slightly lopsided. Its delicate feet were red, and its wings drooped by its sides. As she walked closer, she saw that on its face was embroidered an expression of almost human mournfulness. The room filled up behind her as she stood. Tears came into her eyes and her mouth twisted. When she turned, the room was swimming with children.

In late October, Roddy was lying on the table in the finch room. His eyes were open, and he was looking at a half-opened window in the skylight. A bird flew across it. He heard the door open, but didn't look up. Steps went past him, and through the cages he could see the back of Mary Leibnitz's head. He heard her walk to where José Jacinto Flores kept his lovebirds and tropical fish. Through the cheeping of the birds he could hear Spanish being spoken. He heard a chair scrape, then footsteps. Mary walked into the finch room, and Roddy sat up on the table. He looked at her through an opening in the cages, and she stared back like a startled animal. He could not imagine what she was reading on his face, but when he focused he could see what was on hers. It was pure grief; if he had ever seen it before, he hadn't known what it was. He swung his legs around.

"Please don't get up," she said, in a soft voice, and he watched her as she walked slowly past the cages and out the door.

The Love-Letters of a Clodhopper

by GERTRUDE BROOKE HAMILTON

"There's no use talking—the person who can read this story without feeling a lump in his throat has something wrong with his heart."

—so was this archetype of Love Conquers All
introduced in a 1917 *Redbook*

She selected several letters from the packet and put up a lovely hand to
switch on the drop-light. Its glow vivified her flowing, tawny hair,
waxen skin and black-lashed, coppery eyes—illuminated the bronze
appointments of her ebony writing-table, purpled the pool in her jeweled inkwell and deepened the rich window hangings of her colorful
room. Below the windows the tide of Manhattan broke and thundered
on the shores of Seventy-second Street and Broadway. She spread the
selected letters on the ebony table and began to read:

Dear Miss Gilder.

I rec'd your most helpful letter at 5.40 to-day.

Please excuse pencil. The ink is froze. Also please excuse, as usual, my
uphill fist and bum spelling.

My married sis, Mrs. Pink Tibberly, is in a worrie to know who you are—she has brot me some of your letters from the P. O. But I wont tell her. I want the secret to myself. Just think. for 3 fine yrs you—Zola Gilder, a New York writer and poet—writing cheering letters to me—Martin Redd, a clodhopper!

Ever since I was old enuff to day-dream I have wanted to know some one like you. But when I first writ you in the care of a magazine, because that story of yours "Just Nature" had made me blubber, I calculated I was cutting fodder to rot. That first pretty, polite letter from you I wore under my shirt for 30 days. And then I seen your picture in a magazine. Shivering snakes! I went down on my big knees to what you had writ to me! It was 7:½ months before I hunched up the nerve to fist my pen again. And you writ back. And I writ back. And dearest, we kept company in letters.

Please excuse the "dearest" for you are dear to me. I have never seen you. Calculate I never will. But I don't think you ought to blame me for loving you as much as it is possible for a man to love a woman. You are good and noble. You make the farm chunks around here look like 30 cts. You know something else besides corset covers and boys and baking biscuits. You have told me 50 fine books to read. I love, honor and adoor you.

If this makes you mad, I am realy and truly sorry. also please forgive me.

Have just finished reading your story "Ships That Pass In The Day." I think it the sweetest one yet—a sort of sad-sweet story. Will get the current magazine you mention. As usual, I gave the "Ship" story to my sis, Mrs. Pink Tibberly, to read.

I am very sorry to hear of your having a cold, but it is no surprise to me, as I know you work to hard. You need fresh air and buttermilk. Dearest, I haven't taken a dose of Dr.'s dope for a cold or anything else for over 14 yrs and I hope I never do again.

Does it make you mad for me to call you dearest? If it does, please tell me so and please forgive me. For I would not hurt or harm you in any way, shape or form. Please an'sr soon.

Your humble friend,
MARTIN REDD.

Dear Miss Gilder.

Yours rec'd at 6.27 this evening.

I was beginning to feel that you was mad at me because I told you I loved you. I would like for to tell you heaps of such things, but I calculate you would laugh at me and think me a fool. But honest I could just fairly chaw you up—I like and love you so well.

After I writ that last letter to you I saddled my mare Crystal Herne and rode 16 hrs straight. The coarse grass on the prairie didn't seem no coarser than me handing you—Zola Gilder—a josh word like "dearest." I drove Crystal and myself to a dripping sweat. On the way home I stopped at Tibberly farm. My married sis Pink was feeding her chickens. I grabbed the mush-pot from her, and before I knew it I was telling her who my girl was. Sis sat down hard and took off her glasses to squint at me. Her eyes are so bad now that she can't read much, so she hasn't read your current story "The Shack Woman," but she will now as fast as she can. Sis thinks I ought to worship you (which I do) bow down and say my prayers to you—which I've done.

Please excuse me for calling you *my girl* to Sis. I know you are not for me, only to dream about, but in my dreams you are my girl. I wonder if you will be mad when you read this. I had a dream last night which I would like for to tell you about.

My Dream.

The date sliped up a few notches and it was midsummer, balmy and fair. I rec'd a letter from you saying you was coming out here. I hitched Crystal to the buggy and drove S. E. along the little lane from our house to the road—then turned E. to the big road called Clinton Road in the country and Clinton Ave. in town. I followed the Road to a little hill about ½ mile long. Then I turned E. and drove over a new concrete bridge—the sides big walls of solid concrete and steel. I drove on over the grade, with Salt Creek running E. at the foot of the grade. There was no houses—all farm ground and pasture. Then I left the grade, drove up a hill—and was on the prairie.

You was there waiting for me. You was just what I know you are, a tall, straight-backed girl with fairy feet and flying hair and something that smells of God about you—like the girls you write of in your stories, like your face in the magazine pictures. You come running to meet me, and as you run you threw off your fine New York clothes and underneath them you wore a print dress and under your shirt you wore that picture of me with my best yearling that I sent you 2 yrs ago.

When you got close by me you stopped, sort of shy, and said, "Howdy, Martin Redd."

And I—pretending I was stuck-up and cityish, and wanting the laugh on you said, "Excuse me. At what hog show did we meet? I can't calculate to remember, Miss Zola."

And you hung your head and shook your flying hair over your eyes and you begun to cry.

And *man alive!* I went down on my big fool knees to you right then and there.

And you laughed quicker than you cried. You run—you was lighter than dandelion fluff—to Crystal and kissed the white star on her forehead and you jumped into the buggy and grabbed up the reins and hollered—"Giddap!"

Crystal backed in the traces and begun to skid. I got in and took the reins. Crystal reared, shyed, laid back her ears and let loose! She had us home in about 5 minutes.

Before the buggy quit swaying you was out of it, dancing by the barn, touching the head of my Holstein heifer, kissing the cat that has double-pawed kittens, wading and capering thro the S. W. field of clover, grabbing up apples and pears and biting into them and throwing them over your shoulder and running all the time to my mother, throwing yourself into her arms and crying. And all the time dancing with your feet.

For supper we chawed something. I never dreamed what. After supper I raced you to the barn. You tiptoed into it and kissed Crystal eating oats and corn in her stall. And mooed at the cows, Blossom and Lillian Russell, munching their straw, and shook your hair over the guinea fowls squeaking to get out of the barred back doors. And like a squirrel you scampered to the hay lofts. I climbed after you. You got to the highest loft and spread out your arms like a bird and sailed down 10 ft and lay there for a minute beautiful and rosy and climbed up again, and said, "Unbar the back doors of the barn, Martin Redd. Let the crying guinea fowls out. And show me the view."

I pulled back the wooden bars and opened the whole back of the barn and you spun out on your tiptoes and whirled about and shrieked with joy at the view. You can see 5 counties—a river—and about 1000 acres of heavy timber from the back of our barn. It is like standing in the clouds with the angels so high up that you can't see no people—just spires and the tops of things. You got sort of solemn over it and you cuddled close to my side and your hand stole up to my breast and lay there.

Next thing—you was laughing. I was fixing a swing for you under the stars. It was N. E. of the clover field where the view is high again. You leaped into the swing and swung up touching the trees. Down, brushing by to quick for me to kiss you.

Next Mother was giving you a foaming pitcher of milk to drink. You drunk and drunk till we all laughed and loved you and worshiped you and went clean mad about you. Mother took you to the S. W. bedroom that is next to hers and she give you a lamp. It shed a sort of a glory over you. We like for to have died from *honoring* you.

You said—looking at the flame of the lamp, "Martin Redd, I love you—I love Crystal Herne, and the cows and the heifer, and the guinea fowls and the double-pawed kittens and your Mother and your married sis, Mrs. Pink Tibberly." And sly as a little spider you spun into the S. W. room and shut the door on me. Mother and Sis run down to the kitchen and begun to break eggs and cream butter and sift flour for the wedding cake.

In the night—when I was prowling under the window of the S. W. room—I heard the sash slip up. You put a foot over the sill and jumped down.

I said, "Where are you going?"

And you changed into a farm chunk.

Dearest, I woke up blubbering.

If this dream ofends you I am truly sorry.

The robins have come and the wild duck and geese are going north but we have had several flurries of snow—about 1 inch deep last night.

How is your work getting on? I wonder if when things go wrong you would like for some big strong person to take you in his arms and make you forget worrie—past and future.

I told you about 13 months ago what I look like. I am 6 ft., weigh 170 lbs. have yellow hair and gray eyes, sound teeth, high nose and reddish skin.

Hope you are well and prosperous. Write when you can.

> As ever your humble friend,
>
> MARTIN REDD.

Dear Miss Gilder.

I sent you a letter some months ago. Like to never got it mailed as I was in the woods cutting timber for 2 weeks on a stretch.

We are having some cussed weather. Spring don't seem to be coming this yr. everything is covered with sleet and ice. Telephone lines is nearly all down and things in bum shape generally. I wonder how cold it gets in New York. It gets 30 below real often here, sometimes 35 and 40.

Please forgive me for that last letter. I calculate I deserve the 10 weeks silence you have handed me. Also please excuse ink blots. Time to feed the hogs.

Hope you are well and happy.

Your humble friend,
MARTIN REDD.

Dear Miss Gilder.

Yours of the 22nd arrived on Christmas Day. I am happy to hear about your good luck about your work and sorry you was to busy to write to me for 3 months.

I have lost $400. worth of hogs. That wont seem a very large sum to you.

I read your story "No King But Caesar" and thought it fine. It hits a world of women—the women in the world. As usual, I gave the Caesar story to my sis, Mrs. Pink Tibberly, to read.

Am glad you got a smile off my mare's name. She is all right. When the mare was a baby it seemed that one of her eyes was going to be what people call *glass eye* an eye that is *white*. I decided on the Crystal partly on account of the crystal-like eye and partly for Crystal Herne. I seen her once in a play when I was in Chicago and thought her fine.

I am glad you are coming to the good money. Hope you are able to keep it up. I am not like you for I don't wants heaps of coin or fame.

I wont bother you with any more.

I love you.

Your humble friend,
MARTIN REDD.

Dear Miss Gilder.

I went to a corn-roast in these parts last night.

The men build a big camp fire in the field. The girls bring corn and salt and marshmallows sometimes rolls and hot sausages. They sit around the camp fire and eat and tell stories. There is always a funny fellow and a girl who recites sad pieces. Once I could laugh at that fellow and the pieces always brot tears to my eyes. Last night I sat like a stiff in the crowd. I saw your face in the big camp fire. Your arms reached out to me in the licking flames. Your curling mouth laughed at the bunch I went with—guyed my friends, guyed me, sang up to the stars in the smoke from the fire and made fun of the clodhopper who had gone stargazing. It come to me in a crack that the love making was always on my side and that it wasn't getting me nowhere. I calculated I was getting tired of kisses on paper. I sort of flared up high as the camp fire and put the blame on you. You have crammed my head with 75 books and set me blubbering over your stories and writ me letters to wear under my shirt. And I'll be thirty next birthday.

This is for you *alone*. I want to work for you, to do things to please you. I want you to like the things I like and I like the things you like— to hold you in my arms evenings and tell you that same old sweet story over and over and over. I love you! You can't never marry me. What is the end of real love but marriage?

What did you learn me to love you for?

MARTIN REDD.

Dearest.

I could grab you in my arms and murmur lots of things in your ear and lay your head on my shoulder—and blubber. All of which would make you justly mad!

I am tipping my hat to you for that lock of hair. It is realy beautiful hair. I have your pictures propped up in front of me as I write. The 3 I have cut from magazines. I wish I was at your side that I might stroke that beautiful hair and kiss and caress you. I don't feel like telling you nothing but I love you. I wonder how you would like for me to come into your room and love you savagely, to take up your hair in my hands and bury my face in it, to look into your eyes and find nothing but purity there. But on the other hand if you was the Devil's own Daughter and your hair was coils of glittering snakes I would love you. You couldn't do nothing low or mean enuff to keep me from loving you.

I am going to ride 18 hrs. straight and think it out.

My Thoughts.

At first I thought I would come to New York and give you back your letters and only slightly smile when I saw you and then come back home after having just loved you with my eyes.

And then—dawn was on the prairie when I come to my 2nd thought —I felt my big, young body and the muscles in my arms. I thought of the $3000 I have in the Fairbanks bank in Mansfield and the 200 good acres I own. I looked at my hands—brown and hard enuff to protect any soft white hand that would trust itself to it. I thought of my married sis, Mrs. Pink Tibberly, who thinks me good enuff for any woman. And my Mother who says I am the handsomest man around these parts. And the farm chunks who any one of them would jump at slinging hash for me.

My 3rd thought was about Love.

My 4th thought was You. I read the beautiful things between the lines of your letters. I heard you calling me. I saw you in New York— pestered by men—fighting for your fame and money—and all the while resting in my big ugly arms.

For you are mine by the right of my manhood—by the right that hasn't nothing to do with schooling—by the right that made Eve belong to Adam.

I am coming to New York to pick you up in my arms and bring you back with me. You're mine! My friend! my girl! my ideal! my pal! my saint! my wife! Those fairy feet of yours may run fast, dearest, but they shant outrun your clodhopper's hoofs. In all my dreams you get away from me. I am going to quit dreaming! I am coming to New York to pick you up in my arms and bring you back with me!

I love you so I am sick and humble from love. My knees knock at the thought of coming into your presence. My eyes blubber. I am like an old man with a young man's lungs. I am feeble and powerful—glad and blue—resolute and uncertain—shouting and afraid—bold and hanging back.

Tell me to come. Tell me *you love me.*

MARTIN REDD.

Miss Zola Gilder.

I would like for to kill you for your letter rec'd today at 12.50.

I would like for to come into your room and put the marks of my fingers on your white shoulders and stamp with my feet on your feet and use my horsewhip on your beautiful back.

You begin your letter with some French that I can't read because I don't know no language but my own. You go on to say that you are not the marrying sort—that my letters have been one long, big laugh to you —that the only reason you encouraged them was to get what you call copy—that a clodhopper story you hope to sell for $500. is already in your typewriter—that love is a fairy tale that brings so much a word— that nothing funnier could be imagined than Zola Gilder jumping about in hay lofts and nestling up to a six-foot son of the soil! You end your letter with some Latin that you know I can't read. And with that you are thro.

Well so am I. Here are your letters, the lock of your hair and the magazine pictures of you, you beauty, you she-wolf.

I am glad you got a $500. laugh out of me.

I love you.

THE CLODHOPPER.

She replaced the letters in the packet and put out lovely hands to pick up a pair of crutches. Slowly she got to her feet and crossed her colorful room to an electric button. She punched white light in abundance over the room. At her ebony-framed, full-length mirror she took stock of her flowing, tawny hair, well-chiseled brow, black-lashed, coppery eyes, delicate nose, idealistic nostrils and red, wistful mouth. Pulling a shimmering mass of hair over her shoulder and half turning from her mirror, she gave a slant stare at the hump on her back and at her shrunken legs and crippled, club feet. She spread her hands on her crutches and began to sob.

The telephone rang. Zola Gilder answered it.

"Mr. Martin Redd, of Illinois, calling," came the metallic voice of the hotel clerk.

"Who?" Zola gasped.

"Mr. Martin Redd, of Illinois, calling," replied the mechanical voice.

Zola Gilder's face went white. "Martin Redd—calling!" she repeated. In swift succession, panic, joy, apprehension, despair, possessed her features.

She moistened her lips, and said into the telephone: "Have Mr. Martin Redd shown up to my suite."

Her hand, as she put the receiver into the hook, went weak. Her shoulders rested heavily on her crutches. She seemed about to crumple up like an imperfect rose-petal at the end of a perfect summer.

Then the spirit that shone in her coppery eyes conquered her weakness. Resolutely she moved to the center of the room, where the light from the chandelier fell full upon her.

Outside, in the softly padded corridor, feet passed and repassed. Somewhere a room-telephone tinkled. The heavy sound of a trunk-truck rumbled by.

An elevator-door clanged. A tread, different from the rest, came along the corridor. The knock that smote her door reverberated through the suite.

With wild, uneven steps, hampered by her infirmity, she rushed to her door—and locked it.

The knock came again. It was perhaps, the *rap-rap* of knuckles fisted to strike.

Zola leaned against the door and put her paling lips on the wood where the knock sounded. "Martin Redd," she whispered dryly, "go away! What have you come for?"

A hand wrenched the door-knob. A heavy foot struck against the satin panel of the door. It seemed as if a giant shoulder might be placed against the wood and the door might come crashing in.

Zola Gilder unlocked the door and moved back to her position under the chandelier. "Come in," she said.

Martin Redd opened the door—and was in the room. He carried a rawhide whip.

Zola Gilder spread out her lovely hands on the rungs of her crutches. "Howdy, Clodhopper," she said faintly.

Martin Redd's balked, baffled stare played on her exquisite face and hair—and on her body.

"You see," she said with a three-cornered smile, "I *would* be funny jumping about in hay-lofts."

His look of amazement increased.

She shook back her flowing hair. The movement revealed the nobility of her brow, the beauty of her eyes, the idealism of her nostrils and the redness of her mouth. "You wouldn't want to come into my room and love me savagely, would you?" she faltered.

Martin Redd took a step toward her and stood still.

Zola Gilder smiled. For the second, her face was all that a man might dream of.

Then renunciation leveled and controlled her face. "I am glad you came, Martin Redd," she said slowly. "I am glad I have had the courage to see you. I am glad to be able to tell you that I did not encourage you to obtain what I call copy. I have not written a clodhopper story. I was lying."

Her voice sank, became infinitely sweet. "Now that you have seen me, you can go back and happily marry a 'farm chunk.' Now that you have seen me, you can forget—or laugh. For it is funny!" She pulled a mass of hair over her shoulder, with brave, tragic humor, exposing her deformity. "See how far I am from the woman you have wanted, Martin. Brains I have, and soul, and beauty of face—" Her tragedy shook her.

His arms hung at his sides, inanimate as his stare.

The slow, luminous calm of the spirit challenging the physical composed her. The spirit transcended the physical. "You can never marry me," she said, sadly. Her face colored. "What is the real end of love but marriage?"

She seemed to wither. "I have done wrong in deceiving you," she stammered. "Use your whip on my—back." She hung her head and shook her tawny hair over her eyes and began to cry.

Martin Redd placed the rawhide whip on her ebony writing-table beside the jeweled inkwell.

A step took him to her.

Gently he threw away the crutches and picked her up in his arms. "Blubber on my onery shoulder, dearest," he said, in a rich voice. "Please excuse the 'dearest,' for you are dear to me."

He walked her up and down the gorgeous room, stroking her beautiful hair—kissing and caressing her.

Below the windows, the tides of Manhattan broke and thundered on the shores of Seventy-second Street and Broadway. As an automobile-siren screamed in the streets, Zola laid a hand on Martin's breast.

"You cannot marry me!" she cried.

"I fail for to see why," he answered.

"I am misshapen."

"I calculate that don't make no difference."

"But Martin, I am a cripple!"

"You're my girl." He rocked and cradled her. "You're glad you're where you are, in my big, ugly arms. Aren't you, dearest? Lay your head down on my shoulder. There." The rich voice was humble. "If you will let me take you back with me, you'll do me honor. I love you."

Her hand on his breast, lighter than a snowflake, seemed to melt there. Her face on his shoulder became less the face of a child-sufferer, less the face of a brilliant recluse—more the face of a woman who would play her woman's part.

A delicate and courageous ecstasy flowed through Zola Gilder's whisper, "I could die from honoring you, Martin Redd."

Love: Three Pages From a Sportsman's Book

by GUY DE MAUPASSANT

I have just read among the general news in one of the papers a drama of passion. He killed her and then he killed himself, so he must have loved her. What matters He or She? Their love alone matters to me; and it does not interest me because it moves me or astonishes me, or because it softens me or makes me think, but because it recalls to my mind a remembrance of my youth, a strange recollection of a hunting adventure where Love appeared to me, as the Cross appeared to the early Christians, in the midst of the heavens.

I was born with all the instincts and the senses of primitive man, tempered by the arguments and the restraints of a civilized being. I am passionately fond of shooting, yet the sight of the wounded animal, of the blood on its feathers and on my hands, affects my heart so as almost to make it stop.

That year the cold weather set in suddenly toward the end of autumn, and I was invited by one of my cousins, Karl de Rauville, to go with him and shoot ducks on the marshes, at daybreak.

My cousin was a jolly fellow of forty, with red hair, very stout and bearded, a country gentleman, an amiable semi-brute, of a happy disposition and endowed with that Gallic wit which makes even mediocrity agreeable. He lived in a house, half farmhouse, half château, situated in a broad valley through which a river ran. The hills right and left were covered with woods, old manorial woods where magnificent trees still remained, and where the rarest feathered game in that part of France was to be found. Eagles were shot there occasionally, and birds of passage, such as rarely venture into our overpopulated part of the country, invariably lighted amid these giant oaks, as if they knew or recognized some little corner of a primeval forest which had remained there to serve them as a shelter during their short nocturnal halt.

In the valley there were large meadows watered by trenches and separated by hedges; then, further on, the river, which up to that point had been kept between banks, expanded into a vast marsh. That marsh was the best shooting ground I ever saw. It was my cousin's chief care, and he kept it as a preserve. Through the rushes that covered it, and made it rustling and rough, narrow passages had been cut, through which the flat-bottomed boats, impelled and steered by poles, passed along silently over dead water, brushing up against the reeds and making the swift fish take refuge in the weeds, and the wild fowl, with their pointed, black heads, dive suddenly.

I am passionately fond of the water: of the sea, though it is too vast, too full of movement, impossible to hold; of the rivers which are so beautiful, but which pass on, and flee away; and above all of the marshes, where the whole unknown existence of aquatic animals palpitates. The marsh is an entire world in itself on the world of earth—a different world, which has its own life, its settled inhabitants and its passing travelers, its voices, its noises, and above all its mystery. Nothing is more impressive, nothing more disquieting, more terrifying occasionally, than a fen. Why should a vague terror hang over these low plains covered with water? Is it the low rustling of the rushes, the strange will-o'-the-wisp lights, the silence which prevails on calm nights, the still mists which hang over the surface like a shroud; or is it the almost inaudible splashing, so slight and so gentle, yet sometimes more terrifying than the cannons of men or the thunders of the skies, which make these marshes resemble countries one has dreamed of, terrible countries holding an unknown and dangerous secret?

No, something else belongs to it—another mystery, profounder and graver, floats amid these thick mists, perhaps the mystery of the creation itself! For was it not in stagnant and muddy water, amid the heavy humidity of moist land under the heat of the sun, that the first germ of life pulsated and expanded to the day?

I arrived at my cousin's in the evening. It was freezing hard enough to split the stones.

During dinner, in the large room whose sideboards, walls, and ceiling were covered with stuffed birds, with wings extended or perched on branches to which they were nailed—hawks, herons, owls, nightjars, buzzards, tiercels, vultures, falcons—my cousin who, dressed in a sealskin jacket, himself resembled some strange animal from a cold country, told me what preparations he had made for that same night.

We were to start at half past three in the morning, so as to arrive at the place which he had chosen for our watching-place at about half past four. On that spot a hut had been built of lumps of ice, so as to shelter us somewhat from the trying wind which precedes daybreak, a wind so cold as to tear the flesh like a saw, cut it like the blade of a knife, prick it like a poisoned sting, twist it like a pair of pincers, and burn it like fire.

My cousin rubbed his hands: "I have never known such a frost," he said; "it is already twelve degrees below zero at six o'clock in the evening."

I threw myself on to my bed immediately after we had finished our meal, and went to sleep by the light of a bright fire burning in the grate.

At three o'clock he woke me. In my turn, I put on a sheepskin, and found my cousin Karl covered with a bearskin. After having each swallowed two cups of scalding coffee, followed by glasses of liqueur brandy, we started, accompanied by a gamekeeper and our dogs, Plongeon and Pierrot.

From the first moment that I got outside, I felt chilled to the very marrow. It was one of those nights on which the earth seems dead with cold. The frozen air becomes resisting and palpable, such pain does it cause; no breath of wind moves it, it is fixed and motionless; it bites you, pierces through you, dries you, kills the trees, the plants, the insects, the small birds themselves, who fall from the branches on to the hard ground, and become stiff themselves under the grip of the cold.

The moon, which was in her last quarter and was inclining all to one side, seemed fainting in the midst of space, so weak that she was unable to wane, forced to stay up yonder, seized and paralyzed by the severity of the weather. She shed a cold, mournful light over the world, that dying and wan light which she gives us every month, at the end of her period.

Karl and I walked side by side, our backs bent, our hands in our pockets and our guns under our arms. Our boots, which were wrapped in wool so that we might be able to walk without slipping on the frozen river, made no sound, and I looked at the white vapor which our dogs' breath made.

We were soon on the edge of the marsh, and entered one of the lanes of dry rushes which ran through the low forest.

Our elbows, which touched the long, ribbonlike leaves, left a slight noise behind us, and I was seized, as I had never been before, by the powerful and singular emotion which marshes cause in me. This one was dead, dead from cold, since we were walking on it, in the middle of its population of dried rushes.

Suddenly, at the turn of one of the lanes, I perceived the ice-hut which had been constructed to shelter us. I went in, and as we had nearly an hour to wait before the wandering birds would awake, I rolled myself up in my rug in order to try and get warm. Then, lying on my back, I began to look at the misshapen moon, which had four horns through the vaguely transparent walls of this polar house. But the frost of the frozen marshes, the cold of these walls, the cold from the firmament penetrated me so terribly that I began to cough. My cousin Karl became uneasy.

"No matter if we do not kill much today," he said: "I do not want you to catch cold; we will light a fire." And he told the gamekeeper to cut some rushes.

We made a pile in the middle of our hut which had a hole in the middle of the roof to let out the smoke, and when the red flames rose up to the clear, crystal blocks they began to melt, gently, imperceptibly, as if they were sweating. Karl, who had remained outside, called out to me: "Come and look here!" I went out of the hut and remained struck with astonishment. Our hut, in the shape of a cone, looked like an enormous diamond with a heart of fire, which had been suddenly planted there in the midst of the frozen water of the marsh. And inside, we saw two fantastic forms, those of our dogs, who were warming themselves at the fire.

But a peculiar cry, a lost, a wandering cry, passed over our heads, and the light from our hearth showed us the wild birds. Nothing moves one so much as the first clamor of a life which one does not see, which passes through the somber air so quickly and so far off, just before the first streak of a winter's day appears on the horizon. It seems to me, at this glacial hour of dawn, as if that passing cry which is carried away by the wings of a bird is the sigh of a soul from the world!

"Put out the fire," said Karl, "it is getting daylight."

The sky was, in fact, beginning to grow pale, and the flights of ducks made long, rapid streaks which were soon obliterated on the sky.

A stream of light burst out into the night; Karl had fired, and the two dogs ran forward.

And then, nearly every minute, now he, now I, aimed rapidly as soon as the shadow of a flying flock appeared above the rushes. And Pierrot and Plongeon, out of breath but happy, retrieved the bleeding birds, whose eyes still, occasionally, looked at us.

The sun had risen, and it was a bright day with a blue sky, and we were thinking of taking our departure, when two birds with extended necks and outstretched wings, glided rapidly over our heads. I fired, and one of them fell almost at my feet. It was a teal, with a silver breast, and then, in the blue space above me, I heard a voice, the voice of a bird. It was a short, repeated, heart-rending lament; and the bird, the little animal that had been spared began to turn round in the blue sky, over our heads, looking at its dead companion which I was holding in my hand.

Karl was on his knees, his gun to his shoulder watching it eagerly, until it should be within shot. "You have killed the duck," he said, "and the drake will not fly away."

He certainly did not fly away; he circled over our heads continually, and continued his cries. Never have any groans of suffering pained me so much as that desolate appeal, as that lamentable reproach of this poor bird which was lost in space.

Occasionally he took flight under the menace of the gun which followed his movements, and seemed ready to continue his flight alone, but as he could not make up his mind to this, he returned to find his mate.

"Leave her on the ground," Karl said to me, "he will come within shot by and by." And he did indeed come near us, careless of danger, infatuated by his animal love, by his affection for his mate, which I had just killed.

Karl fired, and it was as if somebody had cut the string which held the bird suspended. I saw something black descend, and I heard the noise of a fall among the rushes. And Pierrot brought it to me.

I put them—they were already cold—into the same game-bag, and I returned to Paris the same evening.

The Fourposter

by JAN DE HARTOG

ACT ONE

SCENE I

1890. Night. Bedroom. Fourposter. Door in arch Center back wall, window in Right; washstand and low chair down Left. Wardrobe above washstand; bed table in front of window, Right; bureau Right of arch. Bed on dais Left of arch; chest at foot of bed; arm chair and trunk, Right Center. Console table and two chairs in rear of hall. The room is dark. Low-burning gaslamps shimmer bluishly Right of arch and at bed Left. The door is opened clumsily, and HE enters, carrying HER in his arms into the room out of the lighted passage. HE wears a top hat on the back of his head; SHE is in her bridal gown. HE stops in the moonlight, kisses her, whirls and carries her to bed.

SHE. Oh, Micky, whoo! Hold me! Hold me! Hold me tight! Whoo! Who! I'm falling. I can't—
    (HE *throws her onto the bed and tries to kiss her again.*)
Michael, the door! The door!
    (HE *runs to the door and closes it.*)
(SHE *gets off the bed, straightens her hat and dress*) Oh, goodness, my

hair—and look at my dress! (SHE *turns on the gas bracket on wall beside the bed.*)

(HE *crosses and turns up gas bracket Right of arch.*)

(SHE *turns toward him.* HE *takes off gloves, puts one in each pocket and kneels before her*) What are you doing?

HE. I'm worshipping you.

SHE. Get up immediately! (*Tries to lift him up*) Michael, get up, I say!

HE. (*Kneeling, hands on her waist*) Can't I worship you?

SHE. Are you out of your senses? If our Lord should see you—

HE. He could only rejoice in such happiness.

SHE. Michael, you mustn't blaspheme. You know you mustn't. Just because you've had a little too much to drink.

HE. I haven't drunk a thing. (*Teeters on his knees*) If I'm drunk, I'm drunk only with happiness—

SHE. You wouldn't be praying with everything on if you weren't. Oh! Goodness! I think I am too.

HE. Happy?

SHE. Tipsy. Let me see if I can stand on one leg. (*Holding her hands out to him, tries and fails*) Whoo!

HE. (*Rises*) Angel! (*Tries to kiss her, but* SHE *dodges.*)

SHE. Michael, that hat—!

HE. What? Oh. (*Takes hat off*) What have you got in your hands?

SHE. A little rose—a little rose from our wedding cake.

HE. Let's eat it.

SHE. No— I want to keep it—always— (SHE *puts it in her dress.*)

HE. (*Puts hat on.*) Agnes, Agnes, tell me that you are happy.

SHE. Please, Michael, do say something else for a change.

HE. I can't. I've only one word left to express what I feel; happy. Happy, happy, happy, happy— Happy! (*Twirls and, stumbling against dais, sprawls back against bed.*)

SHE. Are you all right?

HE. Happy!

SHE. I suddenly feel like saying all sorts of shocking things.

HE. Go on.

SHE. Listen—no, in your ear— (SHE *wants to whisper something but is checked by what she sees*) Oh! Michael—!

HE. What?

SHE. No, don't move. (*Looks at ear again*) Let me see the other one.

(HE *turns his head and* SHE *looks at his other ear.*)

You pig!

He. What is it?

She. Don't you ever wash?

He. Every day.

She. All over?

He. Oh, well—the main things.

She. What *are* the main things?

He. (*Trying to kiss her*) My precious—

She. Your what?

He. You are my precious. Wouldn't you like to kiss me?

She. I would like to go over you from top to bottom, with hot water and soap; that's what I would like to do.

He. Please do.

She. Oh, well—don't let's dwell on it.

(He *puts one foot on dais.*)

(She *sits on trunk*) Ouch!

He. Sweetheart! What's the matter?

She. Ouch! My shoes are hurting me. I must take them off or I'll faint.

He. Let me do it! Please—

(She *puts out her foot.* He *kneels and tenderly pulls her skirt back and kisses her shoe.*)

She. Michael, please, they hurt me so.

He. (*Kisses her foot again; when* She *wants to do it herself*) No, no, dearest! Let me do it, please let me do it. (He *takes her shoe again.*)

She. But you take such a long time.

He. (*Untying bow on shoe*) Isn't that heaven? I could spend the whole night undressing you.

She. I didn't ask you to undress me. I only asked you to help me out of my shoes.

He. I would help you out of anything you ask, dear heart. (*Takes off shoe.*)

She. (*Withdraws her foot*) Now that's one, and now—

(As She *leans forward to take off other shoe herself, sees him, still on his knees, leaning back and staring at her.*)

Please, Michael, don't look at me so creepily. Please get undre—take your hat off!

He. (*Takes hat off, puts it on trunk*) Agnes, do you remember what I told you, when we first met?

She. No—?

He. That we had met in a former existence.

SHE. Oh, that.

HE. I am absolutely certain of it now.

SHE. Of what?

HE. That moment, just now, I suddenly had the feeling of having experienced all this before.

SHE. Did you really?

HE. You sitting here just as you are, I on my knees in front of you in a hired suit, just before we—

SHE. What?

HE. (*Putting shoe down,* HE *leans against her knee*) Oh, darling, I am happy.

SHE. *Must* you make me cry?

HE. You should, you know. This is a very sad occasion, really. Your youth is over.

SHE. (*Pushing him back and getting up*) I want to go home.

HE. What—?

SHE. I can't! I want to go home!

HE. (*Still on knees*) Darling, what's the matter? What have I done?

SHE. (*Picks up shoe*) I want to go home. I should never have married you.

HE. (*Rises*) Agnes—

SHE. How can you! How dare you say such a thing!

HE. But what—? I haven't said a thing all night but that I was—

SHE. My youth over! That's what you would like! Undressing me, the whole night long, with your hat on and unwashed ears and—oh! (*Crosses to him and puts her arms around his neck and weeps.*)

HE. (*Comforting her inexperiencedly*) That's right, darling; that's it; you cry, my dearest; that's the spirit.

SHE. That's—that's why you made me drink such a lot, taking nothing yourself all the time.

HE. Why, I've had at least three bottles.

SHE. (*Breaks away from him and backs up*) Then what did you say? What did you say, when you threw me on the bed?

HE. Threw?

SHE. "If I'm drunk, I'm drunk with happiness." That's what you said.

HE. But, darling, only a minute ago you said yourself—

SHE. I did not!

HE. Well, of all the— (*Takes her by the shoulders*) Here—smell! (*Breathes at her with his mouth wide open*) Ho, ho, ho!

SHE. (*Escaping the kiss she wants by hiding her face against his shoulder*) Oh, I'm so dizzy.

HE. I love you.

SHE. I'm so embarrassed.

HE. Why?

SHE. Because I'm so dizzy.

HE. So am I.

SHE. Dizzy?

HE. Embarrassed.

SHE. Why?

HE. (*Backs away from her*) Oh, well, you know. It would have been such a relief if I could have spent the whole night taking off your shoes.

SHE. And then have breakfast, straight away, yes?

HE. (*Picks up hat*) Yes. Agnes, I— I don't revolt you, do I?

SHE. (*Slips off other shoe, picks it up*) You? Why on earth should you?

HE. Well, I mean—those ears and—things, you know.

SHE. (*Puts shoes on chest at foot of bed*) But, darling, I said that only because of other people. What do I care?

HE. And Agnes—there's something I should tell you.

SHE. Why tell it just now?

HE. You're right. (*Puts hat on*) I'm such a fool that I—

(SHE *frowns*.)

(HE *takes hat off again and puts it on trunk*) Would you like something to drink? (*Crosses to washstand.*)

SHE. Heavens, no. Don't talk about drinking.

HE. A glass of water, I mean. (*Picks up glass and carafe*) After all that champagne.

SHE. Michael, please talk about something else. I— I really couldn't just now, honestly.

HE. Well, I think I will. (*Pours glass of water.*)

SHE. Did you write a poem for tonight?

HE. No.

SHE. What a pity. I thought you would have written something beautiful for our wedding.

HE. (*Drinks*) No.

SHE. Nothing at all?

HE. (*Drinks again and puts glass down*) No.

SHE. You're blushing. Please read it to me.

HE. I haven't got one, darling, really, I haven't.

SHE. You're lying. I can tell by your eyes that you are lying.

HE. As a matter of fact, you wouldn't like it, darling; it's rather modern. There is another one I'm writing just now.

SHE. I want to hear the one about our wedding.

HE. Never before in my whole life have I told anybody anything about a poem I hadn't finished.

SHE. Is it in your pocket? (*Starts to pick his pockets*)

HE. (*Trying to keep her hands back, sits in chair*) Agnes, you can't have it. I think it's going to be wonderful. "The Fountain of the Royal Gardens."

SHE. Why may I not hear the one about our wedding?

HE. Darling, don't you think it much more special, just now, something nobody else has ever heard before?

SHE. Has anybody heard the one about our wedding, then?

HE. (*Takes poems from pocket*) Listen, tell me what you think of the permutation of the consonants, the onomatopoeia, I mean: "Hissing shoots the slender shower; out of shining, slimy stone—"

SHE. (*Steps back*) No.

HE. "Swaying shivers sparkling flower; rainbow shimmers in the foam.

(SHE *starts to door.*)
Flashing, dashing, splashing, crashing—"
(SHE *hurries to the door, picking up suitcase from chest as she goes.*)
Where are you going?

SHE. (*Opens door, taking the key from the lock*) Back in a minute. (*Exits, shuts door, locks it.*)

HE. Why are you taking your suitcase? (*Rises and runs to door; drops poems on chest as he goes*) Agnes, darling! Agnes! Agnes! (*Tries to open the locked door.*)

(HE *turns, sees her shoes, picks them up and smiles. Suddenly, a thought strikes him. He drops the shoes, runs onto dais, picks up suitcase there, starts to put it on bed, stops, turns, then puts suitcase on arms of chair. He opens the case, takes out nightcap and puts it on his head. He rips off his coat and vest, shirt and tie. As he starts to take his trousers off, he stops, listens, runs to door, listens again. He then hurries and takes the trousers off. He takes nightshirt from case, crosses to foot of bed, throws nightshirt on bed and sits on chest and hurriedly takes off his shoes. Then he pauses, looks toward the door in embarrassment. He quickly puts the shoes back on again, gets into the nightshirt, pulls his trousers on over it; then his coat. He moves a few steps, turns, sees*) *his vest, shirt and tie on trunk where he had thrown them. He tosses them into the suitcase, fastens it, puts suitcase in wardrobe; starts to washstand, stops, looks toward door. Then quickly he crosses to washstand, picks up towel, dampens one corner of it in pitcher of water and starts to wash his right ear.)*

(SHE *enters. As* HE *hears door open, he sits in chair and folds his arms.* SHE *closes the door and puts the key back in the lock. Her dress is changed somehow; it looks untidier and she has taken off her wedding hat.* SHE *turns from door, spots him sitting in the chair, the collar of his jacket upturned and the nightcap on his head.)*

HE. Hullo.

SHE. What—what are you doing?

HE. Sitting.

SHE. What on earth is that?

HE. What?

SHE. On your head?

HE. Oh—why—

SHE. Do you wear a nightcap?

HE. Oh, no. Just now when there's a draft. (*Rises, takes cap off and put it in his pocket. Crosses to her.*)

SHE. Is that a nightshirt?

HE. What have you got on?

SHE. My father has been wearing pajamas for ages.

HE. Oh, has he really? Well, I don't.

SHE. Why have you—changed?

HE. Why have you?

SHE. I? Oh— I'm sleepy.

HE. So am I.

SHE. Well, then, shall we—?

HE. Why, yes—let's.

SHE. (*Crossing below him onto dais*) All right. Which side do you want?

HE. I? Oh, well— I don't care, really. Any side that suits you is all right with me.

SHE. I think I would like the far side. Because of the door.

HE. The door?

SHE. (*Turns back quilt*) Because of breakfast, and in case somebody should knock. You could answer it.

HE. I see.

SHE. (*Picks up pillow from bed*) What's this?

HE. What?

SHE. This little pillow? Did you put that there?

HE. Of course not! What's it got written on it?

SHE. "God Is Love." Oh, how sweet! Mother must have done that. Wasn't that lovely of her? (*Puts pillow back on bed.*)

HE. Yes, charming.

(SHE *turns away and starts undressing.* HE *takes off his coat.* SHE *turns. After an embarrassing moment in which neither of them can think of anything to say:*)

SHE. Michael, please turn 'round.

HE. Oh, I'm so sorry— I just didn't realize.

(HE *sits down on the edge of the chest, putting his coat beside him, and takes off his shoes and socks.* SHE *steps out of dress and hangs it in wardrobe.*)

SHE. It's rather a pretty bed, isn't it?

HE. (*Picks up her shoes and places them next to his*) Yes, it is, isn't it? It was my father's, you know.

SHE. Not your mother's?

HE. Yes, of course, my parents. I was born in it, you know.

SHE. (*Taking a step toward him*) Michael—

HE. (*Turning toward her*) Yes, darling?

SHE. (*Backing up*) No, don't look! Michael?

HE. (*Turning away*) Yes?

SHE. Tell me how much you love me, once more.

HE. I can't any more.

SHE. What?

HE. I can't love you any more than I'm doing. I wor— I'm the hap— I'm mad about you.

SHE. That's what I am about you. Honestly.

HE. That is nice, dear.

SHE. I am so happy, I couldn't be happier.

HE. That is lovely, darling.

SHE. And I wouldn't want to be, either.

HE. What?

SHE. Happier.

HE. I see.

SHE. I wish that everything could stay as it was—before today. I couldn't stand any more—happiness. Could you?

He. God, no.

She. How coldly you say that.

He. But what the blazing hell do you expect me to say then?

She. Michael! Is that language for the wedding ni—before going to sleep? You ought to be ashamed of yourself!

He. But damn it, Agnes— (*Sneezes*) I— I've got a splitting headache and I'm dying of cold feet. (*Takes nightcap from pocket and put it on.*)

She. (*Takes off her slippers*) Then why don't you get into bed, silly?

(He *rises, crosses up onto dais.*)

No! A moment! A moment!

(He *turns away.* She *gets into bed, the "God Is Love" pillow beneath her head.* He *stands for a moment in embarrassment, starts to take off his trousers, then realizing that the room is still brightly lit, he crosses to bracket and turns it off.*)

He. May I turn 'round now?

She. Yes.

(He *reaches to turn down the other bracket but is stopped by her interruption.*)

Wait! It can't leak, can it? The lamp, I mean?

He. Of course not.

She. But I think I smell gas.

He. (*Reaches behind him and takes her hand*) Darling, listen. You are an angel, and I'm madly in love with you, and I'm embarrassed to death and so are you, and that's the reason why we— Goodnight. (He *reaches up and turns down the bracket.*)

She. Goodnight.

(He *steps down, takes off his trousers and puts them on chair.*)

Can you find your way?

He. Yes, yes— (*Crossing back up to bed, stubs his toe on the dais*) Ouch!

She. Michael! What are you doing?

He. Nothing. I hurt my toe. (He *gets into bed.*)

She. Oh, I'm so sorry. (*Long silence*) Do get into bed carefully, won't you?

He. I'm in it already.

She. Michael?

He. Yes?

She. Michael, what was it you didn't want to tell me tonight?

He. Ah—

She. You may tell me now, if you like. I'm not embarrassed any more, somehow.

He. Well—

She. If you tell me what it was, I'll tell you something as well.

He. What?

She. But you must tell me as well. Promise me.

He. Yes.

She. No, promise me first.

He. All right. I promise.

She. I— I've never seen a man—before—completely. Never.

He. Oh, well—you haven't missed much.

She. And you?

He. Oh.

She. Have you ever seen a woman before—completely?

He. Well—

She. What does that mean?

He. You know, I once had my fortune told by a gypsy.

She. Oh—

He. She said I'd have a very happy married life, that I'd live to a ripe old age, and she said that everything would turn out all right.

She. And was she—naked?

He. Of course not! She went from house to house with a goat.

She. Oh— Goodnight.

He. Goodnight. (*Pause*) Are you comfy?

She. Oh yes.

He. Not too cold?

She. Heavens, no. I'm simply boiling. And you?

He. Rather cold, really.

She. (*After a silence*) Michael!

He. Yes?

She. Michael! Now I'm sure that I smell gas. (She *sits up*.)

He. That must be the drink.

She. Do you still smell of drink that much? I can't believe it.

He. Yes.

She. Let me smell your breath again.

He. Oh please, Agnes, let's try to go to sleep.

She. No, Michael, I want to smell it. If it is the gas, we may be dead tomorrow, both of us.

He. Oh, well—

She. Oh well? Do you want to die?

He. Sometimes.

She. Now?

He. No, no.

She. Please, Michael, let me have a little sniff before I go to sleep; otherwise, I won't close an eye. (*Lies down*) Please, Michael.

He. (*Sits up and leans over her*) Ho! Ho! Ho! (*Lies back on his pillow*) There.

She. (*Sits up and leans over him*) I don't smell a thing. Do it again.

He. Ho! Ho!

She. Again.

He. Ho, ho.

She. Again—

He. (*Raises his arm to embrace her*) Ho—

CURTAIN

ACT ONE

Scene II

1891. *Late afternoon. The same bedroom. Down Right a bassinette. Right Center chair is now down Right. He is lying in the fourposter, with a towel wrapped around his head. The bed is strewn with books, papers, an over-sized dinner bell and his dressing gown. Heaps of books and papers are on the dais at foot of bed. When the Curtain rises, He awakens.*

He. (*From beneath the blankets*) Agnes! Agnes! (*Sits up*) Agnes! (*Picks up bell and rings loudly and insistently.*)

She. (*Enters arch hurriedly carrying a pile of clean laundry. She is very pregnant*) Yes, yes, yes, yes, yes. What is it? (*Crosses to foot of bed.*)

He. I've got such a pain! I can't stand it any longer!

She. (*Putting laundry on chest*) Now, come, come, darling. Don't dramatize. (*Takes towel from his head*) I'll soak your towel again.

He. No! It isn't my head, it's shifted to here. (*Puts his hand on his back.*)

She. Where?

He. Here! (*Leans forward. Places her hand on the painful spot*) Here! What is there? Do you feel anything?

SHE. You've got a pain there?

HE. As if I'd been stabbed. No, don't take your hand away—oh, that's nice.

SHE. (*Suspiciously*) But what sort of pain? Does it come in—in waves? First almost nothing and then growing until you could scream?

HE. That's right. How do you know—

SHE. Micky, that's impossible.

HE. What's impossible? Do you think I'm shamming?

SHE. You're having labor pains!

HE. You're crazy!

SHE. And all the time—all the time I've put up a brave front because I thought you were really ill! (*Sits on chest, puts towel on chest.*)

HE. But I *am* ill! What do you think? That I lay here groaning and sweating just for the fun of it?

SHE. All the time I've been thinking of *you!*

HE. I've done nothing else, day and night, but think of *you!* How else do you think I got the pains *you're* supposed to have?

(*SHE sobs.*)

Oh hell! This is driving me mad! (*HE jumps out of bed.*)

SHE. Micky! (*HE tears open the wardrobe*) Micky, what are you doing?

HE. Where are my shoes?

SHE. Michael! You aren't running away, are you?

HE. (*Gets clothes from wardrobe*) I'm going to get that doctor.

SHE. (*Rises*) No, Michael, you mustn't.

HE. (*Puts clothes on chair*) If I drop dead on the pavement, I'm going to get that doctor. I'm not going to leave you in this condition a minute longer. He said so himself, the moment you got those pains. (*Crosses onto dais. Kneels, looks under bed.*)

SHE. When *I* got them! Not when you got them!

HE. Don't you feel anything then?

SHE. Nothing! Nothing at all.

HE. Agnes, I don't understand why you were crying just now.

SHE. (*Helps him up*) Please darling, please go back to bed. You'll catch a cold with those bare feet and you're perspiring so freely. Please, darling.

HE. But I don't want to.

SHE. (*Pops him into bed*) I want you to. Uppy-pie, in you go!

HE. Anyone would think you wanted me to be ill.

SHE. No grumbling, no growling. (*Puts "God Is Love" pillow behind his head*) There! Comfy?

HE. No! (HE *throws pillow to floor down Left.*)

(SHE *picks up laundry, crosses to bureau and puts laundry in drawer. Closes drawer.*)

Agnes, I'm scared.

SHE. But what on earth of?

HE. Of—of the baby. Aren't you?

SHE. Good Heavens, no. Why should I? It's the most natural thing in the world, isn't it? And I'm feeling all right. (*Picks up sewing.*)

HE. You have changed a lot, do you know that?

SHE. (*Starts sewing*) Since when?

HE. Since you became a mother.

SHE. But I'm not a mother yet.

HE. Then you don't even realize it yourself. Suddenly you have become a woman.

SHE. Have I ever been anything else?

HE. A silly child.

SHE. So that's what you thought of me when we married?

HE. When we married, my feet were off the ground.

SHE. Well, you've changed a lot, too.

HE. Of course I have. I have become a man.

SHE. Hah!

HE. Well, haven't I? Agnes, aren't I much more calm, composed—

SHE. (*Picks up rattle from bassinette and throws it to him*) You're a baby!

HE. (*Throws covers back and sits on edge of bed*) That's right! Humiliate me! Lose no opportunity of reminding me that I'm the male animal that's done its duty and now can be dismissed. (*Jumps up*)

SHE. (*Sits on chest*) Michael!

HE. Yes! A drone, that's what I am! The one thing lacking is that you should devour me. The bees—

SHE. Michael, Michael, what's the matter? (*Reaches out to him.*)

HE. I'm afraid!

SHE. But I'm not, Michael, honestly, not a bit.

HE. I'm afraid of something else.

SHE. What?

HE. That I've lost you.

SHE. Michael, look at me—what did the doctor tell you?

HE. It's got nothing to do with the doctor. It's got nothing to do with you, either. It's got to do with me.

SHE. (*Puts arms about him*) But you're going to be all right, aren't you?

He. (*Breaks away*) I'd never be all right again, if I've lost you.

She. But what are you talking about? You've got me right here, haven't you?

He. But your heart, that's gone. I wish I was lying in that cradle.

She. (*Puts her arms around him again*) You fool— (*Kisses him*)— you can't be as stupid as all that. No, Michael.

He. (*Breaks away and picks up slippers*) I'm sorry I brought the subject up. Whatever did I do with my shoes?

She. (*Crossing up Center*) Darling, do you mean that you haven't noticed how I've tried every day, all day long to prove to you how much I love you—and I don't understand why I should.

He. Listen! Before that cuckoo pushes me out of the nest, I want to tell you once more that I love you. Love you, just as you are— (*Sits on bed and puts on slippers*) I thought I loved you when I married you, but that wasn't you at all. That was a romantic illusion. I loved a sort of fairy princess with a doll's smile and a—well, anyway not a princess with hiccoughs and cold feet, scratching her stomach in her sleep— (*Takes her hand*) I thought I was marrying a princess and I woke up to find a friend, a wife— You know, sometimes when I lay awake longer than you, with my arm around your shoulder and your head on my chest, I thought with pity of all those lonely men staring at the ceiling or writing poems—pity, and such happiness that I knew at that very moment it wouldn't last. I was right, that's all.

She. Well, if you thought about a princess, I thought about a poet.

He. (*Fixes sleeves in robe right side out*) Oh?

She. You didn't know that I had cold feet and every now and again I get an attack of hiccoughs—

He. (*Putting on robe*) You don't do anything else the whole night long.

She. What?

He. Scratch your stomach and sniff and snort and smack your lips, but go on, go on.

She. And you lie listening to all this without waking me up?

He. Yes. Because I don't know anything in the world I'd rather listen to. (*Kisses her*) Got anything to say to that?

She. Yes, but I won't say it.

He. Why not?

She. Never mind, darling, you stay just as you are.

He. Miserable, deserted, alone? You do nothing else all day and night but fuss over that child—eight months now! First it was knitting panties, then sewing dresses, fitting out the layette, rigging the cradle— (*Ties robe.*)

SHE. And all this time you sat quietly in your corner, didn't you?

HE. I retired into the background as becomes a man who recognizes that he is one too many.

SHE. Oh, angel! (*Puts her arms around his neck and kisses him*) Do you still not understand why I love you so much?

HE. You—you noticed how I blotted myself out?

SHE. Did I?

HE. I didn't think you did.

SHE. You helped me more than all model husbands put together. Without you I would have been frightened to death for eight whole months. But I simply had no time.

HE. (*Turns suddenly to her*) I believe you're teasing me.

SHE. I love you. Do you believe that?

HE. Of course.

SHE. Must I prove it to you?

HE. Oh, no. I'm perfectly prepared to take your word for it.

SHE. All right, if you like, we'll send the child to a home.

HE. What?

SHE. And then we'll go and look at it every Sunday.

HE. Agnes, why do you tease me?

SHE. Darling, I'm not teasing you. I'm telling you the truth. Even if I were going to have twenty children, you are my husband and I'd rather leave them as foundlings— (SHE *grasps at her back and turns up stage.* HE *stares at her in horror.*)

HE. Darling, what—what is it? Agnes!

SHE. (*Clutching the bed post*) Oh!

HE. The doctor! For God's sake, the doctor! (*Frantically unties robe.*)

SHE. No—oh, oh! Don't—not the doctor. Stay here.

HE. Darling, darling! Angel! Agnes, my love! What must I do? For God's sake, I must do something!

SHE. (*Sings, convulsed by pain, loudly*)

> "Yankee Doodle went to town,
> Riding on a pony—"

HE. Agnes!

SHE. (*Sings on*)

> "He stuck a feather in his hat,
> And called it macaroni."

He. (*Takes her by shoulders*) Agnes! (He *slaps her cheek quickly several times.*)

She. (*Regains her senses, slaps back at him*) Oh, Micky— What are you doing?

He. I— I thought you were going mad.

She. I? Why?

He. (*Seats her on chest*) You started to sing.

She. (*Sitting*) Oh, yes. The doctor said if those pains started, I had to sing. That would help. I must have done it automatically.

He. Are you all right now?

She. Oh yes, yes.

He. Now you just sit here quietly. I'll get the doctor.

She. No, Michael, you mustn't. He said we weren't to bother him until the pains came regularly.

He. Regularly? But I won't be a minute.

She. Oh, please, please don't go away. Oh, I wish mother were here.

He. Now, don't worry! This is the most natural thing in the world. You just sit here quietly. I'll put some clothes on and—

She. Oh no, no Micky, please, please don't fuss. I wish it didn't have to happen so soon.

He. (*Turns upstage with back to audience, takes off pajama pants. Puts on trousers*) Yes.

She. I'm not nearly ready for it yet—

He. (*Taking off robe and putting it on bed*) Well, I am. Honestly, I am. I can't wait to—to go fishing with him, if it's a boy, and—and, if it's a girl, go for walks, nature rambles— (*Crosses to wardrobe and gets tie from there.*)

She. But that won't happen for years. First, there will be years of crying and diapers and bottles—

He. (*Ties tie*) I don't mind, darling. Honestly, I don't. I'll—find something to do. I'll work and—and go fishing alone. You're never going to have to worry about—

She. (*In pain again*) Oh!

He. (*Crossing to her, kneels*) Another one?

She. No. No, I don't think so.

He. Now, why don't you go to bed? (*Fixes bed linen*) You go to bed—I'll finish dressing and make you a nice cup of tea, yes?

She. No, no thank you, darling. I think I'll stay right where I am. Oh, I haven't done nearly all the things I should have done. There's still half the laundry out on the roof and—

He. Agnes, do stop worrying. As soon as I've finished dressing, I'll go to the roof and take the washing in for you. (*Seats her on chest.*)

She. (*Puts arms about his waist*) No, please don't leave me alone.

He. (*Puts his arms about her shoulders*) All right, all right. There's nothing to be afraid of. This has been going on for millions and millions of years. Now what would you like? Shall I read you something? (*Picks up books*) "Schopenhauer," "Alice in Wonderland?"

She. No.

He. I know. I've started a new book. It's only half a page. Shall I read you that? Yes? (*He picks up the writing pad.*)

She. (*Biting her lip*) Yes—

He. (*Sits on foot of bed*) It's going to be a trilogy. It's called "Burnt Corn, the Story of a Rural Love." Do you like that as a title?

She. (*Biting her lips*) I think that's wonderful.

He. Now this is how it opens— (*Takes hold of her hand*) Are you all right?

She. Fine.

He. (*Reads*) "When she entered the attic with the double bed, she bent her head, partly out of reverence for the temple where she had worshipped and sacrificed, partly because the ceiling was so low. It was not the first time she had returned to that shrine—"

(*She has a pain.*)
Are you all right?

She. Oh, Micky, I love you so. Don't, don't let's ever— (*She has another pain.*)

(*He helps her like a sweet man. He drops pad and kneels before her.*)
(*She buries her head in his shoulder, then looks up*) No—now, I think you'd better go and call him.

He. I will, my darling. (*Puts on his coat. Crosses up to door, stops, returns to her*) Now, you just sit tight. (*Crosses to door, returns and kisses her. Crosses to door, turns, sees bassinette, runs to it and pulls it over close to her and exits as:*)

CURTAIN

ACT TWO

SCENE I

1901. *Night. The same room, ten years later. The only piece of furniture left from the preceding scene is the fourposter, but it has been fitted out with new brocade curtains. Paintings hang on the walls, expensive furniture crowds the room. Dressing table and chair up Right; sofa Right Center; chair down Right; sofa at foot of bed with tabouret below it; chairs Left Center and Left. Bed table on dais at head of bed. Bureau in dressing room. No washstand any more, but a bathroom down Left. Where the wardrobe stood in the preceding act, the wall has been removed and this has become an entrance to a dressing room. The whole thing is very costly, very grand and very new. Only one side of the bed has been made; there is only one pillow on the bed with the "God Is Love" pillow on top of it.*

At Rise, there is no one in the room. SHE *enters door Center and slams the door behind her.* SHE *stands at the foot of the bed, removing her evening gloves. Crosses to dressing table, throws gloves on the table, and is stopped by a KNOCK at the door.* SHE *stands for a moment. The KNOCK is repeated, more insistently.*

SHE. (*After a pause*) Come in.

HE. (*Enters, closes door*) Excuse me. (*Goes to the dressing room, gets his night clothes, re-enters and crosses to door*) Goodnight.

SHE. (*As* HE *opens door*) You were the life and soul of the party this evening, with your interminable little stories.

HE. (*Starts out, stops, turns*) My dear, if you don't enjoy playing second fiddle, I suggest you either quit the orchestra or form one of your own. (*Goes out and shuts door.*)

SHE. (*Mutters after a moment's stupefaction*) Now, I've had enough! (*Runs to door, rips it open, stands in hallway and calls off*) Michael! (*Then bellows*) Michael! Come here! (*Re-enters, takes off evening wrap, throws it on bed.*)

HE. (*Pops in. Has top hat and cane in hand and evening cape over arm*) Have you taken leave of your senses? The servants?

SHE. I don't care if the whole town hears it.

(HE *exits.*)
Come back, I say!

HE. (*Re-enters*) All right. This situation is no longer bearable! (*Closes door.*)

SHE. What on earth is the matter with you?

HE. Now, let me tell you one thing, calmly.

(SHE *crosses below him to dressing table. Takes off plume, throws it on table.*)

My greatest mistake has been to play up to you, plying you with presents—

SHE. I like that! (*Picks up gloves.*)

HE. Calmly! Do you know what I should have done? I should have packed you off to boarding school, big as you are, to learn deportment.

SHE. Deportment for what?

HE. To be worthy of me.

SHE. The pompous ass whose book sold three hundred thousand copies!

HE. That is entirely beside the point.

SHE. It is right to the point! Before you had written that cursed novel, the rest of the world helped me to keep you sane. Every time you had finished a book or a play or God knows what, and considered yourself to be the greatest genius since Shakespeare—

(HE *says,* "Now really!" HE *puts cape, hat, gloves on wall chair.*)

—I was frightened to death that it might turn out to be a success. But, thank Heaven, it turned out to be such a thorough failure every time, that I won the battle with your megalomania. But now, now this book, the only book you ever confessed to be trash until you read the papers— oh, what's the use!

HE. My dear woman, I may be vain, but you are making a tragic mistake.

SHE. (*Laughs*) Now listen! (*Laughs*) Just listen to him! To be married to a man for eleven years, and then to be addressed like a public meeting. (*Throws gloves on dressing table*) Tragic mistake! Can't you hear yourself, you poor darling idiot, that you've sold your soul to a sentimental novel?

HE. Agnes, are you going on like this, or must I—

SHE. Yes, yes, you must! You *shall* hear it.

(HE *pounds floor with cane.*)

And don't interrupt me! There is only one person in this world who loves you in spite of what you are, and let me tell you—

HE. You are mistaken. There is a person in this world who loves me—because of what I am.

SHE. And what are you, my darling?

HE. Ask her.

SHE. Her—

HE. Yes.

SHE. Oh— Who is she?

HE. You don't know her.

SHE. Is she—young? How young?

HE. No. (*Rises. Picks up clothes*) I'll be damned if I'll go on with this. You look like a corpse.

SHE. A corpse?

HE. So pale, I mean. (*At door*) Agnes, I'm not such a monster, that— (*Crossing to her*) Sit down. Please, Agnes, do sit— Agnes!

SHE. (*Turns away.*) No, no—it's nothing. I'm all right. What do you think? That I should faint in my thirty-first year because of something so—so ordinary?

HE. Ordinary?

SHE. With two children? I didn't faint when Robert had the mumps, did I?

HE. Don't you think this is a little different?

SHE. No, Michael. This belongs to the family medicine chest.

HE. I love her!

SHE. So, not me anymore?

(HE *doesn't reply.*)

I don't mean as a friend, or as—as the mother of your children, but as a wife? You may tell me honestly, really. Is that why you've been sleeping in the study?

HE. I haven't slept a wink.

SHE. I see. It must be Cook who snores.

HE. Since when do I snore?

SHE. Not you, dear, Cook. Every night when I went down the passage.

HE. (*Goes to the door, opens it*) Goodnight!

SHE. Sleep well.

HE. What was that?

SHE. Sleep well.

HE. Oh— (*Stops at door, then slams it shut*) No! (*Throws clothes down on sofa at foot of bed.*) I'll be damned, I won't stand it!

SHE. What is the matter?

HE. Cook snores! Agnes, I love somebody else! It's driving me crazy! You, the children, she, the children, you—for three weeks I have lived through hell, and all you've got to say is "Cook snores!"

SHE. (*Steps toward him*) But darling—

HE. (*Crossing below sofa down Right*) No, no, no, no! You are so damned sure of yourself that it makes me sick! I know you don't take this seriously, but believe me, I love that woman! I must have that woman or I'll go mad!

SHE. Haven't you—had her yet?

HE. At last! Thank God, a sign of life.

(She *sits on sofa at foot of bed.*)
Why haven't you looked at me like that before? I have begged, implored, crawled to you for a little understanding and warmth, and love, and got nothing. Even my book, that was written inspired by you, longing for you—right from the beginning you have seen it as a rival. Whatever I did, whatever I tried: a carriage, servants, money, dresses, paintings, everything—you hated that book. And now? Now you have driven me into somebody else's arms. Somebody else, who understands at least one thing clearly: that she will have to share me with my work.

She. Does she understand that she will have to share you with other women as well?

He. She doesn't need to. At last I found a woman who'll live with my work, and a better guarantee of my faithfulness nobody could have.

She. But how does she live with it? What does she do?

He. She listens. (*Sits on bed*) She encourages me—with a look, a touch, a—well, an encouragement. When I cheer, she cheers with me, when I meditate, she meditates with me—

She. And when you throw cockery, she throws crockery with you?

He. (*Checks himself*) Haven't you understood one single word of what I have been saying? Won't you, can't you see that I have changed?

She. No.

He. (*Rises*) Then you are blind, blind, blind! That's all I can say. At any rate, *you've* changed.

She. I!

He. No, don't let's start that.

She. Go on.

He. No, it's senseless. No reason to torture you any longer, once I have—

She. Once you have tasted blood?

He. (*Crossing around sofa*) Agnes, I'm sorry it was necessary for me to hurt you. It couldn't very well have been done otherwise. I'm at the mercy of a feeling stronger than I. (*Sits on sofa.*)

She. Rotten, isn't it.

He. Horrible.

She. And yet—at the same time not altogether.

He. No. On the other hand, it's delicious.

She. The greatest thing a human being can experience.

He. I'm glad you understand it so well.

She. Understand?—why, of course. It's human, isn't it?

He. How do you come to know that?

She. What?

He. That it's—human?

She. Well, I'm a human being, aren't I?

He. Agnes, I never heard you talk like this before. What's the matter with you?

She. Well, I might have my experience too, mightn't I? (*Rises. Crossing onto dais, picks up clock from bed table*) Goodnight!

He. (*Rises. Crossing to foot of bed*) Just a minute! I want to hear a little more about this.

She. But I know it now, dear.

He. Yes, you do! But I don't! What sort of experiences are you referring to?

She. (*Puts clock on tabouret*) Now listen, my little friend! You have dismissed me without notice, and I haven't complained once as any other housekeeper would have done. I have accepted the facts, because I know a human being is at the mercy of this feeling, however horrible and at the same time delicious it may be.

He. Agnes!

She. I really don't understand you. I am not thwarting you in the least, and instead of your going away happily and relieved that you are not going to leave a helpless wreck behind—

He. You might answer just one plain question before—we finish this business. Have you—aren't you going to be alone, if I leave you?

She. Alone? I've got the children, haven't I?

He. That's not at all certain.

She. (*After a shaky silence*) You had better leave this room very quickly now, before you get to know a side of me that might surprise you a lot.

He. I have, I'm afraid. I demand an answer. Have you a lover?

She. (*Goes to door, opens it.*) Goodnight.

He. For eleven long years I have believed in you! You were the purest, the noblest thing in my life!

She. (*Interrupting, and with him*) —the noblest thing in my life! Goodnight!

He. If you don't answer my question, you'll never see me again.

She. Get out of here.

He. (*Sits sofa at foot of bed*) No.

She. All right. (*Crossing onto dais*) Then there's only one thing left to be done. (*She picks up wrap from bed and exits into dressing room.*)

He. What? What did you want to say?

(SHE *does not answer.* SHE *returns with second wrap and overnight case; puts them both on chair and opens case.*)
What's the meaning of that?

(SHE *goes on, crosses onto dais, picks up nightgown and negligee, packs them in case.*)
Darling, believe me, I won't blame you for anything, only tell me—where are you going?

SHE. (*Crossing to dressing table and getting brushes and comb*) Would you mind calling a cab for me?

HE. Agnes!

SHE. (*Packs brushes and comb in case*) Please, Michael, I can't arrive there too late. It is such an embarrassing time already. Pass me my alarm clock, will you?

HE. No, I can't have been mistaken about you that much! Only yesterday you said that I had qualities—

SHE. Excuse me. (*Passes him, gets her alarm clock from the tabouret.*)

HE. (*Wants to stop her when she passes, but checks himself*) All right. It *is* a solution, anyhow.

SHE. (*Closes overnight case, picks it up, puts wrap over arm, crosses to him and puts out her hand*) Goodbye, Michael.

(HE *blocks her way.*)

HE. Do you really think I'm going to let you do this? Do you?

SHE. A gentleman does not use force when a lady wishes to leave the room.

HE. Oh, I'm so sorry. (*Steps aside*)

SHE. Thank you.

(HE *grabs her arm and pulls her back.* SHE *drops her suitcase and wrap in the struggle.* HE *flings her up onto the bed.*)
Michael! Let me go! Let me go! I—

HE. Now look, I've put up with all the nonsense from you—

(SHE *succeeds in tearing herself free, gets off the bed and kicks his shin.*)
Ouch! (HE *grasps at his shinbone and limps down Right, leans against arm of sofa.*)

SHE. Get out!

HE. Right on my scar!

SHE. Get out!

(HE *takes off his coat, throws it on chair. As* HE *starts toward her:*)
I'll scream the house down if you dare come near me! (SHE *scrambles back up onto bed.*)

HE. Where's my pillow!

SHE. (*Reaching for bell pull*) Get out or I'll ring the bell!

HE. (*As he exits dressing room*) Make up that bed properly.

SHE. You're the vilest swine God ever created.

HE. (*Re-enters carrying pillow. Crossing to foot of bed*) If I have to make you hoarse and broken for the rest of your life, you'll know that I am a man. Make up that bed! (*Throws pillow at her.*)

SHE. I would rather—

HE. And shut up! Get off there!

SHE. (*Strikes at him with "God Is Love" pillow*) You are the silliest hack-writer I ever—

HE. (*Grabs "God Is Love" pillow and throws it*) Get off, or I'll drag you off!

SHE. (*Gets off bed*) And that book of yours is rubbish.

HE. What did I tell you after I finished it? Listening to me once in awhile wouldn't do you any harm. Here! (*Throws comforter at her*) Fold that!

SHE. (*Throws it back*) Fold it yourself!

HE. (*Throws it back*) Fold it!

(SHE *goes at him and* HE *grasps her hands.* SHE *still tries to flail him.* HE *slips in the struggle and sits on dais.* SHE *tries to pound his head.* HE *regains his feet and pinions her arms behind her.*)

SHE. (*As* HE *grasps her face with hand*) I'll bite you!

HE. Oh, no you won't. If you could see your eyes now, you'd close them. They're blinding.

SHE. With hatred!

HE. With love. (*Gives her a quick kiss;* SHE *breaks free.* HE *gets on guard.*)

SHE. (*Looks at him speechless for a moment, then sits on the bed, away from him, sobbing*) I wish I were dead. I want to be dead, dead, dead—

HE. (*Sits on edge of bed, holding shin*) Before you die, look in my eyes, just once. Look! (*Turns her to him*)

(SHE *looks.*)

What do you see there?

SHE. Wrinkles!

HE. (*Crosses down, picks up evening pumps which have come off in the scuffle and crosses back up onto dais*) That's how long it is since you last looked. (*Sits on bed and puts one pump on*) What else?

SHE. But—what about her?

HE. I was lonely.

SHE. (*Stands*) You'd better go now.

HE. Weren't you?

SHE. Please go.

HE. (*Picks up evening coat. Crosses up to door*)

(SHE *picks up his pillow and puts it on chair.*)

(*At archway, as* HE *puts on other pump:*) I've started writing a new book.

SHE. When?

HE. A couple of weeks ago.

SHE. And you haven't read me anything yet? Impossible.

HE. I read it to her.

SHE. Oh—and?

HE. She liked it all right. But she thought it a little—well, coarse.

SHE. You, coarse? What kind of sheep is she?

HE. Shall I go and get the manuscript?

SHE. (*Picks up his pillow*) Tomorrow.

HE. (*Moves quickly to door and puts hand on door knob*) No, now!

SHE. (*Crosses up onto dais, puts his pillow in bed*) Please, tomorrow— Tomorrow.

(HE *throws coat onto sofa at foot of bed and crosses around onto dais and embraces her.*)

CURTAIN

ACT TWO

SCENE II

1908. 4:00 A.M. *to dawn. When the Curtain rises, the stage is dark. The door is opened brusquely and* HE *enters, wearing an overcoat over his pajamas.* HE *is carrying a bourbon bottle and riding crop.* SHE *is asleep in the fourposter.*

HE. (*As* HE *enters*) Agnes! (*Crosses to dressing table, turns on dressing table lamps*) Agnes, Agnes, look at this! (HE *shows her brown bourbon bottle.*)

SHE. (*Waking up and shielding her eyes with arm*) Hunh? What's the matter?

HE. In his drawer, behind a pile of junk—this!

SHE. What?

HE. He's seventeen—eighteen! And it's four o'clock in the morning! And—and now, this!

SHE. (*Sitting up*) What, for Heaven's sake?

HE. (*Hands her the bottle*) Look!

SHE. (*Takes bottle and looks at it*) Bourbon!

HE. Your son. The result of your modern upbringing.

SHE. But what—where— (*Puts bottle down in bed*) —what does all this mean? What's the time? (*Leans over and picks up clock.*)

HE. (*Exits into bathroom*) It's time I took over his education.

SHE. But he told you he would be late tonight. He specially asked permission to go to that dance— I gave him the key myself!

HE. (*Re-enters and exits again into dressing room*) Where did you put that thing?

SHE. What thing?

HE. My old shaving strop.

SHE. What do you want that for? (*Lying back in bed*) Come back to bed.

HE. (*Re-enters*) So you approve of all this? You think it's perfectly natural that a child boozes in his bedroom and paints the town until four o'clock in the morning?

SHE. But darling, he told you! And surely the child has a right to a bit of gaiety.

HE. One day let me explain the difference to you between gaiety and delirium tremens!

SHE. What are you going to do, Michael?

HE. I am going downstairs where I have been since one o'clock this morning. And when he comes home, I—

SHE. (*Climbs out of bed.* SHE *wears a slumber bonnet. Picks up robe*) I won't let you—if you are going to beat that child, you will have to do so over my dead body. (*Putting on robe.*)

HE. Don't interfere, Agnes.

SHE. I mean it, Michael! Whatever happens, even if he has taken to opium, I will not let you beat that child!

HE. All right. In that case, we had better call the police.

SHE. But you knew he was coming in late! These children's parties go on till dawn!

HE. (*With a politician's gesture of despair*) Now, in my young days, if I was told to be in at a certain hour— (*Turns to her for the beginning of a big speech*) I— (*Sees her for the first time*) What in the name of sanity have you got on your head?

SHE. Now, now, that's the very latest thing—everyone's wearing them—

HE. But what *is* it?

SHE. A slumber helmet.

HE. Slumber helmet! Bourbon in the bedroom, children's parties that go on till dawn and slumber helmets. All right. (*Throws riding crop on sofa at foot of bed and rips off overcoat*) I am going to bed.

SHE. Listen to me, will you?

HE. (*Steps out of slippers*) I have the choice between bed and the madhouse— I prefer bed. I have a life to live. Goodnight! (HE *gets into bed and pulls the blanket up.* HE *sits up*) I hope you enjoy being a drunkard's mother! (*Lies back.*)

SHE. (*Crossing to foot of bed*) I don't want to spoil your performance as an irate father, but I can't help thinking what your attitude would be if it were not Robert, but Lizzie who stayed out late.

HE. (*Sits up*) Exactly the same! With this difference, that Lizzie would never do such a thing.

SHE. Ha!

HE. Because she happens to be the only sane member of this family. Except me, of course. (*Lies back.*)

SHE. I could tell you something about her that would—no, I'd better not.

HE. (*Sits up*) If you think that I am going to fall for that stone-age woman's trick of hinting at something and then stopping— That child is as straight and as sensible as—as a glass of milk. (*Lies back.*)

SHE. Milk!

HE. (*Finds bottle in bed, sits up, puts bottle on bed table, lies back*) At least she doesn't go to bed with a bottle of bourbon.

SHE. Hmm—

HE. (*Sitting up*) What—hmm?

SHE. Nothing, nothing. Nothing, nothing.

HE. Agnes, you aren't by any chance suggesting that she goes to bed with anything else, are you?

SHE. (*Crossing to foot of bed*) I am not suggesting anything. I am just sick and tired of your coming down like a ton of bricks on that poor boy every time, while she is allowed to do whatever she pleases.

HE. So! I have an unhealthy preference for my daughter. Is that it?

SHE. I am not saying that. I—

HE. All right, say it! Say it!

SHE. What?

HE. Oedipus! Oh! Leave me alone. (*Under the blankets again.*)

SHE. (*Sits on sofa*) In his drawer, did you say?

HE. Shut up.

SHE. Darling, I know you never concern yourself with the children's education except for an occasional bout of fatherly hysteria, but I think that this time you are going a little too far, if you don't mind my saying so. (*Sits back with feet up on sofa.*)

HE. (*Sitting up*) What else do you want me to do? I have to spend every waking hour earning money. Agnes, you are my second in command— I have to leave certain things to you; but, if I see that they are obviously going wrong, it is my duty to intervene.

SHE. If that is your conception of our relationship, then you ought to think of something better than a shaving crop and a riding strop.

HE. Riding crop! And it's not a matter of thinking of something better, it's— (HE *stops, because she has suddenly got up and gone to the window, as if she heard something.*)

SHE. Michael!

HE. Is that him? (*As* SHE *does not answer,* HE *gets out of bed and grabs his overcoat.*)

SHE. (*Peeking out the window*) I thought I heard the gate.

HE. Robert! (*Exits and calls offstage*) Is that you, Robert? (*No answer, so he comes back*) No. (*Sits down at sofa foot of bed.*)

SHE. (*Sits at dressing table, opens powder box*) Why don't you go back to bed?

HE. Because I'm worried.

SHE. (*Picking up handmirror and puff and powdering face*) Why, that's nonsense!

HE. And so are you.

SHE. (*Turns profile*) What on earth gives you that idea?

HE. That you are powdering your face at four o'clock in the morning.

SHE. (*Puts down mirror, puff. Realizes that there is no use pretending any longer, goes to the bottle and picks it up from bed table*) What drawer was it?

HE. The one where he keeps all his junk.

SHE. I can't believe it. It can't be true.

HE. Well, there you are.

SHE. How did you find it?

HE. I was sitting downstairs waiting— I got more and more worried so I decided to go up to his room and see whether perhaps he had climbed in through the window, and then I happened to glance into an open drawer, and there it was.

SHE. But it isn't possible. A child can't be drinking on the sly without his mother knowing it.

HE. We'll have to face it, my dear. He is no longer a child. When I looked into that drawer and found his old teddy bears, his steam engine and then that bottle, I— I can't tell you what I felt.

SHE. Suppose—of course it isn't—but suppose—it is true, whatever shall we do?

HE. I don't know—see a doctor.

SHE. Nonsense. It's perfectly natural childish curiosity. A boy has to try everything once.

HE. If that's going to be your attitude, he'll end by trying murder once. By the way, what were you going to say about Lizzie?

SHE. (*Smiles*) She is in love.

HE. What?

SHE. She's secretly engaged.

HE. To whom?

SHE. To the boy next door.

HE. To that—ape? To that pie-face?

SHE. I think it's quite serious.

HE. The child is only—nonsense!

SHE. She is not a child anymore. She's—well, the same thing Robert is, I suppose. I wouldn't be surprised if one of these days the boy came to see you to ask for her hand.

HE. If he does, I'll shoot him.

SHE. But darling—

HE. But she's only sixteen! Agnes, this is a nightmare!

SHE. But sweetheart—

HE. She can't be in love and certainly not with *that!*

SHE. Why not?

HE. After spending her whole life with me, she can't fall in love with something hatched out of an egg.

SHE. Are you suggesting that the only person the child will be allowed to fall in love with is a young edition of yourself?

HE. Of course not. Don't be indecent. What I mean is that at least we should have given them taste! They should have inherited our taste.

SHE. Well, he seems to have inherited a taste for bourbon.

HE. I don't understand how you can joke about it. This happens to be the worst night of my life.

SHE. I'm not joking, darling. I just don't think that there's much point in us sitting up all night worrying ourselves sick about something we obviously can't do anything about until the morning. Come, go back to bed.

HE. You go to bed— I'll wait up for him.

SHE. Shall I make you a cup of tea?

HE. Tea! You know, we haven't had a single crisis in our life yet for which your ultimate solution wasn't a cup of tea.

SHE. (*Straightening bed linen*) I'm sorry. I was only trying to be sensible about it.

HE. I know you are. I apologize if I've said things that I didn't mean. (*Picks up the bourbon bottle and uncorks it with his left hand*) I think what we both need is a swig of this. Have we got any glasses up here?

SHE. Only tooth-glasses.

(HE *takes a swig, then with a horrified expression thrusts the bottle and cork into her hands and runs to the bathroom.*)

Michael. (SHE *smells the bottle, grimaces*)

HE. (*Rushing out of bathroom with a nauseated look on his face*) What is that?

SHE. (*Corking bottle*) Cod liver oil!

HE. Ohhh—!! (*Runs back into bathroom.*)

SHE. (*Takes handkerchief from pocket, wipes bottle*) How on earth did it get into this bottle?

HE. God knows! (*Re-enters to just outside bathroom door. HE carries a glass of water*) Agnes, I think that little monster must have been trying to set a trap for me! (*Runs back into bathroom.*)

SHE. (*Holding bottle up, puzzling over contents*) Michael, wait a minute! (SHE *is interrupted by the sound of his gargling*) I know! Well, this is the limit!

HE. (*Re-enters, wiping mouth with towel*) What?

SHE. Do you remember three years ago that he had to take that spoonful of cod liver oil every night and that he didn't want to take it in my presence? Of course I measured the bottle every morning, but he poured it into this!

HE. Agnes, do you mean to say that that stuff I swallowed is three years old?

SHE. The little monkey! Oh, now I am going to wait till he gets home! (*Sits sofa.*)

HE. I think perhaps we'd better call the doctor. This stuff must be putrid by now. (*Throws towel into bathroom.*)

SHE. (*Holding bottle*) You'll have to speak to him, Michael. This is one time that you'll have to speak to him. I— (*Hears something*) Michael, there he is! (*Rises, crosses up to door.*)

(HE *rushes to door, stops, returns to sofa and picks up riding crop. Starts out.*)

(SHE *stops him*) No, Michael, not that! Don't go that far!

HE. Three-year-old cod liver oil! (HE *whips the air with the riding crop. Exits.*)

(SHE *listens for a moment, very worried. Then she runs into the bathroom and leaves the bottle there. Re-enters, crosses to door, listens, crosses to sofa at foot of bed and sits down on end of it, all the while muttering to herself.* HE *appears in the doorway, dejectedly holding his riding crop in his hand.* HE *looks offstage, incredulously.* SHE *turns to him.*)

SHE. Well—what did you say?

HE. (*Closes door; distracted, turns to her*) I beg your pardon?

SHE. What did you *say* to him?

HE. Oh—er— "Good morning."

SHE. Is that all?

HE. (*Throws crop on sofa*) Yes.

SHE. (*Rises*) Well, I must say! To go through all this rigamarole and then to end up with— I honestly think you could have said something more.

HE. (*Sits sofa*) I couldn't.

SHE. Why not?

HE. He was wearing a top hat.

(HE *makes a helpless gesture and rests his head in his hands.* SHE *laughs, crosses to him and puts her arms about him, then kisses him on the top of his head.*)

CURTAIN

ACT THREE

SCENE I

1913. *Late afternoon. The same bedroom. Dressing table and chair at window; tobacco stool at Left of arch; sofa Right Center; bed table as before; chairs Center and Left Center. The bed canopy has been changed as have the drapes and articles of furniture. It is all in more conservative taste now. As the Curtain rises,* SHE *is seated at the dress-*

*ing table, holding a wedding bouquet that matches her gown and hat.
After a moment,* He *is heard humming the Wedding March.*

He. (*From dressing room off Left*) Agnes! (*Hums a bit more, then
whistles for her.* He *enters arranging his smoking jacket. Crosses to foot
of bed, humming again. Sees her*) Oh, there you are. Your hat still on?
Agnes!

She. (*Starts*) Yes?

He. (*Crosses to her*) Hey! Are you asleep?

She. (*Sighs and smiles absently*) Yes—

He. (*Fixing scarf, looking in mirror of dressing table*) Come on,
darling. The only thing to think is: little children grow up. Let's be
glad she ended up so well.

She. Yes—

He. Thank God, Robert is a boy. I couldn't stand to go through
that a second time, to see my child abducted by such a— Oh, well, love
is blind.

She. (*Putting down bouquet*) Michael.

He. Yes? (*Opens humidor and picks up pipe*) What is the matter
with you? The whole day long you've been so—so strange.

She. How?

He. You aren't ill, are you?

She. No.

He. That's all right then. (*Starts filling his pipe*) What did you
want to say?

She. (*Rises*) Today is the first day of Lizzie's marriage.

He. It is. And?

She. (*Crosses and sits sofa*) And the last day of ours.

He. Beg pardon?

She. (*Takes off gloves*) I waited to tell you, perhaps too long. I
didn't want to spoil your fun.

He. My *fun?*

She. Yes. I haven't seen you so cheerful for ages.

He. Well— I'm— (*Closes humidor*) For your sake I have made a
fool of myself. For your sake I have walked around all these days with
the face of a professional comedian, with a flower in my buttonhole and
death in my heart! (*Leans over sofa*) Do you know what I would have
liked to do? To hurl my glass in the pie face of that bore, take my child
under my arm—and as for that couple of parents-in-law— (*Looks heav-*

enward) And now you start telling me that you didn't want to spoil my fun! (*Searches pockets for match.*)

SHE. With the information that I am going away.

HE. You are what—?

SHE. I'm going away.

HE. (*Feeling pockets for match*) Huh?

SHE. Away.

HE. How do you mean?

SHE. Can't you help me just a little by understanding quickly what I mean?

HE. But, darling—

SHE. Michael, I'll say it to you plainly once, and please try to listen quietly. If you don't understand me after having heard it once, I'll— I'll have to write it to you.

HE. But darling, we needn't make such a fuss about it. (*Sits sofa*) You want to have a holiday now the children have left the house; what could be more sensible? No need to announce it to me like an undertaker.

SHE. Not for a holiday, Michael—forever.

HE. You want to move into another house?

SHE. I want to go away from *you*.

HE. From me?

SHE. Yes.

HE. You want to—visit friends, or something?

SHE. Please, darling, stop it. You knew ages ago what I meant; please don't try and play for time, it makes it all so—so difficult.

HE. I don't know a damn thing. What have I done?

SHE. Nothing, nothing. You are an angel. But I am—not.

HE. (*Rises, backs up a step*) Agnes, what is the matter with you?

SHE. I would appreciate it if you would stop asking me what is the matter with me. There never has been anything the matter with me, and there couldn't be less the matter with me now. The only thing is, I can't—

HE. Can't what?

SHE. Die behind the stove, like a domestic animal.

HE. Good Heavens—

SHE. You wouldn't understand. You are a man. You'll be able to do what you like until you are seventy.

HE. But my dear good woman—

SHE. I won't! Today I stopped being a mother; in a few years' time, perhaps next year even, I'll stop being a woman.

HE. And that's what you don't want?

SHE. I can't help it. That happens to be the way a benevolent Providence arranged things.

HE. But darling, then it's madness.

SHE. I want to be a woman just once, before—before I become a grandmother. Is that so unreasonable?

HE. But my angel—

SHE. (*Rises; takes off hat*) For Heaven's sake, stop angeling me! You treat me as if I were sitting in a wheel-chair already. I want to live, can't you understand that?

(HE *backs up, leans on sofa.*)

(SHE *puts hat and gloves on bed*) My life long I have been a mother, my life long I've had to be at somebody's beck and call; I've never been able to be really myself, completely, whole-heartedly. No, never! From the very first day you have handcuffed me and gagged me and shut me in the dark. When I was still a child who didn't even know what it meant to be a woman, you turned me into a mother.

HE. (*Steps toward her*) But darling, you wanted Robert—

SHE. No, not through Robert, not through Lizzie, through yourself, your selfishness, your— Oh, Michael. (*Crossing to him, puts her hand on his shoulder*) I didn't intend to say all this, honestly, I didn't. I only wanted to be honest and quiet and nice about it, but—but I can't help it. I can't! The mere way you look at me, now, this very moment! That amazement, that heartbreaking stupidity—don't you feel yourself that there is nothing between us anymore in the way of tenderness, of real feeling, of love; that we are dead, as dead as doornails, that we move and think and talk like—like puppets? (SHE *sits down*) Making the same gestures every day, the same words, the same kisses— Today, in the carriage, it was sinister. The same, the same, everything was the same; the coachman's boots behind the little window, the sound of the hooves on the pavement, the scent of flowers, the— I wanted to throw open the door, jump out, fall, hurt myself, I don't know what—only to feel that I was alive! (SHE *rises*) I, I, not that innocent, gay child in front, who was experiencing all this for the first time, who played the part I had rehearsed for her, but I couldn't. I said "yes" and "no" and "darling" and "isn't it cold," but I heard my own voice and saw my own face mirrored in the little window, in the coachman's boots, like a ghost, and as I put my hat straight, to prove to myself that I wasn't a ghost, driving to my own burial, I looked at myself in exactly the same way, in the same window perhaps, to see if my bridal veil— (*Her voice breaks*; SHE *covers her face with her hands; crosses up onto dais and falls onto bed, weeping*)

(HE *puts his pipe into his pocket, crosses up onto dais and puts his hands on her waist.*)

No! Don't touch me! (*Sits up, gets handkerchief from bed table drawer and wipes her eyes*) Michael, I don't want to, I don't want to blame you for anything. You've always been an angel to me, you've always done whatever you could, as much as you could—

(HE *sits on bed.*)

—although you never opened a door for me, always got on the street car first, never bought me anything nice—oh yes, I know, darling, you have given me many beautiful presents. But something real—if it had only been one book you didn't want to read yourself; or one box of chocolates you didn't like yourself, but nothing. Absolutely nothing. (*Crosses up to him, shows him her hands*) Look, just look! Only wrinkles and a wedding ring, and a new cash book for the household every year.

(HE *takes her hand, raises it to his lips, kisses the palm of her hand.*) No, Michael. That's so easy, so mean, really. You've always known how to make that one little gesture, say that one little word—but now it doesn't work anymore. This is what I've been trying to tell you all along. It's the most difficult part of all, and I don't know if I—no, I can't. (*Sits sofa.*)

HE. Say it.

SHE. I don't think— I'm sure I don't love you any more. I don't say this to hurt you, darling, honestly I don't. I only want you to understand. (*Turns to him*) Do you? Do you a little?

HE. Yes. I think so.

SHE. I even remember the moment I realized I didn't love you. One clear, terrible moment.

HE. When was that?

SHE. It was about a month ago, one Sunday morning in the bathroom. I came in to bring you your coffee and you were rubbing your head with your scalp lotion. I said something about that boy's poems that you had given me to read; I don't remember what I said—and then you said, "I could tell him where to put them"—with both hands on your head. (*Puts hands on her head*) And then—then it was suddenly as if I were seeing you for the first time. It was horrible.

HE. (*After a silence*) Where had you thought of going?

SHE. Oh, I don't know. I thought a room in a boarding house somewhere.

HE. Not a trip, abroad for instance?

SHE. Good Heavens, no.

HE. Why not?

SHE. Because I don't feel like it— (*Turns to him*) —you don't think that I—that there is something the matter with me?

HE. No.

SHE. Do you understand now why I *must* go away?

HE. (*Sitting on bed*) Well, if I were to come into the bathroom with my head full of love lyrics, like you, only to see you rubbing your face with skin food or shaving your arm pits, I don't think I'd have been overcome by any wave of tenderness for you—but I wouldn't go and live in a boarding house.

SHE. That was not the point. The point was what you said.

HE. "I could tell him where to put them." (*Rises*) H'mm. You're sure that was the point? (*Stands on dais, right hand on bedpost.*)

SHE. Why?

HE. Who wrote those poems you were talking about?

SHE. Well, that boy—that boy, who keeps asking you what you think about his work.

HE. You liked what he wrote, didn't you?

SHE. Oh, yes. I thought it young, promising—honestly. It had something so—so—

HE. So—well?

SHE. Well, what?

HE. (*Crossing down Center to Left of chair*) Well, I seem to remember this same description twenty-three years ago.

SHE. You aren't trying to tell me that I'm in love? I won't say another word to you! The very idea that I, with a boy like that, such a— such— It's just that the boy has talent! At least as much as you had, when you were still rhyming about gazelles with golden horns.

HE. I was rhyming about you.

SHE. He must be rhyming about somebody as well, but—

HE. Of course he is. About you, too.

SHE. Me?

HE. What did he write on the title page— "Dedicated in reverent admiration to the woman who inspired my master." Well, I have been his master only insofar that I wrote him a letter: "Dear Sir, I have read your poems twice. I would advise you to do the same." Still, I don't know. Perhaps I'm growing old-fashioned. After all, he's new-school and all that. I should like to read those poems again. Have you got them here?

SHE. Yes.

HE. Where are they?

SHE. (*Crosses onto dais, gets poems from lower drawer of bed table; crosses to foot of bed and starts to hand him the poems, then stops*) You aren't going to make fun of them, are you?

HE. (*Takes out glasses, puts them on, takes poems from her*) Fun? Why should I? I think this occasion is serious enough for both of us to find out what exactly we're talking about. Perhaps you're right. Perhaps I need this lesson. Well, let's have it. (*Reads the title*) "Flashing Foam —Jetsam on the Beach of Youth." H'm. That seems to cover quite a lot. First Sonnet: "Nocturnal Embrace."

SHE. Michael, if you're going to make a fool of this poor boy who is just starting, only because you—

HE. Who is doing the starting here? Me! After thirty years I'm just starting to discover how difficult it is to write something that is worth reading, and I *shall* write something worth reading one day unless— well, "Nocturnal Embrace." (*Reads*)

> "We are lying in the double bed,
> On the windows have thrown a net
> The dead leaves of an acorn tree."

Do you understand why it has to be an acorn tree? Why not an oak?

SHE. (*Leaning against bedpost*) Because it's beautiful. Because it gives atmosphere.

HE. I see. I'm sorry. (HE *reads*)

> "From a church tower far unseen.
> A solemn bell strikes twelve."

Well, now that rhyme could definitely be improved.

> "From a church tower far unseen,
> A solemn bell strikes just thirteen."

(SHE *doesn't answer.*)

(HE *reads on*)

> "Strikes twelve,
> O'er the darkened fields,
> The silent sea.
> But then we start and clasp
> A frightened, sickening gasp,
> For a foot has stopped behind the door."

Now this I understand. No wonder they are startled. Suppose you're just busy clasping each other, and then a foot walks along the corridor and stops right outside your door— (HE *shudders*)

SHE. I'm not laughing, if that's what you're after.

He. That's not what he was after in any case, but let's see how it ends. (He *reads*)

> "For a foot has stopped behind the door.
> Silence. Thumping. It's our hearts
> Waiting with our breath—"

Wondering where the other foot's got to, I suppose—

She. Michael, please stop it!

He. Why? Am I his master or am I not? And has he got the cheek to dedicate this bad pornography to my Agnes or has he not?

She. He meant it for the best.

He. Oh now, did he really? (*Throws poems on sofa*) Do you call that for the best, to turn the head of a woman, the best wife any man could wish himself, at the moment when she's standing empty-handed because she imagines her job is over? To catch her at a time when she can't think of anything better to do than to become young again and wants to start for a second time fashioning the first damn fool at hand into a writer like me?

She. But you don't need me anymore.

He. (*Crossing to her*) Oh no? Well, let me tell you something. People may buy my books by the thousands, they may write me letters and tell me how I broke their hearts and made them bawl their damn heads off, but I know the truth alright. It's *you* who makes me sing— and if I sing like a frog in a pond, it's not my fault. (*Crosses and sits on sofa. Takes off glasses.*)

She. (*Is so amused and relieved that she cries and laughs at the same time. The laughter gets the upper hand*) Oh, Michael!

He. What are you laughing at?

She. (*Crossing to him and sitting on sofa beside him*) Oh, Michael— I'm not laughing— I'm not laughing. (She *embraces him and sobs on his shoulder.*)

He. (*Comforts her like a man who suddenly feels very tired*) I'll be damned if I understand that. (*Rests his head on her shoulder.*)

CURTAIN

ACT THREE

Scene II

1925. *Dawn. Same bedroom, twelve years later. It is apparent that they are moving out—pictures have been taken off the walls, leaving discolored squares on the wallpaper; a step-ladder leans against the*

*Right wall of archway; all drapes have been removed with the exception
of the bed canopy and spread on the fourposter which is the only piece
of furniture remaining in the room. Several large suitcases, packed and
closed, are sitting down Right Center; a trunk at Right.*

At Rise, HE *is heard messing about in the bathroom. Then* HE *comes
out, humming and carrying toilet articles.* HE *goes to the suitcases,
finds them shut, carries the stuff to the bed.* HE *crosses down Center
again to the suitcases, opens one. It is full.* HE *slams the lid shut and
fastens the locks, at the same time noticing that a small piece of clothing is left hanging.* HE *disregards it and drags a second case on top of
the first one, opens it, finds that it is fully packed as well. However,* HE
rearranges the contents to make room for his toilet articles. As HE *starts
back to bed,* HE *again noticed the piece of clothing hanging out of the
bottom case.* HE *looks toward door, then leans down and rips off the
piece of material, puts it in his pocket and crosses up onto dais.* HE
*picks up his toilet articles from the bed, turns, then drops them on the
floor.* HE *mutters, "Damn!" and gets down on his hands and knees to
pick them up. At that moment, when* HE *is out of sight of the Center
door,* SHE *comes in carrying the little "God Is Love" pillow. The moment* SHE *realizes* HE *is there,* SHE *quickly hides the pillow behind her
back.*

SHE. What are you doing?

HE. (*Rises*) Packing.

SHE. Well, hurry up, darling. The car comes at eight and it's almost twenty of. What have you been doing all this time?

HE. Taking down the soap dish in the bathroom.

SHE. The soap dish? What on earth for?

HE. I thought it might come in useful.

SHE. But darling, you mustn't. It's a fixture.

HE. Nonsense. Anything that is screwed on isn't a fixture. Only
things that are nailed.

SHE. That's not true at all. The agent explained it most carefully.
Anything that's been fixed for more than twenty-five years is a fixture.

HE. (*Hands her the soap dish*) Then I'm a fixture, too.

SHE. (*Crosses to bathroom*) Don't be witty, darling. There isn't
time.

HE. (*Seeing little pillow under her arm*) Hey! Hey! Hey!

(SHE *stops.*)

We don't have to take that little horror with us, do we?

SHE. No. (*Exits into bathroom.*)

He. (*Picks up part of his toilet things*) What about the bed?

She. (*Off*) What?

He. Are you going to unmake the bed or have we sold the blankets and the sheets with it? (*Starts packing toilet things.*)

She. (*Off*) What is it, dear?

He. Have we only sold the horse or the saddle as well?

She. (*Re-enters, stands holding the little pillow*) Horse, what horse?

He. What's to become of those things? Have we sold the bed-clothes or haven't we?

She. Oh, no dear. Only the spread. I'll pack the rest. (*Crosses onto dais. Puts little pillow under arm and strips pillow cases.*)

He. In what? These suitcases are landmines. Why are you nursing that thing?

(She *mumbles something and tucks little pillow more firmly under her arm.*)

(He *crosses up to her*) Just what are you planning to do with it?

She. I thought I'd leave it as a surprise.

He. A surprise?

She. Yes, for the new tenants. Such a nice young couple. (*Places pillow.*)

He. Have you visualized that surprise, may I ask?

She. Why?

He. Two young people entering the bedroom on their first night of their marriage, uncovering the bed and finding a pillow a foot across with "God Is Love" written on it.

She. (*Picks up rest of toilet articles and newspaper from bed. Puts them down on dais, the newspaper on top*) You've got nothing to do with it.

He. (*Crosses up onto dais*) Oh, I haven't, have I? Well, I have. I've only met those people once, but I'm not going to make a fool of myself.

She. But, darling—

He. There's going to be no arguing about it, and that's final. (*Snatches pillow, crosses to suitcases and throws it on trunk. Mutters*) God is Love!

She. (*Stripping blanket and sheets from bed*) All right. Now, why don't you run downstairs and have a look at the cellar.

He. Why?

She. (*Stuffs bed linen in pillow case*) To see if there's anything left there.

HE. Suppose there is something left there, what do you suggest we do with it? Take it with us? You don't seem to realize that the apartment won't hold the stuff from one floor of this house.

SHE. Please, darling, don't bicker. We agreed that it was silly to stay on here with all these empty rooms.

HE. But where are we going to put all this stuff?

SHE. Now, I've arranged all that. Why don't you go down and see if there's anything left in the wine cellar?

HE. Ah, now you're talking! (HE *goes out*.)

(SHE *twirls the pillow case tight and leaves it by the suitcases. Picks up the "God Is Love" pillow, returns to the bed, and places it on top of the regular bed pillows, then stands back and admires it. With one hand on bedpost, SHE glances over the entire bed and smiles fondly. Then straightens the spread, smooths out the cover, goes to foot of bed, stops, hears him coming, and quickly covers the "God Is Love" pillow with spread*.)

HE. (*Entering with champagne bottle*) Look what I've found!

SHE. What?

HE. Champagne! (*Blows dust from bottle*) Must be one that was left over from Robert's wedding.

SHE. Oh.

HE. Have we got any glasses up here?

SHE. Only the tooth glasses.

HE. (*Sits on edge of bed*) All right, get them.

SHE. You aren't going to drink it now?

HE. Of course. Now, don't tell me this is a fixture! (*Tears off foil from bottle*.)

SHE. But darling, we can't drink champagne at eight o'clock in the morning.

HE. Why not?

SHE. We'll be reeling about when we get to that place. That would be a nice first impression to make on the landlady!

HE. I'd be delighted. I'd go up to that female sergeant major and say, "Hiya! Hah! Hah!" (*Blows his breath in her face as in the First Act*.)

(*The memory strikes them* BOTH. THEY *stay for a moment motionless.* SHE *pats his cheek lovingly*.)

SHE. I'll go get those glasses. (SHE *exits into bathroom*.)

(HE *rises, throws the foil into the wastebasket at foot of bed, crosses to suitcases and puts bottle on floor. Goes back to bed and looks for the rest of his toilet articles.* HE *pulls back the spread, picks up the "God Is Love" pillow, looks under it, tosses it back, looks under the other pillows, then suddenly realizes that the "God Is Love" pillow has been put back in the bed. Picks it up and calls:*)

HE. Agnes.

SHE. (*Off*) What?

HE. Agnes.

SHE. (*Re-enters carrying towel and two glasses*) What? Oh— (SHE *is upset when she sees what it is, and very self-conscious.*)

HE. Agnes, did you put this back in the bed?

SHE. Yes.

HE. Why, for Heaven's sake?

SHE. I told you— I wanted to leave something—friendly for that young couple—a sort of message.

HE. What message?

SHE. I'd like to tell them how happy we'd been—and that it was a very good bed— I mean, it's had a very nice history, and that—marriage was a good thing.

HE. Well, believe me, that's not the message they'll read from this pillow. Agnes, we'll do anything you like, we'll write them a letter, or carve our initials in the bed, but I won't let you do this to that boy—

SHE. Why not? (SHE *puts glasses and towel on floor beside knitting bag, takes little pillow from him and crosses up to bed.*) When I found this very same little pillow in this very same bed on the first night of our marriage, I nearly burst into tears!

HE. Oh, you did, did you? Well, so did I! And it's time you heard about it! When, on that night, at that moment, I first saw that pillow, I suddenly felt as if I'd been caught in a world of women. Yes, women! I suddenly saw loom up behind you the biggest trade union in existence, and if I hadn't been a coward in long woolen underwear with my shoes off, I would have made a dive for freedom.

SHE. That's a fine thing to say! After all these years—

HE. Now, we'll have none of that. You can burst into tears, you can stand on your head, you can divorce me, but I'm not going to let you paralyze that boy at a crucial moment.

SHE. But it isn't a crucial moment!

HE. It is *the* crucial moment!

SHE. It is not! She would find it before, when she made the bed.

That's why I put it there. It is meant for her, not for him, not for you, for her from me! (*Puts little pillow on bed as before.*)

HE. Whomever it's for, the answer is NO! (HE *takes the little pillow and puts it on the trunk again.* SHE *pulls the spread up over the bed pillows*) Whatever did I do with the rest of my toilet things?

(HE *is very carefully packing his things. When* HE *is finished,* HE *closes the lid to the suitcase.*)
You'll have to sit on this with me. I'll never get it shut alone.

(SHE *sits down beside him.*)
No, get hold of the lock and when I say "Yes," we'll both do—that. (HE *bounces on the suitcase*) Ready? Yes!

(THEY *bounce.*)

(HE *fastens his lock*) Is it shut?

SHE. (*Trying to fix catch*) Not quite.

HE. What do you mean, not quite? Either it's shut or it isn't.

SHE. It isn't.

HE. All right. Here we go again. Ready? Yes!

(THEY *bounce again.*)
All right?

SHE. Yes.

HE. (*Picks up champagne bottle*) Now, do we drink this champagne or don't we?

SHE. (*Picks up glasses, towel, packs them in knitting bag*) No.

HE. All right. I just thought it would be a nice idea. Sort of round things off. (*Puts champagne bottle back on floor*) Well, what do we do? Sit here on the suitcase till the car comes, or go downstairs and wait in the hall?

SHE. I don't know.

HE. (*Looks at her, then at the little pillow on trunk, then smiles at her anger*) It's odd, you know, how after you have lived in a place for so long, a room gets full of echoes. Almost everything we've said this morning we have said before. It's the bed—

(SHE *lays her head on his shoulder.*)
—it's the bed, really, that I regret most. Pity it wouldn't fit. I wonder how the next couple will get along. Do you know what he does?

SHE. He's a salesman.

HE. A salesman, eh? Well, why not? So was I. Only I realized it too late. The nights that I lay awake in that bed thinking how I'd beat Shakespeare at the game—

SHE. Never mind, darling, you've given a lot of invalids a very nice time.

(*In his reaction, as* HE *turns to reply:* DOORBELL *rings twice.*)

(HE *rises and looks out window. Crosses to door, opens it.* SHE *rises and turns top suitcase up.* HE *crosses, puts bed linen under arm, picks up top suitcase.* SHE *turns up the other suitcase and* HE *picks that one up in his right hand; turns to go.* SHE *quickly gets the knitting bag, stops him and tucks it under his right arm.* HE *exits.*)

(SHE *picks up purse, gloves, from off of trunk, then quickly takes the little pillow and crosses to bed but stops suddenly, hearing him return, and hides the pillow under her coat.* HE *crosses down to trunk, leans over to grasp its handle, sees that the little pillow is not there, but proceeds to drag the trunk out. At the door, as* HE *swings trunk around,* HE *looks back at her.* SHE *is standing, leaning against the bedpost, pulling on her gloves. As soon as* HE *is out of sight,* SHE *hurriedly puts the pillow back into the bed and covers it.*)

(HE *re-enters, wearing his hat, picks up bottle of champagne, crosses up to bed, drops hat on foot of bed, flings back the covers, picks up the little pillow and throws it to her side of the bed; then throws the bottle of champagne down on the pillow on his side, and flips the spread back into place.* HE *picks up his hat and crosses to her.* THEY *stand there for a moment, looking about the room.* HE *puts his hat on, smiles, leans down and hesitantly, but surely, picks her up.* SHE *cries, "Michael!"* HE *stands there for a moment, kisses her, then turns and carries her out of the room.*)

CURTAIN

The Hand

by COLETTE

He had fallen asleep on his young wife's shoulder, and she proudly supported the weight of his head, with its fair hair, his sanguine-complexioned face and closed eyes. He had slipped his large arm beneath the slim, adolescent back and his strong hand lay flat on the sheet, beside the young woman's right elbow. She smiled as she looked at the man's hand emerging there, quite alone and far removed from its owner. Then she let her glance stray round the dimly lit bedroom. A conch-shaped lamp threw a subdued glow of periwinkle-blue over the bed. "Too happy to sleep," she thought.

Too excited also, and often surprised by her new state. For only two weeks she had taken part in the scandalous existence of a honeymoon couple, each of them relishing the pleasure of living with an unknown person they were in love with. To meet a good-looking, fair-haired young man, recently widowed, good at tennis and sailing, and marry him a month later: her conjugal romance fell little short of abduction. Whenever she lay awake beside her husband, like tonight, she would still keep her eyes closed for a long time, then open them and relish with astonishment the blue of the brand-new curtains, replacing the apricot-pink which had filtered with the morning light into the room where she had slept as a girl.

A shudder ran through the sleeping body lying beside her and she tightened her left arm round her husband's neck, with the delightful authority of weak creatures. He did not wake up.

"What long eyelashes he has," she said to herself.

She silently praised also the full, graceful mouth, the brick-red skin and the forehead, neither noble nor lofty, but still free of wrinkles.

Her husband's right hand, beside her, also shuddered, and beneath the curve of her back she felt the right arm, on which her whole weight was resting, come to life.

"I'm heavy . . . I'd like to reach up and put the light out, but he's so fast asleep. . . ."

The arm tensed again, gently, and she arched her back to make herself lighter.

"It's as though I were lying on an animal," she thought.

She turned her head slightly on the pillow and looked at the hand lying beside her.

"How big it is! It's really bigger than my whole head."

The light which crept from under the edge of a blue crystal globe fell on to this hand and showed up the slightest reliefs in the skin, exaggerated the powerful, knotty knuckles and the veins which stood out because of the pressure on the arm. A few russet hairs, at the base of the fingers, all lay in the same direction, like ears of wheat in the wind, and the flat nails, whose ridges had not been smoothed out by the polisher, gleamed beneath their coat of pink varnish.

"I'll tell him not to put varnish on his nails," thought the young wife. "Varnish and carmine don't suit a hand so . . . a hand so . . ."

An electric shock ran through the hand and spared the young woman the trouble of thinking of an adjective. The thumb stiffened until it was horribly long and spatulate, and moved close up against the index finger. In this way the hand suddenly acquired an apelike appearance.

"Oh!" said the young woman quietly, as though faced with some minor indecency.

The horn of a passing car pierced the silence with a noise so shrill that it seemed luminous. The sleeper did not wake but the hand seemed offended and reared up, tensing itself like a crab and waiting for the fray. The piercing sound receded and the hand, gradually relaxing, let fall its claws, became a soft animal, bent double and shaken with faint jerks which looked like a death agony. The flat, cruel nail on the over-long thumb glistened. On the little finger there appeared a slight deviation which the young woman had never noticed, and the sprawling hand revealed its fleshy palm like a red belly.

"And I've kissed that hand! . . . How horrible! I can't ever have looked at it!"

The hand was disturbed by some bad dream, and seemed to respond to this sudden reaction, this disgust. It regrouped its forces, opened out wide, spread out its tendons, its nerves and its hairiness like a panoply of war. Then it slowly withdrew, grasped a piece of sheeting, dug down with its curving fingers and squeezed and squeezed with the methodical pleasure of a strangler. . . .

"Oh!" cried the young woman.

The hand disappeared, the large arm was freed of its burden and in one moment became a protective girdle, a warm bulwark against the terrors of night. But next morning, when the tray with frothing choco-late and toast was on the bed, she saw the hand again, russet and red, and the ghastly thumb crooked over the handle of a knife.

"Do you want this piece of toast, darling? I'm doing it for you."

She shuddered and felt gooseflesh high up on her arms and down her back.

"Oh, no . . . no . . ."

Then she concealed her fear, controlled herself bravely and, begin-ning her life of duplicity, resignation, base and subtle diplomacy, she leant over and humbly kissed the monstrous hand.

Translated by Margaret Crosland

The Wheel of Love

by JOYCE CAROL OATES

Some must break
Upon the wheel of love, but not the strange,
The secret lords, whom only death can change.

—Stanley Kunitz, "Lovers Relentlessly"

He and Nadia turned up the walk to their apartment building.

He and Nadia would go out to dinner that night.

He and Nadia could drive off any time they wanted, go anywhere: they were free.

David caught himself thinking this way, "He and Nadia," thinking about himself in the third person the way he had to think about Nadia, who was dead. She had been dead now for three months. But in his mind the sentences wound on, picking at the past and terrifying him with their hunger for the future. There was no longer any "He and Nadia could drive off any time they wanted. . . ." The fact was that while she had been alive they had not driven off like that; who was he trying to deceive?

So he thought clearly, "I have to be careful. I have to remember what has happened and, because of that, what can no longer happen."

That evening he was on his way to an ex-student's apartment for dinner. To a man so newly lonely, so newly alone, an invitation out meant an evening in other people's lives, and therefore freedom from his own, and it meant the possibility of laughter that would surprise him—how good it was to be alive and healthy, to have a body that had not given up in spite of everything. When he was with other people he realized that he had not really died along with Nadia after all.

The strange thing was that he hated to be invited out. He hated to play the game again, as one hates and fears returning to a childhood game that was once so easy. It was almost too much effort for him to show that he was alive when every cell in his body ached to die and have it over with. But he never turned down any invitations. He never said no because he was the sort of man, kindly and distracted, who would agree to anything; and what if he wanted to join the game again someday and he had no way to get in? He had parked his car down the block and was now walking quickly to his ex-student's apartment building. As he walked he listened to the curious lonely sound of his footsteps, a sound he had truly never heard before Nadia died, and he quelled the panic that rose in him by saying, "The hell with it. The hell with it," telling himself that he could stand anything, now that he had stood so much, that he could get through these few hours with a former student without breaking down.

The apartment building was shabby, and he felt his suit sympathize with the building and grow limp, wrinkled. Yes, he was shabby, he was tired. Why hide it? Everyone who saw him said, "that's the one whose wife killed herself," and made a moist clicking sound with their mouths; they would have wondered had he not been shabby. A young couple on their way out for Saturday night held the door open for him and he mumbled thanks and ducked inside. He probably looked as if he lived here. All his life David had melted into landscapes, just as Nadia had stood out from them. Seen in the foyer of the expensive apartment house where he lived, he looked as if he belonged there; seen in one of the sleazy campus taverns, he looked as if he belonged there too. Nadia had had the gift of eliminating all backgrounds. It had not been her face, exactly, that angular, striking, nervous face that always drew one's eye back to it, and not her long slender body that looked always about to move on, to shift about restlessly . . . but something in her manner, some indefinable impatience or intolerance in her voice. She blotted out landscapes and other people, and she was beginning to blot out, for David, all of the life he had led up to the time of her death.

Time led up a slight incline, like a cracked sidewalk, and at its feeble peak was the top of his life: those several minutes when they had explained to him that she was dead. Then time led downward again, the same modest cracked sidewalk.

In the foyer he pressed the buzzer by Jerry Randolph's name and was answered at once by another buzzer, which unlocked the inner door. All this caution, David thought, in a neighborhood like this? Why would anyone want to break in here? The buzzing had made him nervous and he tried to force the heavy door shut behind him, but it was closing slowly of its own accord and could not be hurried. He was standing there, no longer pushing at it and not quite on his way again, when he heard: "Dr. Hutter? Hello."

Jerry stood on the landing, smiling nervously. "Hello," David said. They both smiled. There was the awkward business of getting up the stairs with Jerry watching, but then they were on a level and it was all right. "We live down here," Jerry said. They walked along briskly. The corridor was gray and made David feel nearsighted: something vague and fuzzy about the way it was lighted. "We were lucky to get in here, so near school. . . . Someone said he was moving out. . . ." David nodded to all this, not really hearing it. He wished suddenly that he had stayed home. He wished that he had stayed safe in his own apartment, wearing out the hours until bedtime without bothering to turn on the lights, just sitting there in the living room that faced the park. . . . But Jerry was talking and David turned to him guiltily. He had always liked the boy and he forced himself to remember this.

"My wife Betty—"

This was a surprise: a wife. "Very pleased to meet you," he heard his voice say. She colored pleasantly, a pretty girl, ordinary and pretty and very young, like all the girls he noticed these days. They ushered him inside the apartment. They chattered together about the room, about Jerry's books and records, he had so many of them, and David gave the impression of listening. If he could get to the moment at which they offered him a drink he would be all right.

Jerry indicated the best chair. He sat. The little girl asked him about drinks and he said, "Yes, anything," and she disappeared. Good. Jerry sat and there was a moment of silence. But fortunately a record was playing and they listened to it carefully.

"Ah, Ives," David said.

"Isn't he wonderful?" said Jerry.

David could let the music answer for him. He sat back and relaxed. But he was such a fake these days, after Nadia had left him for the last time, that even his relaxing was just pretense. He had forgotten how to relax.

". . . eight more credit hours to go. It doesn't seem possible," Jerry was saying. David asked him about his plans for next year. The boy talked and now David had that drink. He smiled up at the girl, what-was-her-name, and accepted it. Because he needed it so much, he forced himself to sit and hear out one of Jerry's sentences to the end. Finally he said, "Here's to your new apartment. It's very nice."

They all drank. The girl smiled and then her smile weakened, became qualified. A tremor in his stomach told David when other people were thinking about Nadia; he looked away.

"What sort of work are you doing this semester?" he asked Jerry.

Jerry sat forward; he could talk for hours. He jumped from topic to topic as he had in class, his conversation a kind of free association of ideas and impressions, like the radical poetry published in the students' literary magazine. The girl was a little embarrassed. David caught something restless in her—she was blond and tanned, not the type David would have guessed for Jerry's kind of quibbling good nature, with a heavy gold bracelet weighing down one wrist. Too good for Jerry. Better background. In a minute Jerry would shift to the University and the class it represented, which had not been his class: his father had been unemployed for years and he, Jerry, was just now finishing up college though he was twenty-six.

". . . the trustees and the Establishment are identical," Jerry was saying.

They talked and the girl listened, fascinated by both husband and professor. When she excused herself and went out into the kitchen, David said, "Very lovely girl." The "very" made it sound insincere and this surprised him, since he had meant it.

"Yes," Jerry said, embarrassed. "She's the one I . . . I mentioned to you a few times. We finally got married in October. I'm afraid I was always bothering you, saying the most self-centered, self-conscious crap, wasting your time. . . . "

"No, not at all," David said vaguely.

"Your advice meant a lot to me. I might not have made it through school without it."

David took a drink, startled. He did not want anything frank or personal said to him this evening. He wanted nothing more than to play the game and hide behind drinks and dinner and ordinary, tedious conversation. Jesus Christ, he thought, does he mean it? He tried to think of what he could have said to this boy, while he himself had been carrying around with him daily the five-hundred-pound burden of a disintegrating marriage, a disintegrating wife. . . .

But Jerry was sensitive enough to switch onto another topic, racial discrimination at the University, which was so familiar that anyone could talk knowledgeably about it. And so on until dinner. They ate in the kitchen, but the overhead light had been turned off and there were candles on the table. David was touched by how hard the little girl was trying.

"More of this sauce?"

"No, thank you."

Eating was a pleasant distraction and he was able to relax a little. He wondered if it was true, what someone had said—that he looked tired, didn't he need a rest? A wave of self-pity swept upon him and he wanted to say, Yes, yes, I am tired, I am tired to death, someone please help me. But when he did speak his voice was as meaningless as the twang of a piece of metal.

". . . What do you think about that new law? Stopping and frisking men on the street?"

David tried to think what this was. He no longer read the newspapers; he had just forgotten about them. "Is it constitutional?" he said. This must have been a good answer, since it got Jerry going. He jiggled the table in his excitement, while David pushed food around on his plate. The girl said, "Oh, honey," and David was able to glance at his watch. It was still early. Jerry was talking about the police abusing a Negro woman, and how she had tried to cut her wrists in her cell. The girl said again, in a sharp surprised voice, "Honey." And all conversation stopped.

David kept on eating. He wanted to explain that it was all right. They need not be concerned. Please talk again. Talk. He ate to show them how composed he was after three months; he was not still thinking of his wife, who had taken every pill in the medicine cabinet, like a child playing a game, flooding her arteries with poisons that must have warred even on one another.

"Do you know Shapero's quartet? I want to play it for you," Jerry said, and when he got up he jiggled the table. The girl steadied it and tried to smile at David, but her smile was unconvincing. From the other room Jerry called in: "Wait till you hear the precision in this—it's stunning."

"Do you like music?" the girl said shyly.

Not really, David thought. Not any more. But he said yes, because only those who are ugly and cruel and are never invited anywhere admit they don't think about music at all—liking it or not liking it.

They listened to the record. They had dessert. David thought, eating, that food was a reality he had almost forgotten about. It was real. Music and talk floated around and got lost, the hell with them, but food was real and proved to him that he was alive. There was always more of it. Music and talk and even people could get lost, but food never.

Jerry got up and played the record again. They listened. The girl pretended to listen and her frown of concentration seemed to David lovely.

After dinner she remained out in the kitchen and he and Jerry sat together, man to man. Jerry said, with the plodding sincerity that had always made David like him, "I was sure sorry to hear about it. I . . . I couldn't believe it at first. . . ." But if he had known Nadia he would have believed it at once. ". . . all the kids . . . I remember that one class, when you talked about Keats. . . ." The class materialized in David's imagination, the roomful of faces he had never realized cared so much about him, were so sympathetic, so nosy. The girl returned, smiling shyly, and Jerry brought that conversation to an undignified halt. He was abrupt, graceless. The little girl stared down at her feet—patent leather shoes, very pretty—and David wanted to take their hands and bring them together, introduce them to each other and leave, get out. What place had he, a forty-year-old wreck still careening along with the force of forty years' momentum, in this crowded happy little apartment? Tonight the girl would huddle in Jerry's arms and maybe even manage to weep, a few tears not for David but for the tragedy of it, how sad it was. . . .

Now they were talking about politics, and David could at least handle his side of the conversation. He felt aged, weary, a tennis player trapped in a game with someone twenty years younger, lunging to get shots no one expected him to get. He drank. Jerry drank and the little girl sat on the floor, her feet tucked primly under her skirt. This was the real thing, this kind of talk. Her eyes shone. She had heard so much about Dr. Hutter, the intellectual Dr. Hutter, and now David could not let her down. He had to perform, weary as he was. Every cell in his body ached but he kept on with the game.

"It really meant a lot—you coming here tonight," Jerry said. "Betty thought we maybe shouldn't bother you, but—" Jerry chattered on without noticing his wife's sharp, warning look. He had a thin, earnest, eager face, this boy who was no longer a boy but a man, growing into manhood and therefore forcing men like David on into middle age before they were ready for it. David felt a stab of sorrow to think that he was not equal to the boy's admiration. He was not equal to anyone's admiration. He wanted to explain this to them but his brain was clouded from the alcohol and the strain of keeping up talk, keeping his face sane and orderly. Jerry faltered, embarrassed and happy in that way only students can be happy, and his wife listened with a small worried smile, hoping he would not make another blunder.

Then it was time to leave. He would be carried along by the current of talk, right out the door and down the corridor into safety. Standing, they talked a little more easily than before. He had stayed late enough. The warm air of the room seemed to push drunkenly at him, pressing against his chest, and he felt as if he were on the brink of something terrible.

"I should—maybe I should explain—" he began.

They waited, but he did not go on. He stared past them and was silent.

Then the chorus of farewells again, and the open door, and the hall that made him feel nearsighted; and at last the night air.

Outside, he knew what he had wanted to tell them. It came to him suddenly, like a blow. They had to know—they shouldn't be fooled—that he was not mourning Nadia's death, but his own. He hated her for the selfishness of her death and for her having eclipsed him forever, obliterated him as if she had smashed an insect under her shoe. He would always be pointed out as the man whose wife had killed herself. That would be the only interesting fact about him, and how could he ever rise above it by anything in his own life?

"Like a slug. A filthy slug," he said aloud. His dead wife was a slug that had trailed its slime across the whiteness of his life, and this was what he had wanted to tell his student and that worried little girl. For a moment he thought about going back to tell them, running back and pounding on the door. "I want you to know the truth! The truth!" Then he recovered and went on home.

II

Three months before, on the day before Nadia died, they had been driving out to her mother's house. It was a Sunday and that day remained in David's mind always blank, blurred, pale, the sky not blue but not white either, overcast by a veil of haze.

She was driving and he didn't like the way she passed everyone, as if she really wanted to get where they were going. But she said, "I can handle the car. I'm fine." She wore a black and white checked coat, of a simple and expensive cut, like all her clothes. When David came home

and found another of those packages on their bed, the long rectangular
cardboard box with flimsy paper inside or lying half-crumpled on the
bed, he always felt a mixture of anger and helplessness. The new suit or
new dress would be in the closet and he could never tell which one it
was, but the box was left out, accidentally, carelessly, as if she had forgotten about how he felt when her mother gave her money. She would
say, her eyes large and restless in their deep sockets, "My mother wants to
do it, why should I refuse her?"

She swung out into the left lane, preparing to pass another car. David
said, "You should have let me drive." She said at once, "Don't talk to
me like that. Don't make me angry." The car gathered power and
rushed forward, leaving the other car behind. David lit a cigarette and
saw how absurdly it trembled in his fingers.

"You keep at me all the time," she said.

"All right."

"You never let me alone." From the side, Nadia's face looked slender
and anxious; she had a gambler's thin, suspicious nose. With her, words
were just sounds to thrust out at David or at anyone—even her doctor,
who had finally contacted David to ask his cooperation—to keep them
at a distance, to distract them. She did not really listen to what she said
and so it was a surprise when she remembered odd, stray little remarks
of his, years old. She would smile at him with her dreamy calculating
smile and recall observations he had made, years ago when he had been
another person. It was the same power she had in her face, something
he could not imagine until he experienced it, again and again: the
power to turn her gaze upon him and excite him so that he felt shaken
and helpless, as innocent as he had been when they had first met.

"Because of the way we came together, you can never respect me,"
she was saying. Their arguments made his head ache because he always
gave in and, in giving in, he knew that the victory was nothing important to her; she was already thinking of something else.

"Look, please," he said. "It's a lovely day. It's Sunday. Why don't
you relax?"

"In every car on this highway someone is telling someone else to
relax," Nadia muttered. "What are you going to say to my mother?
About my going to Toronto?"

"Nothing."

Nadia glanced at him. "Were you really so worried?"

He did not answer. His head was aching.

"David, look," she said. "I know how you feel. I know. But what
about me? I keep thinking of going away, of going to strange places

. . . can't you understand that? You've never tried to understand it. I think of dirty old buses, I think of walking, hitching rides . . . if you woke up one morning and ran outside and ran away from your life, wouldn't you come into a new one? What would it be? And if you had run away a day earlier, wouldn't you have gone to a different life still, a different world? When people know this, how can they stay in one place?"

"Nadia, we don't want to talk about this again. Not now."

"But you stay where you are and you're so permanent," she said, "you seem to me heavy and strange, like a statue. I can feel you behind me when I leave, I circle around you and feel you there, I don't know what happens. . . . He told me to call this Dr. Hack, but I'm not going to. I know very well what Dr. Hack is."

"We'll call him tomorrow."

"Everyone is like me! They want to have other lives, be other people. Don't tell me. If I have to be just one person I'll kill myself—"

"Don't talk like that, Nadia. Please."

"What day is today? Sunday?" She frowned and he saw sharp lines on her forehead, between her eyes. In a few years she would look like a witch, he thought. He was unmoved. The love he felt for this woman was a condition he existed in, the way he existed in a world of gases only accidentally fit to breathe. He needed this love for survival the way he needed air, but it would never have occurred to him to be grateful for it or to feel any affection for Nadia, beneath the surface of his passion. And what a famous passion it must be, he thought—married now for six years and still hollow-eyed with being so alert, with having to see in every stranger an object for Nadia's meticulous and always serious concern.

Right now it was a child on a bicycle, coming toward them. She rode on the muddy shoulder of the highway, a girl of about twelve. Hands firm on the handlebars, on red plastic guards that were probably soiled, body leaning forward, legs pumping . . . she wore sneakers and white socks.

"Wonder where she's going in such a hurry," Nadia said.

He saw her take the time to glance into the rear-view mirror, and he was bitter with jealousy. It was like a taste in his mouth. Her imagination sailed off backward with the child, to what ugly little farmhouse crouched on the edge of this highway, stunned by the road getting so wide and so busy over the years, to what drudge of a mother and what father resting all day from a week in the factory, now that these small old farms were no longer worked. . . ?

"I used to love riding a bicycle," Nadia said softly.

"We could get two bicycles. Keep them in the garage."

"I'm too old for it now. . . ."

"Everyone rides bicycles in the park. Grandfathers. Grandmothers."

"It wouldn't be the same thing," she said.

It was never the "same thing" with them. She was vague and exasperating. Why wouldn't it be the same thing? She was a woman who had abandoned her own life, her own body, and David felt shackled to a corpse.

She disappeared sometimes and when she returned to him, haggard and wistful, he always took her in. She had done nothing wrong, even when there had been other men involved, at least nothing that should not have been done; and if she stayed home for his sake in the apartment she had wanted so badly, she could sit for four, five hours at a time in the bedroom, staring out at the park. The building was expensive because its hundred or so inhabitants could stare out their windows at the jumble of leaves and branches that was the park, but there was a terror to the silence of trees that could never be imagined by one living an ordinary noisy life. He said to her, Call that girl you used to see, what's-her-name, and go shopping. Have lunch. He said, Why don't we have someone over? I can help you with dinner. He bought tickets to plays and concerts, wooing her, luring her out, but he got no happiness from her icy, beautiful face if that drugged look was in it. Neutral to the touch as wax, neither cold nor warm, having neither softness nor hardness—her skin lay on the outermost limits of her body, and that was all. If she did not run away on an impulse to Chicago or Toronto, she could be just as far away lying beside him at night. She said, "I keep wanting to go away but I need you here. I need you back here, waiting."

"Do you think that's healthy? Normal?"

"I don't know what that means, normal," she had said slowly.

He thought that if they went out driving more, went on sudden trips of their own, she would give in to him and become his wife. A wife was a kind of possession and no husband thought that way until something went wrong: there were things in life you had to have, to possess, you had to be able to depend upon. He tried to explain this to her. But his love was the anchor that held her down and kept her safe, no matter how far away she went. Without him, she would have had no one to encircle and she would have kept going forever in one direction, lost.

Now she let her head fall back a little, in a girlish indication of surprise. And chagrin. She said, "David, I don't think this is the right Sunday."

"What?"

"I don't think she meant today. She meant next week."

"Are you sure?" David said.

"I think so. . . . Isn't this silly?"

If she questioned anything, David lost his capacity to be certain about it. She might have doubted his own past, the years before she came into his life, and he would have had to struggle to retain it. So he said, "Well, whatever you say. I'm not very anxious to keep going."

"I know."

"I like your mother, but. . . ."

"Mothers are all the same. Mothers, fathers," she said. "I hate your family and you hate mine, no, don't interrupt. I'm not complaining. Everyone knows these things. Well, what should we do?"

"What do you want to do? Keep on driving?"

"Please don't make fun of me."

"I wasn't. I'm just trying to understand you."

Nadia laughed. "But you're the one who's strange! How anyone can stay in one place, one room, for five years the way you did, the same job, the same life. . . . What should we do now?"

"We can turn around and go back home."

"But maybe it was today? I can't remember," she said. "Today or next Sunday? It's always a Sunday. . . . Why does she bother me, why can't she leave me alone?" she said angrily. "I have you now and I don't need her. I wish she could understand that."

"What did you mean just now?"

"What?"

"Not being able to understand me—"

"Christ, this car is hot," she said. The sun had broken through the haze. Nadia rolled down the window and the air blasted against her face, whipping her short dark hair back. "I can't stand driving, I hate being so hot and sweaty. Tell me what you want to do or I'll drive off the road. I'll turn the car into that field."

"Just slow down," he said. He spoke carefully, though his head was pounding with pain. "It's all right, Nadia. You can park on the edge." She let the car roll to a stop. Now the sunlight pounded onto the hood of the car and through the windshield. "You don't want me to go anywhere again, so why should I? I'll stay in one place forever," she said. She snatched the keys out of the ignition and threw them out the window. They landed on the far side of the highway, with a thin metallic ting.

"It's all right, Nadia."

"Nothing's all right."

"We can just sit here and relax for a minute."

She was breathing hard. Always, confronted with the real woman and not just with the memory of her, David felt how inadequate he was— how little he knew, how little power he had. She was like a rich, complex gift bestowed upon him, one he had received without earning and so could not enjoy. "Please don't leave me again," he said. He took both her hands and turned her to him, he pressed her cold hands against his face. They sat like this for some time, both breathing hard, nervously. He thought, If I look up at her and she looks at me in that certain way, it will mean something.

He looked up and her eyes, in their dark, strained sockets, were fixed on him. She smiled hesitantly.

"Here we are, in this one life," she said.

A surge of love for her rose within him. He loved her and he was not going to let her go. For six years he had been strong enough always to draw her back, and he would be able to save her. Why not? Sunlight flooded the car and pounded on the side of his face, like the strength that coursed through his body and gave him such power.

III

About seven years before that day, in early October, David had been in his old room a few blocks from the University, waiting. He had waited part of a Monday and all day Tuesday, stepping out now and then onto the top of his landlady's back porch, which had been converted into a kind of balcony for anyone who rented the second floor. It looked out and down to a nondescript back yard, mainly crab grass and dandelions, and finally to a board fence; behind that a few yards was a railroad track, on a raised column of ground.

He would have to go out the next day, but Tuesday he could stay home, waiting for her, and at the thought of her coming to him he felt his heart pound violently. He was like a machine or a complicated toy whose parts have begun to speed up inside. In the medicine-cabinet mirror his face looked the same, his skin a little pale but cool, almost clammy. He had the look of a man who is waiting.

Every hour he turned up the radio volume and listened to the news.

Listening to the news was like sliding downhill. At first there was confusion and pain, then you got numb, then you were at the bottom and could not remember how bad it had been. He listened, sweating, to the urgent details of crisis in China, Berlin, Cuba, and then to details of crisis in Washington, and finally to items about little children whose dogs had been found after two weeks, or children whose cats had been rescued from trees by the Fire Department. Then he turned down the volume again. He went out on his makeshift balcony and leaned on the railing, looking out into the rich golden air of early autumn and sometimes not even thinking about Nadia, not even thinking her name.

She did finally come, that evening. She had been breathless, with her long hair disheveled about her face. David stared at her hungrily to see what she was bringing him: and she looked back at him and smiled. It was all right. He drew her into the room and closed the door and they stood looking at each other, afraid to let their excitement show. She said, "We've been talking about it for two days nearly. All last night and today. I told him how I felt and he understands, it's all over. He understands." She half-closed her eyes, those languid bluish lids, in an adolescent expression of relief.

"Here, sit down," David said. They were furtive and bumbling, like children playing at being adults. "I bought this to celebrate. In case there was something to celebrate."

"Did you think I might not come?" she said shyly.

It took him a while to get the cork out and his face flushed. She laughed with him, her own cheeks hectic and red. When she held up her glass for him to fill, he noticed how it trembled in her fingers.

"No, I knew you'd come," he said.

Even now, awkward as she was, this young girl knew the secret rhythm that women have for moments of intimacy; she was awkward but not embarrassed. She sat back with a gesture of exhaustion that was only pretense, childish pretense, and smiled at him over the rim of the glass, a lovely dazzling smile that meant she had come a long way, a very long way to this room. "My God, my God," she whispered. There was so much to say, so much to ask, that David could not begin. He sat smiling as if enchanted, staring into a light that was radiant but blinding.

She had first appeared to him as an indifferently ordinary body, a girl in the company of other people. He could not truly say when he had first seen her, but she remembered her first impression of him because of course he was someone special; even the least of professors is a public personality. All this was teasing, droll, but something in him hungered for it: her heavy antique bracelets, her old-fashioned sapphire ring, and that air she had at all times—even when sloppily dressed—of belonging strangely to both the present and a personal, private past. She was not a college student but instead the wife of a young instructor, and she explained rapidly and defensively that she had not graduated from college, no, she had dropped out in her second year. And then she would pause, as if only now did she recall why she had dropped out, and the recollection was unpleasant. "What I want is to get out of here. This city. I want to go back home, where my mother is," Nadia would say, gently and persistently, so that anyone who heard her knew she was demanding something. Of her husband she said little. "It was a mistake. I was too young. He'll be happy to stay here forever. And he listens to the opera on the radio, any opera, all day Sunday." She spoke in a rapid, clipped voice, flushed at her vulgarity but really not caring, carrying it all off whimsically and brusquely. She had decided to take a night course, not for credit, and so she had walked into David's life, idle and always perfectly dressed, with an odor or look about her of clear, sun-drenched days at the shore and a dark, studious gaze of utter frankness. She had always worn sleek, high-heeled shoes that made her long legs look even longer and more slender than they were, and made her shoulders arch slightly and the curve at the base of her spine show as if she were sucking in her breath. Her hair was loose on her shoulders and it did not make her look casual so much as it made her look impatient, restless.

And so she had run up his stairs and into his room, this elaborately furnished and cluttered room he had had for years all to himself, and changed both their lives. In his arms she was like treasure scooped up and flung upon him by the sea, overwhelming him, sweeping him along with its fragrant odor and its rich, heavy, entwining embrace, something that looked and felt soft but was strangely ornamental, even glittering. No one else eixsted in the world except them. There was no one.

David woke to hear a vague sputtering, some static: just the radio over on his desk. Its dial showed in the dark, a dim orange, but he looked away and forgot it. She asked him something sleepily, and he answered, telling her nothing but giving her all she wanted—the sound of his voice. The moment was sealed within itself, David thought, and nothing could change it, as if he and this girl were on an island together, able to read in each other's eyes the opaque secret of life—huddling together, embracing, loving, thwarted only at having at last to come apart and be two people again. All of the world must be straining against his windows to get a glimpse at them, he thought fiercely; all of the world must be sick with jealousy to know that it could never have what they possessed together.

The Rider Was Lost

by NANCY HALE

*"For want of a nail the shoe was lost,
for want of a shoe the horse was lost, for
want of a horse the rider was lost . . ."*

The last of the dinner-guests had finally driven away down the frosty lane. Even old Harry Dawson, drunk as a goat, had been persuaded by his mild wife to leave off declaiming "How We Beat the Favorite" and be assisted into the driving seat of their ancient dog-cart. Long after the sounds of the departing motors had died away in the November night, their wheels could be heard rattling down the half-frozen ruts, back into the country where they lived in a poverty which demanded the sacrifice of all comforts, but never of necessities like hunters and new top-boots for old Harry. . . .

Mary and Cathcart James stood in the wide doorway of Aspenwall, swallowing slow lungfuls of strong, cold air. They felt the long swells of pasture-land falling away around them in the darkness, the hidden ribbons of icy creeks, the miles of weatherbeaten rail fences, the stone walls, the hillside clumps of brambly thicket, the high, fast-closed gates, the low, dark buildings full of shuffling, breathing horses—all the still, bare beauty of their own land in the night. They stood quiet side by side, bone-satisfied, but they said nothing.

Cathcart closed the door, and they went back across the hall to the lighted library, where a sleepy fire snapped and died down. Mary moved about the corners of the room, turning out lamps. Cathcart picked up his whiskey-glass from the mantel and stood drinking beneath the portrait of themselves mounted on a pair of chestnut hunters, now dead; a drop fell from the bottom of the glass and rolled down the smooth scarlet cloth of his tailcoat; his eyes watched his wife's figure as it moved in and out of the shadows.

"Hounds meet at ten-thirty, or eleven, in the morning?" she asked in her low voice, straightening up and facing him across the room.

"Eleven." His voice had its slight, midnight blur from whiskey. "Mary. . . ."

She went and leaned against the mantel with him. He put one arm around her strong firm waist, and pulled her closer to him; he finished off the whiskey in the glass.

"Do you want another before we go up?"

"Half of one."

She leaned down to a table at the side of the fireplace, and picked up the decanter; Cathcart left his hand resting on her bent back. Then he poured out his drink, and she stood up close to him again; he drank the whiskey slowly, tasting its grainy sweetness. Her quiet eyes looked into the shadows at nothing; in the faint firelight her face was rosy and contented. She was thirty-four years old. He was forty-one.

He drank up the glass and set it down and put his other arm around his wife. He said,

"Mary . . ." and pulled her big warm body to his, that was taller and thicker. His arms were hard and heavy around her, and his ruddy face grew redder, but his eyes were calm and sleepy and undisturbed as he kissed her on her mouth.

". . . Let's go to bed."

They turned out the one last light and left the fire dying on the hearth. In the silent dark they crossed the hall to the stairs. Above, a yellow light burned, and they mounted toward it, their bodies one dark mass against the upper glow. But they climbed their own stairs unhurriedly, in content and comfort, and they said nothing.

Their breakfasts were brought to them on two large trays at nine in the morning. The Negro man-servant pulled out two small tables, put chairs to them, and placed the trays, with oranges, oatmeal, eggs, ham, cornbread, and coffee. Then he went away. There was a low bustle of work going on in the house.

Mary and Cathcart James lay side by side on their backs in their broad poster bed. They were waking with their eyes still closed; they lay as still and firm as those mediæval squires who, with their ladies, sleep a wedded sleep in quiet stone until the last trump shall wake them.

Their faces, side by side, were curiously alike; warm red blood ran close to the surface, the mouths were close-shut, and the skin wind-tanned; they were healthy, vigorous, impassive, and profoundly contented faces; they were powerful and wilful, but there was no dissatisfaction in them. . . .

At quarter to eleven they left their car in the lane at Gresham churchyard, where hounds were meeting, and strode in their boots up the ridge to where their man was waiting with the horses. All around them were big, delicate hunters, gray, chestnut, and bay, nervous and excitable in the frosty morning air, dancing about the black grooms that stood at their heads; and their friends, the farmers, the owners of big houses, and the visitors out for a day's run; in hunt-buttoned pink and varnished top-boots, in ratcatchers, in muddy tweeds; all standing about under the leafless trees, under the watery November sun, standing alert, intent, engrossed; waiting.

Cathcart cupped his hand for his wife to mount, and helped her adjust her dark blue skirt; he stepped cleanly into his own saddle, and the two moved off toward an advantageous corner near the road, out of the way of jostling horses. Their faces were weathered, full, immobile; they waited with each other on the horses they loved, in the country they loved. . . .

By twelve o'clock the hounds were in full cry after a fox that was making straight for the mountains. Harvey the huntsman could be seen two fields away, his flea-bitten gray going hard across country. The first flight of the field kept close in behind him, Cathcart, with his hat jammed down over his ears, helping his excited young horse to head straight at the high chicken-coops over wire, Mary sitting straight as an arrow on her seasoned hunter, a little ahead of her husband. Their faces were red and calm. . . .

There was a fast straightaway to a rail fence at the brim of a hill. Cathcart saw Mary fly over it like a swallow; her back was tall and trim. He saw the muscles in her hunter's quarters work as he galloped thrustingly down the hill at the jagged stone wall at the bottom. Momentarily he heard hoofs rapping the piece of timber that lay along the stones as the horse took the jump.

The next second he was himself in midair over the wall, with a sickening, heaving scramble of horse, woman, blue cloth, saddle, directly under his hunter's stomach.

With a great reach they overtopped the rolling mess; it was half a field before he could pull his horse up. He cantered back, dismounted, pulled the horse off Mary, spoke to her. . . .

It was nearly two o'clock when the ambulance from Washington labored up the narrow, rutted road into the fields and Mary was carried to it.

He rode beside her to the hospital, with his terrified, puzzled eyes on her white face. He had never seen her face white before. He had never heard her scream before, either.

Cathcart James was the son of a horse-dealer who made most of his money from the Northerners who fell in love with the hunting country. They had lived in the casual cabins that edged up to the significant buildings—the vast, orderly stables—and the white-fenced schooling ring. Life was great horses, and enough whiskey, and women—a round that fell into a perfect balance, the satisfying of three appetites.

Cath used to lean against the whitewashed fence with his blue shirt open around his big, red-burned throat, and the sweat separating his black hair into thick locks, watching the Negro boys schooling young hunters over the bars, and shouting at them in his strong, lazy voice. He was good looking and physical and self-confident, and he had never in his life wanted anything enough to try to keep it.

All the Northern women who came down to buy his father's horses fell in love with him, and sometimes he was put to difficult and ruthless resorts to explain that in spite of his responsiveness he did not want to marry them. He really liked the light, easy, chattering Southern girls better. He never doubted that he could have any woman in the county if he wanted her.

In the long, burning, murmurous Virginia summers he used to ride, alone, back into the country towards the mountains, along the clay roads, dusty and red, and through the sweet-scented long grasses of the fields. He carried a switch to brush the crust of flies from his horse's neck, and his horse's feet squelched in the soft black mulch of the bottoms. He rode dripping and relaxed, with a lazy rein, and his eyes drifted along the blue-gray haze of the mountains.

No one ever rode in such weather but the little Calthrope girl from Aspenwall. She rode in any weather. Often they met coming across a field or down the road, and then they would ride along together in the heat, without saying much. The country throbbed and shimmered under the blazing sky, blank blue overhead, and the cicadas shrilled higher and sharper in the golden fields; the walking horses went ta-cla, ta-cla, ta-cla on the baked clay road.

She was skinny and tall and young with the angularity of a young filly; her sunburned face was serious and intent, and she rode better than any girl he had ever known. In the winter he would see her in the hunting field, and they would often be alone together, an acre or two out in front of the rest of the field, she tearing like a breeze along beside him over fences, and her face thin and young and serious. But he never saw her anywhere else, because she stayed with her people back in the old house, Aspenwall, except when she rode out. The Calthropes were very old people and all their children had grown up and married away from Aspenwall except Mary. One spring both of them died, but Mary went on living there alone.

In the summer Cath began riding along on the hot days with her again, when he ran across her out in the back country. She was a nice little girl who knew horses and who didn't want to talk any more than he did, and he never thought of her as a woman at all. Sometimes, lounging along on their dripping horses, they would talk horse to each other, but little even of that because neither had anything to say that the other didn't know. He liked her because he felt that she was as absorbed and content as he was. . . . It was a surprise that jarred him to the core when one day in the afternoon she said she loved him, and rode close and put her face up for him to kiss.

In that shock it came to him solidly that she was the only woman he had ever wanted to marry. He wanted to marry her because he somehow knew her through and through, and she was the same person that he was. After that shock there was never any nervous excitement of the kind that had stimulated but really annoyed him in making love to other women; there was instead something as calm and rhythmic and satisfying as physical health. They were married practically at once, and began living together in a deep, constant, warm tempo that was like a heart-beat vivifying the whole of their active, out-of-door existence.

The money was Mary's, and Aspenwall was Mary's, but neither of them ever thought of separate possession at all. Mary had a man, and Cath a wife, and they possessed each other completely, besides all that they had possessed before: horses, land, a house, and their core-deep health. They were better suited than any couple in the country; everything in the world that either of them needed they had at home. As soon as she was married Mary filled out her angles into a strong solidity; soon they grew to look physically alike. . . . They had lived thirteen years in a physical and emotional accord that had nearly dispensed with the need of language when Mary had the accident which put her, smashed and crumpled below the waist, into the hospital for nearly a year.

The doctor led him out of the ether-smelling private room, and paused in the corridor.

"Your wife's in for a long rest," he said. "It was a nasty fall."

"Won't she be well?" Cath asked. He could not seem to think at all; the significance of his life seemed to be deducted from the remainder; he felt hopelessly confused.

"With care. . . . With time. . . ." the doctor offered inconclusively.

Cath nodded and started toward the elevator. He went out to his car that had been brought, and started to drive back into Virginia. His articulate mind put words in his mouth that he kept saying over and over as he drove—"I want my wife. I want my wife."

That night after dinner he started drinking and by ten he was as drunk as he could make himself. He stood underneath the mantel portrait alone, drinking whiskey that had a dead taste; he could not enjoy it, but he drank it up fast. He poured out some more, and picked up the siphon.

"I want my wife," he whispered to himself like a child, and took a big drink.

Every day he went in to see Mary in the hospital after hunting, and every night he got as drunk as possible. He saw almost nobody besides friends in the hunting-field, and he was not glad to see them; in the mornings now he had a bad head from the night before, so bad that the day's fast run no longer sweated the dead alcohol out of him as it should. He was in a bad temper nearly all the time that he was not at the hospital; he felt dully, helplessly furious that his life was spoiled; drinking hard and riding hard did not seem to rearrange it.

Hounds were not meeting one morning and Cath went out, late, to school a four-year-old in the enclosed paddock behind the stables. The horse was frightened at the fences and tried to run out every time, or he would refuse and Cath would give him a cut and turn him round at the jump, sharply, again. The horse was in a lather.

"Don't ride at 'em so savage, Mr. James, and he'll go better," called Jefferson, the trainer, chewing a straw at the fence-rail.

Cath rode up close to the barrier and pulled in the hysterical horse.

"God damn you to hell, Jeff. Do you think you know more about schooling horses than I do? Do you? Do you?"

"No, *sir!*" said Jefferson promptly, staring at Cath curiously. He rolled himself back on his elbow and lounged off toward the tack-room.

Cath wheeled the four-year-old around and started off in a little whirl of kicked-up dirt to make the circuit of the jumps. He held the horse's head straight, rigidly, and somehow the horse scrambled messily over three jumps in a row. On the fourth he came down hard. Cath jumped up quickly, and turned to the horse, kicking clumsily on the ground. It appeared one leg was broken. After Jefferson had come out to destroy him, Cath went into the house and had a drink.

He was really drunk when he went in that afternoon to see Mary. He walked into the room that smelled so close, so unpleasant to his nostrils, and she was lying there, white and strained and like a stranger. He knew from her face that she was in pain, and he felt angry at her pain; he felt suspicious of pain, and it did something to her face that made her into a different person from his wife, whose real face he knew like the sky or the earth.

"Oh, Cath, you're drunk!" she cried, and turned her face, whittled sharp with suffering, toward the sterile white wall.

Her voice was a stranger's, too, higher than hers, and almost shrilly critical. Mary was never critical. All his discomfort and loneliness and confusion rose like a lump in his throat, and his head swam with the closeness of the room and the whiskey he had drunk.

"I'm not drunk," he said thickly to the white stranger that lay in the bed. "A man's got to do something when his wife goes away and leaves him besides—" he sought in his mind for an expression of what he wanted to say—"knit."

"Oh, Cath! How can you say I went away and left you? You don't think I wanted to be all smashed to pieces, do you?"

"No." He spoke deep, low; he felt ashamed and uncomfortable. What was all this talking for? It was not Mary in the bed there, and he didn't feel as if he were himself, either. He never did, these days.

"My God, Cath, it's such hell to lie here day after day after day, and not be able to do *anything*." Her voice rose. "You don't know what it's like to be helpless. You can hunt every day and be out with the horses and do everything you want."

He patted her hand. He was deeply uneasy. He kept glancing at the woman who had been his own wife, and who was talking so much more than his wife ever talked, and his head whirled dizzily, and he wondered what was the matter with everything.

But she went on talking.

"And I'm missing everything. Everything. I just lie here. You can get drunk or anything you please. You don't care if I'm all busted to pieces."

This certainly was not his wife. His wife had gone away and left him to hang about like a lost dog, without any purpose to his life.

"God damn it," he said, and he jerked his arm away from the bed, "I come in here to see you every day, don't I? Every day and it's three months now, I reckon." He stopped talking abruptly. It seemed as if in this strange life he talked all the time.

"Oh!" Now she had started to cry, weakly.

He thought, "She's a silly woman." Then he almost jumped at the shock and sickness of thinking it. A stiff, white figure slipped creepily into the room and started to murmur.

"Mr. James, I'm afraid you'll have to go now. Mrs. James can't stand excitement; you must be careful. . . ."

He got up and glanced unhappily at the bed, but the woman in it was crying into the pillow. He went out, tiptoeing the way that being in a hospital made him tiptoe. In the elevator he thought:

"I want my wife." It always came to him in words in the elevator in the hospital. "I want my wife," he thought inside his head. His mouth tasted sour and rotten. He drove the car fast and recklessly going back out to Virginia. He wanted to get home quick so he could start drinking.

The hunting season was over in February, and there was a hunt ball at the Tavern to conclude it. Cath had dinner alone in his pink tailcoat at home, but after he had had three highballs he thought, "God damn it, I don't want to go to the God damned ball." All his thoughts were coming out in his head in words nowadays, and he hated the feeling. He sat down in front of the fire with his feet up on the fender, and a full bottle of whiskey at his elbow.

The doorbell rang, and he went and answered it himself. It was old Harry Dawson, already as drunk as a goat, roaring "Hoick!" as soon as the door opened. Dimly Cath saw Mrs. Dawson, quietly holding the reins of the ancient dog-cart, out on the drive.

"Come in," he called down to her.

"No, you come on go to the ball," Harry shouted. "Women, song, and god damned good corn liquor, and all because the hunting of foxes is over. 'And now was the hunting of foxes,'" he began to quote, staggering about on the front steps. "Come on go."

Cath got his coat and battered hunting topper off the hall rack, and went along with them.

He was standing up at the bar, and somebody took his arm.

"Hello, Cath." It was a big, well-made woman with a little gray in her hair, and she smiled at him and squeezed his arm and said:

"Don't remember me, do you? I bought some horses from your father way back in the old days. You were just a young boy, but you had the bluest eyes I ever saw. I was pretty peeved because you wouldn't give me a tumble, Cath! I thought I wasn't bad looking, either."

She said her name was Mrs. Walters. She came from New York, and she wore a shiny white dress cut down to her waist behind, and she held herself up well, and Cath took her out on the floor and danced with her. It felt good to have his arm around a firm, big waist like that.

He was cut in on, and he went away and had two more drinks, and then he went back and looked for her among the dancers. She was standing away from the man she was dancing with, and Cath looked at her fine mature figure across the room, and went and cut back.

She said she wanted to sit down, and they wandered out of the big dancing-room and into one of the smoking rooms and sat on a sofa. All the other people went away, and she put down her drink and leaned over toward Cath. Her voice was a little blurred.

"Cath. . . . I certainly used to be crazy about you."

He put both arms around her and pushed her back into the corner of the sofa and kissed her hard, feeling her big and curved underneath him. They kissed for some time; then somebody came into the room, and they went back and danced close together. But she said she had to go home with her husband.

He was out watching them school horses in the paddock the next afternoon when Mrs. Walters appeared around the back of the stables, walking through the slimy red mud smiling at him. They watched the horses jump, and he liked her; she did not talk too much, though when she did it was with an unfamiliar accent that kept her a stranger; he remembered the Northern women that he used to make love to when he was younger. Mrs. Walters talked like them, she was like them, but somehow he didn't mind as much now.

When they went in the house for a drink he did not wait. He kissed her up against the door to the library, and liked her with a wave of heat for being the way she was, big and laughing. He knew she wanted everything he could give her. They sat down and drank on the sofa, and he kept his arm around her good waist; he felt better than he had for months, and a little flame of delight and relief danced inside him.

"What are you doing tonight? I hear you're a bachelor these days," she said, suddenly.

"I—" he remembered and looked at his watch. "I've got to drive in town and see my wife right now, at the hospital. Do you want to drive to Washington with me?"

She waited in the car while he went up to Mary's room.

Something in him always made him hope, for a minute before he opened the bare white door, that everything would have changed: that Mary would be sitting up, that she would smile silently at him in her own old way, that her face would have its own ruddy fullness.

But nothing was different. Her eyes, strange and dark in that thinning white face, stared at him as he came in with the tense unhappiness that was all of Mary nowadays. He knew that look and hated it because it was something sick; sick animals had it, creatures that were not calm and well. It made him feel uncomfortable and self-conscious, a look like that seemed in a disagreeable way to see right through him; he was conscious of the liquor on his breath, although the real Mary had never cared about liquor on his breath.

She talked so much! He knew that she suffered, and tried to imagine what such suffering would be like, but it made him feel ashamed and guilty when she told him about her dreadful nights, and all the pain she had. He resented feeling guilty, and reacted angrily against it. He sat dumbly in the hospital armchair, and thought confusedly that he had lost the awareness of being a man; most of the time he felt like an unhappy, awkward boy with nothing to do.

"It's so awful, waiting and waiting. Cath, don't you care if I ever get well?"

He saw a kind of blurred, red haze when she asked it, after all the miserable loneliness and the aimlessness that his life had turned into.

"Good God, Mary, what do you mean by a thing like that? Don't you suppose I want my wife? A man doesn't want living alone."

"Cath . . . !"

"What?"

"Have you been untrue to me?"

"No."

"Cath, have you? Have you done that to me, while I'm helpless and can't do anything? Oh, God, don't you know it would kill me to lie here thinking about you and some woman?"

"I told you, I have not been untrue to you."

"It would kill me, Cath. How much do you think I can stand, anyway? Oh, *God*, why did that horse have to fall and spoil my whole life this way?"

"No use fretting over it, Mary. Just try to get well fast."

"How can I get well when I have to think about you and some woman together?"

"God damn it, I told you twice I haven't been with any woman. I swear to God."

"Oh, Cath, I know what you're like. You couldn't get along."

"Mary, I swear you'd drive a man to it."

"Oh, you don't know what it's like. . . ."

"Mary, I think I'd better be going. You're getting excited, and the nurse said. There's someone waiting for me downstairs."

"Who?"

He did not know any way of getting out of it now that he had gotten in.

"A Mrs. Walters. She's visiting down in the country."

"Oh, God! I knew it! . . ." Mary was in her weak sick tears again, the white face thrown back against the pillow.

"Mary, I've told you. . . . Oh, Jesus Christ," he said, and walked out of the room. He felt guilty and in the wrong and yet he had really told the truth.

Mrs. Walters waved to him from the car. "Hel-*lo!*" she called gaily. She smiled and talked a lot on the way home; he listened and drove. He didn't like her voice, but she was cheerful and healthy, and when he took her back to Aspenwall she stayed until after midnight.

He had to lie to Mary, after that.

As it became apparent that Mary's accident had been no minor fracture, as month after month went by and she was no better, and nothing was said about her coming home, the neighborhood began to accept Cath as a semi-permanent bachelor, and he went out a great deal in the evenings. In people's minds he slipped back thirteen years and they thought of him again as the Cathcart James who liked horses and liquor and women. But now he talked much more than young Cathcart had, and drank more, and had a more impatient way with a horse.

It was spring now, and in the big, far-apart houses in the Virginia countryside people sat after dinner and drank peach brandy and talked about polo and breeding, and went and sat out on the verandas under the young May moon. Cath would drive some woman home from a party with the top down on his car, driving fast over the narrow lanes that now began to be domed over with thin leafy boughs; the headlights twinkled through them as the car leapt over the winter's ruts. The crickets began to sing out in the dark spring fields, and the frogs from the shadowy bottoms. Cath would drive with one hand, and the woman would look up at his heavy, handsome profile looking straight ahead, and they would go back up to Aspenwall in the spring night and have a few drinks.

Life had somehow straightened out into an endurable round of horses, whiskey, and women—the ministering to three appetites. It kept the appetites quiet and took care of the days. But Cath had a new, permanent irritability because he never felt satisfied any more. He was restless with everything he did, because nothing seemed to fall into any rhythm any longer; he could never seem to strike a balance in his living. Trying to make himself happier he did more of everything. He rode the horses ragged, his old judgment, that came from a deep, adjusted quietness, gone; he got drunk every night; and he became the beau of the countryside, a dinner-table byword, and took out every visitor to Virginia and made love to her.

People were tolerant in that country, and most of the time they laughed about his bachelor behavior and teased him for being fickle. But some of the older people sometimes took him aside and gave him a talking-to about Mary. He always took it mutely, and he always believed that he was as bad as they said he was. He would go home and get a little drunker and think about Mary and what a rotten time she was having, but he could never see what he could do about it. He had tried different ways, and this was the only way that he could get along without her. He always went in to see her at the hospital every day.

As his existence got gradually more supportable he felt more and more aching pity for his wife. It put his mind in a blur of unhappy confusion when he thought about the fix she was in; he understood more and more sharply that she was getting nothing out of life, and tried oftener to imagine what that would be like. Assuaging his own dissatisfaction made him try to think of things that might be some comfort to Mary, and he began bringing little things to her, books on hounds and breeding that her nurse could read to her in the long nights, and illustrated sporting papers, and a bronze model of one of their hunters to set on the hospital bureau, and even bunches of flowers that he would buy on the way into Washington. He had never in their life thought of her as a separate and feeling being as he did now; before she had been part of their joint satisfaction. Now he felt further and further away from her, and was sorrier for her.

One day in August when it was sultry and breathless he had an idea that made him happy, and he hurried into Washington with a big flask of rye whiskey in his pocket.

"How would you like a little drink?" he asked her with a pleased expression as he came into the room.

She turned her head toward the door and smiled a small, white smile.

"That would be fine."

"Are you supposed to have it?"

"I guess not, but Lord I want it."

They got a little tight together, and they had not gotten along so well for months. Two purply-pink spots appeared in Mary's hollow cheeks, and Cath looked at her through a slight haze and thought that this was what she really needed—she was already looking more like herself. She talked a lot, and it still made him uneasy to hear Mary's voice going on, weakly, in this way that was unlike her, but he did not mind very much because she was smiling at him often, and seemed so much happier.

He moved the chair over nearer to the bed, and took hold of Mary's arm up above the elbow.

"Mary. . . ."

He kissed her hard on her mouth. . . . Her breath smelled of hospital, and her skin was queerly soft and loose.

"Oh, Cath." After months and months her voice was low again. "I am going to get well, aren't I?"

"You're going to get well. You're coming back home soon. I'll be with you—all the time, to make up for all this."

"Yes, Cath." Her low voice made him feel warm and happy, and he put his head down on her breast.

"Mary. . . . I want you back. Nothing is any good without you. Nobody is any good except you."

"Cath!" Now suddenly her voice was high and wild again. He lifted his head out of a swimming daze.

"Cath, you tell me now. You have been untrue to me, haven't you?"

He looked at her in the nakedness of his surprise, and he saw that she saw inside of him. Then her voice began. It frightened him.

"Oh, God damn you, you rotten itching dog, you took everything I had in the world until I got broken to pieces, and then you didn't care, you went on after every bitch that crossed your trail. God damn you, I haven't got anything left, I'm all smashed, and you did that to me.

"You rotten stable-boy, you've taken all your women into my house and slept with them on my bed, haven't you? All these nights I've had to think about them in my house, and you lied to me and lied to me. Oh, you've got everything of mine and you don't give me one thing back. I just lie here.

"You did that to me, everything is all spoiled to hell. . . . Oh, Jesus, Cath!" Her voice went suddenly soft and pleading for a minute. Then it rose and sharpened almost into a scream.

"God damn you, get out of my house! I don't want you in my house, with your women!"

Nurses were hurrying into the room, and everything was a soft blur of whispers, and they were taking away the whiskey and Mary was crying forever and ever on that white bed. Cath went away.

At Aspenwall he had them pack two bags, and said he was going in to stay at the Tavern to be on the main road to Washington. He went and stood in the open doorway of Aspenwall while they brought the bags down. He looked out at the dusk over the late August land, over the fields and the long fences and the creeks, the country falling in swells away from the rise of Aspenwall into the twilight; he looked at it, and none of it meant anything to him at all.

He had dinner at the Tavern and got drunk. Then he went up to his room and Sophy Grainger, who ran the Tavern and was an old girl of Cath's, came up and knocked with a new bottle of rye under her arm for him. She was a big, clumsy, laughing woman, and they sat in his room together and drank a lot more until they groped for each other. . . .

His stubborn loyalty and all his deepening pity made him go in to the hospital the next afternoon, and he was not allowed to see Mary except for a moment. They thought she had pneumonia. The doctor talked to him about it outside the room; Cath could not remember anything the doctor said, only that he must try to make Mary stop worrying about him so much. Cath took a room in the hospital itself to be near her.

She had a high fever and was delirious part of the time, but she always recognized Cath when they let him into the room for a moment, and she always turned her head away into the pillow and refused to speak to him. Only once she looked at him, with her face all purple with fever, and asked him if he had left her house. He said he had, and she turned her face away from him.

He woke up soon after dawn one morning. His small, white enamel room smelled of disinfectant, and his heart gave a great throb of restlessness and he wanted to be out of it. He knew they were cubbing this morning, early, down in the country, and he wanted to be out in the fresh, wet, early autumn fields watching the hounds work through the morning mists, and not here in the cold white hospital.

He took a taxi out from Washington and changed at the Tavern; he kept the taxi and had it drive him back up country to Harry Dawson's place, where they were taking hounds out. Harry lent him a horse, and they rode out and sat on top of a hill watching hounds work deep in a thicket below in the valley.

Cath wondered why it was not what he thought it was going to be, when he had awakened so sharply out of his sleep and wanted to get away. He had felt that everything would be all right and that he would feel better if he could go cubbing that morning, and now that he was out he was still restless and unhappy. He was impatient of the hounds circling about so long; perhaps if they galloped everything would be fixed up in his head.

Harry's stable-boy came tearing up the other side of the hill on an old gray, all sparkling with kicked-up dew.

"Miss Carey the operator's been trying to find you all over the countryside, Mr. James. They want you to go right on in to the hospital. Mrs. James is real bad."

Harry wanted to go in with him, so they took the stable-boy's Ford and drove as fast as the thing would go over the cement road to Washington in the sunny, early morning. When they got there everything was very suppressed and strange. In a little while they told Cath that Mary was dead.

He went in and looked at her for a long time. Then he came out and sat down on a chair in the corridor and looked at his knees.

He felt old Harry's hand on his shoulder after a time, and paid no attention to it. Later Harry's voice said:

"It's hard, Cath. But you've still got a lot to live for."

He thought carefully, in a slow confusion, about the words that old Harry had said.

"No." He spoke slowly. "Nothing is ever any good without Mary."

Then he dropped his head down again, into despair, and his mind went round and round, and he knew it would always go round and round, and he thought, wildly:

"I want my wife. I want my wife."

Boys and Girls Together

by WILLIAM SAROYAN

They were four and a family—the man, the woman, the small boy, the small girl, and [as with all families] there was something wrong with the whole thing, only now it was too late. In each of them there seemed to be a secret anguish about the struggle it was, every day, to understand the others. By turns they were enchanted and perplexed, delighted and outraged, entertained and bored; and yet most of the time in the most unaccountable manner *all* of it was fun of one kind or another, or at any rate could become pleasantly memorable, as when after the stupidest fight imaginable the man and woman began to move about in the house in silence, as if in memory of chances lost from long before they had met, and suddenly they looked at one another and each saw a total stranger but loved the stranger because now they were tangled in time and held captive by the two kids, and therefore laughed softly about it all, or hummed or sang or said strange words.

The man was 39, the woman 24, the boy five, the girl three. They lived in a square two-flat house tightly packed among identical houses on a fog-enveloped street in the Sunset district of San Francisco, less than a mile from the ocean, more than three miles from Nob Hill, more than three *thousand* miles from Times Square.

They lived in the bottom flat; the man worked in the top one. His work was to write, as it had been for 15 years. His stories and plays had earned him a name and more money than he had had in mind at the outset or had known how to manage, money which had in fact made him uncomfortable because it had put him with the successful and secure, but now after three years in the Army he was broke, in debt, bored with his name, with writing, and with art in general, because to the real people, the people in real trouble, what good did art do? All the same, every morning he went upstairs to his work, hoping for something miraculous to come in the mail.

He saw the mail carrier coming down the street, so he went down to the garage, where the mail was dropped. The shelves along the entire far wall were loaded with books and magazines, and the baby-grand Pianola was there beside the gas furnace—the Pianola that had been in his last play on Broadway, the flop, the third flop in a row. The car was there, and all the junk from New York: the baby carriages and other things with wheels that small children are pushed around in; the cribs and canvas bathing tubs for infants, the toys, the tricycles and the boy's bicycle that he couldn't ride yet from the seat but could somehow ride, that he loved so much but could only have when someone was there to help and see that he didn't hurt himself. The garden tools, the pruning shears for the rose trees and bushes, the shovel and rake, the lawn mower.

Lord, he thought, *I ought to get up at seven and be at work in an office in town somewhere by nine and come home at six, and live the way everybody else around here does.*

One day when he was cutting the lawn and letting Johnny help—it was sundown then, about seven in the evening—a man came out onto the service porch of the top flat of the house just like his house, across the way, and called out to him, "What are you writing?"

The mail was good-for-nothing.

A woman in Richmond, Virginia, wrote to say that he had twice described someone as being cultured when the correct term was "cultivated." The woman asked if he had done this on purpose, as part of his style, or because he didn't know any better.

The lecture-bureau man who had been writing him for 15 years wrote again saying that he could arrange for a very profitable series of lectures at a moment's notice, in almost any part of the country, including the Far West.

There was a royalty statement from his publisher in New York which only reminded him that he was still in debt, even though his books had sold fairly well over a period of six months.

There was an invitation from a cousin who lived four or five miles across town to go to the races at Bay Meadows and make a killing.

There was a check for $27.81, which represented his share of the royalties from an anthology of one-act plays.

There was a letter from a girl who had been 11 years old when she had appeared in one of his plays on Broadway and was now 18, and there was a snapshot of her with the letter. She wore a low-cut evening dress so that he could see how nicely she had grown, and she said she would never forget him for picking her out of all the others and giving her a start in the theater. She was in Hollywood now, and when was he coming there to show them how to make moving pictures? She said her mother sent him her love and hoped he would visit them in their nice apartment when he got to Hollywood.

And there was a letter for his wife from her friend Lucretia in New York.

He put the letter with the small check in it, and the one with the snapshot in it, into the back pocket of his trousers, and then went up to the lower flat and let himself in with a key, calling out to the woman first so that she wouldn't be frightened. He handed her the mail, as she liked to look at everything.

"Is this all?"

"What's Lucretia say?"

"Are you sure you haven't kept some of the mail?"

"Go ahead. Open it and see what she's up to."

The woman tore open the fine envelope with the fancy writing all over it and glanced quickly at the first of the five or six pages of very thin paper, and then she said, "They're coming out to pay us a visit."

"The hell they are."

"They can stay upstairs."

"The hell they can. That's where I work. Now listen, I don't want any trouble about your friends. Things are tough enough around here without a couple of phonies from New York."

"They have to go to Hollywood. They only want to stop and say hello."

"Hello for a week? Write and tell her I'm working. I've *got* to work, and you know I'll never be able to with them around. It takes time even to *get ready* to work, and you're always arranging for something to happen that stops me from getting ready."

"Can't they come for just a *little* visit? She's my best friend, and he's such a great man."

"She's a bore and he's a bore."

"I never see anybody out here. Just the people you know. None of my people."

"Your people stink. Your sister was here for ten days a month ago. Two months before that your mother was here. Now don't try to make me put up with these two, too."

"OK. I'll write and tell her the kids are sick, but I think you're mean."

"The kids aren't sick. Tell her I'm working. She'll understand."

"I can't be rude."

"It's not rude to tell the truth. I *am* working. We're broke. I've got to see about getting hold of some money."

"OK, I'll tell her you're working."

"Don't have her drop in on us and then give me a long explanation about how you must have misdirected the letter telling her not to come because she hadn't received it, and now as long as she was here we couldn't turn her away. Don't do anything like that again. That was a dirty trick."

"She didn't get the letter."

"If she didn't, you didn't write a letter."

"You saw me mail it yourself."

"Then you didn't tell her not to come. You told her something else. Maybe you told her to pretend that she hadn't got the letter. All I know is that we agreed that you would write and tell her not to come because I was working, and then a taxi came up to the house and there she was with six suitcases all the way from New York. No more of that."

"OK."

"Just take care of your kids and let me see if I can start writing again."

"I miss my people."

"Your kids are your people now."

He went up the stairs and back to his worktable, but it was no use; he had no heart for the work, for the novel he was writing; he had been fighting the idea of abandoning it for days, and now he knew it was abandoned. He'd worked eight days for nothing. It was the tenth or eleventh job he had abandoned in 10 or 11 weeks. Well, he would have to start again and this time see that it was not a false start. But when he tried to think what would not be a false start, he could think of

nothing that wouldn't; everything would be a false start; anything anybody might do would be a false start; there was no such thing as a true
start.

He took the envelope with the snapshot in it, put a match to it and
tossed it into the fireplace. Then he got the check out of the other envelope and put it in his wallet to have when he went to the bank.

The way things were, he wished his profession weren't writing, but
that was silly. Writing *was* his profession; it had always been his profession, only now he didn't want to write, didn't want to try to write,
never reached his worktable eager to see what he had written the
previous day, the way it had been in the old days. All he wanted was
money because he always needed money; maybe if he had enough of it
once and for all—enough to pay his debts and buy a house somewhere
where she could feel more at home, in Manhattan maybe, or Long Island, or Connecticut—maybe then she would feel at home and be able
to get along with herself and the kids and him.

Maybe then he'd be able to get along with her, maybe help her over
the hard times a little better, maybe find out why she had to bite her
fingernails and be in despair so often; maybe if he could get hold of
enough money all of a sudden, that would be how he would be able to
forget all about money and be free to think about her only, and the
kids, and the work, and she wouldn't be forever discontented, wanting a
better house, better clothes, better times, and all the other things she
seemed to be dreaming about all the time. Maybe then she wouldn't
feel she was losing her youth and beauty for nothing; she'd calm down
and see that what she had was just about as much as any woman could
ever get, and maybe she'd be thankful for it and make the most of it
and not go off by herself in her head dreaming up desperate ways to
make up for the loss of her youth and beauty, writing to her friends as
if she were writing from a penitentiary, asking them to visit her, for
God's sake come and see her, telegraphing them, screaming at them at
the top of her voice on the telephone and then, after talking about hats
and shoes and dresses and who'd cheated on whom and why, hanging
up on a bill for $36.75 and wandering around in despair, unable to fix a
simple supper for the kids, or make a sandwich for herself, or think of
anything to do.

If he could get hold of $30,000 straight off and be out of debt and
have enough left over for a down payment on a new house and $500 to
go in her pocketbook for anything she felt like buying, everything
might straighten out and he might be able to get ready to work and
then actually write again.

He couldn't get to work, the way things were, because he couldn't get ready to. He was willing to believe that it was just as important to work for the family, for the kids and for her, as it was to work at his profession, but the way things were he just couldn't afford not to try to work at his profession, too. If he were rich he'd be glad to help her all the time and let his work go.

There's the typewriter, he thought. *Sit down and write.*

He put paper into the machine and began to work, but after an hour he knew it wouldn't do. He wasn't ready.

He had always believed he could write under any circumstances, any set of circumstances, but now he knew he couldn't.

He could still read a little, but he was finding a lot of fault with everything he was reading too.

He was trying to think of an entire work, something that would turn out to be full, that he could do in two or three months, when she let herself in and said, "What you doing?"

"I'm trying to think of something to write in two or three months in short daily installments."

"I wish you knew how much he admires you."

"Who?"

"Leander."

"They can't come, and I don't want to hear any more about it."

"He told me you're the greatest writer in America."

"For your own sake, stop lying, will you?"

"It's not a lie. He told me at a party, when you were overseas."

"Well, I don't want them here; that's all. If they come to town you can take a taxi and spend an afternoon and evening with them."

"Can I? You said I could. Don't take it back."

"OK."

"And you'll let me buy a new dress so I won't look like a dog when I see them? Nothing expensive, just something new, something under fifty dollars."

"OK."

"And you'll come downstairs and stay with the kids so I can go to the beauty parlor?"

"OK."

"I mean now. My appointment's for eleven, and it's already ten after."

"When did you make it?"

"Half an hour ago."

"Why? You've got to get the kids their lunch and get them in bed for their naps."

"Oh, won't you do it for me, just this once?"

"Why not make the appointment for tomorrow when they're napping, the way you always do once a week when you go to the beauty parlor?"

"Well, after I'm finished at the beauty parlor I thought I'd buy the dress. I don't have to have cash for it. I'll charge it."

"OK, let's have it. What are you trying to tell me?"

"They'll be here tomorrow morning. I telephoned and told them to go to the Fairmont because—"

"The kids are sick?"

"I just *couldn't* tell them you were working. They'd never understand. And Rosey *has* a running nose."

"OK."

They went downstairs to the lower flat.

"Could you let me have some money for the taxi and beauty parlor?"

"OK."

He gave her two tens and a five, but she wanted more, so he gave her another ten. The doorbell rang, and when he opened it he saw that it was a taxi driver. The woman kissed him and said, "About five, I guess, but maybe a little later."

"OK."

He went to the kitchen and looked into the refrigerator to see what might be possible for their lunch, and then into the cupboard, the vegetable bin and everywhere else that food was kept. There wasn't much, but there was enough. He'd give them breakfast again, or some soup out of a can, and mashed potatoes. The back door was open, but he couldn't hear them fighting, so he went out onto the steps and saw that they were lying under an army blanket talking quietly and looking up, either at the sky or at the top of their house or at the houses all around or at nothing. The neighbor on the left, Turandi Turanda, was working quietly in his vegetable garden. Either they had already had their fun with him or they hadn't noticed that he had stepped out of his house, for they always talked with him, the boy climbing the fence and hanging on to see over it, the girl getting up on an apple box to look over and watch and talk too.

He stepped back into the kitchen and began to peel the potatoes. By the time the water was boiling he heard the three of them talking. The man was a plasterer by trade, more or less retired, so he spent a lot of time in his garden, and he either liked the kids or put up with them because they were always there and there was nothing he could do about it. Sometimes he lifted the little girl and walked around with her in his garden, and the boy would hoist himself over the fence and let himself down, falling part of the way and skinning his hands a little.

They seemed to be friends, the three of them, and the man's wife (whenever she came out into the yard) talked with them and admired the girl and teased the boy about putting him in a hole in the ground. But it was all play, and the boy only hollered at her because he knew she would never put him in a hole in the ground.

Their voices grew louder, so he stepped to the door to see what it was all about. Turandi Turanda was standing at the fence, looking down at them and talking. The boy was holding a tennis ball, and the girl wanted it, but he wouldn't let her have it.

"You be a good boy, Johnny," Turanda said. "You give her the ball. You got other things."

The boy handed the ball to the girl. "OK, I'm a good boy," he said.

Turanda smiled and looked around to see if anybody had heard, and then he said, "There, Rosey, see? Johnny's a good boy. Tell him thanks."

"Yes, he is a good boy," the girl said. She said it softly and sweetly. "Thanks, Johnny, my little brother."

The neighbor went back to his garden, and the man thought, *He's a fine man, that Turandi Turanda.*

He got them their lunch and took off their clothes and put them in their beds and went to the living room and turned the radio to the station that gave the race results.

He got the morning paper and turned to the sports section and studied the entries at all of the tracks and picked a horse in the fifth at Laurel. He telephoned the bookie where his credit was good and bet the horse six hundred across the board and began to wait for the results, chain-smoking and feeling sick because all he had in the bank was $140.

The horse wasn't in the money, so he made the same bet on a horse in the seventh, but that horse ran third, so he owed the bookie $820 instead of $1,200, which is what he would have owed if the horse had run out of the money. But that wasn't winning—that wasn't even getting out of debt to the bookie—so he bet a horse in the last race at one of the eastern tracks, but that horse wasn't in the money either, so now he owed the bookie $1,420.

He bet $900 across the board on a horse in the first race at Bay Meadows, post position one, Longden up, maiden three-year-olds, six furlongs.

If it didn't get in the money he would owe the bookie $2,320, which meant that he would have to borrow $2,500 from somebody, only there wasn't anybody to borrow from. But the horse won and paid a pretty good price.

He sat down and tried to think, and then got up and walked around, even though he hadn't figured his winnings yet. When he figured them he was astonished to discover that they came to so much: $1,880, net. Well, he couldn't pay his debts with it, but at least he *had* it, and it was better than needing to go out and try to borrow $2,500.

He got into the shower, put on fresh clothes and felt a little easier. Now, instead of having only $140, he had a little better than $2,000. He could bet another horse and maybe win again, but the hell with it. All he'd wanted was to get something, and he had, he'd gotten more than he had expected to get, so it was enough. Maybe if he could have a little luck like that every day he could get hold of enough money to pay the debts and have something left over for the other things.

He dressed the kids and put the girl in her chair in the car and drove to town. He put the car in the garage a block and a half from the bookie's and asked the man to fill the tank and check the oil and water and tires. He told the kids he was going to get a package of cigarettes and would be back in a minute, and not to move. He went up to the bookie's and chatted with the boys a few minutes, and then Leo looked into his book and said, "Eighteen-eighty, right?" And counted the money out and thanked him, as he always did.

He took the money and put it in his pocket and chatted with the boys some more, and then went back to the car.

The kids were laughing together about something.

He drove out Geary to the ocean, along the ocean four or five miles, and then he stopped where some new houses were being built, and he and the boy piled scraps of lumber in the back of the car for the fireplace, because doing that made the boy happier than anything else he knew how to do. He drove home and left the car out front and took the kids for a walk to a drugstore and got them each, and himself, an ice-cream soda.

It wouldn't be so bad if he could get hold of money that way any time he needed it.

He was clean and calm sitting with the kids in the booth in the ice-cream-parlor part of the drugstore, and that's what a man wanted, that's what he always wanted, to be clean and calm, his kids across a table from him with their new eyes, new voices, hands and fingers, hair and lips, teeth and nostrils and ears, moisture and skin, their new beating hearts and working lungs; that's all any man ever wanted, just to be decently at peace with himself and his woman and to have his kids around and happy about vanilla and chocolate and soda, the long spoon and the straws, and the drama of other people around, the druggist, the girl who brought the stuff, the boy who made it, and the other people having other stuff.

All any man ever wanted was peace, and the only way he could have it was to have money, and now he had a little. Betting the races was the best way to get money if you had to get it that way at all. You never hurt anybody by winning on the races because whatever you got you got anonymously and whoever lost because he had picked another horse in the same race was unknown to you. It was a dirty business, but if you won, it certainly made a difference.

He asked the kids if they would like to go to the notion store across the street and have a look at the junk, and they said they would, so they went there and he let them have one thing each because having too much, or being free to have too much, made them unhappy, confused them, so the girl had a blown-up red balloon on a stick, and the boy had a gyroscope in a square pasteboard box. They stepped out into the street and began to walk home, but the man noticed that the old North Carolina barber whose shop had only one chair had nobody in the chair so he asked the kids if they would sit nicely while he got a haircut, and they said they would, so he got a haircut.

Then he stepped into the Safeway, to the butcher's counter, and bought four thick sirloins and six French lamb chops, but didn't buy anything else because you had to stand in line to pay and have your stuff wrapped everywhere except at the butcher's. In the delicatessen next door, owned by the lady who loved her big ugly cat and was always making rugs out of rags and listening to the radio, he bought six cans of chili with beans, and that was enough to carry, so they walked home. He and the boy unloaded the pieces of lumber from the car to the basement. He took up an armful, put them in the fireplace and lighted the fire, because they all liked to see a fire.

The red balloon popped, and the little girl looked astonished, as she always did when a balloon popped.

"It was *my* balloon," the girl said. "I want my balloon."

She held what was left of it, the thin, limp, absurd-looking rubber and the skinny stick, and she didn't like it. The man examined the wreckage, got a piece of string and tied some of the rubber together. He undid the neck from the stick to which it was attached and blew into it, and the little girl saw the balloon again, lopsided, even the color different, tied ends hanging loose, but she laughed and liked it. When she had her balloon again she squeezed it and let it fall and bounce, but the boy just sat and watched the fire.

"What is fire?" he said.

"What we see there."

"But what is it?"

"What it really is I don't know," the man said. "But I know that the sun in the sky is fire."

"It's my balloon," the girl said. "Johnny can't have it."

"I got this," the boy said. He lifted the square pasteboard box containing the gyroscope. "Whatever it is."

"It's a gyroscope."

"What does it do?"

"It turns."

"What's it for?"

"To look at when it turns. It's beautiful then."

The boy lifted the top off the square pasteboard box and turned the box over so that the gyroscope would slide out into his hand. He held it up and looked at it.

The girl squeezed the lopsided balloon, rubbed it against her face, tossed it up, watched it fall. The boy looked at the gyroscope and then let it rest on the floor and looked back at the fire. He had been sitting on the floor. Now he stretched out full-length on his belly, resting his chin in the palm of his right hand. The man poked the fire and put more wood on it, squares and angles of house lumber, all kinds of shapes piled together.

"It looks like a church burning," the boy said.

The man looked to see if this was so, and it *did* look like a church burning.

"But nobody's in it," the boy said. "They never burn churches with people in them. They always get the people out and then burn them, so the people can see the fires. Do they ring the bells when they burn churches?"

"I don't believe they do," the man said. "But when the bells fall they make quite a lot of noise."

"Did you see a church burn?"

"Yes, I did. I was a little older than you are now. It was at night, and everybody ran. You couldn't go close because the fire made so much heat. You could hear the fire cracking the wood, and things falling inside the church, and then at last the bells fell and rang. We went home then, and the next day it was all black there, like the ashes after a fire burns in a fireplace."

"I don't like it when it's black in the fireplace," the boy said.

They sat and talked quietly for an hour, and then he heard a taxi out front and in a moment the woman let herself in. The taxi driver carried half a dozen packages. The little girl ran, and the woman hugged her and kissed her and talked to her, and then she told the taxi driver where to put the packages, on her bed. She handed him some money, and the man tipped his hat and thanked her and went out. The woman closed the door and stood hushed with excitement and happiness.

"Wait till you see the things I've bought."

She picked up the boy and danced around with him and put him down again. "Do you like my hair?"

She removed the scarf wrapped over her hair, and the red fell down, new and bright.

"It's beautiful, Mamma," the boy said.

"Oh, Johnny. Wait till you see mamma's new dress. Shall I put it on now?"

"Yes, Mamma."

"Shall I?" the woman said to the man.

"Sure. Let's have a look at it. You look fine."

The woman hugged the man, ran off to the bedroom and closed the door, but the little girl opened the door and went on in, and then the boy went in too. The man heard them talking in there, and then the woman came out.

"It cost a hundred, but we've got so many debts anyway I thought you wouldn't care. Do you like it?"

"Yes. You look fine."

"I bought some other things too. I'll show them to you afterwards."

"OK."

"They cost about a hundred, too, but they're things I need, shoes and stockings and brassieres and perfume. You won't make me send them back, will you? It's so humiliating. Just this once more. I've got everything now."

"No. You can keep them."

"Some women spend a thousand for one dress."

"You look fine in this one."

"I thought you'd be angry."

"No, it's OK. I'm glad you got the stuff."

"Really? How come?"

"Take it off now and get supper for the kids. We'll eat after they're in bed. I've bought lamb chops for them and sirloins for us."

"All right," the woman said. . . . "Johnny, Rosey, go to your room and play until mamma gets supper."

The children went down the hall to their room. The woman closed the door behind them, then came to the man and put her arms around him and said, "I love you so much. I love our life together so much. I love Johnny and Rosey so much."

The man held her gently, then tightly.

"Wait till you see me tonight."

She was happy because she had new things to wear and she'd been to the beauty parlor and her friends from New York would be in town to-morrow and she would get all dressed up and go and see them and let them see her.

The woman made the kids a good supper of broiled lamb chops, boiled spinach, stewed fruit out of a can, and milk. They didn't finish everything, but they did pretty well. She gave them each two tea-spoonfuls of the thick brown syrup that was supposed to have every-thing in it, that they seemed to like to take, that she had been giving them every night after supper for more than a month. It had a name that made it sound like it ought to be something somebody had figured out carefully. The doctor said it was a good thing. He gave it to his own kids, he said. It looked like molasses, but didn't smell as good. It didn't smell fishy, but it didn't smell like candy, either.

"Can I have a bath tonight?" the boy said.

"Ask papa."

The boy went into the living room and said, "Can I have a bath to-night, Papa?"

"Ask mamma."

The boy's face winked. "Papa," he said, "I *asked* mamma. She said, 'Ask papa.' I'll ask Rosey."

He ran back to the kitchen, to keep up with the joke. "Rosey," he said, "can I have a bath tonight?"

The little girl looked at him sideways, knowing it was a joke. "Not tonight," she said, "because I'm too tired."

The boy watched her.

"Because you was a bad boy," she said.

He watched some more.

"Because you hit your little sister," she said.

He just had to watch a little longer.

"Because there's no water," she said.

Would there be more?

"Because you're a poopoo," she said.

More?

"Pohpoh," she said.

She ran into the living room with the fun. "Isn't Johnny a pohpoh, Papa?"

"Is he?"

"I saw him. He's a pohpoh and a poopoo and a piepie. That's why he can't have a bath tonight. He's a paypay. He's a peepee," she said and laughed.

"Peepee?" the boy said. "I'll peepee you if you say I'm a peepee."

"Shall I give him a bath?" the woman said. "Shall I give them both a bath? I bathed them both night before last."

"Bathe them," the man said. "I'll straighten out the kitchen."

"What about their sheets? I haven't changed them in days. It must be a week at least."

"Change them. I'll get supper too."

"All right. If they're going to get clean, they might as well get into clean beds too. Will you make a green salad, with the wine vinegar from Vanessi's?"

"Sure."

"Yum, yum," the woman said, "if you know what I mean."

She's happy, all right. She'd be happy all the time if nobody ever had to do anything but have fun and never had to think about anything else. She's right too. She's got a perfect system if it would work. I'd go for that system any day if it would work.

They were eating. It might have been the thousandth time.

"What did you write today?"

"When?"

"This morning, when you went upstairs."

"I've forgotten the precise words, but they were words."

"What did you expect them to be?"

"That's all they were."

"That's all any writing is, isn't it?"

"No, that's precisely what writing isn't."

"Well, what were the words about, then?"

"Nothing. If writing were words, writing would be easy. Writing is stuff that happens in spite of words. There's no other way for writing to happen than with words, but at the same time it's got to happen in spite of them. The thing that gets you in writing is the story the words themselves don't tell but make you know. It's something like that."

"Well, what did you think about, then?"

"I thought about money. It's the only thing I think about. Most people forget it. I can't. I think about it all the time."

"We need an awful lot, don't we?"

"We need thirty thousand. To start, I mean."

"Would that pay the debts and everything?"

"Yes. I figured it out on a piece of paper, and thirty thousand would pay the debts and leave a little."

"How much?"

"About seven thousand."

"What could we do with that?"

"Take it and run. Sit on it. Look at it. Smell it. Put it in silver dollars and stack them up in piles in the living room. I was thinking of paving the hall with them. It wouldn't take more than two thousand, and it would make quite an impression on visitors."

"On me too. What else did you think?"

"I thought if I changed a thousand dollars into dimes—just a measly thousand—this would be a rather petty and annoying thing because they're such small coins."

"What else?"

"I thought if I had a nickel for every dollar I've spent in my life I'd still be rich because twenty nickels makes a dollar and there ought to be at least two hundred thousand of them."

"How did you spend two hundred thousand dollars?"

"You tell me."

"You spent most of it before you met me."

"I spent a little after I met you."

"How much?"

"Thirty thousand a year, I suppose."

"Six years. What's that come to?"

"A hundred and eighty thousand."

"Is that all?"

"Maybe it was forty thousand a year. That would make it two hundred and forty thousand."

"You spent something the year we weren't married too."

"I would have spent that anyway."

"You would have spent the two hundred and forty thousand anyway, too, wouldn't you?"

"I don't know. Anyhow, maybe it's not the spending that makes the difference; maybe it's whether or not you're earning it to spend, and now I'm not. I haven't written anything that has earned anything since I got out of the Army."

"Or since you got in. How many years is that?"

"Three in, three out. Six."

"That's how long we've been married too."

"Yes, it is."

"Have you written anything that has made any money since we met?"

"No, I'm afraid I haven't. The money all came from stuff I wrote before we met."

"I'm hurt. Aren't I inspiring?"

"Awe-inspiring."

"I thought a wife always inspired her husband."

"To think about money, perhaps."

"Do I spend as much as all that?"

"You don't spend much. I just don't write anything. All I do is think about money."

"Do you love money?"

"I *need* money. I don't hate money, but I hate to need it so badly."

"Well, what are we going to do?"

"Be poor, I suppose. Wear out our clothes. Make the most of everything we have. Enjoy the things that don't cost anything or cost only a little. Improve our health. Be happy. Forget money and remember everything else."

"How are we going to pay the debts?"

"Maybe we aren't. At least not for a while. Not until we've forgotten about money for so long that all of a sudden we find that I've written a few things that are worth something."

"Will that happen?"

"It *could* happen; it used to happen all the time."

"I don't like to be poor."

"I know you don't. But it's not nearly as bad as you think."

"I hate being poor."

"It's not so bad. It makes people more alive. Even when I used to get money, I never stopped being poor."

"That's silly."

"What happens is that if you let yourself get rich in money you get poor in living."

"No, you don't. The richer you get in money the richer you get in living and everything else."

"You get poor in living. You get poverty-stricken. The more money you get, the more like a beggar you become. A man who doesn't think about money is a lord. A man who does is a cripple with his hand held out. I think about money all the time. It's humiliating."

"Don't you sometimes think about something else too?"

"No. Everything else I think about turns out to be money too."

"Everything?"

"Everything."

"I think about money a lot, too," the woman said, "but I think more about other things too."

"It's all money you think about," the man said. "You think you think about other things, too, but you don't. You never do. If you did, you'd be a different person."

"Don't you like the person I am?"

"The person you are isn't an easy person to like."

"Well, you can get a divorce, then."

"No, I can't."

"You can get a divorce anytime you feel like it. Get it tomorrow. I don't want to be married to a man who doesn't love me. I don't want a man to make love to me who doesn't love me. Get a divorce tomorrow. Why can't you get a divorce tomorrow?"

"I can't afford it."

"Get a divorce tomorrow."

"I can't leave the kids, either."

"You can leave me, but you can't leave the kids. Get your lousy divorce tomorrow."

"I can't, and shut up."

He left the table, walked around in the living room, poked the fire and put some more wood on it.

"I don't want a man to love me who doesn't love me," the woman screamed.

He went into the kitchen. The woman got up from her chair and ran to the other side of the table, away from him.

"If you don't love me, get out!"

"I told you I don't want the kids to hear that screaming."

"Get out!" the woman screamed, then fell to the floor, sobbing the way that made him think of money all the time and wouldn't let him think of anything else.

He lifted the woman and held her in his arms.

"You mustn't let yourself scream that way. I want to love you. Why don't you let me? It's easy to let me. You don't have to do anything but be on the level and love Johnny and Rosey and not talk about it."

When she had stopped sobbing he walked with her to the living room and sat with her there, looking at the fire. It was a small fire now, barely a fire at all. The door of the bedroom opened and the little girl wandered out into the hall, sobbing the lonely, inconsolable way her mother had just sobbed, naked and sobbing.

The woman ran to the girl and took her in her arms.

"Did you have a bad dream? It's all gone now. You don't have to cry any more. You sit on the toddy, and mamma'll give you some water, and then you go right back to sleep."

He heard the girl stop crying, and then he heard the woman and the girl talking softly.

When the woman came back, she said, "I'm afraid she heard us. I'm so ashamed."

The man was about to say, "What good is it to be ashamed, to *say* you're ashamed, to *talk* your life, and therefore mine, and theirs? *Live* the damned thing, and *don't* be ashamed. Don't give yourself reason to be ashamed. Just stop pretending to be the richest girl in America, and the most beautiful girl in the world, and the wittiest girl since the beginning of time, and just stop being the cleverest, the silliest, the most pathetic psychopathic liar and phony outside any loonybin in the world, and you won't need to scream every other day like a tortured soul in hell," but he remembered that he had said it all before, and it was useless.

He was a writer, but he was also stupid; he knew nothing, he understood nothing, so why should he holler at her again? *If she is in fact mad, be glad she's mad; make being mad a form of genius, the truest superiority, the only royalty.* And so he said nothing, only smiled until she smiled, and then turned away and walked around the house in silence, in memory of chances lost, children never met, churches burning, and the broken tolling of the falling bells, but in the end again he thought, *If I had $30,000 I could straighten this out.*

A Cure for Love

by H. G. WELLS

The excellent Mr. Morris was an Englishman, and he lived in the days of Queen Victoria the Good. He was a prosperous and very sensible man; he read the "Times" and went to church, and as he grew toward middle age an expression of quiet contented contempt for all who were not as himself settled on his face. He was one of those people who do everything that is right and proper and sensible with inevitable regularity. He always wore just the right and proper clothes, steering the narrow way between the smart and the shabby, always subscribed to the right charities, just the judicious compromise between ostentation and meanness, and never failed to have his hair cut to exactly the proper length.

Everything that it was right and proper for a man in his position to possess, he possessed; and everything that it was not right and proper for a man in his position to possess, he did not possess.

And among other right and proper possessions, this Mr. Morris had a wife and children. They were the right sort of wife, and the right sort and number of children, of course; nothing imaginative or highly flighty about any of them, so far as Mr. Morris could see; they wore perfectly correct clothing, neither smart nor hygienic nor faddy in any way, but just sensible; and they lived in a nice sensible house in the later Victorian sham Queen Anne style of architecture, with sham half-timbering of chocolate-painted plaster in the gables, Lincrusta Walton sham carved oak panels, a terrace of terra cotta to imitate stone, and cathedral glass in the front door. His boys went to good solid schools, and were put to respectable professions; his girls, in spite of a fantastic protest or so, were all married to suitable, steady, oldish young men with good prospects. And when it was a fit and proper thing for him to do so, Mr. Morris died. His tomb was of marble, and, without any art nonsense or laudatory inscription, quietly imposing—such being the fashion of his time.

He underwent various changes according to the accepted custom in these cases, and long before this story begins his bones even had become dust, and were scattered to the four quarters of heaven. And his sons and his grandsons and his great-grandsons and his great-great-grandsons, they too were dust and ashes, and were scattered likewise. It was a thing he could not have imagined, that a day would come when even his great-great-grandsons would be scattered to the four winds of heaven. If any one had suggested it to him he would have resented it. He was one of those worthy people who take no interest in the future of mankind at all. He had grave doubts, indeed, if there was any future for mankind after he was dead. It seemed quite impossible and quite uninteresting to imagine anything happening after he was dead. Yet the thing was so, and when even his great-great-grandson was dead and decayed and forgotten, when the sham half-timbered house had gone the way of all shams, and the "Times" was extinct, and the silk hat a ridiculous antiquity, and the modestly imposing stone that had been sacred to Mr. Morris had been burned to make lime for mortar, and all that Mr. Morris had found real and important was sere and dead, the world was still going on, and people were still going about it, just as heedless and impatient of the Future, or, indeed, of anything but their own selves and property, as Mr. Morris had been.

And, strange to tell, and much as Mr. Morris would have been angered if any one had foreshadowed it to him, all over the world there were scattered a multitude of people, filled with the breath of life, in whose veins the blood of Mr. Morris flowed. Just as some day the life which is gathered now in the reader of this very story may also be scattered far and wide about this world, and mingled with a thousand alien strains, beyond all thought and tracing.

And among the descendants of this Mr. Morris was one almost as sensible and clear-headed as his ancestor. He had just the same stout, short frame as that ancient man of the nineteenth century from whom his name of Morris—he spelled it Mwres—came; he had the same half-contemptuous expression of face. He was a prosperous person, too, as times went, and he disliked the "new-fangled," and bothers about the future and the lower classes, just as much as the ancestral Morris had done. He did not read the "Times" indeed, he did not know there ever had been a "Times"—that institution had foundered somewhere in the intervening gulf of years; but the phonograph machine, that talked to him as he made his toilet of a morning, might have been the voice of a reincarnated Blowitz when it dealt with the world's affairs. This phonographic machine was the size and shape of a Dutch clock, and down the front of it were electric barometric indicator, and an electric clock and calendar, and automatic engagement reminders, and where the clock would have been was the mouth of a trumpet. When it had news the trumpet gobbled like a turkey, "Galloop, galloop," and then brayed out its message as, let us say, a trumpet might bray. It would tell Mwres in full, rich, throaty tones about the overnight accidents to the omnibus flying machines that plied around the world, the latest arrivals at the fashionable resorts in Tibet, and of all the great monopolist company meetings of the day before, while he was dressing. If Mwres did not like hearing what it said, he had only to touch a stud, and it would choke a little and talk about something else.

Of course his toilet differed very much from that of his ancestor. It is doubtful which would have been the more shocked and pained to find himself in the clothing of the other. Mwres would certainly have sooner gone forth to the world stark naked than in the silk hat, frock coat, gray trousers and watch-chain that had filled Mr. Morris with sombre self-respect in the past. For Mwres there was no shaving to do: a skilful operator had long ago removed every hair-root from his face. His legs he incased in pleasant pink and amber garments of an air-tight material, which with the help of an ingenious little pump he distended so as to suggest enormous muscles. Above this he also wore pneumatic garments beneath an amber silk tunic, so that he was clothed in air and admirably protected against sudden extremes of heat or cold. Over this he flung a scarlet cloak with its edge fantastically curved. On his head, which had been skilfully deprived of every scrap of hair, he adjusted a pleasant little cap of bright scarlet, held on by suction and inflated with hydrogen, and curiously like the comb of a cock. So his toilet was complete; and, conscious of being soberly and becomingly attired, he was ready to face his fellow-beings with a tranquil eye.

This Mwres—the civility of "Mr." had vanished ages ago—was one of the officials under the Wind Vane and Waterfall Trust, the great company that owned every wind wheel and waterfall in the world, and which pumped all the water and supplied all the electric energy that people in these latter days required. He lived in a vast hotel near that part of London called Seventh Way, and had very large and comfortable apartments on the seventeenth floor. Households and family life had long since disappeared with the progressive refinement of manners; and indeed the steady rise in rents and land values, the disappearance of domestic servants, the elaboration of cookery, had rendered the separate domicile of Victorian times impossible, even had any one desired such a savage seclusion. When his toilet was completed he went toward one of the two doors of his apartment—there were doors at opposite ends, each marked with a huge arrow pointing one one way and one the other—touched a stud to open it, and emerged on a wide passage, the centre of which bore chairs and was moving at a steady pace to the left. On some of these chairs were seated gayly dressed men and women. He nodded to an acquaintance—it was not in those days etiquette to talk before breakfast—and seated himself on one of these chairs, and in a few seconds he had been carried to the doors of a lift, by which he descended to the great and splendid hall in which his breakfast would be automatically served.

It was a very different meal from a Victorian breakfast. The rude masses of bread needing to be carved and smeared over with animal fat before they could be made palatable, the still recognizable fragments of recently killed animals, hideously charred and hacked, the eggs torn ruthlessly from beneath some protesting hen—such things as these, though they constituted the ordinary fare of Victorian times, would have awakened only horror and disgust in the refined minds of the people of these latter days. Instead were pastes and cakes of agreeable and variegated design, without any suggestion in color or form of the unfortunate animals from which their substance and juices were derived. They appeared on little dishes sliding out upon a rail from a little box at one side of the table. The surface of the table, to judge by touch and eye, would have appeared to a nineteenth-century person to be covered with fine white damask, but this was really an oxidized metallic surface, and could be cleaned instantly after a meal. There were hundreds of such little tables in the hall, and at most of them were other latter-day citizens singly or in groups. And as Mwres seated himself before his elegant repast, the invisible orchestra, which had been resting during an interval, resumed and filled the air with music.

But Mwres did not display any great interest either in his breakfast or the music; his eye wandered incessantly about the hall, as though he expected a belated guest. At last he rose eagerly and waved his hand, and simultaneously across the hall appeared a tall dark figure in a costume of yellow and olive green. As this person, walking amid the tables with measured steps, drew near, the pallid earnestness of his face and the unusual intensity of his eyes became apparent. Mwres reseated himself and pointed to a chair beside him.

"I feared you would never come," he said. In spite of the intervening space of time, the English language was still almost exactly the same as it had been in England under Victoria the Good. The invention of the phonograph and suchlike means of recording sound, and the gradual replacement of books by such contrivances, had not only saved the human eyesight from decay, but had also by the establishment of a sure standard arrested the process of change in accent that had hitherto been so inevitable.

"I was delayed by an interesting case," said the man in green and yellow. "A prominent politician—ahem!—suffering from overwork." He glanced at the breakfast and seated himself. "I have been awake for forty hours."

"Eh dear!" said Mwres: "fancy that! You hypnotists have your work to do."

The hypnotist helped himself to some attractive amber-colored jelly. "I happen to be a good deal in request," he said modestly.

"Heaven knows what we should do without you."

"Oh! we're not so indispensable as all that," said the hypnotist, ruminating the flavor of the jelly. "The world did very well without us for some thousands of years. Two hundred years ago even—not one! In practice, that is. Physicians by the thousand, of course—frightfully clumsy brutes for the most part, and following one another like sheep—but doctors of the mind, except a few empirical flounderers, there were none."

He concentrated his mind on the jelly.

"But were people so sane—?" began Mwres.

The hypnotist shook his head. "It didn't matter then if they were a bit silly or faddy. Life was so easy-going then. No competition worth speaking of—no pressure. A human being had to be very lopsided before anything happened. Then, you know they clapped 'em away in what they called a lunatic asylum."

"I know," said Mwres. "In these confounded historical romances that every one is listening to, they always rescue a beautiful girl from an asylum or something of the sort. I don't know if you attend to that rubbish."

"I must confess I do," said the hypnotist. "It carries one out of one's self to hear of those quaint, adventurous, half civilized days of the nineteenth century, when men were stout and women simple. I like a good swaggering story before all things. Curious times they were, with their smutty railways and puffing old iron trains, their rum little houses and their horse vehicles. I suppose you don't read books?"

"Dear, no!" said Mwres, "I went to a modern school and we had none of that old-fashioned nonsense. Phonographs are good enough for me."

"Of course," said the hypnotist, "of course"; and surveyed the table for his next choice. "You know," he said, helping himself to a dark-blue confection that promised well, "in those days our business was scarcely thought of. I dare say if any one had told them that in two hundred years' time a class of men would be entirely occupied in impressing things upon the memory, effacing unpleasant ideas, controlling and overcoming instinctive but undesirable impulses, and so forth, by means of hypnotism, they would have refused to believe the thing possible. Few people knew that an order made during a mesmeric trance, even an order to forget or an order to desire, could be given so as to be obeyed after the trance was over. Yet there were men alive then who could have told them the thing was as absolutely certain to come about as—well, the transit of Venus."

"They knew of hypnotism, then?"

"Oh dear, yes! They used it—for painless dentistry and things like that! This blue stuff is confoundedly good: what is it?"

"Haven't the faintest idea," said Mwres, "but I admit it's very good. Take some more."

The hypnotist repeated his praises, and there was an appreciative pause.

"Speaking of these historical romances," said Mwres, with an attempt at an easy, off-hand manner, "brings me—ah—to the matter I—ah—had in mind when I asked you—when I expressed a wish to see you." He paused and took a deep breath.

"The fact is," said Mwres, "I have a—in fact a—daughter. Well, you know I have given her—ah—every educational advantage. Lectures—not a solitary lecturer of ability in the world but she has had a telephone direct—dancing, deportment, conversation, philosophy, art criticism . . ."

A Cure for Love

229

He indicated catholic culture by a gesture of his hand. "I had intended her to marry a very good friend of mine—Bindon of the Lighting
Commission—plain little man, you know, and a bit unpleasant in some
of his ways, but an excellent fellow really—an excellent fellow."

"Yes," said the hypnotist, "go on. How old is she?"

"Eighteen."

"A dangerous age. Well?"

"Well: it seems that she has been indulging in these historical
romances—excessively. Excessively. Even to the neglect of her philosophy. Filled her mind with unutterable nonsense about soldiers who
fight—what is it?—Etruscans?"

"Egyptians."

"Egyptians—very probably. Hack about with swords and revolvers
and things—bloodshed galore—horrible!—and about young men on tor-
pedo catchers who blow up—Spaniards, I fancy—and all sorts of irregu-
lar adventurers. And she has got it into her head that she must marry
for Love, and that poor little Bindon—"

"I've met similar cases," said the hypnotist. "Who is the other young
man?"

Mwres maintained an appearance of resigned calm. "You may well
ask," he said. "He is"—and his voice sank with shame—"a mere attendant upon the stage on which the flying-machines from Paris alight. He
has—as they say in the romances—good looks. He is quite young and
very eccentric. Affects the antique—he can read and write! So can she.
And instead of communicating by telephone, like sensible people, they
write and deliver—what is it?"

"Notes?"

"No—not notes. . . . Ah—poems."

The hypnotist raised his eyebrows. "How did she meet him?"

"Tripped coming down from the flying-machine from Paris—and fell
into his arms. The mischief was done in a moment!"

"Yes?"

"Well—that's all. Things must be stopped. That is what I want to
consult you about. What must be done? What *can* be done? Of course
I'm not a hypnotist; my knowledge is limited. But you—?"

"Hypnotism is not magic," said the man in green, putting both arms
on the table.

"Oh, precisely! But still—!"

"People cannot be hypnotized without their consent. If she is able to
stand out against marrying Bindon, she will probably stand out against

being hypnotized. But if once she can be hypnotized—even by some-body else—the thing is done."

"You can—?"

"Oh, certainly! Once we get her amenable, then we can suggest that she *must* marry Bindon—that that is her fate; or that the young man is repulsive, and that when she sees him she will be giddy and faint, or any little thing of that sort. Or if we can get her into a sufficiently profound trance we can suggest that she should forget him altogether—"

"Precisely."

"But the problem is to get her hypnotized. Of course no sort of pro-posal or suggestion must come from you—because no doubt she already distrusts you in the matter."

The hypnotist leaned his head upon his arm and thought.

"It's hard a man cannot dispose of his own daughter," said Mwres ir-relevantly.

"You must give me the name and address of the young lady," said the hypnotist, "and any information bearing upon the matter. And, by the by, is there any money in the affair?"

Mwres hesitated.

"There's a sum—in fact, a considerable sum—invested in the Patent Road Company. From her mother. That's what makes the thing so ex-asperating."

"Exactly," said the hypnotist. And he proceeded to cross examine Mwres on the entire affair.

It was a lengthy interview.

And meanwhile "Elizebe*θ* Mwres," as she spelled her name, or "Elizabeth Morris," as a nineteenth-century person would have put it, was sitting in a quiet waiting-place beneath the great stage upon which the flying-machine from Paris descended. And beside her sat her slen-der, handsome lover, reading her the poem he had written that morning while on duty upon the stage. When he had finished they sat for a time in silence; and then, as if for their special entertainment, the great ma-chine that had come flying through the air from America that morning rushed down out of the sky.

At first it was a little oblong, faint and blue amid the distant fleecy clouds; and then it grew swiftly large and white, and larger and whiter, until they could see the separate tiers of sails, each hundreds of feet wide, and the lank body they supported, and at last even the swinging seats of the passengers in a dotted row. Although it was falling it seemed to them to be rushing up the sky, and over the roof-spaces of the city below its shadow leaped toward them. They heard the whistling rush of the air about it and its yelling siren, shrill and swelling, to warn those who were on its landing-stage of its arrival. And abruptly the note fell down a couple of octaves, and it had passed, and the sky was clear and void, and she could turn her sweet eyes again to Denton at her side.

Their silence ended; and Denton, speaking in a little language of broken English that was, they fancied, their private possession—though lovers have used such little languages since the world began—told her how they too would leap into the air one morning out of all the obstacles and difficulties about them, and fly to a sunlight city of delight he knew of in Japan, half-way about the world.

She loved the dream, but she feared the leap; and she put him off with "Some day, dearest one, some day," to all his pleading that it might be soon; and at last came a shrilling of whistles, and it was time for him to go back to his duties on the stage. They parted—as lovers have been wont to part for thousands of years. She walked down a passage to a lift, and so came to one of the streets of that latter-day London, all glazed in with glass from the weather, and with incessant moving platforms that went to all parts of the city. And by one of these she returned to her apartments in the Hotel for Women where she lived, the apartments that were in telephonic communication with all the best lecturers in the world. But the sunlight of the flying stages was in her heart, and the wisdom of all the best lecturers in the world seemed folly in that light.

She spent the middle part of the day in the gymnasium, and took her midday meal with two other girls and their common chaperone—for it was still the custom to have a chaperone in the case of motherless girls of the more prosperous classes. The chaperone had a visitor that day, a man in green and yellow, with a white face and vivid eyes, who talked amazingly. Among other things, he fell to praising a new historical romance that one of the great popular story-tellers of the day had just put forth. It was, of course, about the spacious times of Queen Victoria; and the author, among other pleasing novelties, made a little argument before each section of the story, in imitation of the chapter headings of the old-fashioned books: as, for example, "How the Cabmen of Pimlico stopped the Victoria Omnibuses, and of the Great Fight in Palace Yard," and "How the Piccadilly Policeman was slain in the midst of his Duty." The man in green and yellow praised this innovation. "These pithy sentences," he said, "are admirable. They show at a glance those headlong, tumultuous times, when men and animals jostled in the filthy streets, and death might wait for one at every corner. Life was life then! How great the world must have seemed then! How marvellous! There were still parts of the world absolutely unexplored. Nowadays we have almost abolished wonder, we lead lives so trim and orderly that courage, endurance, faith, all the noble virtues seem fading from mankind."

And so on, taking the girls' thoughts with him, until the life they led, life in the vast and intricate London of the twenty-second century, a life interspersed with soaring excursions to every part of the globe, seemed to them a monotonous misery compared with the dædal past.

At first Elizabeth did not join in the conversation, but after a time the subject became so interesting that she made a few shy interpolations. But he scarcely seemed to notice her as he talked. He went on to describe a new method of entertaining people. They were hypnotized, and then suggestions were made to them so skilfully that they seemed to be living in ancient times again. They played out a little romance in the past as vivid as reality, and when at last they awakened they remembered all they had been through as though it were a real thing.

"It is a thing we have sought to do for years and years," said the hypnotist. "It is practically an artificial dream. And we know the way at last. Think of all it opens out to us—the enrichment of our experience, the recovery of adventure, the refuge it offers from this sordid, competitive life in which we live! Think!"

"And you can do that!" said the chaperone eagerly.

"The thing is possible at last," the hypnotist said. "You may order a dream as you wish."

The chaperone was the first to be hypnotized, and the dream, she said, was wonderful, when she came to again.

The other two girls, encouraged by her enthusiasm, also placed themselves in the hands of the hypnotist and had plunges into the romantic past. No one suggested that Elizabeth should try this novel entertainment; it was at her own request at last that she was taken into that land of dreams where there is neither any freedom of choice nor will. . . .

And so the mischief was done.

One day, when Denton went down to that quiet seat beneath the flying stage, Elizabeth was not in her wonted place. He was disappointed, and a little angry. The next day she did not come, and the next also. He was afraid. To hide his fear from himself, he set to work to write sonnets for her when she should come again. . . .

For three days he fought against his dread by such distraction, and then the truth was before him clear and cold, and would not be denied.

She might be ill, she might be dead; but he would not believe that he had been betrayed. There followed a week of misery. And then he knew she was the only thing on earth worth having, and that he must seek her, however hopeless the search, until she was found once more.

He had some small private means of his own, and so he threw over his appointment on the flying stage, and set himself to find this girl who had become at last all the world to him. He did not know where she lived, and little of her circumstances; for it had been part of the delight of her girlish romance that he should know nothing of her, nothing of the difference of their station. The ways of the city opened before him east and west, north and south. Even in Victorian days London was a maze, that little London with its poor four millions of people; but the London he explored, the London of the twenty-second century, was a London of thirty million souls. At first he was energetic and headlong, taking time neither to eat nor sleep. He sought for weeks and months, he went through every imaginable phase of fatigue and despair, over-excitement and anger. Long after hope was dead, by the sheer inertia of his desire he still went to and fro, peering into faces and looking this way and that, in the incessant ways and lifts and passages of that interminable hive of men.

At last chance was kind to him, and he saw her.

It was in a time of festivity. He was hungry; he had paid the inclusive fee and had gone into one of the gigantic dining-places of the city; he was pushing his way among the tables and scrutinizing by mere force of habit every group he passed.

He stood still, robbed of all power of motion, his eyes wide, his lips apart. Elizabeth sat scarcely twenty yards away from him, looking straight at him. Her eyes were as hard to him, as hard and expressionless and void of recognition, as the eyes of a statue.

She looked at him for a moment, and then her gaze passed beyond him.

Had he had only her eyes to judge by he might have doubted if it was indeed Elizabeth, but he knew her by the gesture of her hand, by the grace of a wanton little curl that floated over her ear as she moved her head. Something was said to her, and she turned, smiling tolerantly, to the man beside her, a little man in foolish raiment knobbed and spiked like some odd reptile with pneumatic horns—the Bindon of her father's choice.

For a moment Denton stood white and wild-eyed; then came a terrible faintness, and he sat before one of the little tables. He sat down with his back to her, and for a time he did not dare to look at her again. When at last he did, she and Bindon and two other people were standing up to go. The others were her father and her chaperone.

He sat as if incapable of action until the four figures were remote and small, and then he rose up possessed with the one idea of pursuit. For a space he feared he had lost them, and then he came upon Elizabeth and her chaperone again in one of the streets of moving platforms that intersected the city. Bindon and Mwres had disappeared.

He could not control himself to patience. He felt he must speak to her forthwith, or die. He pushed forward to where they were seated, and sat down beside them. His white face was convulsed with half-hysterical excitement.

He laid his hand on her wrist. "Elizabeth?" he said.

She turned in unfeigned astonishment. Nothing but the fear of a strange man showed in her face.

"Elizabeth," he cried, and his voice was strange to him: "dearest—you *know* me?"

Elizabeth's face showed nothing but alarm and perplexity. She drew herself away from him. The chaperone, a little gray-headed woman with mobile features, leaned forward to intervene. Her resolute bright eyes examined Denton. "*What* do you say?" she asked.

"This young lady," said Denton—"she knows me."

"Do you know him, dear?"

"No," said Elizabeth in a strange voice, and with a hand to her forehead, speaking almost as one who repeats a lesson. "No, I do not know him. I *know*—I do not know him."

"But—but . . . Not know me! It is I—Denton. Denton! To whom you used to talk. Don't you remember the flying stages? The little seat in the open air? The verses—"

"No," cried Elizabeth—"no. I do not know him. I do not know him. There is something . . . But I don't know. All I know is that I do not know him." Her face was a face of infinite distress.

The sharp eyes of the chaperone flitted to and fro from the girl to the man. "You see?" she said, with the faint shadow of a smile. "She does not know you."

"I do not know you," said Elizabeth. "Of that I am sure."

"But, dear—the songs—the little verses—"

"She does not know you," said the chaperone. "You must not . . . You have made a mistake. You must not go on talking to us after that. You must not annoy us on the public ways."

"But—" said Denton, and for a moment his miserably haggard face appealed against fate.

"You must not persist, young man," protested the chaperone.

"*Elizabeth!*" he cried.

Her face was the face of one who is tormented. "I do not know you," she cried, hand to brow. "Oh, I do not know you!"

For an instant Denton sat stunned. Then he stood up and groaned aloud.

He made a strange gesture of appeal toward the remote glass roof of the public way, then turned and went plunging recklessly from one moving platform to another, and vanished amid the swarms of people going to and fro thereon. The chaperone's eyes followed him, and then she looked at the curious faces about her.

"Dear," asked Elizabeth, clasping her hand, and too deeply moved to heed observation, "who was that man? Who *was* that man?"

The chaperone raised her eyebrows. She spoke in a clear, audible voice. "Some half-witted creature. I have never set eyes on him before."

"Never?"

"Never, dear. Do not trouble your mind about a thing like this."

And soon after this the celebrated hypnotist who dressed in green and yellow had another client. The young man paced his consulting-room, pale and disordered. "I want to forget," he cried. "I *must* forget."

The hypnotist watched him with quiet eyes, studied his face and clothes and bearing. "To forget anything—pleasure or pain—is to be, by so much—*less*. However, you know your own concern. My fee is high."

"If only I can forget—"

"That's easy enough with you. You wish it. I've done much harder things. Quite recently. I hardly expected to do it: the thing was done against the will of the hypnotized person. A love affair too—like yours. A girl. So rest assured."

The young man came and sat beside the hypnotist. His manner was a forced calm. He looked into the hypnotist's eyes. "I will tell you. Of course you will want to know what it is. There was a girl. Her name was Elizabeth Mwres. Well . . ."

He stopped. He had seen the instant surprise on the hypnotist's face. In that instant he knew. He stood up. He seemed to dominate the seated figure by his side. He gripped the shoulder of green and gold. For a time he could not find words.

"*Give her me back!*" he said at last. "Give her me back!"

"What do you mean?" gasped the hypnotist.

"Give her me back."

"Give whom?"

"Elizabeth Mwres—the girl—"

The hypnotist tried to free himself; he rose to his feet. Denton's grip tightened.

"Let go!" cried the hypnotist, thrusting an arm against Denton's chest.

In a moment the two men were locked in a clumsy wrestle. Neither had the slightest training—for athleticism, except for exhibition and to afford opportunity for betting, had faded out of the earth—but Denton was not only the younger but the stronger of the two. They swayed across the room, and then the hypnotist had gone down under his antagonist. They fell together. . . .

Denton leaped to his feet, dismayed at his own fury; but the hypnotist lay still, and suddenly from a little white mark where his forehead had struck a stool shot a hurrying band of red. For a space Denton stood over him irresolute, trembling.

A fear of the consequences entered his gently nurtured mind. He turned toward the door. "No," he said aloud, and came back to the middle of the room. Overcoming the instinctive repugnance of one who had seen no act of violence in all his life before, he knelt down beside his antagonist and felt his heart. Then he peered at the wound. He rose quietly and looked about him. He began to see more of the situation.

When presently the hypnotist recovered his senses, his head ached severely, his back was against Denton's knees and Denton was sponging his face.

The hypnotist did not speak. But presently he indicated by a gesture that in his opinion he had been sponged enough. "Let me get up," he said.

"Not yet," said Denton.

"You have assaulted me, you scoundrel!"

"We are alone," said Denton, "and the door is secure."

There was an interval of thought.

"Unless I sponge," said Denton, "your forehead will develop a tremendous bruise."

"You can go on sponging," said the hypnotist sulkily.

There was another pause.

"We might be in the Stone Age," said the hypnotist. "Violence! Struggle!"

"In the Stone Age no man dared to come between man and woman," said Denton.

The hypnotist thought again.

"What are you going to do?" he asked sulkily.

"While you were insensible I found the girl's address on your tablets. I did not know it before. I telephoned. She will be here soon. Then—"

"She will bring her chaperone."

"That is all right."

"But what—? I don't see. What do you mean to do?"

"I looked about for a weapon also. It is an astonishing thing how few weapons there are nowadays, if you consider that in the Stone Age men owned scarcely anything *but* weapons. I hit at last upon this lamp. I have wrenched off the wires and things, and I hold it so." He extended it over the hypnotist's shoulders. "With that I can quite easily smash your skull. I *will*—unless you do as I tell you."

"Violence is no remedy," said the hypnotist, quoting from the "Modern Man's Book of Moral Maxims."

"It's an undesirable disease," said Denton.

"Well?"

"You will tell that chaperone you are going to order the girl to marry that knobby little brute with the red hair and ferrety eyes. I believe that's how things stand?"

"Yes—that's how things stand."

"And, pretending to do that, you will restore her memory of me."

"It's unprofessional."

"Look here! If I cannot have that girl I would rather die than not. I don't propose to respect your little fancies. If anything goes wrong you shall not live five minutes. This is a rude makeshift of a weapon, and it may quite conceivably be painful to kill you. But I will. It is unusual, I know, nowadays, to do things like this—mainly because there is so little in life that is worth being violent about."

"The chaperone will see you directly she comes—"

"I shall stand in that recess. Behind you."

The hypnotist thought. "You are a determined young man," he said, "and only half civilized. I have tried to do my duty to my client, but in this affair you seem likely to get your own way. . . ."

"You mean to deal straightly?"

"I'm not going to risk having my brains scattered in a petty affair like this."

"And afterward?"

"There is nothing a hypnotist or doctor hates so much as a scandal. I at least am no savage. I am annoyed. . . . But in a day or so I shall bear no malice. . . ."

"Thank you. And now that we understand each other, there is no necessity to keep you sitting any longer on the floor."

The Offshore Pirate

by F. SCOTT FITZGERALD

This unlikely story begins on a sea that was a blue dream, as colorful as blue-silk stockings, and beneath a sky as blue as the irises of children's eyes. From the western half of the sky the sun was shying little golden disks at the sea—if you gazed intently enough you could see them skip from wave tip to wave tip until they joined a broad collar of golden coin that was collecting half a mile out and would eventually be a dazzling sunset. About half-way between the Florida shore and the golden collar a white steam-yacht, very young and graceful, was riding at anchor and under a blue-and-white awning aft a yellow-haired girl reclined in a wicker settee reading The Revolt of the Angels, by Anatole France.

She was about nineteen, slender and supple, with a spoiled alluring mouth and quick gray eyes full of a radiant curiosity. Her feet, stockingless, and adorned rather than clad in blue-satin slippers which swung nonchalantly from her toes, were perched on the arm of a settee adjoining the one she occupied. And as she read she intermittently regaled herself by a faint application to her tongue of a half-lemon that she held in her hand. The other half, sucked dry, lay on the deck at her feet and rocked very gently to and fro at the almost imperceptible motion of the tide.

The second half-lemon was well-nigh pulpless and the golden collar had grown astonishing in width, when suddenly the drowsy silence which enveloped the yacht was broken by the sound of heavy footsteps and an elderly man topped with orderly gray hair and clad in a white-flannel suit appeared at the head of the companionway. There he paused for a moment until his eyes became accustomed to the sun, and then seeing the girl under the awning he uttered a long even grunt of disapproval.

If he had intended thereby to obtain a rise of any sort he was doomed to disappointment. The girl calmly turned over two pages, turned back one, raised the lemon mechanically to tasting distance, and then very faintly but quite unmistakably yawned.

"Ardita!" said the gray-haired man sternly.

Ardita uttered a small sound indicating nothing.

"Ardita!" he repeated. "Ardita!"

Ardita raised the lemon languidly, allowing three words to slip out before it reached her tongue.

"Oh, shut up."

"Ardita!"

"What?"

"Will you listen to me—or will I have to get a servant to hold you while I talk to you?"

The lemon descended slowly and scornfully.

"Put it in writing."

"Will you have the decency to close that abominable book and discard that damn lemon for two minutes?"

"Oh, can't you lemme alone for a second?"

"Ardita, I have just received a telephone message from the shore——"

"Telephone?" She showed for the first time a faint interest.

"Yes, it was——"

"Do you mean to say," she interrupted wonderingly, "'at they let you run a wire out here?"

"Yes, and just now——"

"Won't other boats bump into it?"

"No. It's run along the bottom. Five min——"

"Well, I'll be darned! Gosh! Science is golden or something—isn't it?"

"Will you let me say what I started to?"

"Shoot!"

"Well, it seems—well, I am up here—" He paused and swallowed several times distractedly. "Oh, yes. Young woman, Colonel Moreland has called up again to ask me to be sure to bring you in to dinner. His son Toby has come all the way from New York to meet you and he's invited several other young people. For the last time, will you——"

"No," said Ardita shortly, "I won't. I came along on this darn cruise with the one idea of going to Palm Beach, and you knew it, and I absolutely refuse to meet any darn old colonel or any darn young Toby or any darn old young people or to set foot in any other darn old town in this crazy state. So you either take me to Palm Beach or else shut up and go away."

"Very well. This is the last straw. In your infatuation for this man—a man who is notorious for his excesses, a man your father would not have allowed to so much as mention your name—you have reflected the demimonde rather than the circles in which you have presumably grown up. From now on——"

"I know," interrupted Ardita ironically, "from now on you go your way and I go mine. I've heard that story before. You know I'd like nothing better."

"From now on," he announced grandiloquently, "you are no niece of mine. I——"

"O-o-o-oh!" The cry was wrung from Ardita with the agony of a lost soul. "Will you stop boring me! Will you go 'way! Will you jump overboard and drown! Do you want me to throw this book at you!"

"If you dare do any——"

Smack! The Revolt of the Angels sailed through the air, missed its target by the length of a short nose, and bumped cheerfully down the companionway.

The gray-haired man made an instinctive step backward and then two cautious steps forward. Ardita jumped to her five feet four and stared at him defiantly, her gray eyes blazing.

"Keep off!"

"How dare you!" he cried.

"Because I darn please!"

"You've grown unbearable! Your disposition——"

"You've made me that way! No child ever has a bad disposition unless it's her family's fault! Whatever I am, you did it."

Muttering something under his breath her uncle turned and, walking forward, called in a loud voice for the launch. Then he returned to the awning, where Ardita had again seated herself and resumed her attention to the lemon.

"I am going ashore," he said slowly. "I will be out again at nine o'clock to-night. When I return we will start back to New York, where I shall turn you over to your aunt for the rest of your natural, or rather unnatural, life."

He paused and looked at her, and then all at once something in the utter childishness of her beauty seemed to puncture his anger like an inflated tire and render him helpless, uncertain, utterly fatuous.

"Ardita," he said not unkindly, "I'm no fool. I've been round. I know men. And, child, confirmed libertines don't reform until they're tired—and then they're not themselves—they're husks of themselves." He looked at her as if expecting agreement, but receiving no sight or sound of it he continued. "Perhaps the man loves you—that's possible. He's loved many women and he'll love many more. Less than a month ago, one month, Ardita, he was involved in a notorious affair with that red-haired woman, Mimi Merril; promised to give her the diamond bracelet that the Czar of Russia gave his mother. You know—you read the papers."

"Thrilling scandals by an anxious uncle," yawned Ardita. "Have it filmed. Wicked clubman making eyes at virtuous flapper. Virtuous flapper conclusively vamped by his lurid past. Plans to meet him at Palm Beach. Foiled by anxious uncle."

"Will you tell me why the devil you want to marry him?"

"I'm sure I couldn't say," said Ardita shortly. "Maybe because he's the only man I know, good or bad, who has an imagination and the courage of his convictions. Maybe it's to get away from the young fools that spend their vacuous hours pursuing me around the country. But as for the famous Russian bracelet, you can set your mind at rest on that score. He's going to give it to me at Palm Beach—if you'll show a little intelligence."

"How about the—red-haired woman?"

"He hasn't seen her for six months," she said angrily. "Don't you suppose I have enough pride to see to that? Don't you know by this time that I can do any darn thing with any darn man I want to?"

She put her chin in the air like the statue of France Aroused, and then spoiled the pose somwhat by raising the lemon for action.

"Is it the Russian bracelet that fascinates you?"

"No, I'm merely trying to give you the sort of argument that would appeal to your intelligence. And I wish you'd go 'way," she said, her temper rising again. "You know I never change my mind. You've been boring me for three days until I'm about to go crazy. I won't go ashore! Won't! Do you hear? Won't!"

"Very well," he said, "and you won't go to Palm Beach either. Of all the selfish, spoiled, uncontrolled, disagreeable, impossible girls I have——"

Splash! The half-lemon caught him in the neck. Simultaneously came a hail from over the side.

"The launch is ready, Mr. Farnam."

Too full of words and rage to speak, Mr. Farnam cast one utterly condemning glance at his niece and, turning, ran swiftly down the ladder.

II

Five o'clock rolled down from the sun and plumped soundlessly into the sea. The golden collar widened into a glittering island; and a faint breeze that had been playing with the edges of the awning and swaying one of the dangling blue slippers became suddenly freighted with song. It was a chorus of men in close harmony and in perfect rhythm to an accompanying sound of oars cleaving the blue waters. Ardita lifted her head and listened.

> "Carrots and peas,
> Beans on their knees,
> Pigs in the seas,
>   Lucky fellows!
> Blow us a breeze,
> Blow us a breeze,
> Blow us a breeze,
>   With your bellows."

Ardita's brow wrinkled in astonishment. Sitting very still she listened eagerly as the chorus took up a second verse.

> "Onions and beans,
> Marshalls and Deans,
> Goldbergs and Greens
>   And Costellos.
> Blow us a breeze,
> Blow us a breeze,
> Blow us a breeze,
>   With your bellows."

With an exclamation she tossed her book to the deck, where it sprawled at a straddle, and hurried to the rail. Fifty feet away a large rowboat was approaching containing seven men, six of them rowing and one standing up in the stern keeping time to their song with an orchestra leader's baton.

> "Oysters and rocks,
> Sawdust and socks,
> Who could make clocks
> Out of cellos?—"

The leader's eyes suddenly rested on Ardita, who was leaning over the rail spellbound with curiosity. He made a quick movement with his baton and the singing instantly ceased. She saw that he was the only white man in the boat—the six rowers were Negroes.

"Narcissus ahoy!" he called politely.

"What's the idea of all the discord?" demanded Ardita cheerfully. "Is this the varsity crew from the county nut farm?"

By this time the boat was scraping the side of the yacht and a great hulking Negro in the bow turned round and grasped the ladder. Thereupon the leader left his position in the stern and before Ardita had realized his intention he ran up the ladder and stood breathless before her on the deck.

"The women and children will be spared!" he said briskly. "All crying babies will be immediately drowned and all males put in double irons!"

Digging her hands excitedly down into the pockets of her dress Ardita stared at him, speechless with astonishment.

He was a young man with a scornful mouth and the bright blue eyes of a healthy baby set in a dark sensitive face. His hair was pitch black, damp and curly—the hair of a Grecian statue gone brunette. He was trimly built, trimly dressed, and graceful as an agile quarter-back.

"Well, I'll be a son of a gun!" she said dazedly.

They eyed each other coolly.

"Do you surrender the ship?"

"Is this an outburst of wit?" demanded Ardita. "Are you an idiot—or just being initiated to some fraternity?"

"I asked you if you surrendered the ship."

"I thought the country was dry," said Ardita disdainfully. "Have you been drinking finger-nail enamel? You better get off this yacht!"

"What?" The young man's voice expressed incredulity.

"Get off the yacht! You heard me!"

He looked at her for a moment as if considering what she had said.

"No," said his scornful mouth slowly, "no, I won't get off the yacht. You can get off if you wish."

Going to the rail he gave a curt command and immediately the crew of the rowboat scrambled up the ladder and ranged themselves in line before him, a coal-black and burly darky at one end and a miniature mulatto of four feet nine at the other. They seemed to be uniformly dressed in some sort of blue costume ornamented with dust, mud, and tatters; over the shoulder of each was slung a small, heavy-looking white sack, and under their arms they carried large black cases apparently containing musical instruments.

"'Ten-*shun!*" commanded the young man, snapping his own heels together crisply. "Right *driss!* Front! Step out here, Babe!"

The smallest Negro took a quick step forward and saluted.

"Yas-suh!"

"Take command, go down below, catch the crew and tie 'em up—all except the engineer. Bring him up to me. Oh, and pile those bags by the rail there."

"Yas-suh!"

Babe saluted again and wheeling about motioned for the five others to gather about him. Then after a short whispered consultation they all filed noiselessly down the companionway.

"Now," said the young man cheerfully to Ardita, who had witnessed this last scene in withering silence, "if you will swear on your honor as a flapper—which probably isn't worth much—that you'll keep that spoiled little mouth of yours tight shut for forty-eight hours, you can row yourself ashore in our rowboat."

"Otherwise what?"

"Otherwise you're going to sea in a ship."

With a little sigh as for a crisis well passed, the young man sank into the settee Ardita had lately vacated and stretched his arms lazily. The corners of his mouth relaxed appreciatively as he looked round at the rich striped awning, the polished brass, and the luxurious fittings of the deck. His eye fell on the book, and then on the exhausted lemon.

"Hm," he said, "Stonewall Jackson claimed that lemon-juice cleared his head. Your head feel pretty clear?"

Ardita disdained to answer.

"Because inside of five minutes you'll have to make a clear decision whether it's go or stay."

He picked up the book and opened it curiously.

"The Revolt of the Angels. Sounds pretty good. French, eh?" He stared at her with new interest. "You French?"

"No."

"What's your name?"

"Farnam."

"Farnam what?"

"Ardita Farnam."

"Well, Ardita, no use standing up there and chewing out the insides of your mouth. You ought to break those nervous habits while you're young. Come over here and sit down."

Ardita took a carved jade case from her pocket, extracted a cigarette and lit it with a conscious coolness, though she knew her hand was trembling a little; then she crossed over with her supple, swinging walk, and sitting down in the other settee blew a mouthful of smoke at the awning.

"You can't get me off this yacht," she said steadily, "and you haven't got very much sense if you think you'll get far with it. My uncle'll have wirelesses zigzagging all over this ocean by half past six."

"Hm."

She looked quickly at his face, caught anxiety stamped there plainly in the faintest depression of the mouth's corners.

"It's all the same to me," she said, shrugging her shoulders. "'Tisn't my yacht. I don't mind going for a coupla hours' cruise. I'll even lend you that book so you'll have something to read on the revenue boat that takes you up to Sing Sing."

He laughed scornfully.

"If that's advice you needn't bother. This is part of a plan arranged before I ever knew this yacht existed. If it hadn't been this one it'd have been the next one we passed anchored along the coast."

"Who are you?" demanded Ardita suddenly. "And what are you?"

"You've decided not to go ashore?"

"I never even faintly considered it."

"We're generally known," he said, "all seven of us, as Curtis Carlyle and his Six Black Buddies, late of the Winter Garden and the Midnight Frolic."

"You're singers?"

"We were until to-day. At present, due to those white bags you see there, we're fugitives from justice, and if the reward offered for our capture hasn't by this time reached twenty thousand dollars I miss my guess."

"What's in the bags?" asked Ardita curiously.

"Well," he said, "for the present we'll call it—mud—Florida mud."

III

Within ten minutes after Curtis Carlyle's interview with a very frightened engineer, the yacht Narcissus was under way, steaming south
through a balmy tropical twilight. The little mulatto, Babe, who
seemed to have Carlyle's implicit confidence, took full command of the
situation. Mr. Farnam's valet and the chef, the only members of the
crew on board except the engineer, having shown fight, were now recon-
sidering, strapped securely to their bunks below. Trombone Mose, the
biggest Negro, was set busy with a can of paint obliterating the name
Narcissus from the bow, and substituting the name Hula Hula, and the
others congregated aft and became intently involved in a game of craps.

Having given orders for a meal to be prepared and served on deck at
seven-thirty, Carlyle rejoined Ardita, and, sinking back into his settee,
half closed his eyes and fell into a state of profound abstraction.

Ardita scrutinized him carefully—and classed him immediately as a
romantic figure. He gave the effect of towering self-confidence erected
on a slight foundation—just under the surface of each of his decisions
she discerned a hesitancy that was in decided contrast to the arrogant
curl of his lips.

"He's not like me," she thought. "There's a difference somewhere."

Being a supreme egotist Ardita frequently thought about herself;
never having had her egotism disputed she did it entirely naturally and
with no detraction from her unquestioned charm. Though she was
nineteen she gave the effect of a high-spirited, precocious child, and in
the present glow of her youth and beauty all the men and women she
had known were but driftwood on the ripples of her temperament. She
had met other egotists—in fact she found that selfish people bored her
rather less than unselfish people—but as yet there had not been one she
had not eventually defeated and brought to her feet.

But though she recognized an egotist in the settee next to her, she
felt none of that usual shutting of doors in her mind which meant
clearing ship for action; on the contrary her instinct told her that this
man was somehow completely pregnable and quite defenseless. When
Ardita defied convention—and of late it had been her chief amusement
—it was from an intense desire to be herself, and she felt that this man,
on the contrary, was preoccupied with his own defiance.

She was much more interested in him than she was in her own situation, which affected her as the prospect of a matinée might affect a ten-year-old child. She had implicit confidence in her ability to take care of herself under any and all circumstances.

The night deepened. A pale new moon smiled misty-eyed upon the sea, and as the shore faded dimly out and dark clouds were blown like leaves along the far horizon a great haze of moonshine suddenly bathed the yacht and spread an avenue of glittering mail in her swift path. From time to time there was the bright flare of a match as one of them lighted a cigarette, but except for the low undertone of the throbbing engines and the even wash of the waves about the stern, the yacht was quiet as a dream boat star-bound through the heavens. Round them flowed the smell of the night sea, bringing with it an infinite languor.

Carlyle broke the silence at last.

"Lucky girl," he sighed, "I've always wanted to be rich—and buy all this beauty."

Ardita yawned.

"I'd rather be you," she said frankly.

"You would—for about a day. But you do seem to possess a lot of nerve for a flapper."

"I wish you wouldn't call me that."

"Beg your pardon."

"As to nerve," she continued slowly, "it's my one redeeming feature. I'm not afraid of anything in heaven or earth."

"Hm, I am."

"To be afraid," said Ardita, "a person has either to be very great and strong—or else a coward. I'm neither." She paused for a moment, and eagerness crept into her tone. "But I want to talk about you. What on earth have you done—and how did you do it?"

"Why?" he demanded cynically. "Going to write a movie about me?"

"Go on," she urged. "Lie to me by the moonlight. Do a fabulous story."

A Negro appeared, switched on a string of small lights under the awning, and began setting the wicker table for supper. And while they ate cold sliced chicken, salad, artichokes, and strawberry jam from the plentiful larder below, Carlyle began to talk, hesitantly at first, but eagerly as he saw she was interested. Ardita scarcely touched her food as she watched his dark young face—handsome, ironic, faintly ineffectual.

He began life as a poor kid in a Tennessee town, he said, so poor that his people were the only white family in their street. He never remembered any white children—but there were inevitably a dozen pickaninnies streaming in his trail, passionate admirers whom he kept in tow by the vividness of his imagination and the amount of trouble he was always getting them in and out of. And it seemed that this association diverted a rather unusual musical gift into a strange channel.

There had been a colored woman named Belle Pope Calhoun who played the piano at parties given for white children—nice white children that would have passed Curtis Carlyle with a sniff. But the ragged little "poh white" used to sit beside her piano by the hour and try to get in an alto with one of those kazoos that boys hum through. Before he was thirteen he was picking up a living teasing ragtime out of a battered violin in little cafés round Nashville. Eight years later the ragtime craze hit the country, and he took six darkies on the Orpheum circuit. Five of them were boys he had grown up with; the other was the little mulatto, Babe Divine, who was a wharf nigger round New York, and long before that a plantation hand in Bermuda, until he stuck an eight-inch stiletto in his master's back. Almost before Carlyle realized his good fortune he was on Broadway, with offers of engagements on all sides, and more money than he had ever dreamed of.

It was about then that a change began in his whole attitude, a rather curious, embittering change. It was when he realized that he was spending the golden years of his life gibbering round a stage with a lot of black men. His act was good of its kind—three trombones, three saxophones, and Carlyle's flute—and it was his own peculiar sense of rhythm that made all the difference; but he began to grow strangely sensitive about it, began to hate the thought of appearing, dreaded it from day to day.

They were making money—each contract he signed called for more—but when he went to managers and told them that he wanted to separate from his sextet and go on as a regular pianist, they laughed at him and told him he was crazy—it would be an artistic suicide. He used to laugh afterward at the phrase "artistic suicide." They all used it.

Half a dozen times they played at private dances at three thousand dollars a night, and it seemed as if these crystallized all his distaste for his mode of livelihood. They took place in clubs and houses that he couldn't have gone into in the daytime. After all, he was merely playing the role of the eternal monkey, a sort of sublimated chorus man. He was sick of the very smell of the theatre, of powder and rouge and the chatter of the greenroom, and the patronizing approval of the boxes. He couldn't put his heart into it any more. The idea of a slow approach to the luxury of leisure drove him wild. He was, of course, progressing toward it, but, like a child, eating his ice-cream so slowly that he couldn't taste it at all.

He wanted to have a lot of money and time, and opportunity to read and play, and the sort of men and women round him that he could never have—the kind who, if they thought of him at all, would have considered him rather contemptible; in short he wanted all those things which he was beginning to lump under the general head of aristocracy, an aristocracy which it seemed almost any money could buy except money made as he was making it. He was twenty-five then, without family or education or any promise that he would succeed in a business career. He began speculating wildly, and within three weeks he had lost every cent he had saved.

Then the war came. He went to Plattsburg, and even there his profession followed him. A brigadier-general called him up to head-quarters and told him he could serve the country better as a band leader—so he spent the war entertaining celebrities behind the line with a headquarters band. It was not so bad—except that when the infantry came limping back from the trenches he wanted to be one of them. The sweat and mud they wore seemed only one of those ineffable symbols of aristocracy that were forever eluding him.

"It was the private dances that did it. After I came back from the war the old routine started. We had an offer from a syndicate of Florida hotels. It was only a question of time then."

He broke off and Ardita looked at him expectantly, but he shook his head.

"No," he said, "I'm not going to tell you about it. I'm enjoying it too much, and I'm afraid I'd lose a little of that enjoyment if I shared it with any one else. I want to hang on to those few breathless, heroic moments when I stood out before them all and let them know I was more than a damn bobbing, squawking clown."

From up forward came suddenly the low sound of singing. The Negroes had gathered together on the deck and their voices rose together in a haunting melody that soared in poignant harmonics toward the moon. And Ardita listened in enchantment.

"Oh down—
Oh down,
Mammy wanna take me downa milky way,
Oh down—
Oh down,
Pappy say to-morra-a-a-ah!
But mammy say to-day,
Yes—mammy say to-day!"

Carlyle sighed and was silent for a moment, looking up at the gathered host of stars blinking like arclights in the warm sky. The Negroes' song had died away to a plaintive humming, and it seemed as if minute by minute the brightness and the great silence were increasing until he could almost hear the midnight toilet of the mermaids as they combed their silver dripping curls under the moon and gossiped to each other of the fine wrecks they lived in on the green opalescent avenues below.

"You see," said Carlyle softly, "this is the beauty I want. Beauty has got to be astonishing, astounding—it's got to burst in on you like a dream, like the exquisite eyes of a girl."

He turned to her, but she was silent.

"You see, don't you, Anita—I mean, Ardita?"

Again she made no answer. She had been sound asleep for some time.

IV

In the dense sun-flooded noon of next day a spot in the sea before them resolved casually into a green-and-gray islet, apparently composed of a great granite cliff at its northern end which slanted south through a mile of vivid coppice and grass to a sandy beach melting lazily into the surf. When Ardita, reading in her favorite seat, came to the last page of The Revolt of the Angels and, slamming the book shut, looked up and saw it, she gave a little cry of delight and called to Carlyle, who was standing moodily by the rail.

"Is this it? Is this where you're going?"

Carlyle shrugged his shoulders carelessly.

"You've got me." He raised his voice and called up to the acting skipper: "Oh, Babe, is this your island?"

The mulatto's miniature head appeared from round the corner of the deck-house.

"Yas-suh! This yeah's it."

Carlyle joined Ardita.

"Looks sort of sporting, doesn't it?"

"Yes," she agreed, "but it doesn't look big enough to be much of a hiding-place."

"You still putting your faith in those wirelesses your uncle was going to have zigzagging round?"

"No," said Ardita frankly. "I'm all for you. I'd really like to see you make a get-away."

He laughed.

"You're our Lady Luck. Guess we'll have to keep you with us as a mascot—for the present, anyway."

"You couldn't very well ask me to swim back," she said coolly. "If you do I'm going to start writing dime novels founded on that interminable history of your life you gave me last night."

He flushed and stiffened slightly.

"I'm very sorry I bored you."

"Oh, you didn't—until just at the end with some story about how furious you were because you couldn't dance with the ladies you played music for."

He rose angrily.

"You have got a darn mean little tongue."

"Excuse me," she said, melting into laughter, "but I'm not used to having men regale me with the story of their life ambitions—especially if they've lived such deathly platonic lives."

"Why? What do men usually regale you with?"

"Oh, they talk about me," she yawned. "They tell me I'm the spirit of youth and beauty."

"What do you tell them?"

"Oh, I agree quietly."

"Does every man you meet tell you he loves you?"

Ardita nodded.

"Why shouldn't he? All life is just a progression toward, and then a recession from, one phrase—'I love you.'"

Carlyle laughed and sat down.

"That's very true. That's—that's not bad. Did you make that up?"

"Yes—or rather I found it out. It doesn't mean anything especially. It's just clever."

"It's the sort of remark," he said gravely, "that's typical of your class."

"Oh," she interrupted impatiently, "don't start that lecture on aristocracy again! I distrust people who can be intense at this hour in the morning. It's a mild form of insanity—a sort of breakfast-food jag. Morning's the time to sleep, swim, and be careless."

Ten minutes later they had swung round in a wide circle as if to approach the island from the north.

"There's a trick somewhere," commented Ardita thoughtfully. "He can't mean just to anchor up against this cliff."

They were heading straight in now toward the solid rock, which must have been well over a hundred feet tall, and not until they were within fifty yards of it did Ardita see their objective. Then she clapped her hands in delight. There was a break in the cliff entirely hidden by a curious overlapping of rock, and through this break the yacht entered and very slowly traversed a narrow channel of crystal-clear water between high gray walls. Then they were riding at anchor in a miniature world of green and gold, a gilded bay smooth as glass and set round with tiny palms, the whole resembling the mirror lakes and twig trees that children set up in sand piles.

"Not so darned bad!" said Carlyle excitedly. "I guess that little coon knows his way round this corner of the Atlantic."

His exuberance was contagious, and Ardita became quite jubilant.

"It's an absolutely sure-fire hiding-place!"

"Lordy, yes! It's the sort of island you read about."

The rowboat was lowered into the golden lake and they pulled ashore.

"Come on," said Carlyle as they landed in the slushy sand, "we'll go exploring."

The fringe of palms was in turn ringed in by a round mile of flat, sandy country. They followed it south and brushing through a farther rim of tropical vegetation came out on a pearl-gray virgin beach where Ardita kicked off her brown golf shoes—she seemed to have permanently abandoned stockings—and went wading. Then they sauntered back to the yacht, where the indefatigable Babe had luncheon ready for them. He had posted a lookout on the high cliff to the north to watch the sea on both sides, though he doubted if the entrance to the cliff was generally known—he had never even seen a map on which the island was marked.

"What's its name," asked Ardita—"the island, I mean?"

"No name 'tall," chuckled Babe. "Reckin she jus' island, 'at's all."

In the late afternoon they sat with their backs against great boulders on the highest part of the cliff and Carlyle sketched for her his vague plans. He was sure they were hot after him by this time. The total proceeds of the coup he had pulled off, and concerning which he still refused to enlighten her, he estimated as just under a million dollars. He counted on lying up here several weeks and then setting off southward, keeping well outside the usual channels of travel, rounding the Horn and heading for Callao, in Peru. The details of coaling and provisioning he was leaving entirely to Babe, who, it seemed, had sailed these seas in every capacity from cabin-boy aboard a coffee trader to virtual first mate on a Brazilian pirate craft, whose skipper had long since been hung.

"If he'd been white he'd have been king of South America long ago," said Carlyle emphatically. "When it comes to intelligence he makes Booker T. Washington look like a moron. He's got the guile of every race and nationality whose blood is in his veins, and that's half a dozen or I'm a liar. He worships me because I'm the only man in the world who can play better ragtime than he can. We used to sit together on the wharfs down on the New York water-front, he with a bassoon and me with an oboe, and we'd blend minor keys in African harmonics a thousand years old until the rats would crawl up the posts and sit round groaning and squeaking like dogs will in front of a phonograph."

Ardita roared.

"How you can tell 'em!"

Carlyle grinned.

"I swear that's the gos——"

"What you going to do when you get to Callao?" she interrupted.

"Take ship for India. I want to be a rajah. I mean it. My idea is to go up into Afghanistan somewhere, buy up a palace and a reputation, and then after about five years appear in England with a foreign accent and a mysterious past. But India first. Do you know, they say that all the gold in the world drifts very gradually back to India. Something fascinating about that to me. And I want leisure to read—an immense amount."

"How about after that?"

"Then," he answered defiantly, "comes aristocracy. Laugh if you want to—but at least you'll have to admit that I know what I want—which I imagine is more than you do."

"On the contrary," contradicted Ardita, reaching in her pocket for her cigarette case, "when I met you I was in the midst of a great uproar of all my friends and relatives because I did know what I wanted."

"What was it?"

"A man."

He started.

"You mean you were engaged?"

"After a fashion. If you hadn't come aboard I had every intention of slipping ashore yesterday evening—how long ago it seems—and meeting him in Palm Beach. He's waiting there for me with a bracelet that once belonged to Catherine of Russia. Now don't mutter anything about aristocracy," she put in quickly. "I liked him simply because he had had an imagination and the utter courage of his convictions."

"But your family disapproved, eh?"

"What there is of it—only a silly uncle and a sillier aunt. It seems he got into some scandal with a red-haired woman named Mimi something—it was frightfully exaggerated, he said, and men don't lie to me—and anyway I didn't care what he'd done; it was the future that counted. And I'd see to that. When a man's in love with me he doesn't care for other amusements. I told him to drop her like a hot cake, and he did."

"I feel rather jealous," said Carlyle, frowning—and then he laughed. "I guess I'll just keep you along with us until we get to Callao. Then I'll lend you enough money to get back to the States. By that time you'll have had a chance to think that gentleman over a little more."

"Don't talk to me like that!" fired up Ardita. "I won't tolerate the parental attitude from anybody! Do you understand me?"

He chuckled and then stopped, rather abashed, as her cold anger seemed to fold him about and chill him.

"I'm sorry," he offered uncertainly.

"Oh, don't apologize! I can't stand men who say 'I'm sorry' in that manly, reserved tone. Just shut up!"

A pause ensued, a pause which Carlyle found rather awkward, but which Ardita seemed not to notice at all as she sat contentedly enjoying her cigarette and gazing out at the shining sea. After a minute she crawled out on the rock and lay with her face over the edge looking down. Carlyle, watching her, reflected how it seemed impossible for her to assume an ungraceful attitude.

"Oh, look!" she cried. "There's a lot of sort of ledges down there. Wide ones of all different heights."

He joined her and together they gazed down the dizzy height.

"We'll go swimming to-night!" she said excitedly. "By moonlight."

"Wouldn't you rather go in at the beach on the other end?"

"Not a chance. I like to dive. You can use my uncle's bathing-suit, only it'll fit you like a gunny sack, because he's a very flabby man. I've got a one-piece affair that's shocked the natives all along the Atlantic coast from Biddeford Pool to St. Augustine."

"I suppose you're a shark."

"Yes, I'm pretty good. And I look cute too. A sculptor up at Rye last summer told me my calves were worth five hundred dollars."

There didn't seem to be any answer to this, so Carlyle was silent, permitting himself only a discreet interior smile.

V

When the night crept down in shadowy blue and silver, they threaded the shimmering channel in the rowboat and, tying it to a jutting rock, began climbing the cliff together. The first shelf was ten feet up, wide, and furnishing a natural diving platform. There they sat down in the bright moonlight and watched the faint incessant surge of the waters, almost stilled now as the tide set seaward.

"Are you happy?" he asked suddenly.

She nodded.

"Always happy near the sea. You know," she went on, "I've been thinking all day that you and I are somewhat alike. We're both rebels—only for different reasons. Two years ago, when I was just eighteen, and you were——"

"Twenty-five."

"—well, we were both conventional successes. I was an utterly devastating débutante and you were a prosperous musician just commissioned in the army——"

"Gentleman by act of Congress," he put in ironically.

"Well, at any rate, we both fitted. If our corners were not rubbed off they were at least pulled in. But deep in us both was something that made us require more for happiness. I didn't know what I wanted. I went from man to man, restless, impatient, month by month getting less acquiescent and more dissatisfied. I used to sit sometimes chewing at the insides of my mouth and thinking I was going crazy—I had a frightful sense of transiency. I wanted things now—now—now! Here I was—beautiful—I am, aren't I?"

"Yes," agreed Carlyle tentatively.

Ardita rose suddenly.

"Wait a second. I want to try this delightful-looking sea."

She walked to the end of the ledge and shot out over the sea, doubling up in mid-air and then straightening out and entering the water straight as a blade in a perfect jack-knife dive.

In a minute her voice floated up to him.

"You see, I used to read all day and most of the night. I began to resent society——"

"Come on up here," he interrupted. "What on earth are you doing?"

"Just floating round on my back. I'll be up in a minute. Let me tell you. The only thing I enjoyed was shocking people; wearing something quite impossible and quite charming to a fancy-dress party, going round with the fastest men in New York, and getting into some of the most hellish scrapes imaginable."

The sounds of splashing mingled with her words, and then he heard her hurried breathing as she began climbing up the side of the ledge.

"Go on in!" she called.

Obediently he rose and dived. When he emerged, dripping, and made the climb, he found that she was no longer on the ledge, but after a frightened second he heard her light laughter from another shelf ten feet up. There he joined her and they both sat quietly for a moment, their arms clasped round their knees, panting a little from the climb.

"The family were wild," she said suddenly. "They tried to marry me off. And then when I'd begun to feel that after all life was scarcely worth living I found something"—her eyes went skyward exultantly—"I found something!"

Carlyle waited and her words came with a rush.

"Courage—just that; courage as a rule of life, and something to cling to always. I began to build up this enormous faith in myself. I began to see that in all my idols in the past some manifestation of courage had unconsciously been the thing that attracted me. I began separating courage from the other things of life. All sorts of courage—the beaten, bloody prize-fighter coming up for more—I used to make men take me to prize-fights; the déclassé woman sailing through a nest of cats and looking at them as if they were mud under her feet; the liking what you like always; the utter disregard for other people's opinions—just to live as I liked always and to die in my own way—Did you bring up the cigarettes?"

He handed one over and held a match for her silently.

"Still," Ardita continued, "the men kept gathering—old men and young men, my mental and physical inferiors, most of them, but all intensely desiring to have me—to own this rather magnificent proud tradition I'd built up round me. Do you see?"

"Sort of. You never were beaten and you never apologized."

"Never!"

She sprang to the edge, poised for a moment like a crucified figure against the sky; then describing a dark parabola, plunked without a splash between two silver ripples twenty feet below.

Her voice floated up to him again.

"And courage to me meant ploughing through that dull gray mist that comes down on life—not only overriding people and circumstances but overriding the bleakness of living. A sort of insistence on the value of life and the worth of transient things."

She was climbing up now, and at her last words her head, with the damp yellow hair slicked symmetrically back, appeared on his level.

"All very well," objected Carlyle. "You can call it courage, but your courage is really built, after all, on a pride of birth. You were bred to that defiant attitude. On my gray days even courage is one of the things that's gray and lifeless."

She was sitting near the edge, hugging her knees and gazing abstractedly at the white moon; he was farther back, crammed like a grotesque god into a niche in the rock.

"I don't want to sound like Pollyanna," she began, "but you haven't grasped me yet. My courage is faith—faith in the eternal resilience of me—that joy'll come back, and hope and spontaneity. And I feel that till it does I've got to keep my lips shut and my chin high, and my eyes wide—not necessarily any silly smiling. Oh, I've been through hell without a whine quite often—and the female hell is deadlier than the male."

"But supposing," suggested Carlyle, "that before joy and hope and all that came back the curtain was drawn on you for good?"

Ardita rose, and going to the wall climbed with some difficulty to the next ledge, another ten or fifteen feet above.

"Why," she called back, "then I'd have won!"

He edged out till he could see her.

"Better not dive from there! You'll break your back," he said quickly.

She laughed.

"Not I!"

Slowly she spread her arms and stood there swan-like, radiating a pride in her young perfection that lit a warm glow in Carlyle's heart.

"We're going through the black air with our arms wide," she called, "and our feet straight out behind like a dolphin's tail, and we're going to think we'll never hit the silver down there till suddenly it'll be all warm round us and full of little kissing, caressing waves."

Then she was in the air, and Carlyle involuntarily held his breath. He had not realized that the dive was nearly forty feet. It seemed an eternity before he heard the swift compact sound as she reached the sea.

And it was with his glad sigh of relief when her light watery laughter curled up the side of the cliff and into his anxious ears that he knew he loved her.

VI

Time, having no axe to grind, showered down upon them three days of afternoons. When the sun cleared the port-hole of Ardita's cabin an hour after dawn she rose cheerily, donned her bathing-suit, and went up on deck. The Negroes would leave their work when they saw her, and crowd, chuckling and chattering, to the rail as she floated, an agile minnow, on and under the surface of the clear water. Again in the cool of the afternoon she would swim—and loll and smoke with Carlyle upon the cliff; or else they would lie on their sides in the sands of the southern beach, talking little, but watching the day fade colorfully and tragically into the infinite languor of a tropical evening.

And with the long, sunny hours Ardita's idea of the episode as incidental, madcap, a sprig of romance in a desert of reality, gradually left her. She dreaded the time when he would strike off southward; she dreaded all the eventualities that presented themselves to her; thoughts were suddenly troublesome and decisions odious. Had prayers found place in the pagan rituals of her soul she would have asked of life only to be unmolested for a while, lazily acquiescent to the ready, naïve flow of Carlyle's ideas, his vivid boyish imagination, and the vein of monomania that seemed to run crosswise through his temperament and colored his every action.

But this is not a story of two on an island, nor concerned primarily with love bred of isolation. It is merely the presentation of two personalities, and its idyllic setting among the palms of the Gulf Stream is quite incidental. Most of us are content to exist and breed and fight for the right to do both, and the dominant idea, the foredoomed attempt to control one's destiny, is reserved for the fortunate or unfortunate few. To me the interesting thing about Ardita is the courage that will tarnish with her beauty and youth.

"Take me with you," she said late one night as they sat lazily in the grass under the shadowy spreading palms. The Negroes had brought ashore their musical instruments, and the sound of weird ragtime was drifting softly over on the warm breath of the night. "I'd love to reappear in ten years as a fabulously wealthy high-caste Indian lady," she continued.

Carlyle looked at her quickly.

"You can, you know."

She laughed.

"Is it a proposal of marriage? Extra! Ardita Farnam becomes pirate's bride. Society girl kidnapped by ragtime bank robber."

"It wasn't a bank."

"What was it? Why won't you tell me?"

"I don't want to break down your illusions."

"My dear man, I have no illusions about you."

"I mean your illusions about yourself."

She looked up in surprise.

"About myself! What on earth have I got to do with whatever stray felonies you've committed?"

"That remains to be seen."

She reached over and patted his hand.

"Dear Mr. Curtis Carlyle," she said softly, "are you in love with me?"

"As if it mattered."

"But it does—because I think I'm in love with you."

He looked at her ironically.

"Thus swelling your January total to half a dozen," he suggested. "Suppose I call your bluff and ask you to come to India with me?"

"Shall I?"

He shrugged his shoulders.

"We can get married in Callao."

"What sort of life can you offer me? I don't mean that unkindly, but seriously; what would become of me if the people who want that twenty-thousand-dollar reward ever catch up with you?"

"I thought you weren't afraid."

"I never am—but I won't throw my life away just to show one man I'm not."

"I wish you'd been poor. Just a little poor girl dreaming over a fence in a warm cow country."

"Wouldn't it have been nice?"

"I'd have enjoyed astonishing you—watching your eyes open on things. If you only wanted things! Don't you see?"

"I know—like girls who stare into the windows of jewelry-stores."

"Yes—and want the big oblong watch that's platinum and has diamonds all round the edge. Only you'd decide it was too expensive and choose one of white gold for a hundred dollars. Then I'd say: 'Expensive? I should say not!' And we'd go into the store and pretty soon the platinum one would be gleaming on your wrist."

"That sounds so nice and vulgar—and fun, doesn't it?" murmured Ardita.

"Doesn't it? Can't you see us travelling round and spending money right and left, and being worshipped by bell-boys and waiters? Oh, blessed are the simple rich, for they inherit the earth!"

"I honestly wish we were that way."

"I love you, Ardita," he said gently.

Her face lost its childish look for a moment and become oddly grave.

"I love to be with you," she said, "more than with any man I've ever met. And I like your looks and your dark old hair, and the way you go over the side of the rail when we come ashore. In fact, Curtis Carlyle, I like all the things you do when you're perfectly natural. I think you've got nerve, and you know how I feel about that. Sometimes when you're around I've been tempted to kiss you suddenly and tell you that you were just an idealistic boy with a lot of caste nonsense in his head. Perhaps if I were just a little bit older and a little more bored I'd go with you. As it is, I think I'll go back and marry—that other man."

Over across the silver lake the figures of the Negroes writhed and squirmed in the moonlight, like acrobats who, having been too long inactive, must go through their tricks from sheer surplus energy. In single file they marched, weaving in concentric circles, now with their heads thrown back, now bent over their instruments like piping fauns. And from trombone and saxophone ceaselessly whined a blended melody, sometimes riotous and jubilant, sometimes haunting and plaintive as a death-dance from the Congo's heart.

"Let's dance!" cried Ardita. "I can't sit still with that perfect jazz going on."

Taking her hand he led her out into a broad stretch of hard sandy soil that the moon flooded with great splendor. They floated out like drifting moths under the rich hazy light, and as the fantastic symphony wept and exulted and wavered and despaired, Ardita's last sense of reality dropped away, and she abandoned her imagination to the dreamy summer scents of tropical flowers and the infinite starry spaces overhead, feeling that if she opened her eyes it would be to find herself dancing with a ghost in a land created by her own fancy.

"This is what I should call an exclusive private dance," he whispered.

"I feel quite mad—but delightfully mad!"

"We're enchanted. The shades of unnumbered generations of cannibals are watching us from high up on the side of the cliff there."

"And I'll bet the cannibal women are saying that we dance too close, and that it was immodest of me to come without my nose-ring."

They both laughed softly—and then their laughter died as over across the lake they heard the trombone stop in the middle of a bar, and the saxophones give a startled moan and fade out.

"What's the matter?" called Carlyle.

After a moment's silence they made out the dark figure of a man rounding the silver lake at a run. As he came closer they saw it was Babe in a state of unusual excitement. He drew up before them and gasped out his news in a breath.

"Ship stan'in' off sho' 'bout half a mile, suh. Mose, he uz on watch, he say look's if she's done ancho'd."

"A ship—what kind of a ship?" demanded Carlyle anxiously.

Dismay was in his voice, and Ardita's heart gave a sudden wrench as she saw his whole face suddenly droop.

"He say he don't know, suh."

"Are they landing a boat?"

"No, suh."

"We'll go up," said Carlyle.

They ascended the hill in silence, Ardita's hand still resting in Carlyle's as it had when they finished dancing. She felt it clinch nervously from time to time as though he were unaware of the contact, but though he hurt her she made no attempt to remove it. It seemed an hour's climb before they reached the top and crept cautiously across the silhouetted plateau to the edge of the cliff. After one short look Carlyle involuntarily gave a little cry. It was a revenue boat with six-inch guns mounted fore and aft.

"They know!" he said with a short intake of breath. "They know! They picked up the trail somewhere."

"Are you sure they know about the channel? They may be only standing by to take a look at the island in the morning. From where they are they couldn't see the opening in the cliff."

"They could with field-glasses," he said hopelessly. He looked at his wrist-watch. "It's nearly two now. They won't do anything until dawn, that's certain. Of course there's always the faint possibility that they're waiting for some other ship to join; or for a coaler."

"I suppose we may as well stay right here."

The hours passed and they lay there side by side, very silently, their chins in their hands like dreaming children. In back of them squatted the Negroes, patient, resigned, acquiescent, announcing now and then with sonorous snores that not even the presence of danger could subdue their unconquerable African craving for sleep.

Just before five o'clock Babe approached Carlyle. There were half a dozen rifles aboard the Narcissus he said. Had it been decided to offer no resistance? A pretty good fight might be made, he thought, if they worked out some plan.

Carlyle laughed and shook his head.

"That isn't a Spic army out there, Babe. That's a revenue boat. It'd be like a bow and arrow trying to fight a machine-gun. If you want to bury those bags somewhere and take a chance on recovering them later, go on and do it. But it won't work—they'd dig this island over from one end to the other. It's a lost battle all round, Babe."

Babe inclined his head silently and turned away, and Carlyle's voice was husky as he turned to Ardita.

"There's the best friend I ever had. He'd die for me, and be proud to, if I'd let him."

"You've given up?"

"I've no choice. Of course there's always one way out—the sure way—but that can wait. I wouldn't miss my trial for anything—it'll be an interesting experiment in notoriety. 'Miss Farnam testifies that the pirate's attitude to her was at all times that of a gentleman'."

"Don't!" she said. "I'm awfully sorry."

When the color faded from the sky and lustreless blue changed to leaden gray a commotion was visible on the ship's deck, and they made out a group of officers clad in white duck, gathered near the rail. They had field-glasses in their hands and were attentively examining the islet.

"It's all up," said Carlyle grimly.

"Damn!" whispered Ardita. She felt tears gathering in her eyes.

"We'll go back to the yacht," he said. "I prefer that to being hunted out up here like a 'possum."

Leaving the plateau they descended the hill, and reaching the lake were rowed out to the yacht by the silent Negroes. Then, pale and weary, they sank into the settees and waited.

Half an hour later, in the dim gray light, the nose of the revenue boat appeared in the channel and stopped, evidently fearing that the bay might be too shallow. From the peaceful look of the yacht, the man and the girl in the settees, and the Negroes lounging curiously against the rail, they evidently judged that there would be no resistance, for two boats were lowered casually over the side, one containing an officer and six bluejackets, and the other, four rowers and, in the stern, two gray-haired men in yachting flannels. Ardita and Carlyle stood up, and half unconsciously started toward each other. Then he paused and putting his hand suddenly into his pocket he pulled out a round, glittering object and held it out to her.

"What is it?" she asked wonderingly.

"I'm not positive, but I think from the Russian inscription inside that it's your promised bracelet."

"Where—where on earth——"

"It came out of one of those bags. You see, Curtis Carlyle and his Six Black Buddies, in the middle of their performance in the tearoom of the hotel at Palm Beach, suddenly changed their instruments for automatics and held up the crowd. I took this bracelet from a pretty, over-rouged woman with red hair."

Ardita frowned and then smiled.

"So that's what you did! You *have* got nerve!"

He bowed.

"A well-known bourgeois quality," he said.

And then dawn slanted dynamically across the deck and flung the shadows reeling into gray corners. The dew rose and turned to golden mist, thin as a dream, enveloping them until they seemed gossamer relics of the late night, infinitely transient and already fading. For a moment sea and sky were breathless, and dawn held a pink hand over the young mouth of life—then from out in the lake came the complaint of a rowboat and the swish of oars.

Suddenly against the golden furnace low in the east their two graceful figures melted into one, and he was kissing her spoiled young mouth.

"It's a sort of glory," he murmured after a second.

She smiled up at him.

"Happy, are you?"

Her sigh was a benediction—an ecstatic surety that she was youth and beauty now as much as she would ever know. For another instant life was radiant and time a phantom and their strength eternal—then there was a bumping, scraping sound as the rowboat scraped alongside.

Up the ladder scrambled the two gray-haired men, the officer and two of the sailors with their hands on their revolvers. Mr. Farnam folded his arms and stood looking at his niece.

"So," he said, nodding his head slowly.

With a sigh her arms unwound from Carlyle's neck, and her eyes, transfigured and far away, fell upon the boarding party. Her uncle saw her upper lip slowly swell into that arrogant pout he knew so well.

"So," he repeated savagely. "So this is your idea of—of romance. A runaway affair, with a high-seas pirate."

Ardita glanced at him carelessly.

"What an old fool you are!" she said quietly.

"Is that the best you can say for yourself?"

"No," she said, as if considering. "No, there's something else. There's that well-known phrase with which I have ended most of our conversations for the past few years—'Shut up!'"

And with that she turned, included the two old men, the officer, and the two sailors in a curt glance of contempt, and walked proudly down the companionway.

But had she waited an instant longer she would have heard a sound from her uncle quite unfamiliar in most of their interviews. He gave vent to a whole-hearted amused chuckle, in which the second old man joined.

The latter turned briskly to Carlyle, who had been regarding this scene with an air of cryptic amusement.

"Well, Toby," he said genially, "you incurable, hare-brained, romantic chaser of rainbows, did you find that she was the person you wanted?"

Carlyle smiled confidently.

"Why—naturally," he said. "I've been perfectly sure ever since I first heard tell of her wild career. That's why I had Babe send up the rocket last night."

"I'm glad you did," said Colonel Moreland gravely. "We've been keeping pretty close to you in case you should have trouble with those six strange niggers. And we hoped we'd find you two in some such compromising position," he sighed. "Well, set a crank to catch a crank!"

"Your father and I sat up all night hoping for the best—or perhaps it's the worst. Lord knows you're welcome to her, my boy. She's run me crazy. Did you give her the Russian bracelet my detective got from that Mimi woman?"

Carlyle nodded.

"Sh!" he said. "She's coming on deck."

Ardita appeared at the head of the companionway and gave a quick involuntary glance at Carlyle's wrists. A puzzled look passed across her face. Back aft the Negroes had begun to sing, and the cool lake, fresh with dawn, echoed serenely to their low voices.

"Ardita," said Carlyle unsteadily.

She swayed a step toward him.

"Ardita," he repeated breathlessly, "I've got to tell you the—the truth. It was all a plant, Ardita. My name isn't Carlyle. It's Moreland, Toby Moreland. The story was invented, Ardita, invented out of thin Florida air."

She stared at him, bewildered amazement, disbelief, and anger flowing in quick waves across her face. The three men held their breaths. Moreland, Senior, took a step toward her; Mr. Farnam's mouth dropped a little open as he waited, panic-stricken, for the expected crash.

But it did not come. Ardita's face became suddenly radiant, and with a little laugh she went swiftly to young Moreland and looked up at him without a trace of wrath in her gray eyes.

"Will you swear," she said quietly, "that it was entirely a product of your own brain?"

"I swear," said young Moreland eagerly.

She drew his head down and kissed him gently.

"What an imagination!" she said softly and almost enviously. "I want you to lie to me just as sweetly as you know how for the rest of my life."

The Negroes' voices floated drowsily back, mingled in an air that she had heard them sing before.

> "Time is a thief;
> Gladness and grief
> Cling to the leaf
> As it yellows——"

"What was in the bags?" she asked softly.

"Florida mud," he answered. "That was one of the two true things I told you."

"Perhaps I can guess the other one," she said; and reaching up on her tiptoes she kissed him softly in the illustration.

About Two Nice People

by SHIRLEY JACKSON

A problem of some importance, certainly, these days, is that of anger. When one half of the world is angry at the other half, or one half of a nation is angry at the rest, or one side of town feuds with the other side, it is hardly surprising, when you stop to think about it, that so many people lose their tempers with so many other people. Even if, as in this case, they are two people not usually angry, two people whose lives are obscure and whose emotions are gentle, whose smiles are amiable and whose voices are more apt to be cheerful than raised in fury. Two people, in other words, who would much rather be friends than not and who yet, for some reason, perhaps chemical or sociological or environmental, enter upon a mutual feeling of dislike so intense that only a very drastic means can bring them out of it.

Take two such people:

Ellen Webster was what is referred to among her friends as a "sweet" girl. She had pretty, soft hair and dark, soft eyes, and she dressed in soft colors and wore frequently a lovely old-fashioned brooch which had belonged to her grandmother. Ellen thought of herself as a very happy and very lucky person, because she had a good job, was able to buy herself a fair number of soft-colored dresses and skirts and sweaters and coats and hats; she had, by working hard at it evenings, transformed her one-room apartment from a bare, neat place into a charming little refuge with her sewing basket on the table and a canary at the window; she had a reasonable conviction that someday, perhaps soon, she would fall in love with a nice young man and they would be married and Ellen would devote herself wholeheartedly to children and baking cakes and mending socks. This not-very-unusual situation, with its perfectly ordinary state of mind, was a source of great happiness to Ellen. She was, in a word, not one of those who rail against their fate, who live in sullen hatred of the world. She was—her friends were right—a sweet girl.

On the other hand, even if you would not have called Walter Nesmith sweet, you would very readily have thought of him as a "nice" fellow, or an "agreeable" person, or even—if you happened to be a little old white-haired lady—a "dear boy." There was a subtle resemblance between Ellen Webster and Walter Nesmith. Both of them were the first resort of their friends in trouble, for instance. Walter's ambitions, which included the rest of his life, were refreshingly similar to Ellen's: Walter thought that someday he might meet some sweet girl, and would then devote himself wholeheartedly to coming home of an evening to read his paper and perhaps work in the garden on Sundays.

Walter thought that he would like to have two children, a boy and a girl. Ellen thought that she would like to have three children, a boy and two girls. Walter was very fond of cherry pie, Ellen preferred Boston cream. Ellen enjoyed romantic movies, Walter preferred Westerns. They read almost exactly the same books.

In the ordinary course of events, the friction between Ellen and Walter would have been very slight. But—and what could cause a thing like this?—the ordinary course of events was shattered by a trifle like a telephone call.

Ellen's telephone number was 3—4126. Walter's telephone number was 3—4216. Ellen lived in apartment 3-A and Walter lived in apartment 3-B; these apartments were across the hall from each other and very often Ellen, opening her door at precisely quarter of nine in the morning and going toward the elevator, met Walter, who opened *his* door at precisely quarter of nine in the morning and went toward the elevator. On these occasions Ellen customarily said "Good morning" and looked steadfastly the other way, Walter usually answered "Good morning," and avoided looking in her direction. Ellen thought that a girl who allowed herself to be informal with strangers created a bad impression, and Walter thought that a man who took advantage of living in the same building to strike up an acquaintance with a girl was a man of little principle. One particularly fine morning, he said to Ellen in the elevator, "Lovely day," and she replied, "Yes, isn't it?" and both of them felt scarcely that they had been bold. How this mutual respect for each other's dignity could have degenerated into fury is a mystery not easily understood.

It happened that one evening—and, to do her strict justice, Ellen had had a hard day, she was coming down with a cold, it had rained steadily for a week, her stockings were unwashed, and she had broken a fingernail—the phone which had the number 3—4126 rang. Ellen had been opening a can of chicken soup in the kitchenette, and she had her hands full; she said "Darn," and managed to drop and break a cup in her hurry to answer the phone.

"Hello?" she said, thinking, *This is going to be something cheerful.*

"Hello, is Walter there?"

"Walter?"

"Walter Nesmith. I want to speak to Walter, please."

"This is the wrong number," Ellen said thinking with the self-pity that comes with the first stages of a head cold that no one ever called *her.*

"Is this three—four two one six?"

"This is three four one two six," Ellen said, and hung up.

At that time, although she knew that the person in the apartment across the hall was named Walter Nesmith, she could not have told the color of his hair or even of the outside of his apartment door. She went back to her soup and had a match in her hand to light the stove when the phone rang again.

"Hello?" Ellen said without enthusiasm; this *could* be someone cheerful, she was thinking.

"Hello, is Walter there?"

"This is the wrong number again," Ellen said; if she had not been such a very sweet girl she might have let more irritation show in her voice.

"I *want* to *speak* to Walter Nesmith, *please.*"

"This is three—four one two six again," Ellen said patiently. "You want three—four two one six."

"What?" said the voice.

"This," said Ellen, "is number three—four one two six. The number you want is three—four two one six." Like anyone who has tried to say a series of numbers several times, she found her anger growing. Surely anyone of *normal* intelligence, she was thinking, surely anyone *ought* to be able to dial a phone, anyone who can't dial a phone shouldn't be allowed to have a nickel.

She had got all the way back into the kitchenette and was reaching out for the can of soup before the phone rang again. This time when she answered she said "Hello?" rather sharply for Ellen, and with no illusions about who it was going to be.

"Hello, may I please speak to Walter?"

At that point it started. Ellen had a headache and it was raining and she was tired and she was apparently not going to get any chicken soup until this annoyance was stopped.

"Just a minute," she said into the phone.

She put the phone down with an understandable bang on the table, and marched, without taking time to think, out of her apartment and up to the door across the hall. "Walter Nesmith" said a small card at the doorbell. Ellen rang the doorbell with what was, for her, a vicious poke. When the door opened she said immediately, without looking at him:

"Are you Walter Nesmith?"

Now Walter had had a hard day, too, and *he* was coming down with a cold, and *he* had been trying ineffectually to make himself a cup of hot tea in which he intended to put a spoonful of honey to ease his throat, that being a remedy his aunt had always recommended for the first onslaught of a cold. If there had been one fraction less irritation in Ellen's voice, or if Walter had not taken off his shoes when he came home that night, it might very probably have turned out to be a pleasant introduction, with Walter and Ellen dining together on chicken soup and hot tea, and perhaps even sharing a bottle of cough medicine. But when Walter opened the door and heard Ellen's voice, he was unable to answer her cordially, and so he said briefly:

"I am. Why?"

"Will you please come and answer my phone?" said Ellen, too annoyed to realize that this request might perhaps bewilder Walter.

"Answer your phone?" said Walter stupidly.

"Answer my phone," said Ellen firmly. She turned and went back across the hall, and Walter stood in his doorway in his stocking feet and watched her numbly. "Come on," she said sharply, as she went into her own apartment, and Walter, wondering briefly if they allowed harmless lunatics to live alone as though they were just like other people, hesitated for an instant and then followed her, on the theory that it would be wiser to do what she said when she seemed so cross, and reassuring himself that he could leave the door open and yell for help if necessary. Ellen stamped into her apartment and pointed at the phone where it lay on the table. "There. Answer it."

Eying her sideways, Walter edged over to the phone and picked it up. "Hello," he said nervously. Then, "Hello? Hello?" Looking at her over the top of the phone, he said, "What do you want me to do now?"

"Do you mean to say," said Ellen ominously, "that that terrible terrible person has hung up?"

"I guess so," said Walter, and fled back to his apartment.

The door had only just closed behind him when the phone rang again, and Ellen, answering it, heard, "May I speak to Walter, please?"

Not a very serious mischance, surely. But the next morning Walter pointedly avoided going down in the elevator with Ellen, and sometime during that day the deliveryman left a package addressed to Ellen at Walter's door.

When Walter found the package he took it manfully under his arm and went boldly across the hall, and rang Ellen's doorbell. When Ellen opened her door she thought at first—and she may have been justified—that Walter had come to apologize for the phone call the evening before, and she even thought that the package under his arm might contain something delightfully unexpected, like a box of candy. They lost another chance then; if Walter had not held out the package and said "Here," Ellen would not have gone on thinking that he was trying to apologize in his own shy way, and she would certainly not have smiled warmly, and said, "You *shouldn't* have bothered."

Walter, who regarded transporting a misdelivered parcel across the hall as relatively little bother, said blankly, "No bother at all," and Ellen, still deceived, said, "But it really wasn't *that* important."

Walter went back into his own apartment convinced that this was a very odd girl indeed, and Ellen, finding that the package had been mailed to her and contained a wool scarf knitted by a cousin, was as much angry as embarrassed because, once having imagined that an apology is forthcoming, it is very annoying not to have one after all, and particularly to have a wool scarf instead of a box of candy.

How this situation disintegrated into the white-hot fury which rose between these two is a puzzle, except for the basic fact that when once a series of misadventures has begun between two people, everything tends to contribute further to a state of misunderstanding. Thus, Ellen opened a letter of Walter's by mistake, and Walter dropped a bottle of milk—he was still trying to cure his cold, and thought that perhaps milk toast was the thing—directly outside Ellen's door, so that even after his nervous attempts to clear it up, the floor was still littered with fragments of glass, and puddled with milk.

Then Ellen—who believed by now that Walter had thrown the bottle of milk against her door—allowed herself to become so far confused by this succession of small annoyances that she actually wrote and mailed a letter to Walter, asking politely that he try to turn down his radio a little in the late evenings. Walter replied with a frigid letter to the effect that certainly if he had known that she was bothered by his radio, he should surely never have dreamed——

That evening, perhaps by accident, his radio was so loud that Ellen's canary woke up and chirped hysterically, and Ellen, pacing her floor in incoherent fury, might have been heard—if there had been anyone to hear her, and if Walter's radio had not been so loud—to say, "I'll get even with him!" A phrase, it must be said, which Ellen had never used before in her life.

Ellen made her preparations with a sort of loving care that might well have been lavished on some more worthy object. When the alarm went off she turned in her sleep and smiled before quite waking up, and, once awake and the alarm turned off, she almost laughed out loud. In her slippers and gown, the clock in her hand, she went across her small apartment to the phone; the number was one she was not soon apt to forget. The dial tone sounded amazingly loud, and for a minute she was almost frightened out of her resolution. Then, setting her teeth, she dialed the number, her hand steady. After a second's interminable wait, the ringing began. The phone at the other end rang three times, four times, with what seemed interminable waits between, as though even the mechanical phone system hesitated at this act. Then, at last, there was an irritable crash at the other end of the line, and a voice said, "Wah?"

"Good morning," said Ellen brightly. "I'm so terribly sorry to disturb you at this hour."

"Wah?"

"This is Ellen Webster," said Ellen still brightly. "I called to tell you that my clock has stopped——"

"Wah?"

"—and I wonder if you could tell me what time it is?"

There was a short pause at the other end of the line. Then after a minute, his voice came back: "Tenny minna fah."

"I beg your pardon?"

There was another short pause at the other end of the line, as of someone opening his eyes with a shock. "Twenty minutes after four," he said. *"Twenty minutes after four."*

"The reason I thought of asking you," Ellen said sweetly, "was that you were so *very* obliging before. About the radio, I mean."

"——calling a person at——"

"Thanks so much," said Ellen. "Good-by."

She felt fairly certain that he would not call her back, but she sat on her bed and giggled a little before she went back to sleep.

Walter's response to this was miserably weak: he contacted a neighboring delicatessen a day or so later, and had an assortment of evil-smelling cheese left in Ellen's apartment while she was out. This, which required persuading the superintendent to open Ellen's apartment so that the package might be left inside, was a poor revenge but a monstrous exercise of imagination upon Walter's part, so that, in one sense, Ellen was already bringing out in him qualities he never knew he had. The cheese, it turned out, more than evened the score: the apartment was small, the day was warm, and Ellen did not get home until late, and long after most of the other tenants on the floor had gone to the superintendent with their complaints about something dead in the woodwork.

Since breaking and entering had thus become one of the rules of their game, Ellen felt privileged to retaliate in kind upon Walter. It was with great joy, some evenings later, that Ellen, sitting in her odorous apartment, heard Walter's scream of pure terror when he put his feet into his slippers and found a raw egg in each.

Walter had another weapon, however, which he had been so far reluctant to use; it was a howitzer of such proportions that Walter felt its use would end warfare utterly. After the raw eggs he felt no compunction whatever in bringing out his heavy artillery.

It seemed to Ellen, at first, as though peace had been declared. For almost a week things went along smoothly; Walter kept his radio tuned down almost to inaudibility, so that Ellen got plenty of sleep. She was over her cold, the sun had come out, and on Saturday morning she spent three hours shopping, and found exactly the dress she wanted at less than she expected to pay.

About Saturday noon she stepped out of the elevator, her packages under her arm, and walked briskly down the hall to her apartment, making, as usual, a wide half circle to avoid coming into contact with the area around Walter's door.

Her apartment door, to her surprise, was open, but before she had time to phrase a question in her own mind, she had stepped inside and come face to face with a lady who—not to make any more mysteries—was Walter Nesmith's aunt, and a wicked old lady in her own way, possessing none of Walter's timidity and none of his tact.

"Who?" said Ellen weakly, standing in the doorway.

"Come in and close the door," said the old lady darkly. "I don't think you'll want your neighbors to hear what I have to say. I," she continued as Ellen obeyed mechanically, "am Mrs. Harold Vongarten Nesmith. Walter Nesmith, young woman, is my nephew."

"Then you are in the wrong apartment," said Ellen, quite politely considering the reaction which Walter Nesmith's name was beginning by now to arouse in her. "You want Apartment Three-B, across the hall."

"I do *not*," said the old lady firmly. "I came here to see the designing young woman who has been shamelessly pursuing my nephew, and to warn her"—the old lady shook her gloves menacingly—"to warn her that *not one cent* shall she have from me if she marries Walter Nesmith."

"Marries?" said Ellen, thoughts too great for words in her heart.

"It has long been my opinion that some young woman would be after Walter Nesmith for his money," said Walter's aunt with satisfaction.

"Believe me," said Ellen wholeheartedly, "there is not that much money in the world."

"You deny it?" The old lady leaned back and smiled triumphantly. "I expected something of the sort. Walter," she called suddenly, and then, putting her head back and howling, "Wal-l-l-l-ter."

"Sh-h-h," said Ellen fearfully. "They'll hear you all over."

"I expect them to," said the old lady. "Wal-l-l-l—— Oh, there you are."

Ellen turned, and saw Walter Nesmith, with triumph in his eyes, peering around the edge of the door. "Did it work?" he asked.

"She denies everything," said his aunt.

"About the eggs?" Walter said, confused. "You mean, she denies about the eggs and the phone call and——"

"Look," Ellen said to Walter, stamping across the floor to look him straight in the eye, "of all the insufferable, conceited, rude, self-satisfied——"

"What?" said Walter.

"I wouldn't want to marry you," said Ellen, "if—if——" She stopped for a word, helpless.

"If he were the last man on earth," Walter's aunt supplied obligingly. "I think she's really after your *money*, Walter."

Walter stared at his aunt. "I didn't tell you to tell her——" he began. He gasped, and tried again. "I mean," he said, "I never thought——" He appealed to Ellen. "I don't want to marry you, either," he said, and then gasped again, and said, "I mean, I told my aunt to come and tell you——"

"If this is a proposal," Ellen said coldly, "I decline."

"All I wanted her to do was scare you," Walter said finally.

"It's a good way," his aunt said complacently. "Turned out to be the only way with your Uncle Charles and a Hungarian adventuress."

"I mean," Walter said desperately to Ellen, "she owns this building. I mean, I wanted her to tell you that if you didn't stop—I mean, I wanted her to scare you——"

"Apartments are too hard to get these days," his aunt said. "That would have been *too* unkind."

"That's how I got my apartment at all, you see," Walter said to Ellen, still under the impression he was explaining something Ellen wanted to understand.

"Since you have an apartment," Ellen said with restraint, "may I suggest that you take your aunt and the both of you——"

The phone rang.

"Excuse me," said Ellen mechanically, moving to answer it. "Hello?" she said.

"Hello, may I speak to Walter, please?"

Ellen smiled rather in the manner that Lady Macbeth might have smiled if she found a run in her stocking.

"It's for you," she said, holding the phone out to Walter.

"For me?" he said, surprised. "Who is it?"

"I really could not say," said Ellen sweetly. "Since you have so many friends that one phone is not adequate to answer all their calls——"

Since Walter made no move to take the phone, she put it gently back on the hook.

"They'll call again," she assured him, still smiling in that terrible fashion.

"I ought to turn you both out," said Walter's aunt. She turned to Ellen. "Young woman," she said, "do you deny that all this nonsense with eggs and telephone calls is an attempt to entangle my nephew into matrimony?"

"Certainly not," Ellen said. "I mean, I *do* deny it."

"Walter Nesmith," said his aunt, "do you admit that all your finagling with cheeses and radios is an attempt to strike up an acquaintance with this young woman?"

"Certainly," said Walter. "I mean, I do *not* admit it."

"Good," said Walter's aunt. "You are precisely the pair of silly fools I would have picked out for each other." She rose with great dignity, motioned Walter away from her, and started for the door. "Remember," she said, shaking her gloves again at Ellen, "not one cent."

She opened the door and started down the hall, her handkerchief over her eyes, and—a sorry thing in such an old lady—laughing until she had to stop and lean against the wall near the elevator.

"I'm sorry," Walter was saying to Ellen, almost babbling, "I'm *really* sorry this time—please believe me, I had *no* idea—I wouldn't for the world—nothing but the most profound respect—a joke, you know—hope you didn't really think——"

"I understand perfectly," Ellen said icily. "It is all perfectly clear. It only goes to show what I have always believed about young men who think that all they have to do is——"

The phone rang.

Ellen waited a minute before she spoke. Then she said, "You might as well answer it."

"I'm *terribly* sorry," Walter said, not moving toward the phone. "I mean, I'm *terribly* sorry." He waved his hands in the air. "About what she said about what she thought about what you wanted me to do——" His voice trailed off miserably.

Suddenly Ellen began to giggle.

Anger is certainly a problem that will bear much analysis. It is hardly surprising that one person may be angry at another, particularly if these are two people who are gentle, usually, and rarely angry, whose emotions tend to be mild and who would rather be friends with everyone than be enemies with anyone. Such an anger argues a situation so acute that only the most drastic readjustment can remedy it.

Either Walter Nesmith or Ellen Webster could have moved, of course. But, as Walter's aunt had pointed out, apartments are not that easy to come by, and their motives and their telephone numbers were by now so inextricably mixed that on the whole it seemed more reasonable not to bother.

Moreover, Walter's aunt, who still snickers when her nephew's name is mentioned, did not keep them long in suspense, after all. She was not lavish, certainly, but she wrote them a letter which both of them found completely confusing and which enclosed a check adequate for a down payment on the extremely modest house in the country they decided upon without disagreement. They even compromised and had four children—two boys and two girls.

L'Elégance

by RUMER GODDEN

"It's so queer not to tell," said Madeleine. "Everyone says where they are going for their summer holidays."

It was tossed into the air for Miss Mountfort to pick up—if she chose. Miss Mountfort did not choose, but went on winding the wide satin ribbon on to its card. The ribbon was fuchsia coloured, Swiss, with a central stripe of grey embroidered with black and silver. "But *wickedly expensive!*" the client had said, fingering it wistfully. The simple Madeleine would have agreed from her heart, but Miss Mountfort was one of the best saleswomen in Pope and Ransome's and, "It is elegant, Madam," she had said austerely. "One must expect to pay for that." The client had bought the ribbon.

Elegant was a word Miss Mountfort used often. Her favourite magazine, that she lived by, was *Elegance, The Way to Gracious Living.* One of the *Elegance* maxims was: A lady never gossips about her private affairs; and now Miss Mountfort noted the measure on the ribbon card, deducted—in her head—the length she had just sold, carefully wrote in the stock figure, returned the ribbon to the drawer, all without speaking. "Everyone tells where they are going," said Madeleine again. Miss Mountfort did not answer that either.

Madeleine knew Miss Mountfort went to an hotel in France but in five years' prying she had not been able to find out where it was. "Why won't you tell?" she asked exasperated.

"Why do you want to know?"

"I might come with you."

Heaven forbid! But Miss Mountfort did not say it. She pressed the ribbon drawer to, very firmly, and said instead, "That would be impossible."

"Why?"

Miss Mountfort and Madeleine not only worked on the same counter, at home they lived on the same landing—in fact it was Madeleine who had found the house in Howard Road where the bed-sitting rooms were large, passably clean and comfortable, each with a gas-ring and ventilated cupboard for food. Miss Mountfort and Madeleine came to work together, and if Madeleine were not going out, went home together as well. If either had anything especial to eat or drink they shared it—"though our tastes are not the same," Miss Mountfort told everyone who knew them. She said no more than that but her pursed mouth was expressive. She and Madeleine were, Miss Mountfort supposed, friends—almost cronies, she had to admit reluctantly—but "friends" does not mean "peers" and, "There wouldn't be room in the hotel," said Miss Mountfort.

"Hasn't it chalets or camping?"

Chalets or camping! The Pierrefonds! But again she did not say it; it would have been a waste of time to try and explain to Madeleine what the Hotel Pierrefonds was.

It had been the private home of a cabinet minister. That, to Miss Mountfort, summed it up; even at the station his aura seemed to meet her. The minister had travelled up to Paris every day; "They stopped the Express for him morning and evening," Madame Voday, the manageress, had told her. Miss Mountfort had never met a French cabinet minister, but every year as she stepped off the train she remembered him with satisfaction. She saw him always with a grey top hat, a frock coat, striped morning trousers, grey spats, white linen, and a dispatch case with a golden crest; he wore a small white goatee and the slip of red ribbon in his buttonhole, the Legion of Honour. He was surrounded, of course, by railway officials; Miss Mountfort always bowed most graciously to right and left as she walked across the platform to her taxi.

The minister's exclusiveness was in the hotel still. For instance, August was not its busy time. "No, we are not for trippers," said Madame Voday. The Pierrefonds' clientele drove out from Paris at weekends to lunch or dine in quiet; a few took weekend fishing rights. In the shooting season it was full, and it was here that the agents and big customers of the champagne companies stayed, so that their wives could enjoy the garden and river walks while they did their business at the great houses at Pommery, Krüg, or Moët et Chandon—Miss Mountfort enjoyed saying those names, especially Veuve Clicquot. Of course, all summer long there were the motorists who stayed only for a night; English on their way to Italy or Switzerland, or rich touring Americans—to Miss Mountfort all Americans were rich and touring—"I have experience of them," she could say with pride.

She had had experience of several foreigners, for at Pope and Ransome's Miss Mountfort was often sent for from other departments to deal with overseas visitors. "It's an advantage speaking French," she said modestly, "and of course, having travelled, I understand currencies and the export regulations."

"You have travelled a great deal?" the customers would ask, surprised, and it was with peculiar pleasure that she could say, "I take my holiday on the Continent each year."

She had read of the Pierrefonds in a travel article in *Elegance* five years ago. The hotel was on the Marne just outside the little town that to Madeleine would have been dull. . . . "Of course. It is a connoisseur's, a vintage town," said Miss Mountfort. She did not really know if a town could be so described but it seemed to her to fit the quiet mellowness of this little place among the cherry orchards and vineyards. Had the hotel been on the coast or nearer Paris or close to the race course of Chantilly its prices would have been so high that Miss Mountfort could not have stayed there at all: as it was, she could manage one week and every year she took the same room, a third floor room, it was true, but it overlooked the garden and had a balcony. For the second week of the holidays she stayed at home. "I ask you!" cried Madeleine. "Stewing in London when you can get away!"

"I can't," said Miss Mountfort. "I can't afford another week."

"You don't have to go to such an expensive hotel."

"I like it expensive."

Madeleine had never heard of that as a reason for liking before. "But what do you *do* among all those grand people?" she said. "You must be miserably lonely."

Miss Mountfort preferred to say nothing to that.

Early on the next Sunday morning she left Victoria station for Paris. She stayed the night in Paris at a small hotel on the Left Bank, but she carefully eschewed places that would, for instance, have amused Madeleine: the raffish Deux Magots, or the book stalls on the Quais. She dined at a small restaurant near the hotel and went to bed early. Next morning was spent walking in the Champs Elysées and down the rue de la Paix and Faubourg St. Honoré, studying elegance. She always allowed herself a treat by buying a handkerchief at the Maison Blanc, paying particular attention to the manners of the saleswomen. Lunch was a cake and a cup of coffee at a *salon de thé*. In the afternoon she crossed Paris to the Gare de l'Est, took the three-thirty train, and in the station taxi as usual, arrived just after five at the Pierrefonds.

As soon as she saw it her heart lifted. How much she liked it! It was not a large house but it was pretty; its white walls and green shutters matched the chestnut trees in the gravelled courtyard that lay between it and the road. At the back the lawns sloped down to a private walk along the river. There was a little boat-house, a pool with water lilies; the terrace below the house was set with white-painted iron tables and chairs under blue garden umbrellas; the terrace was edged with arches of white scrolled iron, up which morning-glory creepers climbed. Each afternoon, in supreme satisfaction, Miss Mountfort would drink a *citron pressé* at the third table from the left.

Her routine was established. She arrived always on the afternoon of the third Monday in August, and left on the following Monday morning. If I went on Sunday night, she thought, they might guess I have to work. She flattered herself that she looked a woman of means—means for a week anyhow—leisured, single, but quite self-contained. She knew she looked refined; she was lucky in being small, with small bones and little hands and feet. She was not quite as pleased with her figure, which was undeniably plump, "especially in places," teased Madeleine, which upset Miss Mountfort. "Why do you mind? It's nice," said Madeleine. Miss Mountfort's skin was pale and covered with green-gold freckles, a green-gold that picked up the colour of her eyes, green as gooseberries behind her spectacles; her hair was mouse colour but with a soft curl that she spoilt by frizzing it and putting it under a net. Madeleine was always trying to make her wear rouge: "You need colour," Madeleine often told her, and Miss Mountfort said, just as often, "No thank you." She disapproved of Madeleine's heavy rouge and lipstick, though they set off her dark hair and great black eyes.

"But don't you *want* to be pretty?" asked Madeleine. Miss Mountfort preferred to be what Madame Voday called "*bien.*"

Her blue leather suitcase, though old, was good—it had belonged to her mother; her stocking and handkerchief cases matched her rose-coloured sponge bag and her quilted rose silk dressing jacket—she had made that herself from an *Elegance* pattern. Her bedroom slippers were rose-coloured too, and it all looked perfectly presentable and well-to-do, unless the chambermaid noticed everything was the same and unused from year to year. As for clothes, Miss Mountfort patronized a second-hand shop where she bought models and she had always known how to look after them. Her gloves were French and she bought her shoes at Pope and Ransome's—"even with our discount they're too expensive," Madeleine said, but Miss Mountfort made each pair last a long time. Every year, before her holiday, she bought a cake of expensive soap.

There was, to her, an infinite satisfaction in these minuscule arrangements. Her daily plan at the Pierrefonds was apt to be minuscule too: she had her morning coffee on her balcony—or in bed if the weather were not kind. She dressed, and leaving her room neat, walked slowly into the town—slowly to make the walk last—took more coffee at the patisserie in the square and walked slowly back to luncheon. In the afternoon she had a short sleep, then sat on the balcony and read the *Elegance* serials—the numbers saved all the year round for this. Later, she washed her face and hands, redid her hair, and descended to the garden where, under her particular umbrella, she added two inches to her crocheted lace. At four o'clock she ordered her lemon, after which she went for a walk along the river, preferring to take several turns on the private way rather than cross the small bridge over a dyke and walk on the public path which was used for towing barges and fishing, public fishing; "public" instantly condemned it in Miss Mountfort's eyes. At five-thirty she went in, had another rest, and an hour later dressed for dinner and came down into the lounge. This was the time the motorists arrived and the residents came in—the interesting time, thought Miss Mountfort. She could not have an aperitif—it would have been too much for her finances—but she found enjoyment in watching the other guests drink theirs. Dinner was late, too late for her comfort; she and Madeleine, when they came home from work, had a tea-supper at half past six. Miss Mountfort would have liked to forget that fact at the Pierrefonds, but her empty stomach rumbled rudely and loudly to remind her; often it had to stay empty until half past eight or even nine, and it was usually ten o'clock before she returned to the lounge, ordered a *filtre*, and read the papers other people had left behind in the hotel. There was a stack of them—careless, Miss Mountfort thought;

her own copy of Elegance lay carefully guarded on her knee. When the lounge emptied, as it did soon after dinner, she went up to bed.

It sometimes occurred to her that in this programme there was a great deal of rest. Well, I go there to rest, she thought; yet every year, in her lonely room, Miss Mountfort, with a surprising stab of jealousy, could not help remembering Madeleine's tales of the holiday camp where they danced and picnicked at night. "Barbecues, moonlight excursions," Madeleine had told her. "You can't imagine what fun."

"I can imagine!" Miss Mountfort had answered in her primmest voice.

"But you do talk to people in that hotel of yours?" Madeleine had once asked.

"Of course," said Miss Mountfort but that was not true; speaking French at Pope and Ransome's was one thing, speaking it at the Pierrefonds was another; and though occasionally Miss Mountfort came to the rescue of a tongue-tied Englishman or American, mostly she did no more than bow, morning and evening, to the other guests.

In the dining-room hers was often the only table laid for one; she could see her loneliness reflected over and over again in the Empire mirrors that hung on the green-and-gold walls, but she saw nothing to pity in it. "Myself with napery," she might have said—Elegance always called it napery—"Myself with silver and glass . . . with my own half bottle of wine, with the vase that holds a single red rose—such excellent taste." As she watched herself eat she became more and more mannered and as she held her fork her little finger waved daintily in the air.

"But what will you get out of it?" asked Madeleine. Miss Mountfort could have answered, quite simply, "It." It, itself; "A Way of Gracious Living." This week would last her all the year, endow her, make her different, but, "You are getting older," Madeleine said often and Miss Mountfort knew very well that "What will you get out of it?" meant, not "What" but "Who."

Madeleine had a friend, "Which means more than a friend," said Miss Mountfort dryly. Madeleine and her Stan made no bones about how they felt; even in front of a third person—me, said Miss Mountfort —Stan would pull Madeleine down on his knee; even in the street he would put his arm round her and let his hand play on her big breasts. That had a strangely strong effect on Miss Mountfort; it filled her with anger in which tremors would shake her and give her physical heartburn. "He is drunk!" she would say furiously.

"Then I like him drunk," said Madeleine and as he rocked her she would croon, "Stan. My great big Stan! Teddybear, Stan!"

"You might at least call him Stanley," Miss Mountfort had once snapped out. Madeleine had looked at Miss Mountfort with eyes that were so honest that Miss Mountfort could not encounter them. "Why do you hate us?" asked Madeleine.

She was not always as mild. It was she who had discovered that Miss Mountfort's name was Aimée; it had been Amy but Miss Mountfort had changed it—it was ironic that it was Madeleine who had been given a French name. "Aimée and never been loved!" taunted Madeleine.

"I do not wish to be loved," said Miss Mountfort. It upheld her to add, "by anyone you are likely to know."

"But it seems a queer way to enjoy oneself," Stan himself had said, "to go off by yourself all alone."

Miss Mountfort did not answer that either. If they had only known it, she was not alone—there was one final luxury she permitted herself in this week of holiday: the luxury of Raoul.

Raoul de Malencourt. That was his name. He came down every evening from Paris; the Express was not stopped for him because he came by car. The car was left under the chestnut trees. "What is the most expensive car?" she had once asked Stan. "A Cad—Cadillac or a Rolls," Stan had said, and sometimes Raoul had a Cadillac, sometimes a Rolls Royce. Raoul wore . . . "perfectly cut clothes," said Miss Mountfort uncertainly—she was not versed in gentlemen's clothes—but his height and leanness showed them off. Sometimes he wore a blazer, dark blue, with a crest—as on the minister's dispatch-case—embroidered on the pocket. Raoul was bronzed, his dark hair just touched with grey. He had small humorous wrinkles round his eyes when he laughed. Miss Mountfort was proud of Raoul—Madeleine, who did not read *Elegance*, could not possibly have imagined him. When he walked into the lounge he knew at once where Miss Mountfort was; as he sat down by her, his eyes . . . *devoured* her, thought Miss Mountfort, and here she had a tremor, a small delicious one, not at all like the painful upsets caused by Stan. "Did you have your rest, my darling?" "Darling" was said very low because of Paul the garçon: "Never show your feelings in public," taught *Elegance*. Raoul did not kiss her, or touch her—yet.

Madame Voday always gave them the best table in the dining-room, the small one in the window. From her lonely one Miss Mountfort could almost see her head bending to his, his to hers; their reflections seemed to be in the panes as they watched the sunset, a brilliant deep pink sunset to match the long, hot, rosy day. "What did you do all day?" "Walked and lazed. And you?" "A hundred and one things.

They are not important now." They ate the menu at twelve hundred francs—Miss Mountfort, as a resident *en pension*, was only entitled to the one at eight hundred and fifty. They drank . . . a Chambertin, thought Miss Mountfort, or *blanc-de-blanc* or pink champagne—she had never even seen pink champagne. "You spoil me, Raoul." "Nothing is too good for you." Sometimes at dinner the Pierrefonds waiters found Miss Mountfort sitting at her table with her eyes tightly shut.

When she ordered her coffee in the lounge she often almost said "*Deux filtres, une fine.*" "Only one brandy?" Madeleine would have asked, and Miss Mountfort could imagine herself explaining, "Raoul does not like me to smell of spirits" and, with another *Elegance* maxim: "A lady should eat or drink nothing that taints the breath."

Then they went upstairs to bed. . . . Here Miss Mountfort had always to break off. She had to wait until she had locked the door, burrowed under the bedclothes and turned off the light before she dared to think those hot beating thoughts. "*Aimée, Aimée chérie, bien Aimée.*" It was a whisper, fragrant in the dark. In the dark she could forget that the whisper was her own.

It was on the second day that Madame Voday told her, "We have a new chef, a new chef and trouble!" She sighed.

"I had noticed a difference," said Miss Mountfort.

The Pierrefonds was one of those hotels in which no trace of the ruder side of service was allowed to be seen. Cleaning was done before the guests were up; no one caught sight of as much as a vacuum cleaner in action. The bedrooms were done behind closed doors when the guests were downstairs; did anyone surprise a chambermaid making a bed, a porter with a pail, they vanished like wraiths; like wraiths they would appear at the sound of the right bell. In the dining-room the food came in as if it had fallen as manna just outside the service door; no sound or smell announced it; but this year the dining-room, even the lounge and hall were filled with an unmistakable clatter; there was also the sound of a loud voice singing. Then that is the new chef, thought Miss Mountfort, marvelling. She soon learned that he would bang open any of the doors that led from the kitchen wing and walk calmly through the lounge or hall to the bar to fetch a fresh bottle of rum or kirsch or brandy; he was accompanied by the flapping of comfortably loose slippers, and he would nod familiarly to a client as he came and went.

"He is always drunk, and on red wine!" said Madame Voday in despair.

"A bad kind of drinking, I believe," said Miss Mountfort primly.

At dinner, that second night, he burst into the dining-room wiping his hands on his trousers as he stood watching them eat, and smacking his lips, an unspeakably vulgar noise. Miss Mountfort ate on, her finger daintily raised, her eyes looking steadily into the sunset, but she wished he would go away; he disturbed her thoughts.

"*Ça va?*" His booming great voice came across her ears. It was not addressed to her, of course, but to the tables where special food had been ordered.

All the food was special—"When he cooks it," said Madame Voday. "But he is lazy!" The cuisine at the Pierrefonds had been good before but now it was outstanding.

Miss Mountfort had always pronounced that it was unladylike to care about food, perhaps as a reaction from Madeleine and Stan. They liked such vulgar food: steak and kidney pie, tripe and onions, roast beef and Yorkshire pudding, chitterlings. Miss Mountfort shuddered. "Well, what kind of food do you like?" Stan had asked her, and Miss Mountfort had answered distantly, "I like real French cooking."

Stan had looked at her in a queer kind of way. "I'm surprised you do," he said, and thoughtfully, "I've been in France myself. I wonder if you really do?"

Miss Mountfort certainly did now. She had always picked at her food but on this holiday she found herself looking forward from one meal to the next—almost greedily, she thought, distressed. She could not help it; juices she had not known she possessed had woken in her mouth.

"If Chef did not drink," said Madame Voday, "he would be in Paris or Monte Carlo." She hesitated and added, "It's not only drink"—she had lowered her voice—"You may have noticed that we have only elderly maids now. I have had to send four girls away. You remember Mauricette . . ." As Miss Mountfort listened, the kind of tremors she thought she had left behind with Stan began to shake her again.

On Wednesday evening, the third of her stay, the chef came into the dining-room with his, by now, familiar smell; he reeked of wine and—man, thought Miss Mountfort. She would not call it "sweat." Gentlemen, like Raoul, smelled of clean linen, eau de cologne, and good tobacco perhaps—she was prepared to allow tobacco, providing it were good. Her nostrils twitched, offended, and she held her napkin up to her lips.

"Well, *mes lapins,*" came the big voice. *Lapins!* That meant rabbits, and to guests! "You eat well." He surveyed them benevolently, beaming at the whole room. "You eat well." It was a statement, not a question.

A party of Americans was at the next table to Miss Mountfort and one of them—an ignorant man, she thought—found fit to raise his glass to the chef. "*Formidable!*" he called, and asked how the dish was made —it was strange what fluent French the ignorant American spoke. The chef immediately crossed the room to him.

A mastodon, not a man, thought Miss Mountfort distastefully, and indeed among the small tables it was an elephant's progress, powerful but soft-footed. To her, anything unusually large was vulgar and there was something most unhappily vulgar about the man in the blue-and-white checked cook's trousers, blue shirt with rolled-up sleeves, thick white apron, handkerchief tied round the neck, and high white cap.

The chef had twinkling eyes, a low twinkle, thought Miss Mountfort. They were fixed now on the American girls whose necklines were decidedly too low. From the back of his trousers another handkerchief hung; he pulled it out as he stood talking and there, in the dining-room in front of them all, rubbed his hands and mopped his face, then unbuttoned his shirt and fanned his chest. The Americans only laughed. Miss Mountfort picked up her fork and began coldly to eat her fish.

The chef seemed to sense her. He stopped talking and turned himself round so that he faced her table. Miss Mountfort caught her breath and the tines of her fork sounded against her plate but she continued to eat. "I *beg* your pardon," said the chef, "I did not know Madame la Duchesse anglaise was staying in the hotel." Miss Mountfort heard a laugh and looked up quickly. He was holding his two little fingers stiffly out in imitation of hers.

She tried to look unmoved—absolutely indifferent, wished Miss Mountfort—but she felt a deep, painfully hot blush rise up her neck and stain her face. The chef must have seen it too for he dropped his hands at once and turned to go; but he was not abashed; as if he were sorry—sorry, thought Miss Mountfort, and a choking sound rose up in her—as he went, and in front of everyone, he patted her consolingly on the shoulder. Then, as if it were a signal for her alone, he let his fingers linger for a moment on her bare neck.

Miss Mountfort could not sleep that night. Her neck, where he had touched it, burned; she burned all over. "Raoul would have knocked him down," she said, but it was strangely little comfort. How could an ephemeral Raoul knock down an actual chef? "Great bloated fat man!" she cried aloud in her agitation, "Bloated fat man!" but that made no impact at all. She tried to make herself laugh, "As the Americans do," but she could not laugh. "Treat him as a character," but he was not a character to her. He had touched her—she shuddered—how could she ever face the dining-room again?

It was a tired Miss Mountfort, with eyelids that ached, who dragged herself next morning to her coffee in the town.

The chef did not cook lunch; "not unless several visitors are in," Madame Voday had confided to Miss Mountfort in despair. "He says the boys can cook for the old hens. Of course, he did not mean you, Mademoiselle."

"He meant me," said Miss Mountfort and she tried to smile tolerantly.

"You are very magnanimous, Mademoiselle."

"Not at all. I don't let servants upset me," said Miss Mountfort. How she wished that were true.

The chef was very lazy. He had a long siesta after lunch and before lunch too, if he could. "He would sleep all day if he could," said Madame Voday. "Drink and sleep." Miss Mountfort had seen him asleep, not only outside the kitchen but even on the bench under the chestnut trees inside the front gate.

"The front gate!" she exclaimed.

Miss Mountfort had never seen an elephant lying down but she had seen pictures of a whale washed up on a beach. Asleep on the bench the chef looked just like a whale, and though the work he was paid to do was being done by the boys, in his sleep he had an animal innocence. He slept, flushed and happy, his snores filling the whole forecourt.

When Miss Mountfort came back from the town next day he was on the bench, and making her way in from the road, she had to pass him close by; she walked on tiptoe but gravel has its effect on high heels and a pebble rolled under her foot so that she lurched suddenly. Big mammals are light sleepers and the chef awoke. He opened his eyes and stretched.

Miss Mountfort was so close that, as he looked up at her, she could catch his reek of garlic, wine, and sweat. His eyes went over her lazily, then recognition came and he laughed. "Ah! *la petite duchesse!*" he said.

She drew herself up to pass immediately towards the house but before she could move, with the agility of a fat man he had jumped up and caught her. He held her by her dress, drawing it tightly backwards so that it showed the shape of her thighs and legs. "Kiss me," said the chef.

She made a stifled small sound between a squeak and a gasp, and as she tried to get away, her feet scrabbled wildly on the gravel. He drew her steadily backwards. "Let me go!" gasped Miss Mountfort.

"When you kiss me," said the chef.

She beat at him with her sunshade but the thwacks did not seem to hurt him. He roared with laughter. "Someone will come!" cried Miss Mountfort in agony.

"Let them come," and then she was close to him; she could feel his heat, his dampness. He reminded her of Stan. "No! No! No!" cried Miss Mountfort.

"Next time you will kiss me," said the chef and he let her go.

I shall not complain to Madame Voday: by five o'clock that afternoon Miss Mountfort had reached that decision. I shall take not the slightest notice. I shall do as I said, refuse to let a servant upset me . . . and she sat down in her chair on the balcony and firmly opened the pages of the serial, but she found she could not read it; it was a story of —of love, she thought, flinching, and she turned to "Answers to Correspondents." She always liked the correspondence columns where there were soothing questions about etiquette: "Should asparagus be eaten with the fingers or a fork?" "Are finger bowls placed to the right or the left?" But the letters this month were about deeper questions than that. ". . . You must remember, my dear," read Miss Mountfort, "in these things it is the woman who leads. Are you sure, quite sure, there was nothing in your behavior . . ." "But nothing, absolutely nothing!" cried Miss Mountfort, and perhaps for the tenth time that afternoon found she was in tears.

When half past six came, she felt so low that she knew she had been silly to miss lunch, and "Just for once, because of the shock," she said aloud, "I shall give myself an aperitif."

That was wise. The vermouth warmed and softened her, yet, mysteriously, made her take a stronger view of things. The man was half asleep, she was able to tell herself. He did not know what he was doing. After she had finished the glass, she could smile and say, "Did you think he was making a set at you?" and it was quite calmly that, at her usual time, she was able to make her way into dinner.

"But . . . what *is* it?" asked Miss Mountfort, staring down at the dish.

The whole dining-room was staring too, had been staring all through dinner. As ill luck would have it, the room was full that evening, of

people with *no* manners, Miss Mountfort thought indignantly. Yet
there was something to stare at.

She had sat down at her table and had picked up the menu when she
had smelled an unmistakable smell and heard a soft, powerful tread;
she flinched as the waiter was pushed aside; then the menu was taken
out of her hand and the silver swept off the table. "I have cooked a special little dinner for you," said the chef.

"I don't want . . . I can't afford . . . I take the menu . . . I refuse . . ." The words might have been small sizzles of fat in a pan for all
the notice he took. He unfolded her napkin and put it across her knees.
"*Taistoi*," he said gently.

To *tutoyer*—! . . . But Miss Mountfort could not speak. If she had
been in the pillory it would not have been possible for her to suffer
more; paying not the slightest attention to anyone else, this man, this
. . . servant, stood over her and . . . What will they *think?* she thought
in agony.

He was in a beaming humour, directing the waiters who brought
flowers in a vase, white carnations, then a bottle of wine, then soup;
after the soup there was sole with white grapes, but Miss Mountfort
hardly knew what it was, she was so nearly choked with mortification.
"You should pray when you drink that wine," said the chef, sniffing the
glass before he gave it to her.

"Perhaps they will think I have tipped him," thought Miss Mountfort, and as he suggested, she prayed, but her prayer was: "Make them
think it is because I tipped him."

She did not see the sunset. The flowers on her table smelled so
strongly she felt faint. "I picked them," said the chef, "I did not let the
boy pick them," and he leaned down and said softly, "Take them up to
bed." Miss Mountfort had always thought it would be wonderful to be
given flowers by a man—the *Elegance* heroes always gave flowers—now
she was given them by a chef; the bitterness of that humiliation had
made her sit upright, but there were scarlet patches on her face and
neck.

Then, as a final touch, this dish had been brought, a dark-looking
pancake with rashers of bacon on top; it was served with potatoes in
their jackets, "*à la paysanne*," said the chef. Proudly he showed it
round. "They do them like this where I come from," he said and then,
winking, "It is good for a duchess now and then to taste a little peasant
food," and to her he said, "It is truly French."

"But what *is* it?"

It looked like something Madeleine might have enjoyed. "I like

French cooking," Miss Mountfort had said and into her ears came Stan's thoughtful, "I wonder if you really do?"

"Eat it up," said the chef, and bite by bite, with the eyes of everyone on her, Miss Mountfort had, willy-nilly, to eat it up.

"Is it good?" asked the American, the one who spoke French.

For the first time she was on a friendly footing with the other guests, and she had to admit that the dish was far better than it looked.

"It wasn't so difficult to eat after all?" asked the chef tenderly. The tenderness in this case was for the food, not for her.

"Now what was it?" asked the American. "I'm sure the little lady wants to know."

"It's a *sanguette*, a blood pancake."

The room grew warm with interest but Miss Mountfort faintly asked, "Blood?"

"Yes. Blood."

"I have eaten *blood*?"

"Of course you have . . . often. Eaten and enjoyed it." And seeing her face, he laughed. "It's only chicken blood. You take onions and fry them," he said to the room, "and breadcrumbs and chopped parsley and slowly the blood of a chicken. It makes a pancake. She needs blood," and he put his hand on Miss Mountfort's shoulder, "for those pale city cheeks." Miss Mountfort made, again, her queer little half-stifled noise.

"Well, I must say!" said the American, pulling a face.

"But look," said the chef, "last night you had *poulet à l'estragon*."

"Well, yes, we did."

"You enjoyed it?"

"Very much."

"But there was blood in that chicken just the same. What is the difference?" and he asked Miss Mountfort, "What difference is there?" No answer came from any of the tables. "*Merde!*" shouted the chef. "You will not have facts." Then he looked down at Miss Mountfort and softened. "But you ate it," he said, and his voice was oddly tender. "You were a good little cannibal hen and ate it all up."

She shook off his hand, pushed back her chair, clapped her napkin over her mouth, and ran out of the room.

It was not till eleven the next morning that Miss Mountfort crept out and came down. There was no one about, only Madame Voday in the office. The house was strangely quiet, quiet as it had been in other years. Then . . . has he gone? thought Miss Mountfort. Perhaps Madame Voday had dismissed him; perhaps someone had reported what had happened in the dining-room? There was a moment's wild hope, then Miss Mountfort's sense reasserted itself; Madame Voday would hardly dismiss a good chef, however troublesome, for an obscure client; Madame Voday, Miss Mountfort suspected, saw a long way through Miss Mountfort.

All the same, it was an odd silence. There was no clatter in the kitchen; there were no sudden eruptions towards the bar, nor, as the morning grew hotter and the shadows under the chestnut trees shortened, was there a whale asleep on the bench. Perhaps he has gone fishing, thought Miss Mountfort; I must avoid the river. It was time and past for her walk into the town; why then did she turn across the lawns?

The river bank was deserted, and on this golden day there were no residents in for lunch. She ate solitarily in the dining-room. The second waiter served her but hardly a word passed between them; the lunch itself was bad; the chef had obviously not even planned it. Miss Mountfort soon folded her napkin and went upstairs.

In her room she had another fit of weeping. Her nerves were completely upset. Though she had come up to rest she could not keep still.

The bedroom seemed dull and hot; she could not open a magazine; her tongue felt stiff from days of silence. The afternoon stretched long and empty. Suddenly she would have given anything to see Madeleine.

All her beloved arrangements were there; she was free, unmolested, to carry them out; no impudent servant had worried her today. Then why did she feel so flattened and, yes, dull?

What did she want? She did not know. She only knew she felt what Madeleine had said she would feel, "miserably lonely." "He made a fool of you," she told herself and it was true; she still scalded and writhed with shame and yet, persistently, she said, "He meant well and he was very drunk." Immediately the unkind question arose, "Can a drunken man mean anything?" She did not know but, "I like him drunk," she said and stopped, appalled. Those were Madeleine's words!

The afternoon dragged on as other afternoons, but none, she was sure, had ever been as long as this; it lasted—from Egypt, thought Miss Mountfort, trying to remember the farthest-away point she had learned in history. Thinking of Egypt she thought of sand, dry, arid sand, deserts. Deserts of afternoon, she thought, deserts, with a merciless glare in which she saw herself, Miss Mountfort of the careful little arrangements, the finger-in-air, she who was made sick by chicken blood, she who was called Aimée, yet had had to invent a Raoul because she had never been loved. "Tomorrow," whispered Miss Mountfort, "tomorrow

I shall go home," but sometimes life does not only pierce; it hammers the nail in.

That evening in the lounge she took another aperitif. "As I'm leaving I can afford it," she said, forcing back the tears. She was sipping it when the new couple came in.

They had left their car in the courtyard, a long low car, and to take a breath of air, perhaps too from curiosity, Miss Mountfort went out and walked around it. She was afraid to leave her glass in case Paul whisked it away, and carried it with her. The car was a Bristol. She had never heard of one but she took note of the long bonnet, the white paint and dark green leather. "It's a speed car," said Paul when she went in.

The couple were English, not young, not yet middle-aged. "Thirty and thirty-six," decided Miss Mountfort. "A perfect age." She peeped over her glass at the man's height in the dark grey flannels and tweed coat; he had the bronzed skin, the dear quizzical wrinkles, the silver-grey hair, but he made Raoul seem like some film actor; no, Raoul could not compete. As for the lady . . . Miss Mountfort was suddenly heart-sick. It was for women such as this that exclusive shops like Pope and Ransome's were run and in that world she, Miss Mountfort, belonged on the other side of the counter; she had a vision of herself selling that fuchsia ribbon. "Bring me another vermouth," she said.

In the dining-room she was glad she had had that extra drink, for Madame Voday led the newcomers to the table by the window. The room was quiet and though the dinner bore every trace of the chef's presence, he did not come in. "What a relief!" said Miss Mountfort under her breath, but as she said it, she remembered the big tenderness of his voice. "I will have a bottle of—of Chambertin," she told the waiter.

"A demi, Mademoiselle?"

"A whole."

The two in the window had the menu at twelve hundred francs. They ordered *blanc-de-blanc*. "You spoil me, Peter." Had Miss Mountfort really heard that or was it because her head was beginning to swim? Peter was a far, far better name than Raoul.

"Darling." She certainly heard that. A *bouchée* crust stuck in her throat, which was sore from her crying upstairs. At the hurt, the tears began to run down her face again. She wiped them on her napkin and drank some more wine.

When Miss Mountfort got up to leave the dining-room she staggered. She heard the waiters titter. I must look very funny, she thought. I have become a figure of fun for the whole hotel, and she said aloud,

"What does it matter?" Her spectacles had fallen awry. That did not matter either. She had not needed spectacles to see what she had been forced to look at all through dinner, two heads against the panes, against the rosy sunset.

She succeeded in getting herself to the lounge and sat down. "A *filtre* and a *fine*," she said.

"*Une fine*, Mademoiselle?" The waiter sounded disapproving.

"*Une fine*." Miss Mountfort rapped out.

Then the two came in. She kept behind the paper but she heard what they said.

"Pete, I'll go up to bed."

"I'll just see to the car and come up."

A pause, and then, "Come soon."

Miss Mountfort turned her head against her chair and closed her eyes. A tear ran out from under her lids. She heard the woman get up to go, pause and say "Good night." Miss Mountfort did not answer. More tears came.

"Phizzt!"

It was an unbearably rude noise but Miss Mountfort opened her eyes.

"Phizzt!"

She sat up and looked towards the service door. The chef was standing there. He was in his trousers and shirt but without his apron and handkerchief and cap. He looked curiously undressed as if . . . he were wearing pyjamas? thought Miss Mountfort. Giddily she noticed his ruffled dark head.

"Phizzt!" and he jerked his head over his shoulder. Miss Mountfort knew that gesture. It was one that Stan used when he . . . *wanted* Madeleine.

Dazed, Miss Mountfort found herself standing up and in a curiously zigzag fashion she went across the lounge. She reached the green baize door and the chef put out his hand, his great flipper; it fell on her shoulder; he pulled her to him and shut the door.

Presently Paul came and took away the unused *filtre* that had gone cold. The *fine* he drank. Then he picked up *Elegance* where it had fallen to the floor and put it on the stack of other papers that the Pierrefonds visitors had left behind.

A Short Walk From the Station

by JOHN O'HARA

On a Friday evening in February this year Francis King dozed off just after his train left the 30th Street Station, and he would have slept all the way to Paoli had it not been for Joe Dybert. Joe Dybert shook him gently. "Wake up, Francis," said Joe Dybert. "Show momma the blue."

"Huh? . . . Oh. Oh, hello, Joe. We here?" said Francis King.

"Think you can make it? What'd you have for lunch, boy?" said Joe Dybert.

The two men left the station together, walking in step but without conversation until they reached the street. "Give you a ride up the hill?"

"No thanks," said Francis King. "See you tomorrow."

"Tomorrow's Saturday. You won't see *me* tomorrow."

"What did *you* have for lunch? We're going to your house for dinner tomorrow night. Drive carefully, Mr. Dybert. Drive carefully." Francis King turned up the collar of his topcoat and put on his gloves, but now that he was alone the thought of walking up the short incline to Cardiff Road sickened him. It was only a short walk, three blocks, and the times he had made it automatically surely numbered well up in the thousands; nevertheless his legs weighed a ton. He had no sensation of dizziness, he felt no pain. It was just that he wanted to stand there a couple of minutes.

Friends of his and their wives waved to him and tapped their horns in goodnight salute, all knowing that Francis King never accepted the offer of a lift in the evening. "Forget something, Francis?" said one such friend, on foot and not waiting for an answer.

"Just trying to think," said Francis King, and it was the truth: he was trying to understand the leaden immobility of his legs. He knew he could walk only so far—to Arlington Drive, which was at the bottom of the incline. He knew he could get that far, that his legs would let him get that far, but not beyond. And then, in shame and embarrassment, he saw the truth: it was not the short incline to Cardiff Road that was so formidable; it was the thought of once more, for the many-thousandth time, walking past Lydia Brown's shop with his eyes averted, pretending the shop did not exist, pretending there was no Lydia Brown.

The Tack Room was hideously expensive. Lydia Brown's prices for everything were really out of this world. You could get cashmere things much cheaper almost anywhere on Chestnut Street, and the horse things she still carried—to justify the original name of the shop—cost less on Walnut Street. The presents for men were higher than in the New York stores, the children's things were ridiculously overpriced. But Lydia Brown's friends went on buying from her whenever they could, partly out of admiration for her courage, partly because her old friends approved of the appearance of her shop and the way she kept it up in among the cluster of real estate offices, liquor stores, drug stores, hairdressers' salons in the vicinity of the station. The Tack Room was a convenient and pleasant place to drop in for a cigarette, a cup of coffee in the mid-morning, a cup of tea in the afternoon. Old friends could borrow an umbrella there, leave their bundles there, make a telephone call. The fieldstone and white trim house was inviting. And if the mounting block at the curb got in the way of off-side car doors, what were a few scratches nowadays, when every anonymous parking attendant did worse than scratch your door? All her old friends wanted Lyd Brown to stay in business, and she always took it with a smile when they kidded her about overcharging them for chutney and English biscuits and Italian leather and Swedish woodwork. Sometimes in the Philadelphia shops a salesperson would say, "We don't carry that any more. The only place I can think of where you might find it is Lydia Brown's store, the Tack Room, you know?" Everything in the Tack Room was the best.

Francis King made straight for the Tack Room, and climbing the three steps from the sidewalk level did not tax his strength. The shop was brightly lighted by three frosted globes hanging from the ceiling, but as he entered he saw no one. Then, from a room at the rear of the store, Lydia Brown came forth.

"Hello, Francis," she said. "Is there something the matter?"

He nodded. "I don't know what it is. I just want to sit down a minute."

"Would you like a glass of water? Brandy? Can I call a doctor?"

"I just want to sit down a minute. It isn't anything. Not a heart attack."

"I'll get you a brandy," she said.

He sat down and opened his coat, took off his hat and gloves and put them on a display table. She brought him a pony of brandy from the back room, and as he took a sip she lowered the Venetian blinds at all the windows. "I was about ready to close up anyway," she said, and stood in front of him with her arms folded and looked down at him over the rims of her glasses.

"If you could see yourself," he said.

"You didn't look so hot when you came in. What did you have for lunch?"

"You're the second one asked me that. I fell asleep on the train, and Joe Dybert asked me the same question. I had oyster stew, apple pie, and two cups of coffee. What I've had for lunch every Friday for thirty years, with time out for the war. What did *you* have for lunch, Lyd?"

"A chicken sandwich and a glass of milk. Why?"

"I don't know. I just thought I'd ask you. *You* asked *me*."

She took a chair facing him and lit a cigarette. "Nobody would believe it, that the first conversation we have after all these years consists of what we had for lunch."

"Well, I guess after all these years that's just about all we have to talk about."

"You have a point. How are you feeling?"

"Much better, thanks. I'll leave, don't worry."

"Don't hurry. I have nothing to do till seven."

"And then what do you do?"

"What?"

"I'm not just being inquisitive. I've often wondered what you do when you're not being a business woman."

"Terribly nice of you, Francis. I'm touched."

"You have a nice store," he said.

"I like it."

"You must do pretty well."

"Pretty well. I had the best Christmas since I opened the shop."

"Good."

"Rose helped," said Lydia Brown.

"You don't have to tell me that. I'm the one that pays the bills. Why the smile?"

"The only communication we ever have, your name at the bottom of a check. Francis D. B. King. Francis D. B. King. I remember I used to write Mr. and Mrs. Francis D. B. King, to see how it would look. Lydia B. King. Mrs. Francis D. B. King. Mrs. F. D. B. King. L. B. K. I guess every girl that ever lived did that."

"I did it too. I wrote Mrs. Francis D. B. King with you in mind."

"You did, really?"

"Sure. And Lydia B. King, and Lydia King. I don't remember writing L. B. K., but possibly I did."

"I just can't imagine you being so sentimental. Romantic."

"You forget," said Francis King.

"Do I, indeed? I—forget. What an unearthly nerve you have, to say a thing like that. The one thing I've never had a chance to do was forget. Do you realize that every morning, when I'm opening up my shop, for close to thirty years I see you walking past here on your way to the train. You've never looked in, not even looked in this direction. But I'm the one that forgets? You don't even see the shop."

"I've always known it was here. During the war I remember I'd be at my battle station, pitch dark in the early morning, and I'd think of how it was at home. I'd think of all the houses in the neighborhood, all the stores. And I always thought of your shop."

"I was hoping you'd be killed in the war."

"What?"

"You find that hard to believe?"

"I find it impossible to believe. By the time the war started it was already a good ten years since we'd had our quarrel. It was one thing to stop speaking to me, but to hate me enough to want me killed, ten years later! I never did anything that bad, Lydia."

"You did to me, Francis. You as good as killed me. Look at me. What am I? Close to sixty years old, no chance of ever having children and I love children. An apartment over my shop instead of a nice home of my own."

"That part isn't hard to understand, being bitter. But hating me enough to want me killed. Do you know, if I'd known that I might have obliged you."

"Oh, come, Francis."

"Oh, yes. When I went out to the Pacific I arranged all my affairs. Made my will, provided for Rose and the children. I put everything in order, so to speak. But I couldn't undo what I'd done to you. I guess it's very seldom a man is so completely in the wrong that there's nothing he can do, absolutely nothing. But I didn't realize you hated me that much."

"Oh, yes."

"And do you now?"

"Right now? This minute? No." She looked away, reflectively. "When you came in here you looked as though you might fall over dead right here."

"That would have been awkward."

"Yes, it would have been. But you asked me a question. Do I hate you now? And the answer is no."

"Why not?"

"You must figure that out for yourself, Francis."

"Because you don't feel anything. Is that why?"

"Yes."

"I looked so nearly dead that you couldn't hate me any more? Is that it?"

"Yes."

"How do I look now?"

"Oh, you're all right now, I suppose."

"Therefore you ought to be hating me again."

She shook her head. "No. Nothing. Absolutely nothing. I'll never hate you again."

Her face was suddenly bright and beautiful, her eyes as blue as her cashmere slip-on and as bright as her necklace of pearls. "Lydia," he said.

"What?"

"Would it be all right if I stopped in again, once in a while?"

"No."

"Never?"

"Never," she said. "I really don't want to see you again, Francis."

"I see," he said. "Well—thanks for the brandy." He rose and picked up his hat and gloves.

"Would you like me to call you a taxi?" she said.

"No thanks," he said.

She held the door open for him, and after he passed through it he heard the spring lock. Even before he reached Arlington Drive she had turned out the lights in her shop, and it was very dark going up to Cardiff Road. Dark and cold, and the wind was strong.

An Unposted Love Letter

by DORIS LESSING

Yes, I saw the look your wife's face put on when I said, "I have so many husbands, I don't need a husband." She did not exchange a look with you, but that was because she did not need to—later when you got home she said, "What an affected thing to say!" and you replied, "Don't forget she is an actress." You said this meaning exactly what I would mean if I had said it, I am certain of that. And perhaps she heard it like that, I do hope so, *because I know what you are* and if your wife does not hear what you say then this is a smallness on your part that I don't forgive you. If I can live alone, and out of fastidiousness, then you must have a wife as good as you are. My husbands, the men who set light to my soul (yes, I know how your wife would smile if I used that phrase) are worthy of you . . . I know that I am giving myself away now, confessing how much that look on your wife's face hurt. *Didn't she know that even then I was playing my part?* Oh no, after all, I don't forgive you your wife, no I don't.

If I said, "I don't need a husband, I have so many lovers," then of course everyone at the dinner table would have laughed in just such a way: it would have been the rather banal "outrageousness" expected of

me. An ageing star, the fading beauty . . . "I have so many lovers"—
pathetic, and brave too. Yes, that remark would have been too apt, too
smooth, right for just any "beautiful but fading" actress. But not right
for me, no, because after all, I am not just any actress, I am Victoria
Carrington, and I know exactly what is due to me. I know what is
fitting (not for *me*, that is not important) but for what I stand for. Do
you imagine I couldn't have said it differently—like this, for instance:
"I am an artist and therefore androgynous." Or: "I have created inside
myself Man who plays opposite to my Woman." Or: "I have ob-
jectified in myself the male components of my soul and it is from this
source that I create." Oh, I'm not stupid, not ignorant, I know the
different dialects of our time and even how to use them. But imagine if
I had said any of these things last night! It would have been a false
note, you would all have been uncomfortable, irritated, and afterwards
you would have said: "Actresses shouldn't try to be intelligent." (Not
you, the others.) Probably they don't believe it, not really, that an actress must be stupid, but their sense of discrepancy, of discordance,
would have expressed itself in such a way. Whereas their silence when I
said, "I don't need a husband, I have so many husbands," was right, for
it was *the remark right for me*—it was more than "affected," or "out-
rageous"—*it was making a claim that they had to recognise.*

That word affected, have you ever really thought why it is applied to
actresses? (You have of course, I'm no foreign country to you, I felt
that, but it gives me pleasure to talk to you like this.) The other afternoon I went to see Irma Painter in her new play, and afterwards I went
back to congratulate her (for she had heard, of course, that I was in the
auditorium and would have felt insulted if I hadn't gone—I'm different,
I hate it when people feel obliged to come back). We were sitting in
her dressingroom and I was looking at her face as she wiped the
makeup off. We are about the same age, and we have both been acting
since the year . . . I recognised her face as mine, we have the same face,
and I understood that it is the face of every real actress. No, it is not
"masklike," my face, her face. Rather, it is that our basic face is so worn
down to its essentials because of its permanent readiness to take other
guises, become other people, it is almost like something hung up on the
wall of a dressingroom ready to take down and use. Our face is—it has a
scrubbed, honest, bare look, like a deal table, or a wooden floor. It has
modesty, a humility, our face, as time wears on, wearing out of her, out
of me, our "personality," our "individuality."

I looked at her face (we are called rivals, we are both called "great"
actresses) and I suddenly wanted to pay homage to it, since I knew

what that scoured plain look cost her—what it costs me, who have played a thousand beautiful women, to keep my features sober and decent under the painted shell of my makeup ready for other souls to use.

At a party, all dressed up, when I'm a "person," then I try to disguise the essential plainness and anonymity of my features by holding together the "beauty" I am known for, creating it out of my own and other people's memories. Of course it is almost gone now, nearly all gone the sharp, sweet, poignant face that so many men loved (not knowing it was not me, it was only what was given to me to consume slowly for the scrubbed face I must use for work). While I sat last night opposite you and your wife, she so pretty and *human*, her prettiness no mask, but expressing every shade of what she felt, and you being yourself only, I was conscious of how I looked. I could see my very white flesh that is guttering down away from its "beauty"; I could see my smile that even now has moments of its "piercing sweetness"; I could see my eyes, "dewy and shadowed," even now . . . but I also knew that everyone there, even if they were not aware of it, was conscious of that hard, honest workaday face that lies ready for use under this ruin, and it is the discrepancy between that working face and the "personality" of the famous actress that makes everything I do and say affected, that makes it inevitable and right that I should say, "I don't want a husband, I have so many husbands." And I tell you, if I had said nothing, not one word, the whole evening, the result would have been the same: "How affected she is, but of course she *is* an actress."

Yet it was the exact truth, what I said: I no longer have lovers, I have husbands, and that has been true ever since . . .

That is why I am writing this letter to you; this letter is a sort of homage, giving you your due in my life. Or perhaps, simply, I cannot tonight stand the loneliness of my role (my role in life).

When I was a girl it seemed that every man I met, or even heard of, or whose picture I saw in the paper, was my lover. I took him as my lover, *because it was my right.* He may never have heard of me, he might have thought me hideous (and I wasn't very attractive as a girl— my kind of looks, striking, white-fleshed, red-haired, needed maturity, as a girl I was a milk-faced, scarlet-haired creature whose features were all at odds with each other, I was pretty only when made up for the stage) . . . he may have found me positively repulsive, but I took him. Yes, at that time I had lovers in imagination, but none in reality. No man in the flesh could be as good as what I could invent, no real lips, hands, could affect me as those that I created, like God. And this remained true when I married my first husband, and then my second, for I loved neither of them, and I didn't know what the word meant for years. Until, to be precise, I was thirty-two and got very ill that year. No one knew why, or how, but *I* know it was because I did not get a big part I wanted badly. So I got ill from disappointment, but now I see how right it was I didn't get the part. I was too old—if I had played her, the charming ingenuous girl (which is how I saw myself then, God forgive me) I would have had to play her for three or four years, because the play ran for ever, and I would have been too vain to stop. And then what? I would have been nearly forty, too old for charming girls, and then, like so many actresses who have not burned the charming girl out of themselves, cauterised that wound with pain like styptic, I would have found myself playing smaller and smaller parts, and then I would have become a "character" actress, and then . . .

Instead, I lay very ill, not wanting to get better, ill with frustration, I thought, but really with the weight of years I did not know how to consume, how to include in how I saw myself, and then I fell in love with my doctor, inevitable I see now, but then a miracle, for that was the first time, and the reason I said the word "love" to myself, just as if I had not been married twice and had a score of men in my imagination was because *I could not manipulate him,* for the first time a man remained himself, I could not make him move as I wanted, and I did not know his lips and hands. No, I had to wait for *him* to decide, to move, and when he did become my lover I was like a young girl, awkward, I could only wait for his actions to spring mine.

He loved me, certainly, but not as I loved him, and in due course he left me. I wished I could die, but it was then I understood, with gratitude, what had happened—I played, for the first time, a woman, as distinct from that fatal creature, "A charming girl," as distinct from "the heroine"—and I and everyone else knew that I had moved into a new dimension of myself, I was born again, and only I knew it was out of love for that man, my first husband (so I called him, though everyone else saw him as my doctor with whom I rather amusingly had had an affair).

For he was my first husband. He changed me and my whole life. After him, in my frenzy of lonely unhappiness, I believed I could return to what I had been before he had married me, and I would take men to bed (in reality now, just as I had, before, in imagination) but it was no longer possible, it did not work, for I had been possessed by a man, the Man had created in me himself, had left himself in me, and so I could never again use a man, possess one, manipulate him, make him do what I wanted.

For a long time it was as if I was dead, empty, sterile. (That is, *I* was, my work was at its peak.) I had no lovers, in fact or in imagination, and it was like being a nun or a virgin.

Strange it was, that at the age of thirty-five it was for the first time I felt virgin, chaste, untouched, I was absolutely alone. The men who wanted me, courted me, it was as if they moved and smiled and stretched out their hands through a glass wall which was my absolute inviolability. Was this how I should have felt when I was a girl? Yes, I believe that's it—that at thirty-five I was a girl for the first time. Surely this is how ordinary "normal" girls feel?—they carry a circle of chastity around with them through which the one man, the hero, must break? But it was not so with me, I was never a chaste girl, not until I had known what it was to remain still, waiting for the man to set me in motion in answer to him.

A long time went by, and I began to feel I would soon be an old woman. I was without love, and I would not be a good artist, not really, the touch of the man who loved me was fading off me, *had* faded, there was something lacking in my work now, it was beginning to be mechanical.

And so I resigned myself. I could no longer choose a man; and no man chose me. So I said, "Very well then, there is nothing to be done." Above all, I understand the relation between myself and life, I understand the logic of what I am, must be, I know there is nothing to be done about the shape of fate: my truth is that I have been loved once, and now that is the end, and I must let myself sink towards a certain dryness, a coldness of intelligence—yes, you will soon develop into an upright, red-headed, very intelligent lady (though, of course, affected!) whose green eyes flash the sober fires of humorous comprehension. All the rest is over for you, now accept it and be done and do as well as you can the work you are given.

And then one night . . .

What? All that happened outwardly was that I sat opposite a man at a dinner party in a restaurant, and we talked and laughed as people do who meet each other casually at a dinner table. But afterwards I went home with my soul on fire. I was on fire, being consumed . . . And what a miracle it was to me, being able to say, not: That is an attractive man, I want him, I shall have him, but: My house is on fire, that was the man, yes, it was he again, there he was, he has set light to my soul.

I simply let myself suffer for him, knowing he was worth it *because* I suffered—it had come to this, my soul had become its own gauge, its own measure of what was good: I knew that *he* was because of how my work was afterwards.

I knew him better than his wife did, or could (she was there too, a nice woman in such beautiful pearls)—I knew him better than he does himself. I sat opposite him all evening. What was there to notice? An ageing actress, pretty still, beautifully dressed (that winter I had a beautiful violet suit with mink cuffs) sitting opposite a charming man—handsome, intelligent, and so on. One can use these adjectives of half the men one meets. But somewhere in him, in his being, something matched something in me, he had come into me, he had set me in motion. I remember looking down the table at his wife and thinking: Yes, my dear, but your husband is also my husband, for he walked into me and made himself at home in me, and because of him I shall act again from the depths of myself, I am sure of it, and I am sure it will be the best work I can do. Though I won't know until tomorrow night, on the stage.

For instance, there was one night when I stood on the stage and stretched up my slender white arms to the audience and (that is how they saw it, what *I* saw were two white-caked, raddled-with-cold arms that were, moreover, rather flabby) and I knew that I was, that night, nothing but an amateur. I stood there on the stage, *as a woman* holding out my pretty arms, it was Victoria Carrington saying: Look how poignantly I hold out my arms, don't you long to have them around you, my slender white arms, look how beautiful, how enticing Victoria is! And then, in my dressingroom afterwards I was ashamed, it was years since I had stood on the stage with nothing between me, the woman, and the audience—not since I was a green girl had I acted so—why, then, tonight?

I thought, and I understood. The afternoon before a man (a producer from America, but *that* doesn't matter) had come to see me in my dressingroom and after he left I thought: Yes, here it is again, I know that sensation, that means he has set the forces in motion and so I can expect my work to show it . . . it showed it, with a vengeance! Well, and so that taught me to discriminate, I learned I must be careful, must allow no secondrate man to come near me. And so put up barriers, strengthened around me the circle of cold, of impersonality, that should always lie between me and people, between me and the auditorium; I made a cool, bare space no man could enter, could break across, unless his power, his magic, was very strong, the true complement to mine.

Very seldom now do I feel my self alight, on fire, touched awake, created again by—what?

I live alone now. No, *you* would never be able to imagine how. For I knew when I saw you this evening that you exist, you are, only in relation to other people, you are always giving out to your work, your wife, friends, children, your wife has the face of a woman who gives, who is confident that what she gives will be received. Yes, I understand all that, I know how it would be living with you, I *know* you.

After we had all separated, and I had watched you drive off with your wife, I came home and . . . no, it would be no use telling you, after all. (Or anyone, except, perhaps, my colleague and rival Irma Painter!) But what if I said to you—but no, there are certain disciplines which no one can understand but those who use them.

So I will translate into your language, I'll translate the truth so that it has the *affected*, almost embarrassing, exaggerated ring that goes with the actress Victoria Carrington, and I'll tell you how when I came home after meeting you my whole body was wrenched with anguish, and I lay on the floor sweating and shaking as if I had bad malaria, it was like knives of deprivation going through me, for, meeting you, it was being reminded again what it would be like to be with a man, really with him, so that the rhythm of every day, every night, carried us both like the waves of a sea.

Everything I am most proud of seemed nothing at all—what I have worked to achieve, what I *have* achieved, even the very core of what I am, the inner sensitive balance that exists like a sort of self-invented super instrument, or a fantastically receptive and cherished animal—this creation of myself, which every day becomes more involved, sensitive, and delicate, seemed absurd, paltry, spinsterish, a shameful excuse for cowardice. And my life, which so contents me because of its balance, its order, its steadily growing fastidiousness, seemed eccentrically solitary. Every particle of my being screamed out, wanting, needing—I was like an addict deprived of his drug.

I picked myself off the floor, I bathed myself, I looked after myself like an invalid or like a—yes, like a pregnant woman. These extra-ordinary fertilisations happen so seldom now that I cherish them, waste nothing of them, and I both long for and dread them. Every time it is like being killed, like being torn open while I am forced to remember what it is I voluntarily do without.

Every time it happens I swear I can never let it happen again, the pain is too terrible. What a flower, what a fire, what a miracle it would be if, instead of smiling (the "sweetly piercing" smile of my dying beauty) instead of accepting, submitting, I should turn to you and say . . .

But I shall not, and so something very rare (something much more beautiful than your wife could ever give you, or any of the day by day wives could imagine) will never come into being.

Instead . . . I sit and consume my pain, I sit and hold it, I sit and clench my teeth and . . .

It is dark, it is very early in the morning, the light in my room is a transparent grey, like the ghost of water or of air, there are no lights in the windows I see from my own. I sit in my bed, and watch the shadows of the tree moving on the brick wall of the garden, and I contain pain and . . .

Oh my dear one, my dear one, I am a tent under which you lie, I am the sky across which you fly like a bird, I am . . .

My soul is a room, a great room, a hall—it is empty, waiting. Sometimes a fly buzzes across it, bringing summer mornings in another continent, sometimes a child laughs in it, and it is like the generations chiming together, child, youth, and old woman as one being. Sometimes you walk into it and stand there. You stand here in me and smile and I shut my eyes because of the sweet recognition in me of what you are, I feel what you are as if I stood near a tree and put my hand on its breathing trunk.

I am a pool of water in which fantastic creatures move, in which you play, a young boy, your brown skin glistening, and the water moves over your limbs like hands, my hands, that will never touch you, my hands that tomorrow night, in a pool of listening silence, will stretch up towards the thousand people in the auditorium, creating love for them from the consumed pain of my denial.

I am a room in which an old man sits, smiling, as he has smiled for fifty centuries, you, whose bearded loins created me.

I am a world into which you breathed life, have smiled life, have made me. I am, with you, what creates, every moment, a thousand animalculae, the creatures of our dispensation, and every one we have both touched with our hands and let go into space like freed birds.

I am a great space that enlarges, that grows, that spreads with the steady lightening of the human soul, and in the space, squatting in the corner, is a thing, an object, a dark, slow, coiled, amorphous heaviness, embodied sleep, a cold stupid sleep, a heaviness like the dark in a stale room—this thing stirs in its sleep where it squats in my soul, and I put all my muscles, all my force, into defeating it. For this was what I was born for, this is what I am, to fight embodied sleep, putting around it a confining girdle of light, of intelligence, so that it cannot spread its slow stain of ugliness over the trees, over the stars, over you.

It is as if, since you turned towards me and smiled letting light go through me again, it is as if a King had taken a Queen's hand and set her on his throne: a King and his Queen, hand in hand on top of my mountain sit smiling at ease in their country.

The morning is coming on the brick wall, the shadow of the tree has gone, and I think of how today I will walk out onto the stage, surrounded by the cool circle of my chastity, the circle of my discipline, and how I will raise my face (the flower face of my girlhood) and how I will raise my arms from which will flow the warmth you have given me.

And so, my dear one, turn now to your wife, and take her head on to your shoulder, and both sleep sweetly in the sleep of your love. I release you to go to your joys without me. I leave you to your love. I leave you to your life.

The Actress

by KATHARINE BRUSH

The last letter in the little pile on the corner of the breakfast tray was a buff-colored letter, plump and stiff and square and from a man. Obviously from a man. Over the delicate gilded rim of her morning coffee cup the actress regarded it casually. It bore two stamps and had been mailed at New Haven.

The coffee was too hot to drink. The actress set the cup down—*klink* —in the shining saucer and patted her lips with a lace-edged napkin. She picked up the letter, opened it, glanced at the first page, turned to the final (the seventh) one, and examined the signature. "Brock Henderson."

Below this, at the side, was written, "922 Yale Station, April third." The actress smiled slightly. A *young* man.

Settling herself more comfortably into the pillows heaped high at her back, she began to read:

"Please," (no other salutation) "PLEASE" (printed large) "don't think I'm the sort of twirp who does this sort of thing. I mean habitually. Cross my heart, I never wrote a fan letter before in my life; I never dreamed of writing one; I never could see how anybody could be such an ass. But that, as the movie titles would say, was before You came.

"Remember the night you played in New Haven last October, before your show opened in New York? That was the night. I was the fellow breathing hard in the fourth row on the aisle. The one who had to be nudged by his roommate when it was time to stop clapping. I had never seen you before, you see, and I felt—but never mind that. The point is that ever since then I've had just three things on my mind; and one is you, and another is you, and the third is you."

Here page one ended. The actress thumbed it aside and slid it under the last page. Holding the letter in her left hand on the taffeta puff that covered her, she stirred her coffee and tasted a spoonful speculatively. And put the spoon down.

She read on:

"Of course I know it's an old, old story. Maybe you're yawning. Probably you are. But I can't help telling you anyway. . . ."

He had, it appeared, seen her play over and over again since October. Every weekend he could get off he came to New York and saw it. And once (there were two full pages about this) he had watched her emerge from the stage door after a performance and get into her car and drive away. She had worn "a white fur wrap like a snowdrift" and she had looked "even more marvelous" off the stage than on. He had wanted terribly to speak to her, to say *something*—but he hadn't dared. "I was afraid you'd think I was just fresh."

He devoured everything he could find about her in the papers and magazines; every news note, every interview. He knew what her apartment looked like; what cigarettes she smoked. He knew that, for all her fame, she was "hardly more than a kid—about my age," and somehow he got a tremendous kick out of that.

He knew her life, her glittering life, and the things of it: the parties, the perfumes, the flowers, the flattery. She was to him a gay and golden person, born to laugh and dance and to be loved. "An orchid person—if that isn't too trite. Exquisite and exotic and rare."

This part of the letter forgot flippancy, neglected self-ridicule. It was painfully in earnest. The meticulous handwriting of the first page or two hurried now, went tumbling along. . . .

"I don't suppose I'll ever really meet you. Optimistic as I am about most things in life, I can't honestly hope ever to bridge the illimitable chasm that lies between a girl like you and a boy like me. Some fellows would manage it, I know, but I haven't the ingenuity to think up a way, and besides, I wouldn't want to risk your indifference. Or your amusement.

"But whether or not I ever meet you—you belong to me, sort of. You're part of my life, and the things I do, and the things I dream. You're in music and in moonlight. When I'm kissing somebody I shut my eyes, and you're there. The *glamour* of you. I suppose that's what I'm in love with. Nothing can ever take that away from me.

"I'm not going to read this over because I know if I do I won't send it." . . .

The actress folded the pages slowly and laid the letter above her other mail. For a moment she thought about it; her lips curved a little, in a gentle little smile.

Then she forgot it.

She drank her coffee and lit a cigarette. She had ceased to smile. Her face was serious now, absorbed, the forehead faintly puckered.

Presently she took a pencil from the bedside table, and the letter from the top of the pile. With heedless hasty fingers she ripped a strip of paper from it, and on the blank side she scribbled:

> Shower curtains
> Dish towels
> New cord elec. iron
> Socks, shirts, pantie-waists for Patty. . . .

Make Me Real

by VICTORIA LINCOLN

It was another world, but it was the same world. Calvin Coolidge was President, and in Italy a man named Mussolini had come into power. We did not read the papers. We shingled our heads, and bound our young breasts flat, and concealed the woman curve of waist and hip in sack-shaped dresses, short to the knee; and we tried to look clever and cool, and as if we had tasted life and found it stale.

But in spring, the trees came into leaf, and we walked by the river and heard the marsh peepers; and we forgot that we were young and clever in a world of emptiness, and became as our parents had been and as our children are. Young and defenseless, young and tender, we breathed the May air and heard the voices of the night. And the young man's hand that shook with eagerness, and the lips of the girl that clung in kissing, cried, "Give me assurance of my power to love and be loved. Tell me that I am part of the night, of the springtime, of the living world. Make me real, make me real."

Do you remember? That is how it was with Rose Carrington. For almost four years she had created a world and a myth. But the four years were almost over, it was May; the world was waiting, the real world, the other world outside.

"If he had really loved me," Rose Carrington whispered suddenly, "if he had gone on loving me, I wouldn't have had to go back to Charleswood, ever. It wouldn't matter if mamma's money didn't hold out until I got a job, it wouldn't matter if I couldn't manage to find one or to keep one. I wouldn't have had to go back."

And as if her own words had shocked her, she lifted her head, high and startled, and then bowed it down.

"But it wasn't ever for that," she whispered. "It wasn't even partly for that. I loved him, I really loved him. Russ——"

She sprang to her feet and opened the door of her room. She called down the hall, toward another open door at the end of it. She called in the soft, musical voice that was still, after four years, so ineradicably Southern, a continual source, to her friends, of tender and delighted mockery, though never a conscious stock in trade.

"Karen," she called. "Karen, do you think they'll want to go anywhere dressy? What are you wearing tonight?"

And another voice, not Karen's, laughed down the corridor:

"If you want to play it safe, Rose, Karen, lovies, I suggest a suit of armor. This is the mating season."

But when she had closed the door again, she opened her closet very deliberately and, as if she had known that she would wear it all along, she took out the dress that she had not worn for months gone by, the straight little tunic of blue gray and silvery green that Russ had always called "your sexy dress."

She was a tall girl, but not very tall; naturally straight-backed and flat-chested in the style of the day. "Poor little Rose," they had often said in her hearing around Charleswood. "Pity she didn't favor her mother. Pity she's so plain."

But she had never been really plain, even as a child, though she had only one striking, positive beauty: the long, black, heavy hair which she had never cut, like her contemporaries, but only parted in the middle and coiled, in its thick knot, low on her neck. As a thin, lank-locked child her features had looked, somehow, too big for her face. But they had taken on a certain harmony of proportion, now; though they were still of the kind that is most beautiful in middle age, the strong and simple features which time and emotion refine until people say, "She is lovely to look at, she must have been a beauty when she was young." Now her face simply waited, more attractive at second glance than at first, and still drawing a dateless elegance from the heavy coil of the black, Madonna hair, and the habitual lifted, half-listening carriage of the head.

Her mother had died when she was only nine. She had not missed her as much as she felt that she should. She continued to live as she had, in the shadowy, cool, big plantation house, with her shadowy, alcoholic father and his gentle, mildly alcoholic sister who came to them when her mother died. They were the Carringtons, all that was left of the family.

The Archer kinfolk—and there were many of them—were like her mother: pretty, vague, dove-voiced women in big hats and ruffled dresses.

"Poor little Rose," she would hear them say; "poor little plain thing, wanderin' round like a lost soul. Y'ought to send her to Briargrove, really y'ought. Lily's money'd take care of that much. I declare, it's too bad, keepin' her around here to get odd as Dick's hatband and lettin' her go to that village school like she was a sharecropper's child. Appears to me you've got that much plain responsibility to Lily, Charles. How's she ever going to get a husband, a little thing without looks or money, if she isn't even raised to fix herself up and have pretty ways?"

But her father would only smile and sweeten his tall drink, accepting them like a fact in nature, as if their voices meant no more than the whistle of the mockingbird in the syringa, or the pattering of a light summer shower.

"We're doing all right, Belle. Now, Carol Anne, don't fuss like that and get wrinkles before your time."

And they would drive off in the big touring car, crying, "I declare to goodness, it's a disgrace. I declare, you might as well talk to the wind in the trees. Every mortal soul of the Carringtons has been like that."

Her mother had been tender in manner but not really affectionate. It was frightening to know that someone could be alive and then dead. It meant that death was real. But no matter how Rose tried to remember her and weep properly, her mother was an easy person to forget.

The days were long and happy, papa and Aunt Lila did not make a bother if you played with the sharecropper's children, and nights they often forgot to tell you to go to bed, and you could sneak down to the cabins and hear the help sing. Old Tizzie had her cabin there. She had belonged to grandfather's father for the first month of her life, and when she got big she worked in the kitchen until she was too old. She had a big, soft lap; even when your legs had got so long they trailed on the ground, she liked you to sit in it and listen to the singing.

"Tizzie, tell them to sing 'Wouldn't mind dyin'.'"

"Tell 'em youself, Rose. Who's boss round here?"

"Papa. You tell them, Tizzie."

"You ol' baby, when you aimin' to grow up?" And then they would sing it for her:

"Wouldn't mind dyin', but I got to go by myself.
Wouldn't mind dyin', but I got to stay so long.
Grave, grave, sure is a lonesome place,
Oh, I wouldn't mind dyin', if dyin' was all."

She liked it because it made her forget for a moment how happy she was, and then she could cry about her mother.

But when she was fourteen they sent her to Briargrove, after all.

The Archer kinfolk had all gone to Briargrove, and all the girls at Briargrove were indistinguishable from the Archer kinfolk. If they had been unkind, she could have hated them and developed a lonely superiority. But they were all gentle and sweet and pitying, they fed their egos with a communal project of being nice to poor Rose Carrington, and it destroyed her.

She had stood outside a closed door, once, in a corridor and heard the voices:

"The poor, skinny little old thing, I declare, I want to cry when I see her. My mother has a friend that's kin to the Archers, she says it's a crime the life that child has had, her mother dead and her father always tipsy."

"Do you guess she minds? She's right smart with her lessons. Maybe she doesn't mind lookin' like she does."

And another voice, cruelly gentle:

"I don't see how any girl could help mindin' it, knowin' she was just a natural-born old maid."

And then Nan Laurence, the cleverest of the seniors:

"You know what I'd do if it was me? I'd go up North to college and then I'd just get me a job and stay there. Lots of things don't matter, up North."

That afternoon she had gone to her favorite teacher. "Would Briargrove prepare me for a Northern college?"

"Briargrove is a finishing school. You couldn't be certified, but you could take examinations. I would like to see you learn something, Rose. I have watched you, I have liked to hope that your intelligence would not be wasted."

At Christmas she hesitated how to approach her father; but fortunately, Aunt Belle and Aunt Pris' Austen, who dropped in one afternoon, were persuaded to have a glass of wine and neither of them had a head for it. They began to fuss at papa and Aunt Lila for the way they lived and said that poor Lily would turn over in her grave if she could see them, always poked in there, never entertaining a soul, drink, drink, drink and ruining their health. Papa was courteous, he was always courteous, but you could see how they made him feel. And for the first time in her life, Rose played a woman's trick.

She waited until they were gone, and she sweetened papa's glass for him herself.

"I love school," she said. "I'm glad you sent me to Briargrove, papa. The—the teachers think I'm so good at my books I ought to go on up North to college. If mamma's money would be enough, that is."

She saw his look of startled hesitation, and laid her ace of trumps gently before him.

"Of course the Archer kinfolk would all think you were right stark out of your head to let me go," she said mournfully. "I didn't think of that. I—I suppose I shouldn't have asked you. I wouldn't want to make trouble for you with Aunt Belle and the rest of them, tiresome as they can be."

He smiled.

"Yes, they think they know everything, don't they? They think they know more than Lila and me and the teachers at Briargrove about raisin' a child."

And then she was part of another world. She had not known what she hoped of it. She only knew, quite simply, that she could not go back to Charleswood and get to be like Aunt Lila, an old maid, disregarded even in her gentle self-destruction, tippling the day's emptiness into a half-semblance of the night's sleep.

At least, she had thought, *I can amount to something. I'm not just a girl, I'm human. I can stay human.*

But the girls she had found were as pretty as the ones that she had left. Their clothes were plainer and smarter, they used rouge less and lipstick more, their talk sounded more like clever people in books, but that was all. She had looked around the dining room, searching for the Northern old maids, the foredoomed spinsters, and found not one.

Places are all the same, she thought. *You don't get out of anything by running away.*

Her senior adviser was a stylish girl called Sue; she was kind, as the girls at Briargrove had been kind, but when the meal was over Rose had said to her, "I got a headache from that old train. Is it all right if I just go and lie down?"

An hour later she went into the bathroom and closed the door of a cubicle. She was lying in her tub when the two girls came in.

"What's your freshman like, Gin?"

"Oh, Sue, she's ghastly. A little number from Lynn, or Lowell or somewhere, all bangles. How's yours?"

"Heaven. From this huge plantation in Mississippi, and just like something out of a book. Her *voice*——"

"A Southern belle, eh?"

"Not exactly. A sheltered exotic. Slender, masses of wonderful hair in a knot. Native dress, of course, rouge and ruffles, but I can fix that tactfully."

"Sounds like a potential killer."

"All that. Intelligent too."

"Oh, dear, I envy you. Mine will probably go right out and pick up a feeble-minded shoe clerk somewhere."

And the door closed behind them.

Rose Carrington lay in the warm tub and shut her eyes. She had not known that standards of beauty vary from place to place, or from period to period. Poor little skinny thing with that straight hair. . . . Slender, masses of wonderful hair in a knot.

She got out of the tub and began to dry herself. She was quite pale, and her eyes looked twice their normal size. After a few moments she spoke, under her breath.

"A couple of plain sweaters," she whispered. "A sort of beige one, like Sue has."

And suddenly, under her breath, she began to cry.

"Oh, please, God," she whispered, over and over, "oh, please, God, please . . . please——"

And it had all happened three, almost four years ago, and except when she went home for vacations, she could hardly remember it.

"I used to be a terribly shy little girl," she once said.

"You must have been," returned her crony, Karen, grinning. "I remember you on our first date, shy as a queen."

And how could she explain what had once been without destroying what now was?

She had not become the most popular girl in her dormitory. Karen, eventually, was that. But there were always presentable, nice boys, three or four on tap at a time, usually, for concerts and theaters, dancing, walks by the river, long talk over restaurant tables. At first it was hard to believe in. The first time she went home for vacation, the time away, the new time was like a dream, and when the Archer kinfolk came to coax her over to Wateroaks for the Christmas dance, she pretended to be sick.

But in the spring, it was Charleswood and Wateroaks that had become the dream. She was affectionate with papa and Aunt Lila now, as she had never been, kissing them good night as a grown woman might kiss an old doll, long forgotten and found in an attic. The very static meaninglessness of their lives, the incessant, undramatic drinking, the vague words and vague silences, had become strange, like something in a book that she read without shock or censure.

And when Aunt Belle, dove-voiced and fluttering, came to ask her to a dance once more, it was only a part of the same story.

She dressed for the evening carefully but not anxiously. The dress was white, girdled at the hips in the new style that was so cruel to all but the very slender, and it was very short.

They'll think I'm a freak, she thought. *And it doesn't matter*.

She remembered the rouged cheeks and small, pale, rosebud pouts that were worn by the girls at Briargrove, and deliberately used no make-up except for the white nose and narrow, brilliant mouth of the metropolitan North.

The girls were just as she remembered them, but they, too, were part of the book. They were overdressed and fluttery. The boys, however, looked like boys anywhere. *It's too bad*, she thought quietly, and with no sense of personal failure, *that they won't ask me to dance*.

Her Cousin Justin was standing before her.

"Rosie?"

She got up. "Take big steps, Juddy. Just to the beat of the music. It's the only way I'm used to."

And, without conscious effort, she moved closer in his arms.

They had gone a little way before they were cut in upon. And then, again.

Toward the end of the evening she let one of them take her into the shadowy part of the veranda.

"Rose——"

But she was funny about kissing. It was not that she had not liked it, from the first time it had happened; but that she always felt that she would like it more with someone else. It felt, always, as she imagined it would if you were in love with someone and being kissed by a stranger.

"I——" She hesitated.

"Rose, please——"

She was ashamed, and gave him her cold, unresponsing lips.

"You're not like that . . . cold. . . . Look, you—you've got someone back up there you like, haven't you?"

"I—I . . . yes."

"I should have known. I'm sorry. You're a terribly sweet girl, Rose."

"Thank you, Carroll. I like you."

But there was nobody. There were always boys, but there was nobody, really, until the beginning of her senior year, when she met Russ. He wasn't handsome, his lips and his nose were too flat, his red hair too wild and wiry. He wasn't very tall, or very clever; but the minute she looked at him the world was changed because she had never known him before, and now she did. And she knew, without question, that it was so for him too.

She knew before he drew her onto another dark veranda, the little porch of the fraternity house, and said, just as the boy at Wateroaks had said, "Rose . . . Rose——"

"Russ?"

But she kept herself stubbornly turned away, refusing to believe in the moment, the holy blessed moment that the weeping child from Briargrove, the lost and buried girl within her, had known would never come.

"Rose . . . oh, darling . . . oh, beautiful."

Then she kissed him, and it was no longer like being in love with someone else and suffering herself to be kissed by a stranger.

"And I heard you were a cold potato," he said. The words were a shock.

"You—you talked about me?"

"Fellows do. Oh, Rose, it doesn't matter. Nothing before this minute matters. Rose——"

And she knew that he was right.

They would be married when college was over. He had a little money, not much but enough to tide them over until he got a job.

He was a chemical engineer, with no interest in the books and the pictures and music that meant so much to her. And she, for her part, took no share in his absorption in world affairs.

"Coolidge is crazy to play ball with that guy Mussolini the way he does. Leaving right and wrong out of it, it's bad business."

"It is?"

But she would find herself simply looking at him, marveling at his face, his shoulders, his hands, forgetting to listen.

They had nothing in common, really, but the intense and highly personalized quality of their desire. They lacked even the gentle, probing, personal interest common to most lovers. She knew that he came from a Middle Western suburb, he knew that she came from a plantation. That was all.

"Our folks will be horrified by each other," she said.

"Sounds likely." And then, at once, "You have the straightest little fingers I ever saw."

They were happiest together in the country. They had a phrase taken from a nursery classic that she had loved in childhood, the tale of Jemima Puddleduck. When they had walked until they were tired, they would say, "Let us look for a convenient, dry nesting place." Then, in a sheltered corner, safe from the wind and the world's eye, they would sit, side by side and face to face, as in an old-fashioned love seat, lips and breasts together, their eyes closed, the world contracted to an awareness of moving hands and lips.

Sometimes they would kiss to the point of anger, of weary staleness.

"Why do you feel you've got to hold out on me? You don't want to yourself. We'll be married in June, what's the difference?"

"Oh, Russ, please don't make it harder for me. Russ, I love you so."

Sometimes they would walk home rigid and silent with anger, wide apart on the road. Sometimes she would weep, and the tears would shock him to a new helplessness, so that they found themselves once more kissing, kissing through a new, blind softness of wonder to a new anger and staleness.

They had still another source of quarreling.

"Don't let's tell anybody yet," she would say. "Our families, our friends, anybody."

"But why? I want to do things properly, get you a ring and all. Why?"

"Not yet, Russ. I like it, secret like this. Not yet."

"But why?"

She could not tell him why. She did not know. She only knew that often, at night, she dreamed that she was in Charleswood, or at Briargrove, and that the hem was torn from her dress, or that she had spilled ink on herself, and that everyone was laughing at her, laughing. And she would wake, possessed anew by that wild, irrational feeling: that so long as love was secret, it was safe; but that if it were discovered, something would happen to separate them.

She even continued, in spite of his protests, to go out with other men. But Karen would not go on foursomes with Russ.

"Not that darned redheaded engineer," she said. "He's a bore. What do you see in him, Rose?"

And because it was secret, it was safe.

"What do you think, ducky? We go out in the country and study nature."

"Oh, Rose, you're shameless."

"Ain't I, just?"

Shortly before the Christmas holidays she went to a party given by some friends who shared a study in a Harvard dormitory.

"Just records, and a couple of bottles of Dago red I sneaked out of the North End, and a stale gingersnap or two."

"Music with wine and gingersnaps? Jim, it's a date."

She knew all the boys in the study but one, a tall, thin, silent young man; shy but rather attractive, she thought, in an odd, individual way. A long face, and extremely large, green-brown, mottled eyes under curious, too heavy lids. The color of his hair was like wet sand; coarse hair, with a hard, springy curl, but clipped close and brushed hard.

Russ would look nice with his hair like that, she thought, idly; *but he wouldn't be bothered.*

The young man, however, did not appear to notice her. He only bowed his head in acknowledgment of her name and looked away. His name she forgot at once.

They played a Brandenburg first, and the Mozart clarinet quintet. She was happy. She sat relaxed and smiling, the toes of one foot curling in her shoe.

"And now," said Jim, "Beethoven, Opus One-thirty-one. Prepare to meet thy God."

The first notes of the opening fugue spoke, and her face changed. It was music, and it was more than music. It was a statement, a grave astonishing statement. But of what? She did not know. It is this, the music said, to be alive; this is the meaning of our journey between birth and death. But, this? What is *this*? She sat forward, struggling, intent.

But the music went on and on. It was too involved, too difficult. At last, it was simply too long. She leaned back in her chair, conscious of the falsity of her own face, frozen, now, in its first spontaneity of intent listening.

And then her eyes fell on the shy young man; and she saw to her surprise that he was remarkably attractive, almost beautiful. The heavy lids were lifted, the too large, mottled eyes, at once brilliant and grave, were like the eyes of a saint in ecstasy.

For an instant she stared at him, and then she averted her eyes, with an uncomfortable feeling of shame, as if she had spied upon him naked.

And then it was over and Jim was waiting, smiling like the magician with silk hat in one hand and rabbit in the other.

"It's wonderful," she said honestly, "but it's too hard, it's beyond me. After half an hour or so I couldn't really listen."

"You'll try again. It takes time."

"How did you find out about it?"

"Oliver." He jerked his head toward the tall young man, and she followed his eyes. However, she barely noticed him. She was thinking, again, about the music.

"You know," she said, "it was queer. . . . I kept feeling that if I could get it, it would take in what art always leaves out . . . you know, headaches, little frustrations, the hour-to-hour part of being alive. As if it made it all fit in . . . everything."

The large, mottled eyes of the quiet young man lifted and looked at her intently. He lifted his head as if he were about to speak. Then his face closed.

"Give me a cigarette, Jim," he said. "I must have smoked my last."

It was the only thing that she heard him say during the afternoon.

Russ came early the next afternoon. He was taking the midnight for Chicago, going home for Christmas.

"What weather! Raw, fog. Not a convenient dry nesting place left above the equator."

"Why don't we go in to the art museum?"

"I hate museums. Full of pictures."

"Oh, all right." She laughed, singing: *"Take your girlie to the movies, when you can't make love at home——"*

He shrugged, his face suddenly angry.

"What is it, Russ? Dear?"

"You know. I've got a warm room, a landlady who doesn't mind——"

"Oh, Russ, please."

"Have it your own way."

They sat through the movie, erect and apart. Afterward neither of them could have told what it had been about.

"It's too early for dinner, not six yet."

"Let's eat anyway, Russ. I didn't have much lunch."

The meal went slowly.

"Russ, I heard the strangest piece of music, yesterday."

"What do you mean, strange?"

"I don't know. It was a Beethoven quartet——"

"Strange is good!"

And there didn't, after all, seem to be anything that you could say about it. There didn't, really, seem to be much of anything to say about anything. For the first time she found herself thinking the thought that she had never let herself think.

We haven't anything in common, except that we love each other. We'll never have anything in common, as long as we live, anything. . . .

"Russ," she said; and her voice was sharp, almost shrewish, and as if she were saying anything but the words she actually said. "Russ . . . look. . . . If you'll understand that it's just the same as if we were outdoors . . . that it's no different . . . that I can't . . . we can't——"

"What?" He stared at her, bewildered. "What?"

"Russ . . . I'll go back to Cambridge. I'll go up to your room."

He looked at her. He smiled.

"Thank you, Rose. It will be all right. I promise."

She felt as if the air were full of sun. She felt gentle and secure. It didn't matter that they couldn't talk to each other. People don't talk about *subjects*, when they're married. They talk about life, day to day. Everything was all right.

I'll tell Karen about us tonight, she thought. *I'll write to papa. I've been so silly . . . silly.*

She rose to her feet and held out her hand, laughing.

"Come on then," she said. "Next stop, convenient, dry nesting place."

They went into the room and shut the door. It was bare and small, a cot, a desk, a straight chair, an unshaded bulb hanging from the ceiling.

She looked around, shaking her head. "My, my, what a little home-maker you are!"

Then she turned, looking for a place to put her coat, and saw, with a start of surprise and pleasure, the picture on the wall behind her.

"Oh," she cried. "The nude Maja! And so big, and in color. How lovely, where did you get her?"

He flushed.

"You like it? Be darned, you're such a straitlaced little somebody, I thought it'd shock you."

"Shock me? Goya?"

She loved pictures. She turned again to the voluptuous richness, the Maja lying on her great, ruffled cushion. And suddenly she saw it as

Russ saw it; the innocent pleasure gone. She felt herself thin and sexless, meager. When she turned back he saw the change in her face.

"Changed your mind? You said yourself it's by a famous painter."

She swallowed.

"Russ, do you wish I looked like that?"

He burst into a roar of laughter, loud with relief.

"Be darned, you're jealous! Jealous of a picture!"

"Russ, it's only—only . . . that I want——"

But she did not know how to say it: *only that I want to be everything a man could want, everything I'm always afraid I'm not.*

"You don't want enough, that's your trouble."

Her face worked.

At once, he was kind.

"Don't worry, darling. I like 'em skinny too. And you don't feel skinny. You feel soft. Rose——"

And suddenly he had reached up and turned off the light.

But the other dark, the inner dark of their lovemaking would not come. She could feel nothing but an emptiness of self-doubt. She tried to hide it from him, letting herself go soft in his arms, opening her lips as she had never done before. She felt him respond to her. After a time she felt him drawing the pins from the knot on her neck, stroking the heavy fall from temple to waist.

"So very long," he said, over and over, softly. "So much, so soft. I never dreamed . . . wonderful——"

Then she was struggling against him.

"Rose, you've got to. You kissed me like that, you let me take your hair down. Rose . . . Rose——"

But he had become completely strange to her and she struggled against him in real terror.

He's forgotten it's me, she thought. *Anyone, I could be anyone. A girl he'd picked up in the street and would never want to see again. I could be hideous . . . old——*

She wrenched and slipped from him and found the lamp on the desk.

They looked at each other, dull-eyed, white-faced. After a little, without a word, she stooped and picked up the scattered pins and wound her hair back into its knot. The sleeve of her dress had torn at the shoulder as she pulled away. She put on her coat.

He was the first to speak, his voice perfectly flat.

"You know, there's an extremely dirty word for girls who start something they don't intend to finish."

"Is there?" Her voice was lifeless as his own.

She turned to the door and opened it.

He let her go into the corridor and start down the steps before he made a motion. But then he hurried toward her and she thought that she was forgiven. However, he had only followed to strike the final blow.

"I had you completely wrong," he said. "You're half-alive, that's what's the matter with you. You ought to go into a convent where you'll be safe. A convent or an old maids' home."

And he went back to his room and shut the door.

She wrote to him once, from Charleswood.

It was only a thing that happened. I got frightened. Perhaps it is always like that for men, impersonal, and I was wrong. Please see me again when you come back. I love you, and I think that you love me.

His own letter crossed hers in the mail.

Dear Rose: I guess we both made a mistake. As I think back, I see you sort of knew it all along, the way you wouldn't go steady or tell anybody. I'm sorry for the things I said up at my place, it wasn't your fault, you just didn't know the score.

Anyway, what I'm trying to say is this. I have patched things up with an old girl out here. She has been very wonderful about understanding that I sort of got off my track out East. We have a great deal in common, folks, upbringing and so forth. But I would feel very bad about this if I wasn't sure that you won't much care. I really did love you, Rose, that's what I want you to know, I loved you right up to almost the end.

Russ.

One of the field hands had brought the mail up from the road and given it to her as she stood alone on the veranda. She read the letter through slowly, once, and then tore it across, dropping the pieces through a crack in the floor boards.

Then she stood straight, with her back against one of the big white pillars, looking across the lawn, across the plowed bottom lands, to the river. She stood so for a long time, not knowing what she thought or felt.

Then her lips moved.

"He couldn't love me. I loved him. But he couldn't love me." And then, "Russ . . . Russ——" And then, quietly, over and over, her own name. "Rose Carrington. Rose Carrington of Charleswood."

At last she went into the house, into her own room, and looked into the mirror.

I didn't tell anyone, she thought. *I can play backgammon with papa, I can go over to Wateroaks, I can go back when vacation is over, and I will be all right, because no one will ever know.*

But that night she dreamed again that she was back at Briargrove, the hem of her dress was torn, and the air was loud with laughter.

It was not until she had come back to Cambridge that she began to cry for Russ at night.

And the year pulled forward into spring. Jim was nice. She saw a lot of Jim.

"Rose, do you remember Oliver?"

"Oliver, Jim?"

"You met him once last winter, over at our place. We were playing records."

"Long legs, didn't talk?"

"The very one. Look, would you take him on for a, well, not blind, a highly astigmatic double date?"

"Oh, mercy, Jim, why?"

"Because . . . I don't know. It's a hunch I've got. If you knew him, if he knew you, you'd be friends."

She laughed. "Looked that way, didn't it? Well, O.K. But if the evening's a flop, don't blame me. Who's the fourth," she asked him; "Karen?"

And she stood by the bed, in her slip and dressing gown, fingering the dress that she had taken from the closet, the tunic, blue gray and silvery green, that Russ had always called "your sexy dress."

I didn't love him because I was afraid to go back to Charleswood, she thought. *I would have loved him just as much if I had never been afraid of anything.*

But for the first time, she had wondered, as she said it, if it were really so.

And it was then that one of the girls called, "Rose! Rose Carrington! Telephone!"

The voice on the other end of the wire was deep and hesitant.

"This . . . this is Miss Carrington?"

"Yes."

Then, in a rush, "This is Oliver Adams. I'm afraid it's off for this evening. Jim tripped on a step, sprained ankle. The doctor's strapped it, but he's got to keep it up for a few days."

"Oh, what a shame. Does it hurt a lot?"

"I expect so. Sprained ankles do. Well——"

She could tell that he was about to hang up. She spoke suddenly, impulsively. "Is it six, then, that you want me to be ready?"

"I . . . why, I——"

"Had you made plans? Because, look, I don't want to influence you or anything, but the Pro Arte Quartette are playing in Sanders Theater tonight."

"Then—then I'll come around at six, as we planned?"

"Six is fine."

And she hung up at once, before he could collect himself.

"The poor thing," she whispered, turning away. "The poor thing. He's scared, the way I used to be."

And for the first time since she had torn the letter from Russ across and dropped it, bit by bit, between the boards of the veranda at Charleswood, her face was warm and bright with self-confidence. She thought, she really thought, that it was for poor Oliver Adams that she was happy.

But the evening was awkward, a failure. The dinner dragged. The conversation was all on her side, too bright and forced. Her face grew stiff with the effort of it, and after a time she began to hear her own voice.

I sound fantastic, she thought angrily. *I sound like a desperate old maid, trying to catch a beau.*

She avoided looking at him through the music, and after it was over they walked home rapidly, almost without a word, as if they were hurrying to an engagement for which they must not be late.

"Good night," she said at the door. "Thank you for a lovely concert."

"Good night." He hesitated for a moment, as if there were something more that he wanted to say. But he only moistened his lips, said once more, "Well, good night," and walked away.

She got into bed, conscious only of a weary exasperation. But tired as she was, sleep did not come.

My legs ache . . . I wonder if I'm catching flu? I feel as if I'd been walking through sand. Jim and his bright ideas.

It was almost two when the tears came at last, the luxurious tears that washed her to sleep.

"Oh, Russ," she sobbed. "You did love me, Russ. You did love me."

And it was flu, after all. Karen brought aspirin, magazines.

"What luck, darling," she said. "What a shame."

"I don't know. It feels sort of nice, now. Watery-weak, and sun in the room, and no need to cope."

"Weren't you going out with Jim tonight?"

"His ankle's sprained. But look, call him for me, will you, and tell him I'm dying too?"

In the late afternoon, a maid came into her room with a florist's box.

"Oh, thank you, Nellie."

"Ah, it's great to be young and it's great to be rich. I told Miss Karen to stop by in a bit and see can she get the right size of a vase from somewhere."

"It's a corsage box, of all things!" Rose exclaimed.

"He expects ye to pin it on your nightgown and die in style."

Of course, it was from Jim. She opened the box, smiling.

It was not a corsage. Lying in the box was a miniature sheaf of sweetheart roses, gypsophila, short side sprays of blue delphinium.

She drew out the card.

"For heaven's sake," she said. "Well, for heaven's sake."

It was from Oliver.

"Thank you for the lovely evening," it said. "Please get well soon. Oliver Adams."

"Oh," she said. "Oh——"

It was a strange little half-rueful sound that caught in her throat.

The afternoon of the day after that was warm and sunny. And Oliver telephoned.

"I've got hold of a car for the day. Do you feel like a little ride, maybe out toward Lincoln? It's very warm and we needn't go far."

"Right away. I feel like a used dishrag and look worse, but I'd love it."

She brushed her long hair and knotted it, smooth and soft.

But when she went down into the hall and found him waiting he stood awkwardly; and when she smiled at him he turned away and walked down the steps to the car with no more than a vague sound of greeting.

Nor, when she was at his side, when she made herself talk, did he seem to feel it necessary to answer in more than the briefest words.

The silences were not comfortable. Under them, the pleasant lassitude of her convalescence changed to a weak-nerved excitement. She heard her own compulsive, high-pitched chatter with shame, and yet she could not be still.

I haven't acted like this for years, she thought. *This is how I would have acted at Briargrove, if anyone had been fool enough to try to find me a beau. I know how he feels, and I can't help him. He brings it all back so.*

They were driving slowly when they passed the old house that looked like Charleswood and Wateroaks, an old white house, the front enclosed in the two-story, pillared porch of the Greek revival. It looked as if nobody had lived in it for a long time. The shutters were closed, and on either side of the tree-lined drive the lawns had become tangled meadows.

"Oh," she cried. "Slow down."

"What is it?"

"That house, that old house. It looks like the place where I grew up."

He drove over to the side of the road.

"Look at that house, Oliver. Can't you imagine it overlooking the cotton fields and the cypress swamps? It doesn't belong here."

But though he had stopped the car for her, and followed her glance with his own eyes, his silence was so odd, so intense, that she turned her head sharply to look at him.

"Oliver, what is it?"

"It's odd that you noticed that house," he said slowly. "It's odd that you said it was like yours."

"Odd? Why?"

"Because it is my house. I grew up there. When I've failed in the world, I shall come back to it and live here, with a cooking pot and a barrel of beans."

She made herself laugh. "Nonsense. Could we get out? Could we walk a little?"

"If you want to."

"Don't you love it?"

"My mother ran away with another man when I was about two, my father died suddenly. I think he killed himself, I'm not sure. My grandmother brought me up. She played solitaire, and talked to herself and read me the more frightening parts of the Bible. I couldn't bring friends home, ever."

He got out of the car.

"No, I don't love it. I haven't been near it for years, except to drive by and look the other way. Come on."

He had come around to her side of the car and opened the door.

"The lane's in too bad shape to drive. Are you up to walking?"

"Not . . . not if it will make you uncomfortable."

"There's a little pond, down the slope at the back. I'd like to see it again. Come on."

He walked slightly ahead of her down the avenue.

"Yes, when I've gone out into the world and failed there, this place will be waiting."

"Don't talk like that," she said sharply. Then she followed him in silence, her head bent.

They walked slowly around one wing of the house; they passed stables, a gingerbread summerhouse with a cupola. There was an overgrown path through the field, down the slope, and the pond lay at the foot, not sprawling and swampy, as she had expected, but deep, fed and drained by a stream, with pebbly banks. There were willows around it.

"Oh," she cried. "What a lovely place!"

He was not looking at her.

"A million miles from the house, that's how I always felt. What seas, what islands? Even in winter, when it froze over. . . . Not to sail boats on, not to skate on, you understand. Just here. Mine."

"I used to go down to the cabins, like that. I used to sit in old Aunt Tizzie's lap and hear the singing. It—it was like a sea."

He was standing behind her, and suddenly she was aware of his hand on her shoulder. His fingers were long and powerful. She looked down at his hand for a moment, and then, hardly knowing what she did, she dropped her cheek upon it. She stood still, feeling his fingers, cold and slowly warming with the warmth of her cheek.

When at length his hand moved, she thought that he would turn her toward him, that he would kiss her. But he only looked at his watch and said, "We should be heading back, shouldn't we?"

I shouldn't have done that, she thought slowly. *He didn't want me to do that.*

She nodded her head and started at once, slowly, back to the car. On the way home they talked about music, briskly, too briskly.

"A good recording. Jim should lend it to you. You heard the C sharp minor, I remember; we have the Budapest records of the Grosse Fugue, now."

Funny, she thought. *Funny. Now he's the one who's sweating to let no ugly silence fall.*

She did not hear from him again for a week. He called, unexpectedly, one night just before dinner. It was an unseasonably soft evening, like full summer.

"Jim says you like to walk by the river. Are you just sitting down to eat? Could I call for you in an hour?"

They walked down Sparks Street and headed up beside the river toward Watertown. They talked easily. It was as if in the week that had separated them, they had become casual old friends. There was still a little evening light by the river, and the air was shrill with marsh peepers.

"Look, Rose, come down here. I'll show you my place. My private point of land."

They sat down, side by side. She looked at him. *Handsome eyes*, she thought, idly. *Funny, you never notice their color, that mottled, bright effect, except when he's happy. He's funny; a difficult, funny person. Funny how last week I was letting myself get ideas about him.*

The air was soft. A vesper sparrow sang from across the water. Russ had taught her so many of the bird songs. *It was autumn*, she thought, *when I used to come here with Russ.* Autumn, the sun still warm, the leaves falling. A convenient, dry nesting place——

And suddenly, silently, she began to cry. As if a film of ice had melted, as if a barrier that she had built had fallen down, she remembered Russ, the shape of his head, the feel of his mouth. If there had never been any friendship, what did it matter? Love, there had been love, and she had been safe in it, secure against everything past and to come. Russ——

She sat quiet, the tears coming faster and faster. The loss and the shame of that loss which she had never dared to let herself admit poured down her cheeks now in a softening, a quickening of sorrow so intense that it was like joy.

"You're crying."

"It doesn't matter," she told him. "Just—just for something that was a long time ago."

"Don't cry."

He had turned toward her, struggling awkwardly to his knees, and she thought, *I can't let him touch me. Russ . . . Russ*——

A week before, by the pond, she had laid her cheek upon his hand, inviting the kiss from which she now shrank in waiting. *It is my fault*, she thought. *I made him want to kiss me. I started it. If I turn away now, he will be so angry. So angry, and so hurt.*

But he did not kiss her. Instead, with a strange, clumsy violence, he threw himself forward, hiding his face in her lap, shuddering. And after a long time, delicately, almost as if she were conquering a repulsion, she raised her hand and laid it on his head.

"What is it?" she whispered. "What is it, Oliver?"

But he only lay, shuddering, his face on her lap, while his long hands moved again and again over her hips and her thighs. And after a little he got to his feet.

"I'm sorry," he said. "Let me take you back to your place. I know it isn't decent, begging like this. I know you're out of my class."

And he walked back to the path. She stumbled after him.

"Oliver, wait . . . wait——"

"What is it?"

"I don't know."

He bowed his head and slackened his pace until they walked side by side, but he did not look down at her, or speak, until they had come to her door again.

"What did you do it for?" he said, then. "What were you trying to do?"

She could only stare at him.

"You made me take you to that concert, when I tried to call it off. You made me stop at my old house, you put your face on my hands, asking me to kiss you. Reflex, I suppose. Collecting another, in spite of yourself. Jim told me how many men you always have. But to let me see you cry, like that, to show me your face like that for someone else . . . that was cruel."

She was too bewildered to answer.

"Think about it," he said abruptly; and walked down the steps.

She went into her room and sat perfectly still on the edge of the bed, staring before her. After a little, clumsily and absently, she drew the pins from her hair and let it fall down about her.

She had sat so, for almost an hour, without moving, when the telephone rang in the upper hall.

"Rose? This is Oliver Adams. I don't know what got into me tonight. Will you forget it, will you let me see you again?"

"You didn't say anything that—that wasn't true."

"And so what? Can you help being yourself, and lovely? Rose, may I see you tomorrow?"

"Yes."

"May I come early and drive you out to the pond?"

She was silent for a moment. Then she said, "I'll try to be ready about nine."

And she hung up without another word.

She looked at herself in the mirror. "I do not love him," she said to her reflection.

She walked about the room.

"It would be catastrophic if I did," she said.

"Penniless, mixed up inside. Both from the same kind of rotten, crazy family. And I made him love me. I did it deliberately, to give myself a build-up, to have someone need me terribly, more than I needed him."

She lay down upon her bed and fell asleep, suddenly and heavily. It was almost morning when she woke with a start. The words in her head spoke themselves so clearly that for an instant she was startled, believing herself to have spoken them aloud.

If I say "I love you," I shall love him. If I say it again and again, "I love you, Oliver, I love you," it will be true.

Then she stood up and pulled off her clothes, opened the bed, and lay down in it. She was asleep again almost at once.

In the morning she did not remember having wakened, but she remembered everything else well enough.

I don't want breakfast, she thought. *I'm not hungry.*

She pulled on a woolen dress, and then, feeling chilly, a light tweed coat.

She looked in the mirror, touched her hair, and sat down on the stiff chair by the desk as if she were waiting for a train.

This is absurd, she said to herself over and over. *Absurd. What am I tearing out to the country for at this hour of the day? To go on making scenes about nothing? Well, I won't.*

"Rose . . . Rose Carrington. . . . Caller."

She ran down the stairs.

He was standing in the lower hall, his head erect and his shoulders back.

"Oliver! I didn't recognize you for a minute. You look . . . you look——"

He laughed, and she realized that she had never heard him laugh before.

"I feel too. I feel. Come out, Rose. It's a perfect day."

He helped her into the car.

"Talk to me while I drive. Tell me about Mississippi."

"I forget about it. It doesn't seem real, up here."

"What are your family like? Your mother?"

"She died when I was little. She had more sisters and cousins than

anybody who ever lived. They're all in the neighborhood, as you count
a neighborhood out there."

"Parties? Ante-bellum stuff?"

"Not at our house. Just the others'."

"Why? Why not?"

"My father's sister keeps house, in a way of speaking. That is, she
lives there. She and my father—they're a lot alike."

"Alike?"

"They drink too much," she said shortly.

He was silent, but the silence was so kind that she was ashamed.

What am I doing? she thought. *Why am I telling him things that I
never told anyone? I will walk down to the pool and we will stand by it,
and he will be like this, happy, and talking, and confident. And I will
say, "It's no use, it's my fault, I made you get fond of me, but it's no
use."*

They drove off the highroad into the long, willow-lined side way. The
house on the hill rose up ahead of them. She got out as he stopped the
car and stood looking up at it.

"Listen," she said suddenly, fiercely. "They're too strong for us,
places like this. They're too strong for people. My father and Aunt Lila
just sit, and sort of nod at each other and drink. And I like them, I love
them, but the silliest one of the Archer kinfolk amounts to more than
both of them put together ten times over."

"Rose, what's the matter?"

"Oliver, promise me . . . before we get to the pond, promise me that
whatever happens, ever, you won't ever come back here."

"What in the world?"

He walked down the path ahead of her.

"I'm sorry . . . I know I sound foolish."

They had come to the edge of the pond. He stood on the edge of it,
smiling as if he had forgotten her.

"What seas, what islands? And you used to run down to the cabins
to hear the singing. Such a long time ago."

"Yes."

"Rose?"

She turned sharply at the sound of his voice. She looked at his face,
and saw, to her utter anguish of shame, that he was happy.

*He thinks that I am beginning to love him. Oh, why did I do it, why
did I make him love me? Because he was so lonely, because I wanted to
save myself by triumphing over an abject need.*

"Rose. Rose who came from a house like mine and never let it hurt her because she was deep and good and sure in herself. Kind, kind Rose, who put out her hand to me."

She looked at the happy shine of the mottled eyes, at the outstretched hands, at the lips smiling. And suddenly she was filled with an amazing sense of power.

I am not a Carrington, she thought. *I am not an Archer. I am myself. I will go on and on, stronger and stronger.*

And suddenly she leaned forward, lifting her mouth. She felt his hands on her, she closed her eyes.

She spoke, moving her lips beneath his, not knowing that she had ever spoken the words before, not knowing that she spoke them now.

"I love you," said the soundless lips. "I love you, Oliver. I love you."

"Rose."

But she had thrown back her head suddenly, joyfully, and was staring into his face.

"Oh, Oliver, I do love you. I do. I do."

They sat down together, hand in hand, by the pond. It was a brilliant morning. They sat motionless for a long time, except that occasionally one or the other laid a cheek upon the interlaced fingers, or raised the free hand to touch the other's hair.

And once or twice Rose thought, *Why have I done this, what am I doing?* But each time she thought again, *Oliver, I love you, Oliver.* And, again, it was true.

She would forget, before a week was past, that her love, her happiness, her coming marriage were of her own making, her own deliberate act.

She looked back up the slope, past the gingerbread summerhouse, past the stables to the house that was like Charleswood, Oliver's house.

"If we ever had money," she said slowly, "you know, it would, it would make a wonderful place for children."

The Liberation

by JEAN STAFFORD

On the day Polly Bay decided to tell her Uncle Francis and his sister, her Aunt Jane, that in a week's time she was leaving their house and was going East to be married and to live in Boston, she walked very slowly home from Nevilles College, where she taught, dreading the startled look in their eyes and the woe and the indignation with which they would take her news. Hating any derangement of the status quo, her uncle, once a judge, was bound to cross-examine her intensively, and Aunt Jane, his perfect complement, would bolster him and baffle her. It was going to be an emotional and argumentative scene; her hands, which now were damp, would presently be dripping. She shivered with apprehension, fearing her aunt's asthma and her uncle's polemic, and she shook with rebellion, knowing how they would succeed in making her feel a traitor to her family, to the town, and to Colorado, and, obscurely, to her country.

Uncle Francis and Aunt Jane, like their dead kinsmen, Polly's father and her grandfather and her great-grandmother, had a vehement family and regional pride, and they counted it virtue in themselves that they had never been east of the Mississippi. They had looked on the departures of Polly's sisters and her cousins as acts of betrayal and even of disobedience. They had been distressed particularly by removals to the East, which were, they felt, iconoclastic and, worse, rude; how, they marveled, could this new generation be so ungrateful to those intrepid early Bays who in the forties had toiled in such peril and with such fortitude across the plains in a covered wagon and who with such perseverance had put down the roots for their traditions in this town that they had virtually made? Uncle Francis and Aunt Jane had done all in their power—through threats and sudden illnesses and cries of "Shame!"—to prevent these desertions, but, nevertheless, one by one, the members of the scapegrace generation had managed to fly, cut off without a penny, scolded to death, and spoken of thereafter as if they were unredeemed, treasonous, and debauched. Polly was the last, and her position, therefore, was the most uncomfortable of all; she and her aunt and uncle were the only Bays left in Adams, and she knew that because she was nearly thirty they had long ago stopped fearing that she, too, might go. As they frequently told her, in their candid way, they felt she had reached "a sensible age"—it was a struggle for them not to use the word "spinster" when they paid her this devious and crushing compliment. She knew perfectly well, because this, too, they spoke of, that they imagined she would still be teaching *Immensee* in German I years after they were dead, and would return each evening to the big, drafty house where they were born, and from which they expected to be carried in coffins ordered for them by Polly from Leonard Harper, the undertaker, whose mealy mouth and shifty eye they often talked about with detestation as they rocked and rocked through their long afternoons.

Polly had been engaged to Robert Fair for five months now and had kept his pretty ring in the desk in her office at college; she had not breathed a word to a soul. If she had spoken out when she came back from the Christmas holidays in her sister's Boston house, her uncle and aunt, with a margin of so much time for their forensic pleas before the college year was over, might have driven her to desperate measures; she might have had to flee, without baggage, in the middle of the night on a bus. Not wanting to begin her new life so haphazardly, she had guarded her secret, and had felt a hypocrite.

But she could not keep silent any longer; she had to tell them and start to pack her bags. She did not know how to present her announcement—whether to disarm them with joy or to stun them with a voice of adamant intention. Resenting the predicament, which so occupied her that her love was brusquely pushed aside, and feeling years younger

than she was—an irritable adolescent, nerve-racked by growing pains—
she now snatched leaves from the springtime bushes and tore them into
shreds. It was late May and the purple lilacs were densely in blossom,
offering their virtuous fragrance on the wind; the sun was tender on the
yellow willow trees; the mountain range was blue and fair and free of
haze. But Polly's senses were not at liberty today to take in these
demure delights; she could not respond today at all to the flattering fortune that was to make her a June bride; she could not remember of her
fiancé anything beyond his name, and, a little ruefully and a little
cynically, she wondered if it was love of him or boredom with freshmen
and with her aunt and uncle that had caused her to get engaged to him.

Although she loitered like a school child, she had at last to confront
the house behind whose drawn blinds her aunt and uncle awaited her
return, innocent of the scare they were presently to get and anticipating
the modest academic news she brought each day to serve them with
their tea. She was so unwilling that when she came in sight of the
house she sat down on a bench at a trolley stop, under the dragging
branches of a spruce tree, and opened the book her uncle had asked her
to bring from the library. It was *The Heart of Midlothian.* She read
with distaste; her uncle's pleasures were different from her own.

Neither the book, though, nor the green needles could hide from her
interior eye that house where she had lived for seven years, since her father had died; her mother had been dead for many years and her sisters
had long been gone—Fanny to Washington and Mary to Boston—but
she had stayed on, quiet and unquestioning. Polly was an undemanding
girl and she liked to teach and she had not been inspired to escape; she
had had, until now, no reason to go elsewhere although, to be sure,
these years had not been exclusively agreeable. For a short time, she
had lived happily in an apartment by herself, waking each morning to
the charming novelty of being her own mistress. But Uncle Francis and
Aunt Jane, both widowed and both bereft of their heartless children,
had cajoled her and played tricks upon her will until she had consented
to go and live with them. It was not so much because she was weak as
it was because they were so extremely strong that she had at last capitu-
lated out of fatigue and had brought her things in a van to unpack
them, sighing, in two wall-papered rooms at the top of the stout brown
house. This odious house, her grandfather's, was covered with broad,
unkempt shingles; it had a turret, and two bow windows within which
begonia and heliotrope fed on the powerful mountain sun. Its rooms
were huge, but since they were gorged with furniture and with garnish-
ments and clumps and hoards of artifacts of Bays, you had no sense of

space in them and, on the contrary, felt cornered and nudged and threatened by hanging lamps with dangerous dependencies and by the dark, bucolic pictures of Polly's forebears that leaned forward from the walls in their insculptured brassy frames.

The house stood at the corner of Oxford Street and Pine, and at the opposite end of the block, at the corner of Pine and Plato (the college had sponsored the brainy place names), there was another one exactly like it. It had been built as a wedding present for Uncle Francis by Polly's grandfather, and here Uncle Francis and his wife, Aunt Lacy, had reared an unnatural daughter and two unnatural sons, who had flown the coop, as he crossly said, the moment they legally could; there was in his tone the implication that if they had gone before they had come of age, he would have haled them back, calling on the police if they offered to resist. Uncle Francis had been born litigious; he had been predestined to arraign and complain, to sue and sentence.

Aunt Jane and Uncle Richard had lived in Grandpa's house, and their two cowed, effeminate sons had likewise vanished when they reached the age of franchise. When both Uncle Richard and Aunt Lacy had been sealed into the Bay plot, Uncle Francis had moved down the street to be with his sister for the sake of economy and company, taking with him his legal library, which, to this day, was still in boxes in the back hall, in spite of the protests of Mildred, their truculent housekeeper. Uncle Francis had then, at little cost, converted his own house into four inconvenient apartments, from which he derived a shockingly high income. A sign over the front door read, "The Bay Arms."

Polly's parents' red brick house, across the street from Uncle Francis's —not built but bought for them, also as a wedding present—had been torn down. And behind the trolley bench on which she sat there was the biggest and oldest family house of all, the original Bay residence, a vast grotesquerie of native stone, and in it, in the beginning of Polly's life, Great-grandmother had imperiously lived, with huge, sharp diamonds on her fichus and her velvet, talking without pause of red Indians and storms on the plains, because she could remember nothing else. The house was now a historical museum; it was called, not surprisingly, the Bay. Polly never looked at it without immediately remembering the intricate smell of the parlor, which had in it moss, must, belladonna, dry leaves, wet dust, oil of peppermint, and something that bound them all together—a smell of tribal history, perhaps, or the smell of a house where lived a half-cracked and haughty old woman who had come to the end of the line.

In those early days, there had been no other houses in this block, and the Bay children had had no playmates except each other. Four generations sat down to Sunday midday dinner every week at Great-grandmother's enormous table; the Presbyterian grace was half as long as a sermon; the fried rabbit was dry. On Christmas Eve, beneath a towering tree in Grandpa's house, sheepish Uncle Richard, as Santa Claus, handed round the presents while Grandpa sat in a central chair like a king on a throne and stroked his proud goatee. They ate turkey on Thanksgiving with Uncle Francis and Aunt Lacy, shot rockets and pinwheels off on the Fourth of July in Polly's family's back yard. Even now, though one of the houses was gone and another was given over to the display of minerals and wagon wheels, and though pressed-brick bungalows had sprung up all along the block, Polly never entered the street without the feeling that she came into a zone restricted for the use of her blood kin, for there lingered in it some energy, some air, some admonition that this was the territory of Bays and that Bays and ghosts of Bays were, and forever would be, in residence. It was easy for her to vest the wind in the spruce tree with her great-grandmother's voice and to hear it say, "Not a one of you knows the sensation of having a red Indian arrow whiz by your sunbonnet with wind enough to make the ribbons wave." On reflection, she understood the claustrophobia that had sent her sisters and cousins all but screaming out of town; horrified, she felt that her own life had been like a dream of smothering.

She was only pretending to read Walter Scott and the sun was setting and she was growing cold. She could not postpone any longer the discharge of the thunderbolt, and at last she weakly rose and crossed the street, feeling a convulsion of panic grind in her throat like a hard sob. Besides the panic, there was a heavy depression, an ebbing away of self-respect, a regret for the waste of so many years. Generations should not be mingled for daily fare, she thought; they are really contemptuous of one another, and the strong individuals, whether they belong to the older or the younger, impose on the meek their creeds and opinions, and, if they are strong enough, brook no dissent. Nothing can more totally subdue the passions than familial piety. Now Polly saw, appalled and miserably ashamed of herself, that she had never once insisted on her own identity in this house. She had dishonestly, supinely (thinking, however, that she was only being polite), allowed her aunt and uncle to believe that she was contented in their house, in sympathy with them,

and keenly interested in the minutiae that preoccupied them: their os-
sifying arteries and their weakening eyes, their dizzy spells and migrant
pains, their thrice-daily eucharist of pills and drops, the twinges in their
old, uncovered bones. She had never disagreed with them, so how could
they know that she did not, as they did, hate the weather? They assumed that she was as scandalized as they by Uncle Francis's tenants'
dogs and children. They had no way of knowing that she was bored
nearly to frenzy by their vicious quarrels with Mildred over the way she
cooked their food.

In the tenebrous hall lined with closed doors, she took off her gloves
and coat, and, squinting through the shadows, saw in the mirror that
her wretchedness was plain in her drooping lips and her frowning forehead; certainly there was no sign at all upon her face that she was in
love. She fixed her mouth into a bogus smile of courage, she
straightened out her brow; with the faintest heart in the world she entered the dark front parlor, where the windows were always closed and
the shades drawn nearly to the sill. A coal fire on this mild May day
burned hot and blue in the grate.

They sat opposite each other at a round, splayfooted table under a
dim lamp with a beaded fringe. On the table, amid the tea things, there
was a little mahogany casket containing the props with which, each
day, they documented their reminiscences of murders, fires, marriages,
bankruptcies, and of the triumphs and the rewards of the departed
Bays. It was open, showing cracked photographs, letters sallow-inked
with age, flaccid and furry newspaper clippings, souvenir spoons flecked
with venomous green, little white boxes holding petrified morsels of
wedding cake. As Polly came into the room, Aunt Jane reached out her
hand and, as if she were pulling a chance from a hat, she picked a newspaper clipping out of the box and said, "I don't think you have ever
told Polly the story of the time you were in that train accident in the
Royal Gorge. It's such a yarn."

Her uncle heard Polly then and chivalrously half rose from his chair;
tall and white-haired, he was distinguished, in a dour way, and dapper
in his stiff collar and his waistcoat piped with white. He said, "At last
our strayed lamb is back in the fold." The figure made Polly shiver.

"How late you are!" cried Aunt Jane, thrilled at this small deviation
from routine. "A department meeting?" If there had been a department
meeting, the wreck in the Royal Gorge might be saved for another day.

But they did not wait for her answer. They were impelled, egocen-
trically and at length, to tell their own news, to explain why it was that
they had not waited for her but had begun their tea. Uncle Francis had

been hungry, not having felt quite himself earlier in the day and having, therefore, eaten next to nothing at lunch, although the soufflé that Mildred had made was far more edible than customary. He had several new symptoms and was going to the doctor tomorrow; he spoke with infinite peace of mind. Painstakingly then, between themselves, they discussed the advisability of Aunt Jane's making an appointment at the beauty parlor for the same hour Uncle Francis was seeing Dr. Wilder; they could in this way share a taxi. And what was the name of that fellow who drove the Town Taxi whom they both found so cautious and well-mannered? Bradley, was it? They might have him drive them up a little way into the mountains for the view; but, no, Francis might have got a bad report and Jane might be tired after her baking under the dryer. It would be better if they came straight home. Sometimes they went on in this way for hours.

Polly poured herself a cup of tea, and Aunt Jane said, as she had said probably three thousand times in the past seven years, "You may say what you like, there is simply nothing to take the place of a cup of tea at the end of the day."

Uncle Francis reached across the table and took the newspaper clipping from under his sister's hand. He adjusted his glasses and glanced at the headlines, smiling. "There was a great deal of comedy in that tragedy," he said.

"Tell Polly about it," said Aunt Jane. Polly knew the details of this story by heart—the number of the locomotive and the name of the engineer and the passengers' injuries, particularly her uncle's, which, though minor, had been multitudinous.

Amazing herself, Polly said, "Don't!" And, amazed by her, they stared.

"Why, Polly, what an odd thing to say!" exclaimed Aunt Jane. "My dear, is something wrong?"

She decided to take them aback without preamble—it was the only way—and so she said, "Nothing's wrong. Everything's right at last. I am going to be married ten days from today to a teacher at Harvard and I am going to Boston to live."

They behaved like people on a stage; Aunt Jane put her teacup down, rattling her spoon, and began to wring her hands; Uncle Francis, holding his butter knife as if it were a gavel, glared.

"What are you talking about, darling?" he cried. "Married? What do you mean?"

Aunt Jane wheezed, signaling her useful asthma, which, however, did not oblige her. "Boston!" she gasped. "What ever for?"

Polly returned her uncle's magisterial look, but she did so obliquely, and she spoke to her cuffs when she said, "I mean 'married,' the way you were married to Aunt Lacy and the way Aunt Jane was married to Uncle Richard. I am in love with a man named Robert Fair and *he* is with *me* and we're going to be married."

"How lovely," said Aunt Jane, who, sight unseen, hated Robert Fair.

"Lovely perhaps," said Uncle Francis the magistrate, "and perhaps not. You might, if you please, do us the honor of enlightening us as to the qualifications of Mr. Fair to marry and export you. To the best of my knowledge, I have never heard of him."

"I'm quite sure we don't know him," said Aunt Jane; she coughed experimentally, but her asthma was still in hiding.

"No, you don't know him," Polly said. "He has never been in the West." She wished she could serenely drink her tea while she talked, but she did not trust her hand. Fixing her eyes on a maidenhair fern in a brass jardiniere on the floor, she told them how she had first met Robert Fair at her sister Mary's cottage in Edgartown the summer before.

"You never told us," said Uncle Francis reprovingly. "I thought you said the summer had been a mistake. Too expensive. Too hot. I thought you agreed with Jane and me that summer in the East was hard on the constitution." (She had; out of habit she had let them deprecate the East, which she had loved at first sight, had allowed them to tell her that she had had a poor time when, in truth, she had never been so happy.)

Shocked by her duplicity, Aunt Jane said, "We ought to have suspected something when you went back to Boston for Christmas with Mary instead of resting here beside your own hearth fire."

Ignoring this sanctimonious accusation, Polly continued, and told them as much of Robert Fair as she thought they deserved to know, eliding some of his history—for there was a divorce in it—but as she spoke, she could not conjure his voice or his face, and he remained as hypothetical to her as to them, a circumstance that alarmed her and one that her astute uncle sensed.

"You don't seem head over heels about this Boston fellow," he said.

"I'm nearly thirty," replied his niece. "I'm not sixteen. Wouldn't it be unbecoming at my age if I *were* lovesick?" She was by no means convinced of her argument, for her uncle had that effect on her; he could make her doubt anything—the testimony of her own eyes, the judgments of her own intellect. Again, and in vain, she called on Robert Fair to materialize in this room that was so hostile to him and, through his affection, bring a persuasive color to her cheeks. She did not question the power of love nor did she question, specifically, the steadfastness of her own love, but she did observe, with some dismay, that, far from conquering all, love lazily sidestepped practical problems; it was no help in this interview; it seemed not to cease but to be temporarily at a standstill.

Her uncle said, "Sixteen, thirty, sixty, it makes no difference. It's true I wouldn't like it if you were wearing your heart on your sleeve, but, my Lord, dear, I don't see the semblance of a light in your eye. You look quite sad. Doesn't Polly strike you as looking downright blue, Jane? If Mr. Fair makes you so doleful, it seems to me you're better off with us."

"It's not a laughing matter," snapped Aunt Jane, for Uncle Francis, maddeningly, had chuckled. It was a way he had in disputation; it was intended to enrage and thereby rattle his adversary. He kept his smile, but for a moment he held his tongue while his sister tried a different tack. "What I don't see is why you have to go to Boston, Polly," she said. "Couldn't he teach Italian at Nevilles just as well as at Harvard?"

Their chauvinism was really staggering. When Roddy, Uncle Francis's son, went off to take a glittering job in Brazil, Aunt Jane and his father had nearly reduced this stalwart boy to kicks and tears by reiterating that if there had been anything of worth or virtue in South America, the grandparent Bays would have settled there instead of in the Rocky Mountains.

"I don't think Robert would like it here," said Polly.

"What wouldn't he like about it?" Aunt Jane bridled. "I thought our college had a distinguished reputation. Your great-grandfather, one of the leading founders of it, was a man of culture, and unless I am sadly misinformed, his humanistic spirit is still felt on the campus. Did you know that his critical study of Isocrates is *highly* esteemed among classical scholars?"

"I mean I don't think he would like the West," said Polly, rash in her frustration.

She could have bitten her tongue out for the indiscretion, because her jingoistic uncle reddened instantly and menacingly, and he banged on the table and shouted, "How does he know he doesn't like the West? You've just told us he's never been farther west than Ohio. How does he dare to presume to damn what he doesn't know?"

"I didn't say he damned the West. I didn't even say he didn't like it. I said *I* thought he wouldn't."

"Then *you* are presuming," he scolded. "I am impatient with Easterners who look down their noses at the West and call us crude and barbaric. But Westerners who renounce and denounce and derogate their native ground are worse."

"Far worse," agreed Aunt Jane. "What can have come over you to turn the man you intend to marry against the land of your forebears?"

Polly had heard it all before. She wanted to clutch her head in her hands and groan with helplessness; even more, she wished that this were the middle of next week.

"We three are the last left of the Bays in Adams," pursued Aunt Jane, insinuating a quaver into her firm, stern voice. "And Francis and I will not last long. You'll only be burdened and bored with us a little while longer."

"We have meant to reward you liberally for your loyalty," said her uncle. "The houses will be yours when we join our ancestors."

In the dark parlor, they leaned toward her over their cups of cold tea, so tireless in their fusillade that she had no chance to deny them or to defend herself. Was there to be, they mourned, at last not one Bay left to lend his name and presence to municipal celebrations, to the laying of cornerstones and the opening of fairs? Polly thought they were probably already fretting over who would see that the grass between the family graves was mown.

Panicked, she tried to recall how other members of her family had extricated themselves from these webs of casuistry. Now she wished that she had more fully explained her circumstances to Robert Fair and had told him to come and fetch her away, for he, uninvolved, could afford to pay the ransom more easily than she. But she had wanted to spare him such a scene as this; they would not have been any more reticent with him; they would have, with this same arrogance—and this underhandedness—used their advanced age and family honor to twist the argument away from its premise.

Darkness had shrunk the room to the small circle where they sat in the thin light of the lamp; it seemed to her that their reproaches and their jeremiads took hours before they recommenced the bargaining Aunt Jane had started.

Reasonably, in a judicious voice, Uncle Francis said, "There is no reason at all, if Mr. Fair's attainments are as you describe, that he can't be got an appointment to our Romance Language Department. What is the good of my being a trustee if I can't render such a service once in a way?"

As if this were a perfectly wonderful and perfectly surprising solution, Aunt Jane enthusiastically cried, "But of course you can! That would settle everything. Polly can eat her cake and have it, too. Wouldn't you give them your house, Francis?"

"I'd propose an even better arrangement. Alone here, Jane, you and I would rattle. Perhaps we would move into one of my apartments and the Robert Fairs could have this house. Would that suit you?"

"It would, indeed it would," said Aunt Jane. "I have been noticing the drafts here more and more."

"I don't ask you to agree today, Polly," said Uncle Francis. "But think it over. Write your boy a letter tonight and tell him what your aunt and I are willing to do for him. The gift of a house, as big a house as this, is not to be scoffed at by young people just starting out."

Her "boy," Robert, had a tall son who in the autumn would enter Harvard. "Robert has a house," said Polly, and she thought of its dark-green front door with the brilliant brass trimmings; on Brimmer Street, at the foot of Beacon Hill, its garden faced the Charles. Nothing made her feel more safe and more mature than the image of that old and handsome house.

"He could sell it," said her indomitable aunt.

"He could rent it," said her practical uncle. "That would give you additional revenue."

The air was close; it was like the dead of night in a sealed room and Polly wanted to cry for help. She had not hated the West till now, she had not hated her relatives till now; indeed, till now she had had no experience of hate at all. Surprising as the emotion was—for it came swiftly and authoritatively—it nevertheless cleared her mind and, outraged, she got up and flicked the master switch to light up the chandelier. Her aunt and uncle blinked. She did not sit down again but stood in the doorway to deliver her valediction. "I don't want Robert to come here because I don't want to live here any longer. I want to live my own life."

"Being married is hardly living one's own life," said Aunt Jane.

At the end of her tether now, Polly all but screamed at them, "We *won't* live here and that's that! You talk of my presuming, but how can *you* presume to boss not only me but a man you've never even seen? I don't want your houses! I hate these houses! It's true—I hate, I despise, I abominate the West!"

So new to the articulation of anger, she did it badly and, ashamed to death, began to cry. Though they were hurt, they were forgiving, and both of them rose and came across the room, and Aunt Jane, taking her in a spidery embrace, said, "There. You go upstairs and have a bath and rest and we'll discuss it later. Couldn't we have some sherry, Francis? It seems to me that all our nerves are unstrung."

Polly's breath toiled against her sobs, but all the same she took her life in her hands and she said, "There's nothing further to discuss. I am leaving. I am not coming back."

Now, for the first time, the old brother and sister exchanged a look of real anxiety; they seemed, at last, to take her seriously; each waited for the other to speak. It was Aunt Jane who hit upon the new gambit. "I mean dear, that we will discuss the wedding. You have given us very short notice but I daresay we can manage."

"There is to be no wedding," said Polly. "We are just going to be married at Mary's house. Fanny is coming up to Boston."

"Fanny has known all along?" Aunt Jane was insulted. "And all this time you've lived under our roof and sat at our table and never told *us* but told your sisters, who abandoned you?"

"Abandoned me? For God's sake, Aunt Jane, they had their lives to lead!"

"Don't use that sort of language in this house, young lady," said Uncle Francis.

"I apologize. I'm sorry. I am just so sick and tired of—"

"Of course you're sick and tired," said the adroit old woman. "You've had a heavy schedule this semester. No wonder you're all nerves and tears."

"Oh, it isn't that! Oh, leave me alone!"

And, unable to withstand a fresh onslaught of tears, she rushed to the door. When she had closed it upon them, she heard her aunt say, "I simply can't believe it. There must be some way out. Why, Francis, we would be left altogether *alone*," and there was real terror in her voice.

Polly locked the door to her bedroom and dried her eyes and bathed their lids with witch hazel, the odor of which made her think of her Aunt Lacy, who, poor simple creature, had had to die to escape this family. Polly remembered that every autumn Aunt Lacy had petitioned Uncle Francis to let her take her children home for a visit to her native Vermont, but she had never been allowed to go. Grandpa, roaring, thumping his stick, Uncle Francis bombarding her with rhetoric and using the word "duty" repeatedly, Polly's father scathing her with sarcasm, Aunt Jane slyly confusing her with red herrings had kept her an exhausted prisoner. Her children, as a result, had scorned their passive mother and had wounded her, and once they finally escaped, they had not come back—not for so much as a visit. Aunt Lacy had died not having seen any of her grandchildren; in the last years of her life she did nothing but cry. Polly's heart ached for the plight of that gentle, frightened woman. How lucky *she* was that the means of escape had come to her before it was too late! In her sister's Boston drawing room, in a snowy twilight, Robert Fair's proposal of marriage had seemed to release in her an inexhaustible wellspring of life; until that moment she had not known that she was dying, that she was being killed—by inches, but surely killed—by her aunt and uncle and by the green yearlings in her German classes and by the dogmatic monotony of the town's provincialism. She shuddered to think of her narrow escape from wasting away in these arid foothills, never knowing the cause or the name of her disease.

Quiet, herself again, Polly sat beside the window and looked out at the early stars and the crescent moon. Now that she had finally taken her stand, she was invulnerable, even though she knew that the brown sherry was being put ceremoniously on a tray, together with ancestral Waterford glasses, and though she knew that her aunt and uncle had not given up—that they had, on the contrary, just begun. And though she knew that for the last seven days of her life in this house she would be bludgeoned with the most splenetic and most defacing of emotions, she knew that the worst was over; she knew that she would survive, as her sisters and her cousins had survived. In the end, her aunt and uncle only *seemed* to survive; dead on their feet for most of their lives, they had no personal history; their genesis had not been individual—it had only been a part of a dull and factual plan. And they had been too busy honoring their family to love it, too busy defending the West even to look at it. For all their pride in their surroundings, they had never contemplated them at all but had sat with the shades drawn, huddled under the steel engravings. They and her father had lived their whole lives on the laurels of their grandparents; their goal had already been reached long before their birth.

The mountains had never looked so superb to her. She imagined a time, after Uncle Francis and Aunt Jane were dead, when the young Bays and their wives and husbands might come back, free at last to admire the landscape, free to go swiftly through the town in the foothills without so much as a glance at the family memorials and to gain the high passes and the peaks and the glaciers. They would breathe in the thin, lovely air of summits, and in their mouths there would not be a trace of the dust of the prairies where, as on a treadmill, Great-grandfather Bay's oxen plodded on and on into eternity.

The next days were for Polly at once harrowing and delightful. She suffered at the twilight hour (the brown sherry had become a daily custom, and she wondered if her aunt and uncle naïvely considered getting her drunk and, in this condition, persuading her to sign an unconditional indenture) and all through dinner as, by turns self-pitying and contentious, they sought to make her change her mind. Or, as they put it, "come to her senses." At no time did they accept the fact that she was going. They wrangled over summer plans in which she was included; they plotted anniversary speeches in the Bay museum; one afternoon Aunt Jane even started making a list of miners' families among whom Polly was to distribute Christmas baskets.

But when they were out of her sight and their nagging voices were out of her hearing, they were out of her mind, and in it, instead, was Robert Fair, in his rightful place. She graded examination papers tolerantly, through a haze; she packed her new clothes into her new suitcases and emptied her writing desk completely. On these starry, handsome nights, her dreams were charming, although, to be sure, she sometimes woke from them to hear the shuffle of carpet slippers on the floor below her as her insomniac aunt or uncle paced. But before sadness or rue could overtake her, she burrowed into the memory of her late dream.

The strain of her euphoria and her aunt's and uncle's antipodean gloom began at last to make her edgy, and she commenced to mark the days off on her calendar and even to reckon the hours. On the day she met her classes for the last time and told her colleagues goodbye and quit the campus forever, she did not stop on the first floor of the house but went directly to her room, only pausing at the parlor door to tell Aunt Jane and Uncle Francis that she had a letter to get off. Fraudulently humble, sighing, they begged her to join them later on for sherry. "The days are growing longer," said Aunt Jane plaintively, "but they are growing fewer."

Polly had no letter to write. She had a letter from Robert Fair to read, and although she knew it by heart already, she read it again several times. He shared her impatience; his students bored him, too; he said he had tried to envision her uncle's house, so that he could imagine her in a specific place, but he had not been able to succeed, even with the help of her sister. He wrote, "The house your malicious sister Mary describes could not exist. Does Aunt Jane *really* read Ouida?"

She laughed aloud. She felt light and purged, as if she had finished a fever. She went to her dressing table and began to brush her hair and to gaze, comforted, upon her young and loving face. She was so lost in her relief that she was pretty, and that she was going to be married and was going away, that she heard neither the telephone nor Mildred's feet upon the stairs, and the housekeeper was in the room before Polly had turned from her pool.

"It's your sister calling you from Boston," said Mildred with ice-cold contempt; she mirrored her employers. "I heard those operators back East giving themselves *some* airs with their la-di-da way of talking."

Clumsy with surprise and confusion (Mary's calls to her were rare and never frivolous), and sorry that exigency and not calm plan took her downstairs again, she reeled into that smothering front hall where hat trees and cane stands stood like people. The door to the parlor was closed, but she knew that behind it Aunt Jane and Uncle Francis were listening.

When Mary's far-off, mourning voice broke to Polly the awful, the impossible, the unbelievable news that Robert Fair had died that morning of the heart disease from which he had intermittently suffered for some years, Polly, wordless and dry-eyed, contracted into a nonsensical, contorted position and gripped the telephone as if this alone could keep her from drowning in the savage flood that had come from nowhere.

"Are you there, Polly? Can you hear me, darling?" Mary's anxious voice came louder and faster. "Do you want me to come out to you? Or can you come on here now?"

"I can't come now," said Polly. "There's nothing you can do for me." There had always been rapport between these sisters, and it had been deeper in the months since Robert Fair had appeared upon the scene to rescue and reward the younger woman. But it was shattered; the bearer of ill tidings is seldom thanked. "How can you help me?" Polly demanded, shocked and furious. "You can't bring him back to life."

"I can help bring you back to life," her sister said. "You must get out of *there*, Polly. It's more important now than ever."

"Do you think that was why I was going to marry him? Just to escape this house and this town?"

"No, no! Control yourself! We'd better not try to talk any more —you call me when you can."

The parlor door opened, revealing Uncle Francis with a glass of sherry in his hand.

"Wait, Mary! Don't hang up!" Polly cried. There was a facetious air about her uncle; there was something smug. "I'll get the sleeper from Denver tonight," she said.

When she hung up, her uncle opened the door wider to welcome her to bad brown sherry; they had not turned on the lights, and Aunt Jane, in the twilight, sat in her accustomed place.

"Poor angel," said Uncle Francis.

"I am so sorry, so very sorry," said Aunt Jane.

When Polly said nothing but simply stared at their impassive faces, Uncle Francis said, "I think I'd better call up Wilder. You ought to have a sedative and go straight to bed."

"I'm going straight to Boston," said Polly.

"But why?" said Aunt Jane.

"Because he's there. I love him and he's there."

They tried to detain her; they tried to force the sherry down her throat; they told her she must be calm and they asked her to remember that at times like this one needed the love and the support of one's blood kin.

"I am going straight to Boston," she repeated, and turned and went quickly up the stairs. They stood at the bottom, calling to her: "You haven't settled your affairs. What about the bank?" "Polly, get hold of yourself! It's terrible, I'm heartbroken for you, but it's not the end of the world."

She packed nothing; she wanted nothing here—not even the new clothes she had bought in which to be a bride. She put on a coat and a hat and gloves and a scarf and put all the money she had in her purse and went downstairs again. Stricken but diehard, they were beside the front door.

"Don't go!" implored Aunt Jane.

"You need us now more than ever!" her uncle cried.

"And we need you. Does that make no impression on you, Polly? Is your heart that cold?"

She paid no attention to them at all and pushed them aside and left the house. She ran to the station to get the last train to Denver, and once she had boarded it, she allowed her grief to overwhelm her. She felt chewed and mauled by the niggling hypochondriacs she had left behind, who had fussily tried to appropriate even her own tragedy. She felt sullied by their disrespect and greed.

How lonely I have been, she thought. And then, not fully knowing what she meant by it but believing in it faithfully, she said half aloud, "I am not lonely now."

❧

Fifty-Fifty

by LEONARD WOLF

❧

Of love, repeat to yourself that it can only be a disaster; throw in the sponge, give up, back away—quit. Whatever you decide, you will come back to it, with or without advice, and, when you do, there she will be, waiting for you in some place she has no business to be, smiling, looking rueful, already with that expectant look in her eyes while you, who have also lived through various permutations of forgetfulness and taken vows never to see or imagine her again, give up. There's a busy destiny here that doesn't like frayed ends and therefore plaits away, braiding, braiding.

You think it's sex, the bitten lower lip, the profile of the bosom behind the translucent pane of glass where an inexpensive lamp makes a silhouette. I know. Of that and those I know all; but that's not it; not the panting, the haste, the motels, the frantic swiftness in a parked car under a wet oak tree in a corner of a public park; not even the yearning moments in a cornfield under the stars while the flashlights of private detectives moved among the broken stalks, row by row, and missed us. Not the yells of triumph or rage; not, sometimes, the silent weeping.

It has nothing to do with that. That's easy. It happens at 10:00

o'clock on any Monday morning; it happens in the dark or daylight; skinny children do it backstage in the local high school while the principal exhorts the day's assembly.

No. No. No. No. No. No. No.

We're all weary of that, and it isn't the truth. I'm talking about love, the higher cataclysm, the whole shebang.

Watch this: I say "Put on your coat."

She is in the other room, still combing her hair, and says, "Wait a minute."

I don't need to look at that hair, thick, wavy, forever perfumed with God knows what—dreadful, lovely. I turn the pages of a book and say, "Okay. But we don't want to get there late."

To which she replies, "We won't be late. Don't rush me."

Without a moment's hesitation, I say, "Who's rushing you?"

I can hear the comb, caught in the hair; the eyes are squinting a little as she looks in her mirror in that small room, too dark for comfort in the tiny squalor where she sleeps. The comb stops, and there are suddenly lines, like the staff of a musical score, waving slowly toward me. Then they turn to wires. Trouble. A living snarl of tons of wire whirling about, surrounding her at her mirror, me at my book.

I don't need to see her put the comb down. She pushes her way as she can through the wire (which has turned barbed as well), clambers into the room where I sit with the book whose title I don't know, and climbs up on the high stool beside the table she made at the Adult Education Center. She made, that is to say, by an ineptitude that wrung sweetly the hearts of instructor, neighbor on the right, neighbor on the left, principal, janitor, rodent in the cellar, cricket on the wall; in short, every creature, male, in the building. Her table was wrought out of such innocence; but, with all that help, made of plywood, rickety, and not a perfect square. She sits precariously at that table and replies to my question: "*You* are rushing me."

To which I say, "Oh, for Christ's sake, forget it. I'm not rushing you." And I reach for that book, knowing that the wires in the room are now going to stay, since one strand has just neatly wound itself around not my skull but the brain proper, the soft cerebrum, cerebellum, medulla oblongata, cortex, and whatever yielding elements there are inside that bone that wire may constrict. And there's a twinge, gentle at first, but it soon gives way to a skilful throbbing.

"That's right," she says; and it's true that her lower lip is delicious; that it does pout; that it is impossible not to think of biting it; but that is not the point. Not now. "That's right," she says. "You're not rushing me."

So I must look up from that book, lifting my head, pushing against the resistance of tons of wire as well as the fine, determined tugging of the strand inside my skull. I look up to see her, dark, small, slim, ready to go, dressed; fresh lipstick, earrings in place; the dewy look of her eye-lids (applied, but nonetheless!); and I hear myself getting ready to ask, "What do you mean?" And, lo and behold, I do.

"I'm not going," she says.

And like a logical machine, having received my appropriate coin, I spit out the appropriate gum ball, this time colored red. "Why not?"

Do you see how it was? The right thing, you might say, was to smack her. Like that: smack, bang. And then to the party or to bed: high-handed and rough. A useful way to deal with a woman. But, remember, I'm talking about love itself.

And, what's more, I did smack her once. And I did the entire prescription. It was a waste of time. She was way ahead of me, betraying the whole psychology—not laughing, but letting me know she knew what page in the book the method came from; calling the shots.

So I didn't smack her, but let her sit on her high chair at her rickety, unsquare table. First we were late to the party to which, of course, we never went. But at least, during that first interval, the party was the myth that buoyed us up; it was the goal of the conversation. If we could only make the idea of the party seem real, we might have a chance to get out of the apartment (her husband was still paying the rent . . . and that's another thing: she was helping me out because I was poor. We split the cost of our evenings, trips, motels, dinners in ob-scure restaurants. Fifty-fifty. My half; her half. And her half—where do you suppose it came from? He was a stickler for propriety and she was still his wife). As I say, we both thought that, if we could only get back to the idea of the party, we might have a chance. But first she had to maintain her integrity, and I, clutching the book whose title I now remembered (*Love in a Darkling Cavern*), hung onto mine. It all seemed logical.

Our words made the case out that she wouldn't be bullied, on the one hand, and that I wasn't a bully, on the other. Don't imagine that this was a spat, either. It was a reasoned analysis of each other's motivations. You've gathered from what I've already told you that we are both sensitive. She wanted me to understand what was *not* bothering her at the same time as I tried to explain, with the greatest detachment, what seemed to me to be our real motivations.

By this time, night had fallen. The lights along the bridge were turned on. It was that trembling time when they have not yet turned the harsh yellow that they become, but hesitate, a lovely amber-red; and the bay, instead of being a body of water, for half an hour announces itself as clean obsidian. Up and down the hill we could hear the prowl cars moving slowly, whining softly, mewing with their gentlest sirens, like kittens. They were looking for a poor Negro who had murdered a policeman early in the morning. "Hey, you, what are you doing there?" the cop is supposed to have said, and the Negro, doing something in the back seat of an automobile, alone, had leapt in panic from the car and driven a six-inch knife into the cop. We'd watched the helicopters searching for him all afternoon.

I suppose I should say "the poor cop," too. Why more pity for the Negro? I suppose because he was asked; he was the one intruded upon. Isn't the asker always stronger? Isn't he?

I'm sorry the cop died. We knew him—a nice boy, much like the decent folk who helped her make the table. He used, sometimes, to carry up her groceries. It was a long flight of steps from the street to her porch and she was often loaded down. You know, living alone as she did, there was something natural and even, if you like, heartwarming about all that. A kind of Greek chorus of decent men developed around her, showing up at odd times to give her a hand. They all knew about me, but a lover isn't the same as a husband, even if he pays some of the bills. So this nice cop helped her out; and the milkman; even the crazy queer next door who lived with his grandmother; and the groceryman down the hill who called me her "friend." But nobody sniggered. Love has its way of disarming comment.

Night had fallen, and it was clearly too late to get to the party. I made some sort of an attempt to phone the hostess—that is, the idea occurred to me, but by then we were up to our skulls in wire and accusations. The book became part of it all. It turned out to be a library book I had forgotten to return for her—its author a sometime friend of mine who had blown into town for a brief visit. A clever young man with lots of books under his belt, and something of a gift. Garrulous and, in his own way, brave. The women reviewers praised his understanding of their sex; the men preferred his style and called it swift, lean, alert. He traveled widely and liked to set his stories in exotic lands. He was still young and wanted to do the talking.

I rather liked him, and brought him around; though liked is a stronger word than I would use if this were fifty years ago. We got along; he was famous; I wasn't . . . there was a kind of swinging interchange between us—friendly, anxious, contemptuous, condescending, and a small bit of respect on both sides. He was rich, and when he came to town usually needed a woman. On occasion, I had done some genteel pandering for him—the usual thing: one of that new breed of employed, clever women with some ambition in the arts who read the latest books and will lie down for literate, sufficient reasons for young men much farther out on the fringes of fame than, for instance, even I was.

A sprightly, vivacious girl. We went out, the four of us, to various places where we could be aloof and bitter and amused while we waited to be rid of each other, to get back to whatever caverns, dens, shacks where they could be simple and quick and we would manage our complex affairs till dawn.

Though even for them it probably turned out not as simple as he would say. The girl came from a terribly respectable Cincinnati family and made her living as the naked swimmer in Bimbo's fishbowl. It's a nice stunt that sets the tourists off. You sit around the bar and drink and wait for the floorshow to begin; it's pleasant and wistful, when you haven't got a girl, or if you have and are not yet warm enough together; so, with your drink in your hand, you watch this mirror panorama—like looking through the portholes of a miniature Beebe diving bell. The effect *is* a little like being under water, and all of a sudden a naked girl appears, evidently swimming. Six inches from crown to toe, swimming, swimming, being very careful of her thighs, or else she breaks the law. Of course, it's all done with mirrors, and everybody except the worst of the yokels knows it. It comes on every hour, and a public intimacy grows, part shame, part bravado, a very small part lust. A roomful of peeping toms peeping also at each other. Respectable Cincinnati family or not, from end to end she looked quite good. The whole act lasts four minutes, and for a girl with ambitions in the theatre, who spent the intervals between appearances reading *Doctor Zhivago*, it was an easy way to make a living (though later the whole thing tumbled down on her head when her uncle, attending a medical convention, caught the act and wired the bad news home. They shipped her off to a psychiatrist—which is one more indication of what has happened to the idea of free will in our time). Lovely shoulders; under glass, her breasts looked better than they were.

Well, I've gone the long way around to make the point that, while the police were driving up and down our hill looking for that poor damned Negro and we were tangled in our wire maze and I was holding onto the book I had failed to take back to the library, it occurred to me at last that her sudden interest in his fiction was more than literary and less than pure. You know how a bubble can burst in the brain, and suddenly you have knowledge. But I resisted. I said to myself, "Hell, that's an unworthy suspicion." Then I remembered the Greek chorus of helpful men, and her fierce protection of her privacy. I didn't live there, you know. And I was never supposed to come without telephoning. When, on some of our angry days, I did, she just damn well didn't let me in. I had no evidence there was anyone with her, and as things turned out I never did, then or later; still, some suspicions become facts whether they can be proved or no.

On the whole, I behaved honorably; I never taxed her. The one thing I never did was spy on her.

We continued to quarrel about the book. I said, with some violence, that my not returning it was a trivial oversight, to which she replied that it was like me to be so petty as to subject her to a daily fine of two cents out of pique with her pleasure in a writer of better (or wider—which word did she use?) reputation than my own. By this time, the room felt as if it existed on a tilted floor; tilted a full forty-five degrees, like the crazy floors in the house in San Jose that the lunatic built who was afraid to die. At the upper end, she sat on her high stool, accusing me in her hushed voice; at the lower end I sat, not quite so calmly, and replied.

At last, she said, "I'm tired. I don't want to talk anymore. It's no use."

And I said, "Come sit here. Let's not go on with this."

"That's always your way, isn't it? Put me on a couch so you can use me. It's disgusting."

But it wasn't. Sometimes the simplest touch could turn her on, and, when she was, it seemed to me that everything but that was mad. During those wild moments, each of us believed—I swear—that we could build a life on that. On that alone.

After one of those beautiful weekends evading her husband's private detectives (fools, by the way: we weren't hiding anything. Everyone in town, including the most widely read gossip columnist, knew about us; but her husband had a New England conscience and wanted, in all things, to be thorough; as he figured it, what was generally known was not necessarily courtroom evidence) . . . The detectives, as I say, were fools, and we evaded them as a sort of game: to see if we could, to add the touch of humor that we both felt was missing in our affair. What oafs they were; eyeing us out of jealous, greasy eyes; scratching at a crotch mournfully in lonely hotel lobbies as we, clean, bathed, slept out, spent, passed them by. One knew, always, what they were imagining; both more and less than the truth. Fat men; fat men; so lonely they were available for following. After one of those beautiful weekends, as I started to say, we were driving north along the coast in her car (mine didn't have a spare tire—it was being retreaded and I'd forgot to get it back before the weekend was on us). It was late afternoon and spring, with the sun not brilliant—calm over the water and shimmering out at sea; inshore, the waves were breaking. Not angrily, but with a friendly, spent motion, curling and dissipating whitely in toward shore. From time to time, as we rounded a curve, we looked north and saw the cliffs where the land broke finally, perhaps a little brusquely, but without accusation on this sunny day. We passed rare, weatherbeaten ranchhouses; aging horses in clusters browsing among furze and heather, content and waiting to die in the ocean-and-broom scented air. Sometimes, to the left, a few hundred yards offshore, there would rise the kind of hunk of island that looks as if it has been yanked away from the land, standing there, tall as the plateau on which we were driving, but separated now by quiet water which could, I knew, rage in the gap between. Worn with love-making and the gentle ending of the day, the car quiet, humming, the spring air flowing through the windows, bringing us the scent the horses breathed, we were quiet and, you would have thought, perfectly at peace.

And so I said of one of them, "Isn't that a fine island?"

She took her hand from mine. We were getting closer to it, and I could see the rank broom in yellow flower surrounding three tall cypresses. "What a great place," I said.

To which she replied, "Why do you always want to own everything? Can't you just let it be? Why must you want it for yourself?"

She was so bitter that I knew she'd guessed what I hadn't, this time, said—that I imagined building a cabin on that island. Moving to it with my typewriter and my imagination; secluding myself where I could watch the ocean every morning, every night. That I wanted to be there in the winter storms when the waves came so high they pounded the windows of my invented cabin; that I had already figured out a way of getting water to the island by means of hanging pipes that would, somehow, be led to a perpetual spring on shore. That I wanted to grow old there (or in any of the scores of other such places I had had this yearning for) while I picked out of the surge of language and the sea the shape of all creation.

I felt my chest grow empty while my hands handled the wheel; we made our way around curves at forty miles an hour, and the sun slipped steadily downward. Some kind of important reply wanted to come up out of that hollow place; it should be witty or deft or scathing or cruel or like a knotted rope pulled through the heart. But a bee flew into the car and, bewildered by the glass and steel, could not find its way out. It circled, humming its minor anger round our heads. She panicked, and I stepped on the gas. The swift burst of air produced by the speed dizzied the bee or frightened it; the buzzing quickened and it flew more fiercely round and round.

"For God's sake, stop the car!" she cried as I twice veered, first right, then left.

"Don't be absurd," I answered. "Sit still. It'll fly out." I waved my hand slowly toward the bee, which merely increased its unhappy buzzing.

"Stop the car," she demanded, cowering to her side of the seat, her hands to her hair.

I said, "Just relax. There's nothing to worry about." I couldn't bring myself to obey her. There was something here; something important. The honey-laden animal held to its murmuring rage, swooping in the closed space like a tiny pursuit plane—and I could not stop the car. It had to leave as it came; it was not to shame me before her; it had to stand for the witty, the deft, the scathing, the cruel reply I had not made. An ordinary honeybee, now miles from home, trying to see the world out of its compound eyes, bumping at glass and steel and an insane dimension of speed. What must it have thought?

She bent far forward, as if she meant to be sick. Her voice came flat and low; her hands were spread over her ears and hair, her elbows meeting over her chest. "It's my car," she said. "Stop it."

And that was that. I stopped the car. I got out and so did she. In a minute, the bee also found its way out, lifted into the air, made two or three circles, and started back over the hopeless miles where, I suppose, it passed the tired detectives driving through the dusk in their rented Chevrolet, munching their cold chicken sandwiches, staring ahead in the falling dark toward love.

Past 9:00 o'clock, she was still sitting at her rickety table. Neither of us had thought to turn on a light. Our anger was going on and on, perfectly content not to be seen. Without meaning to, I'd begun to tear small corner strips from the pages of my friend's book. A shaft of moonlight, coming through her street window, fell diagonally across the room, dividing her neatly from me. The whiteness lay between us, cool, inert; it seemed to me that we would soon resemble a painting by Pieter de Hooch, though there was no checkerboard tile floor, no butter churn, no grieving picture on the wall.

There was a knock at the door, and I answered it. She only leaned against the wall; her backless stool was hard to sit on, but she wouldn't move. It was a policeman, carrying a flashlight.

"Would you folks mind turning on your porch light?" he asked. "That nigger's sure to be in one of these blocks. We're trying to cut down the places he can hide." He said no word about the obscurity in which we sat. I turned on the porch light; he thanked me and left, looking scared.

When I turned back to her, she was gone, evidently to the bedroom. I went to my corner of the couch; with the porch light on, I could now see well enough to read, and I glanced down at a page in the book my friend had written. I read, "She seduced me quite openly, almost avariciously; and, at the same time, as if she hardly noticed me. I was standing on a ladder adjusting a water bottle over the cage of a family of mice when she looked up at me, a fine glaze of impersonality across her eyes, and said, 'Come down off that ladder.' I came down and lost my virginity in a roomful of mice, behind a locked door, while in forty-seven cages hundreds of rodents rustled and tittered on their shelves.

"From then, it is not as if she taught me all I know, but for a few months, on river banks, in hayfields, behind fences, beside the stadium —everywhere, indeed, except a common bed—she emphasized the single advantage that we have in youth. On really cold nights, she taught me that it is better to love than to freeze.

"But I did not want anything from her. I hardly called her by name, and she merely gritted her teeth at the familiar moment and cried out once, after which she wanted nothing more than her delicious sleep."

It seemed to me that "it is better to love than to freeze" was a good line, but not nearly good enough to support the sudden reputation that had come to my friend recently. As for the rest, wasn't it really rather empty?

She came back into the room and resumed her seat. "Aren't you hungry?" I asked her.

"No," she said, smiling wolfishly. "Wolfish" is the right word, too. That beautiful, oval face, now touched by the light that came into the room from the porch, simply opened into a smile that had neither love nor humor in it. It came to me that she was frightened . . . triumphant and frightened.

"What have you done?" I asked.

"What do you care?" She had her hands folded in her lap, her shoulders slumped forward.

"What have you done?" I demanded.

"It isn't polite to ask a lady, but, if you must know, I've been to the bathroom." It was a wretched reply; indelicate; not like her.

"No," I said. "That's not what you've done." The secret hung between us; I was already beginning to guess—pushed along by that wolflike smile, the hysterical contentment, the grim happiness of her folded hands.

Urgently, wearily, she whispered, "What do you care?" And, again, "What do you care? All you've done all evening is grind and grind at me. Why don't you go home and let me sleep?"

"Are you sleepy?" I said, catching the clue.

"No, but I will be."

"What does that mean?"

"Nothing. Nothing." She leaned her back and shoulders heavily against the wall, letting her eyes open to their fullest—wide, dark, at moments so plunged in melancholy I would have died to take that sorrow from her; now, so wide and glittering; expanded with her secret; joyful, and instinct with harm.

"Have you taken a sleeping pill?"

"Five," she replied.

I got to my feet. "Goddamn it. For God's sake, what are you trying to do?"

"I want you to go home," she said.

"I can't go home now," I shouted.

"Why not? You could go home and let me sleep. You could go away. You could go to a show. You could go to the party. I'm tired. I've been tired. I told you a long time ago I was tired. Go home."

"Did you really take five tablets?"

"Yes. I want to sleep."

"Come on," I said. "I'll get your coat. I'm taking you to the hospital."

"I won't go," she whispered. "No, I won't go."

I put my hand on her shoulder; that thin shoulder— I could feel the fragile collarbone under my fingers, my thumb on the delicate skin at her throat, feeling her pulse throbbing. "Come *on*," I said. "Come on."

I let her go and found her coat.

"I won't go. This is my house. Go away. Why won't you go away? Why must you sit here and torment me? Couldn't you have gone away long ago?" The words came low and secret, spoken to the darkest corners of the room.

"I can't go away. I love you."

"If you love me, you'll go away and let me sleep."

"Have you taken five sleeping tablets?"

"Do I ever lie to you?"

I answered truthfully, "Never." But she didn't need to lie; whenever she wanted to keep something from me, she simply said nothing, or ruled the question out of order. If I asked her about my friend, for instance, she would say that if I trusted her I had no right to ask; and if I didn't trust her—what was the point of our relationship? And that was true, too.

"Five?" I said, expecting God knows what reply.

"Yes. But I don't want to go to the hospital. I don't need to."

That sounded reasonable. "All right," I said. I hung her coat back up. From the couch, I telephoned the emergency department at the local hospital, where I explained to an intern that my wife had accidentally taken five sleeping pills. I wanted to know what to do.

"Five isn't deadly," he said, "but you really ought to bring her in, anyhow."

"Suppose she won't come in?" It was hard to remember that the telephone was anonymous; he couldn't know her or me.

"Don't ask her, Mac. Bring her."

I shivered. "She won't come. What can I do at home?"

"Watch her. Watch her closely; but it would be better if she came in. What's the address where you are?"

I hung up, wondering if he would trace the call. She had her head in her hands and was already getting drowsy. I stood beside her and stroked her hair because she did not resist. I asked, "Will you have some black coffee?"

"No," she said.

"Why did you do it?"

Without anger, she said, "I don't know. I just got tired . . ."

"Come with me." I lifted her off the chair and crossed the ray of moonlight, taking her with me to the couch where I sat at one end, her head in my lap. I stroked her forehead; a little later, I loosened her clothes when I felt her beginning to relax.

For a while, she lay with her eyes open, staring across the room at the stool from which I had carried her. I felt her body grow warm as the sleepiness spread, and I leaned down to kiss her. "Do you think they'll catch the boy?" she wanted to know.

I looked out across the lighted porch. The bridge lights were burning brightly and the late night traffic was sweeping back and forth. "I don't know," I answered. "I suppose they will." I felt the stiffness, the resentment passing out of her body as the drug took over. Again, I bent to kiss her, and her lips parted, ever so gently, to mine. She was already drifting away. The weight of her head and shoulders in my lap was marvelous. I felt that we were dreaming lovers. Very carefully, I held her head while I got up from the couch and bent to gather her in my arms so I could cradle her completely. She whispered in my ear, "Why do you always have to move; why can't we just be?" But her sleep muffled the complaint, and I sat down with her in my arms.

I could see the flashlights of the policemen as they quartered the hillside hunting for their murderer. I put my head to her cheek, to her hair. From time to time, I put soft kisses on her lips or touched her throat. Sometimes, I touched her body, but without desire, moving her limbs, touching her side, her shoulders, smoothing her forehead, holding her waist. She lay in my arms, utterly asleep. I had her and I breathed her breath.

The moonlight crossing the coffee table caught the random pattern of the page corners I had torn out of my friend's weak book. The trouble was, he had insufficient needs; they could be satisfied. The insufficiency and satisfaction crept into his book, rendering it thin. A brief seduction in a roomful of mice; a pathetic, stage-struck girl who kept her thighs closed not to break the law as she pretended to paddle about in an imitation sea: his world. A world without disaster.

I had her; held her; rocked her in my arms. Toward midnight, there were shots, but I didn't bother to turn out the light. It kept the shadows from the porch till dawn.

Maud

by LOUIS AUCHINCLOSS

All Maud's life it had seemed to her that she was like a dried-up spring
at the edge of which her devoted relatives and friends used to gather
hopefully in the expectation that at least a faint trickle might appear.
Their own natures, it seemed, were rich with the bubbling fluid of
hearty emotion, and their very repleteness made her own sterility the
more remarkable. She gazed back at them; she tried to feel what they
felt, tried to respond to their yearning glances. But what was the use? It
had been her lot to live alone, surrounded by smiles and love, by sports
and games and homely affection, through cold winters with warm fires
and long, bright boisterous summers. To Maud, the Spreddons seemed
to be always circling, hand in hand, the bonfire of their own joy in life.
Could they mean it? she would sometimes ask herself. Yet in sober
truth they seemed to be what they appeared. Daddy, large and hearty,
was always spoken of as one of the best lawyers downtown and was certainly a rich man, too, despite his eternal jangle about being the average
father of an average American family. Mummie, stout and handsome,
bustled with good works, and the morning mail was always filled with
invitations to accept the chairmanship of worthy drives. Brother Fred
was captain of his school football team; brother Sam was head of his

class; Grandpapa was the good old judge whom all had revered, and beautiful Granny one of the "last" of the great ladies—there was no end to it.

But why did they always think that they had to draw *her* in, make *her* part of it? Why did they all turn to her on those ghastly Christmas Eves, when they gathered around the piano to bray out their carols, and cry: "Maud, sing this," and "Maud, isn't it lovely?" And why, when, with the devil in her soul, she raised her uncertain voice to sing the page's part in "Good King Wenceslaus," did they say? "That was *really* nice, Maud. You do like Christmas, don't you, after all?" It was the "after all" that gave them away. They smelled her out, spotted her for what she was, a rank intruder in their midst; but at the same time, with inexhaustible generosity, they held open the gate and continued to shout their welcome.

"Damn you! Damn all of you!"

There. She had said it, and she had said it, too, on Christmas Eve, one week after her thirteenth birthday. Not as long as she lived would she forget the shocked hush that fell over the family group, the stern amazement of her father, the delighted animosity of the boys. It was out at last.

"Maud!" her father exclaimed. "Where did you ever pick up language like that?"

"From Nannie," she answered.

"From Nannie!"

"Darling!" cried her mother, enveloping her with arms of steel. "Darling child, what's wrong? Aren't you happy? Tell Mummie, dearest."

"Maud's wicked," said brother Sam.

"Shut up, Sam," his father snapped.

Pressed to the lacy warmness of her mother's bosom, Maud felt welling up within herself the almost irresistible tide of surrender, but when she closed her eyes and clenched her fists, her own little granite integrity was able, after all, to have its day. She tore herself out of her mother's arms.

"I hate you all!" she screamed.

This time there was no sternness or hostility in the eyes around her. There was only concern, deep concern.

"I'll take her up to her room," she heard her mother tell her father. "You stay here. Tell Nannie, if she hasn't already gone out, to stay."

Her mother took her upstairs and tried to reason with her. She talked to her very gently and told her how much they all loved her and how much they would do for her, and didn't she love them back just a little, tiny, tiny bit? Didn't she really, darling? But Maud was able to shake her head. It was difficult; it cost her much. Everything that was in her was yearning to have things the way they had always been, to be approved and smiled at, even critically, but she knew how base it would be to give in to the yearning, even if everything that stood for resistance was baser yet. She was a bad girl, a very bad one, but to go back now, to retrace her steps, after the passionately desired and unbelievably actual stand of defiance, to merge once more with that foolish sea of smiles and kisses, to lose forever her own little ego in the consuming fire of family admiration—no, this she would not do.

Alone in the dark she flung herself upon her pillow and made it damp with her tears, tears that for the first time in her life came from her own causing. Why she was taking this dark and lonely course, why she should have to persist in setting herself apart from all that was warm and beckoning, she could only wonder, but that she *was* doing it and would continue to do it and would live by it was now her dusky faith. "I will. I will. I *will!*" she repeated over and over, until she had worked herself into a sort of frenzy and was banging her head against the bedpost. Then the door opened, swiftly, as though they had been standing just outside, and her mother and father and Nannie came in and looked at her in dismay.

2

Mrs. Spreddon had certainly no idea what had possessed her daughter. She was not without intelligence or sympathy, and responsibility sat easily with the furs on her ample shoulders, but there was little imagination and no humor in her make-up, and she could not comprehend any refusal of others to participate in that portion of the good of the universe which had been so generously allotted to herself. The disappointments that resulted from a failure to achieve an aim, any aim, were well within her comprehension, and when her son Sammy had failed to be elected head monitor of his school she and Mr. Spreddon had journeyed to New England to be at his side; but misery without a cause or misery with bitterness was to her unfathomable. She discussed it with her husband's sister, Mrs. Lane, who was in New York on a visit from Paris. Lila Lane was pretty, diminutive, and very chatty. She laughed at herself and the world and pretended to worship politics when she really worshiped good food. She dressed perfectly, always in black, with many small diamonds.

"It isn't as if the child didn't have everything she wanted," Mrs. Spreddon pointed out. "All she has to do is ask, and she gets it. Within limits, of course. I'm not one to spoil a child. What could it be that she's dissatisfied with?"

Mrs. Lane, taking in the detail of her sister-in-law's redecorated parlor, heavily and perfectly Georgian, all gleaming mahogany and bright new needlework, reflected that Maud might, after all, have something to be dissatisfied with.

"Is she ever alone?" she asked.

"Why should she be alone?" Mrs. Spreddon demanded. "She's far too shy as it is. She hates playing with other children. She hasn't a single friend at school that I know of."

"Neither did I. At that age."

Mrs. Spreddon was not surprised to hear this, but then she had no intention of having her Maud grow up like Lila and perhaps live in Paris and buy a Monet every fifth year with the money that she saved by not having children.

"But Maud doesn't like *anybody*," she protested. "Not even me."

"Why should she?"

"Oh, Lila. You've been abroad too long. Whoever heard of a child not liking her own family when they've been good to her?"

"I have. Just now."

Mrs. Spreddon frowned at her. "You seem to think it's my fault," she said.

"It isn't anyone's fault, Mary," Mrs. Lane assured her. "Maud didn't choose you for a mother. There's no reason she should like you."

"And what should I do about it?"

Mrs. Lane shrugged her shoulders. "Is there anything to be done?" she asked. "Isn't the milk pretty well spilled by now?"

"That's all very well for you to say," Mrs. Spreddon retorted. "But a parent can't take that point of view. A parent has to believe."

"I don't mean that she's hopeless," Mrs. Lane said quickly. "I just mean that she's different. There's nothing so terrible about that, Mary. Maud's more like her grandfather."

"The Judge? But he was such an old dear, Lila!"

Mrs. Lane placed a cigarette carefully in her ivory holder and held it for several seconds before lighting it. She hated disputes, but the refusal of her sister-in-law to face any facts at all in the personalities around her other than the cheerful ones that she attributed to them, a refusal that Mrs. Lane felt to be indigenous to the stratum of American life that she had abandoned for Paris, irritated her almost beyond endurance.

"My father was not an 'old dear,' Mary," she said in a rather metallic tone. "He was a very intellectual and a very strange man. He was never really happy until they made him a judge, and he could sit on a bench, huddled in his black robes, and look out at the world."

"You have such a peculiar way of looking at things, Lila," Mrs. Spreddon retorted. "Judge Spreddon was a great man. Certainly, I never knew a man who was more loved."

Mrs. Lane inhaled deeply. "Maybe Maud's daughters-in-law will say the same about her."

"Maybe they will," Mrs. Spreddon agreed. "If she ever has any."

Mr. Spreddon worried even more than his wife, but he knew better than to expose himself to the chilly wind of his sister's skepticism. When he sought consolation it was in the sympathetic male atmosphere of his downtown world where he could always be sure of a friendly indifference and an easy optimism to reassure his troubled mind. Mr. Spreddon at fifty-five showed no outward symptoms of any inner insecurity. He was a big man of magnificent health, with gray hair and red cheeks, who had succeeded to his father's position in the great law firm that bore his name. Not that this had been an easy or automatic step, or that it could have been accomplished without the distinct ability that Mr. Spreddon possessed. He was an affable and practical-minded man whose advice was listened to with respect at directors' meetings and by the widows and daughters of the rich. But it was true, nevertheless, that beneath the joviality of his exterior he carried a variegated sense of guilt: guilt at having succeeded a father whose name was so famous in the annals of law, guilt at having leisure in an office where people worked so hard, guilt at being a successful lawyer without having ever argued a case, guilt at suspecting that the sound practical judgment for which he was reputed was, in the last analysis, nothing but a miscellany of easy generalities. It may have been for this reason that he took so paternal an interest in the younger lawyers in his office, particularly in Halsted Nicholas, the prodigy from Yonkers who had started as an office boy and had been Judge Spreddon's law clerk when the old man died.

"I tell you she's all right, Bill," Halsted said with his usual familiarity when Mr. Spreddon came into the little office where he was working surrounded by piles of photostatic exhibits, both feet on his desk. "You ought to be proud of her. She's got spunk, that girl."

"You'll admit it's an unusual way to show it."

"All the better. Originality should be watered." Halsted swung around in his chair to face the large ascetic features of the late Judge

Spreddon in the photograph over his bookcase. "The old boy would have approved," he added irreverently. "He always said it was hate that made the world go round."

Mr. Spreddon never quite knew what to make of Halsted's remarks. "But I don't want her to be abnormal," he said. "If she goes on hating everybody, how is she ever going to grow up and get married?"

"Oh, she'll get married," Halsted said.

"Well, sure. If she changes."

"Even if she doesn't."

Mr. Spreddon stared. "Now, what makes you say that?" he demanded.

"Take me. I'll marry her."

Mr. Spreddon laughed. "You'll have to wait quite a bit, my boy," he said. "She's only thirteen."

3

Mr. and Mrs. Spreddon were not content with the passive view recommended by Mrs. Lane and Halsted Nicholas. Conscientious and loving parents as they were, they recognized that what ailed Maud was certainly something beyond their own limited control, and they turned, accordingly, in full humility and with open purses, to the psychiatrist, the special school, the tutor, the traveling companion. In fact, the whole paraphernalia of our modern effort to adjust the unadjusted was brought to bear on their sulking daughter. Nobody ever spoke to Maud now except with predetermined cheerfulness. She was taken out of the home that she had so disliked and sent to different schools in different climates, always in the smiling company of a competent woman beneath whose comfortable old-maid exterior was hidden a wealth of expensive psychological experience, and whose well-paid task it was to see if somehow it was not possible to pry open poor tightened Maud and permit the entry of at least a trickle of spontaneity. Maud spent a year in Switzerland under the care of one of the greatest of doctors, who regularly devoted one morning a week to walking with her in a Geneva park; she spent a year in Austria under equally famous auspices, and she passed two long years in Arizona in a small private school where she rode and walked with her companion and enjoyed something like peace. During visits home she was treated with a very special consideration, and her brothers were instructed always to be nice to her.

Maud saw through it all, however, from the very first and resented it with a continuing intensity. It was the old battle that had always raged between herself and her family; of this she never lost sight, and to give in because the struggle had changed its form would have been to lose the only fierce little logic that existed in her drab life. To this she clung with the dedication of a vestal virgin, wrapping herself each year more securely in the coating of her own isolation. Maud learned a certain adjustment to life, but she lost none of the bitterness of her conflict in the process. At nineteen she still faced the world with defiance in her eyes.

When she returned from the last of her many schools and excursions and came home to live with her family in New York, it was just six years from the ugly Christmas Eve of her original explosion. She had grown up into a girl whose appearance might have been handsome had one not been vaguely conscious of a presence somehow behind her holding her back—a person, so to speak, to whom one could imagine her referring questions over her shoulder and whose answer always seemed to be no. She had lovely, long, dark hair which she wore, smooth and uncurled, almost to her shoulders; she was very thin, and her skin was a clear white. Her eyes, large and brown, had a steady, uncompromising stare. She gave all the appearance of great shyness and reserve, for she hardly spoke at all, but the settled quality of her stare made it evident that any reluctance on her part to join in general conversation did not have its origin in timidity. Maud had established her individuality and her prejudices, and it was felt that this time she had come home to stay. Her parents still made spasmodic efforts to induce her to do this thing or that, but essentially her objectives had been attained. Nobody expected anything of her. Nobody was surprised when she did not kiss them.

She adopted for herself an unvarying routine. Three days a week she worked at a hospital; she rode in Central Park; she read and played the piano and occasionally visited the Metropolitan. Mrs. Spreddon continued the busy whirl of her life and reserved teatime every evening as her time for Maud. What more could she do? It was difficult to work up any sort of social life for a daughter so reluctant, but she did make occasional efforts and managed once in a while to assemble a stiff little dinner for Maud where the guests would be taken on, immediately upon rising from table, to the best musical comedy of the season, the only bait that could have lured them there. Maud endured it without comment. She was willing to pay an occasional tax for her otherwise unruffled existence.

At one of these dinners, she found Halsted Nicholas seated on her right. She remembered him from earlier days when he had spent summers with them as her brothers' tutor, and her memories of that summer were pleasanter than most. He was, of course, no longer a boy, being close to thirty-five, and a junior partner now of her father's; but his face had lost none of the sensitivity and charm, none of the uncompromising youth that she dimly remembered. He seemed an odd combination of ease and tension; one could tell that his reserve and even his air of gentle timidity were the product of manners; for when he spoke, it was with a certain roughness that indicated assurance. This was reinforced by the intent stare with which he fastened his very round and dark eyes on his plate and the manner in which his black eyebrows seemed to ripple with his thick black hair. She would have liked to talk to him, but that, of course, was not her way, and she watched him carefully as he crumbled his roll on the thick white tablecloth.

"You've certainly been taking your own sweet time to grow up, Maud," he said in a familiar tone, breaking a cracker into several pieces and dropping them into his soup as Maud had been taught never to do. "This makes it six years that I've been waiting for you."

"Six years?" she repeated in surprise.

He nodded, looking at her gravely. "Six years," he said. "Ever since that wonderful Christmas Eve when you told the assembled Spreddon family to put on their best bib and tucker and jump in the lake."

Maud turned pale. Even the heavy silver service on the long table seemed to be jumping back and forth. She put down her spoon. "So you know that," she said in a low voice. "They talk about it. They tell strangers."

He laughed his loud, easy laugh. "I'm hardly a stranger, Maud," he said. "I've been working as a lawyer in your father's office for twelve years and before that I was there as an office boy. And you're wrong about their telling people, too. They didn't have to tell me. I was there."

She gasped. "You couldn't have been," she protested. "I remember it so well." She paused. "But why are you saying this anyway? What's the point?"

Again he laughed. "You don't believe me," he said. "But it's so simple. It was Christmas Eve and I was all alone in town, and your old man, who, in case you don't know it, is one prince of a guy, took pity on me and asked me up. I told him I'd come in a Santa Claus get-up and surprise you kids. Anyway I was right in here, in this very dining room, sticking my beard on and peering through the crack in those double doors to watch for my cue from your father when—bingo!—you pulled that scene. Right there before my eyes and ears! Oh, Maud! You were terrific!"

Even with his eyes, his sure but friendly eyes, upon her as he said all this, it was as if it were Christmas again, Christmas with every stocking crammed and to be emptied, item by item, before the shining and expectant parental faces. Maud felt her stomach muscles suddenly tighten in anguished humiliation. She put her napkin on the table and looked desperately about her.

"Now Maud," he said, putting his firm hand on hers. "Take it easy."

"Leave me alone," she said in a rough whisper. "Leave me be."

"You're not going to be angry with me?" he protested. "After all these years? All these years that I've been waiting for the little girl with the big temper to grow up? Maud, how unkind."

She gave him a swift look. "I've been back home and grown up for several months," she pointed out ungraciously. "If you know Father so well, you must have known that. And this is the first time you've been to the house."

He shrugged his shoulders. "Lawyers are busy men, Maud," he said. "We can't get off every night. Besides, I'm shy."

She was not to be appeased so lightly. "You didn't come to see me, anyway," she retorted. "You came because Daddy begged you to." She smiled sourly. "He probably went down on his knees."

"Nothing of the sort," he said coolly. "If you must know, I came because I heard we were going to *Roll Out the Barrel.*"

Maud stared at him for a second and then burst out laughing. "Then you're in for a sad disappointment, Mr. Nicholas," she said, "because Daddy couldn't get seats. We're going to *Doubles or Quits.* I do hope you haven't seen it."

He covered his face with his napkin. "But I have," he groaned. "Twice!"

Maud, of course, did not know it, but Halsted Nicholas was the partner who, more than any other, held the clients of Spreddon & Spreddon. Mr. Spreddon increasingly accepted positions of public trust; he was now president of a museum, a hospital, and a zoo, all the biggest of their kind; he represented to his partners that this sort of thing, although unremunerative and time-consuming, "paid dividends in the long run." If anyone grumbled, it was not Halsted, whose industry was prodigious. What drove him so hard nobody knew. He never showed ambition of the ordinary sort, as, for example, wanting his name at the top of the firm letterhead or asking for paneling in his office. He felt, it was true, the deepest gratitude to Mr. Spreddon and to his late father, the Judge, who had seen promise in him and who had sent him to college and law school, but this he had already repaid a hundredfold. He loved the law, it was true, but he was already one of the ablest trial lawyers in the city and could certainly have held his position without quite so liberal an expenditure of energy. No, if Halsted was industrious it was probably by habit. He may have lacked the courage to stop and look into himself. He was a man who had met and undertaken many responsibilities; he had supported his friends with advice and his parents with money; he was considered to be—and, indeed, he was—an admirable character, unspoiled even by a Manhattan success; but whatever part of himself he revealed, it was a public part. His private self was unshared.

He left the theater that night after the second act to go down to his office and work on a brief, but the following Sunday he called at the Spreddons' and took Maud for a walk around the reservoir. A week later he invited her to come to Wall Street to dine with him, on the excuse that he had to work after dinner and could not get uptown, and after she had done this, which he said no other girl would have done, even for Clark Gable, he became a steady caller at the Spreddons'. Maud found herself in the unprecedented situation of having a beau.

He was not a very ceremonious beau; he never sent her flowers or whispered silly things in her ear, and not infrequently, at the very last moment, when they had planned an evening at the theater or the opera, he would call up to say that he couldn't get away from the office. Maud, however, saw nothing unusual in this. What mattered to her was that he expected so little. He never pried into her past or demanded her agreement or enthusiasm over anything; he never asked her to meet groups of his friends or to go to crowded night clubs. He never, furthermore, offered the slightest criticism of her way of living or made suggestions as to how she might enlarge its scope. He took her entirely for granted and would, without any semblance of apology, talk for an entire evening about his own life and struggles and the wonderful things that he had done in court. She was a slow talker, and he a fast one; it was easier for both if he held forth alone on the subjects closest to his heart. In short, she became accustomed to him; he fitted in with her riding and her hospital work. She had been worried at first, particularly in view of his initial revelation, never thereafter alluded to, of what he had once witnessed, but soon afterwards she had been reassured. It was all right. He would let her be.

4

Mr. and Mrs. Spreddon, in the meantime, were holding their breath. They had almost given up the idea that Maud would ever attract any man, much less a bachelor as eligible as Halsted. It was decided, after several conferences, that what nature had so miraculously started, nature might finish herself, and they resolved not to interfere. This, unfortunately, they were not able to do without a certain ostentation, and Maud became aware of an increasing failure on the part of her family to ask their usual questions about what she had done the night before and what meals she expected to eat at home the following day. If she referred to Halsted, her comment received the briefest of nods or answers. Nobody observing the fleeting references with which his name was dismissed at the Spreddon board would ever have guessed that the parental hearts were throbbing at the mere possibility of his assimilation into the family.

Maud, however, was not to be fooled. The suppressed wink behind the family conspiracy of silence was almost lewd to her, and it brought up poignantly the possibility that Halsted might be thinking of their friendship in the same way. It was true that he had said nothing to her that could even remotely be construed as sentimental, but it was also true, she realized ruefully, that she knew very little of such things, and the effusive, confiding creature to whom her brother Sammy was engaged, who frequently made her uncomfortable by trying to drag her into long intimate chats "just between us girls," had told her that when men took one out it was never for one's society alone and that this went for a certain "you know who" in the legal world as well as anyone else, even if he *was* somewhat older. Maud seemed to feel her breath stop at this new complication in a life settled after so many disturbances. Was this not the very thing that she had always feared, carried to its worst extreme? Was this not the emotion that was reputedly the most demanding, the most exacting of all the impulses of the heart? She had a vision of bridesmaids reaching for a thrown bouquet and faces looking up at her to where she was standing in unbecoming satin on a high stair—faces covered with frozen smiles and eyes, seas of eyes, black and staring and united to convey the same sharp, hysterical message: Aren't you happy? Aren't you in love? Now, then, didn't we *tell* you?

The next time Halsted called up she told him flatly that she had a headache. He took it very casually and called again about a week later. She didn't dare use the same excuse, and she couldn't think of another, so she met him for dinner at a French restaurant. She nibbled nervously on an olive while he drank his second cocktail in silence, watching her.

"Somebody's gone and frightened you again," he said with just an edge of roughness in his voice. "What's it all about? Why did you fake that headache last week?"

She looked at him miserably. "I didn't."

"Why did you have it then?"

"Oh." She raised her hand to her brow and rubbed it in a preoccupied manner. "Well, I guess I thought we were going out too much together."

"Too much for what?"

"Oh. You know."

"Were you afraid of being compromised?" he asked sarcastically.

"Please, Halsted," she begged him. "You know how people are. I like going out with you. I love it, really. But the family all wink and nod. They can't believe that you and I are just good friends. They'll be expecting you—well, to say something."

He burst out laughing. "And you're afraid I won't. I see."

She shook her head. "No," she said gravely, looking down at her plate; "I'm afraid you will."

He stopped laughing and looked at her intently. Then he gave a low whistle. "Well!" he exclaimed. "So that's how it is. And this is the girl whose father used to say that she had no self-confidence! Well, I'll be damned!"

Maud blushed. "You mustn't think I'm conceited," she said with embarrassment. "It's not that at all. I just don't understand these things. Really." She looked at him, imploring him not to take it amiss.

"Look, Maud," he said more gently, taking her hand in his. "Can't you trust me? I know all about it. Honest."

"All about what, Halsted?"

"What you're afraid of. Listen to me, my sweet. Nobody's going to make you do any falling in love. Nobody could. Yet. Do you get that? It's just possible that I may ask you to marry me. We'll see. But in any case I'm not going to ask you how you feel about me. That's your affair. Is that clear?"

She looked into his large and serious eyes and felt her fears subside. It was true that he was completely honest. He did not even tighten his grip on her hand.

"But why should you ever want to marry me?" she asked. "Nobody likes me."

"Give them time, darling," he said, smiling as she withdrew her hand from his. "They will. You want to know why I should be thinking about marrying you? Very well. That's a fair question. I'm thirty-four. There's one reason. It's high time, you'll admit. And I'm not so attractive that I can pick anyone I want. I have to take what I can get." And again he laughed.

"But don't you feel you could do better than me?" she asked seriously. "I'm really a terrible poke. Besides, Sammy says you make all sorts of money. That should help."

He shrugged his shoulders. "Oh, I haven't quite given up," he said cheerfully. "Don't get your hopes too high."

This time she smiled too. "You mean I'm only a last resort?"

Again he put his hand on hers, "Not quite. There's another point in your favor, Maud," he said. "If you must know."

"And what's that?"

He looked at her for a moment, and she suddenly knew that they were going to be very serious indeed.

"I wasn't going to mention it," he continued, "but I might as well now. I'm in love with you, Maud."

She could only shake her head several times in quick succession as if to stop him. "Why?" she asked. "What do you see in me?"

He shrugged his shoulders. "Who knows?" he said. "Call it the desire to protect. Or the mother instinct. Or just plain middle-aged folly. It might be anything. But, Maud, you wouldn't believe it. I can even catch myself thinking about you in court."

They looked at each other gravely for several seconds.

"Well, I suppose that does it," she said, smiling. "I'll have to marry you now."

He raised his hand. "Wait a moment!" he warned her. "First you've got to be asked. And after that you've got to think it over. For several days. I want no fly-by-night answer."

Halsted did things in his own way, and he adhered strictly to a program laid down by himself. Three days later she received a telegram from Chicago, where he had gone on business, saying: "This is the formal offer. Think it over. See you Friday."

Maud did think it over. In fact, she had thought of nothing else since it had first occurred to her that he might do this. She examined the state of her heart and asked herself if her feeling for Halsted could, even by the watered-down standards of her own emotions, be called

love, and she decided that it probably could not. She then tried to ana-
lyze what it was that she did feel for him; it was certainly the friendliest
feeling that she had ever experienced for another human being. She
asked herself if she was not lucky indeed—miraculously lucky—to have
run into the one man, probably in the whole country, who wanted her
as she was. She visualized the joy of sudden and final liberation from
her family. And then, too, undeniably, she felt stirring within her the
first faint manifestations of a new little pride in her own self that she
could pull this off, that she could mean so much to a man like Halsted,
a good man, an able man, a man whom people looked up to; she
thought of Sammy and his silly little fiancée, and of her worried parents and their hopelessness about her; she pictured the amazement of
the family friends. She stood before her mirror and pushed the hair out
of her face and tossed her head in sudden resolution.

When Halsted called for her on Friday night she was waiting for him
in the front hall with her hat and coat on. She was so nervous that she
didn't even allow him to speak.

"Halsted," she said, and the words tumbled out. "I've decided. I will.
Definitely."

He walked slowly across the front hall to the bottom step of the cir-
cular stairway where she was standing and took both her hands in his.
For a long tense moment he looked at her.

"Darling," he said and then laughed. "I thought you'd never make
up your mind!"

5

Halsted's courtship occurred during the winter of the first year of the
war in Europe. It was the period of the "phony war," which, however
much it may have bothered Halsted, was of little concern to Maud. For
her the fall of France had as its immediate consequence the precipitous
return of her father's sister, Lila Lane, from Paris. Aunt Lila took up
her residence, as was to be expected, with her brother, and family meals
came to be held in respectful silence while she expounded in her own
graphic fashion on her hasty departure from Paris, the forced abandonment of her Renault in a roadside ditch, and her successful arrival, half-
starved but with all her diamonds, in an unfamiliar and unfriendly
Madrid.

It was not an easy time for her unenthusiastic sister-in-law. Mrs.
Spreddon was hardly able, in the untroubled safety of her New York

home, to debunk these experiences, simply because they had happened to Lila. She was obliged to give lip service to the family idea that Lila for once in her life had come up against the fundamentals, things that in the Spreddon mind loomed as vast round bollards on the long dock of a routine existence. Maud's mother could only bide her time, provoking as it might be, and stop for a bit to listen to Lila's tales.

Maud, as might have been expected, did not think as her mother did. Feeling as she had always felt about the restricted atmosphere of her family life, she thought of this aunt in Paris, with perfect clothes and no children, as the desired antithesis of the boisterous and the vulgar. The vision of Lila's garden and the marble fountain surrounded by the bit of lawn, so closely cut and brightly green, which Maud had seen as a child from the grilled balcony of the exquisite house on the rue de Varenne had always lingered in her mind as the essence of everything that was cool and formal and wonderfully independent. It was no wonder that she hovered expectantly before the exotic gateway of her aunt's existence. And Lila, in her turn, appreciating this silent devotion, particularly from a Spreddon, and having always regarded Maud's troubles as the result of a life spent in the limelight of her sister-in-law's exuberant wealth and bad taste, turned as much of her attention as she could spare from hats to Maud and her singular love life. There were long morning conferences in Lila's littered room over a very little toast and a great deal of coffee.

She had, of course, insisted on meeting Halsted; they lunched, the three of them, one Saturday noon at a small French midtown restaurant, and, as poor Maud could clearly see, it had not gone well. Lila had spent the meal telling Halsted the well-known story, already published in a women's magazine, of her arduous escape from the Germans. Halsted, taciturn and obviously unimpressed, had said almost nothing. But it was later, when Maud was having tea and an early cocktail alone with her aunt, that the important conversation occurred.

"I hope you like him, Aunt Lila," Maud said timidly. "Mother and Daddy do, of course, they would. He's a wonderful lawyer. But you've lived abroad and know about people."

Lila Lane inserted a cigarette in her holder and surveyed her niece's almost expressionless face. She prided herself on being the one member of the family who had a kindred sense of the deep antipathies that had gone into Maud's make-up, and she saw her niece's solution along the lines of her own life. "I certainly like him, my dear," she said in a definite tone. "He's obviously a very fine and a very intelligent man. In fact, I shouldn't be surprised if I'm not a little afraid of him. He's *un peu farouche*, if you see what I mean. But attractive. Undeniably."

"Oh, he is, isn't he?"

Lila hesitated a moment before trying a stroke of sophistication. To clear the air. "All in all, my dear," she said with a smile, "an excellent first marriage."

"Oh, Aunt Lila!" Maud's eyes were filled with protest. "What do you mean?"

Her aunt reached over and patted her hand. "Now there, dear, don't get excited. You must let the old Paris aunt have her little joke. You see, Maud, as you say, I've lived abroad. A long time. I've been used to people who are, well—to say the least—stimulating. Your young man, who isn't, by the way, so frightfully young, is more of your father's world. Of course it was my father's world, too. But it's certainly a world that I myself could never be happy in. And I hope you'll forgive me for saying so, my dear, but I have my doubts if you ever could, either. It's a dull world, Maud."

"But I'm dull, Aunt Lila!" Maud protested. "I'm a thousand times duller than Halsted!"

Her aunt looked suddenly stern. "Don't let me ever hear you say that again!" she exclaimed. She got up and took Maud to the mirror over the mantel. "Take a good look at yourself! Your skin. Those eyes. They're good, my dear. Very good." She took Maud's long hair and arranged it in a sort of pompadour over her forehead. "You haven't tried, Maud. That's all. You could be beautiful."

Maud stared at her reflection with momentary fascination, and then turned abruptly away. She shrugged her shoulders. "I'd still be dull."

"Beautiful women are never dull," Lila said, sitting down again at the tea table. "But now I'm sounding like a rather bad Oscar Wilde. Tell me, my dear. In all seriousness. Are you in love with this wonderful lawyer?"

Maud's face was filled with dismay as she stared down at the floor. Neither her mother nor Halsted had presumed to ask her such a question, but there was no escaping it. Now she had to hear it from the lips of Aunt Lila, who spoke, she felt, with an authority that could not be resented. Whatever love may have been to the Spreddons—and Maud, when she thought of it, had a sense of something thick and stifling like a blanket—to Aunt Lila it was a free and glorious emotion that knew no restraint and graced those whom it touched. She was not sure that Aunt Lila had been one so graced, but she had infinite faith in her aunt's ability to observe.

Venus had risen, so to speak, on a shell from the sea and was awaiting her answer.

"I really can't say that I am," she answered at last in a low voice. "The way you use the word, anyway."

"The way *I* use the word, Maud! But there's only one way to use it. Either you are or you aren't."

"Oh, Aunt Lila." Maud's eyes filled with tears.

"Listen to me, Maud." Lila had moved over to the sofa and put her arm around her niece. "You know that I love you dearly. Do you think I'd have asked you such an impertinent question if I hadn't been sure that the answer was no?"

Maud shook her head. "Everyone knows about me," she said despairingly. "What should I do?"

"Do?" Lila queried. "You don't have to *do* anything at all. You certainly don't have to marry Halsted because you're *not* in love with him. Maud, darling, if you only knew how I understood! You think you're always going to be bottled up like a clam and that this is the way to make the best of it. But it's not. You're just beginning to stick your head out and peer around. It's absurd to be snapped up by the first one of your father's partners who comes along! Before you've even had a chance to take your bearings!"

But if Maud accepted her aunt as an expert in love, it did not mean that she accepted her as a judge of her own character. She had no interest in her own future, but a very deep interest in her duty to Halsted. Getting up, she went to her room. She sat there by herself for an hour. Then, for the first time in her life, she went to her mother for advice. Mrs. Spreddon was sitting at her dressing table, getting ready for dinner.

"Mother, I'm going to break my engagement to Halsted," she said abruptly.

Mrs. Spreddon eyed her closely in the glass as she fastened a pearl bracelet on her wrist. "May I ask you why?"

"I'm not in love with him."

Mrs. Spreddon was silent for a moment. Then she nodded. "Let me ask you one thing," she said. "Have you been talking to your aunt?"

"I have. But it's not her fault. She said nothing I didn't know already."

"I see."

There was a pause. Then poor Maud blurted forth her appeal. "Mother, what should I do?"

Mrs. Spreddon stood up, very slowly, and turned around. She faced her daughter with dignity, but her voice was trembling. "I'm sorry, Maud," she said. "I'd give anything in the world to be able to help you. You know how your father and I love Halsted. We think he'd be the perfect husband. But this is your life, my dear. Not mine. If we'd had more of a relationship, you and I, we might have been able to work this thing out. God knows I've tried. But parents can take only so much, Maud, and then they're through. You've always wanted to work things out your own way. I'm afraid that now it's too late for me to butt in."

For a long moment they looked at each other, almost in surprise and a little fear at the sudden reclarification of the gulf between them.

6

It was dark and cool inside the little restaurant where she was to meet Halsted for lunch. When her eyes were adjusted to it, she saw him sitting at the bar talking to the bartender. She went up and sat on the stool beside him, and he smiled and ordered her a drink. Then she told him, straight away. She did it very clearly and rather coldly; she was sure as she looked into his large hurt eyes that she had been convincing.

"But Maud," he protested in a tone almost of exasperation, "we've been through all this before! You know I don't expect anything of you. We can leave that to the future."

"I don't trust the future," she said. "I want to know more about it first."

"Maud, have you gone crazy?"

"It may well be."

There was a pause.

"How can you talk that way, Maud?" he asked suddenly. "How can you be such a smug little—? Good God! Maud, have you really never given a damn about me? Even one little damn?"

She looked at him steadily. From way back in her past she felt the stirrings of that almost irresistible tide of surrender, the tide that she had dammed so desperately and so decisively on that long ago Christmas Eve. But once again she was the mistress of her fate. "Not in that way, Halsted," she said.

He turned to his unfinished cocktail. "Well, I'll be damned," he said, almost to himself. "I'll be damned."

"You believe me, Halsted, don't you?"

He turned back to her. "I guess I'll have to, Maud," he said. "Maybe I had you doped out all wrong." He shrugged his shoulders. "Lawyers can be persistent," he continued, "but even they know when the game's really up. You'd better go home, Maud. I'll get you a taxi."

He got up and left her, and she knew, as she stared at her reflection in the mirror across the bar, that she was at last doing penance for what she had done that Christmas Eve.

Halsted disappeared from her life as suddenly as he had come into it. Shortly after the fateful meeting, he came into Mr. Spreddon's office, sat down, and putting one leg as usual over the arm of the chair, asked "Got another litigator around here, Bill? You'll be needing one."

"Oh, Halsted. You too?"

"Me too. I've decided to take that War Department job, after all. Maybe after I've been around there a few months they'll give me a commission. Just to get rid of me."

"Can't you get a commission now?"

"Eyes."

Mr. Spreddon looked broodingly at the photograph of his daughter which stood on his desk between him and Halsted. His heart was heavy. "You must do what you think best, of course," he said sadly. "We'll make out. I'm not trying to hide the fact that it'll be difficult. You know how we stand. This is your firm, Halsted."

Halsted's face clouded with embarrassment. "Cut it out, will you, Bill!" he protested. "You're the whole business around here, and that's the way it should be."

Mr. Spreddon shook his head. "Just a name, my boy. But I won't embarrass you. There's only one thing I'd like to know. Your going to Washington isn't because of Maud, is it?"

Halsted stood up and sauntered around the big office. "Like everyone else," he said in a rather rough tone, while his back was turned to Mr. Spreddon, "I have my own feelings about this war. And they happen to have nothing under the sun to do with your daughter."

"I'm sorry," Mr. Spreddon said meekly. "I shouldn't have mentioned it. But you know how I feel about that. It was the hope of my life."

Halsted shrugged his shoulders and left the room.

Mrs. Spreddon said nothing to Maud when the engagement was broken. She gave her a kiss and offered to send her on a trip. She was seething, however, against her sister-in-law, who, she felt, had betrayed her hospitality. She determined to break openly with her and debated for two days how most cuttingly to accomplish it. Then she went, without consulting her husband, to her sister-in-law's room.

"I hope, Lila," she said in a voice that trembled slightly, "that it gives you some satisfaction to reflect that in all probability you've ruined whatever slight chances Maud may have had for a normal and happy life."

Lila flushed deeply. "I wouldn't expect you to understand, Mary," she answered in a hurt but lofty tone. "All I can say is that anything I may have said to Maud was with her best interests at heart. We differ too fundamentally to make explanations worth while. Under the circumstances I think it would be best if I moved to the Pierre."

"Under the circumstances, I must agree with you."

And so it ended. Halsted wrote Maud from time to time, amusing, impersonal letters, but he never called at the Spreddons' when he came to New York. Then we entered the war, and he got his commission and was one of the first to be sent overseas. Lila tried to cheer Maud up by giving a cocktail party for her at her hotel, but Maud would not even go. Despite what her aunt had said about beautiful women, she still knew that she was dull.

7

Maud joined the Red Cross shortly after the attack on Pearl Harbor. She worked for two years in New York, after which she was sent to Southampton, England. She worked hard and well, serving coffee to literally thousands of young men. When she looked back over her time in uniform she pictured a sea of faces, young and healthy faces; it seemed to her as if there would never be an end to the pressure of youth and vigor and courage upon the barred doors of her heart. But she never yielded, never opened—and anyway, she sometimes wondered, did it matter? They kept passing her tumultuously, and if she had opened the door, just the tiniest crack, and peered out for a glimpse of the surging throng, would anyone have stopped to look or listen, to reach out a hand to her and cry: "Maud, come on! Can't you see us? We're on our *way!*"

If Maud, however, was uncompromising in her attitude towards the future, she was learning, nonetheless, a new latitude in the examination of her past. She was perfectly willing, even eager, to entertain the possibility that she had, after all, been in love with Halsted from the beginning and still was, but she was afraid to fall into the over-simplifications of wishful thinking. She still had no referent by which to judge love, and though she realized from time to time that she might be losing herself in the forests of introspection, she was capable, in spite of her doubts, of a fierce single-mindedness. There could be no question of other men. If Halsted had been dead she would still have felt an obligation to resolve the incomprehensible problem of her own determination.

Halsted, however, was far from dead. He was in London, and she actually had his address, though she dared not go to see him. She had not even let him know that she was in England. Their correspondence, in fact, had entirely ceased. Now she could see dimly that life might be offering her that rarest of all things, a second and final chance, and she hardly dared face the fact that, in her usual fashion, she was going to let it pass.

Her brother Sammy's destroyer had put in to Southampton at this time, and she was seeing a good deal of him. They had had little enough to say to each other before the war, but now that they were both three thousand miles from their family, they met in the evening in pubs and exchanged confidences with some of the excitement that is shared by new and congenial friends. They drank gin when they could get it and ale when they couldn't, and discussed their parents and themselves with detachment and impartiality. Sammy and his wife were not getting on, and this lent to his conversation the flavor of a superior disillusionment.

"The trouble with you, Maud," he told her one night, "is that you take everything too seriously. You're always analyzing your own emotions. Hell. The thing to do is to grab fun where you can get it. You ought to write Halsted and tell him you're crazy about him."

She looked skeptically at his blond, undoubting face. "But do you really think I am?" she asked.

He shrugged his shoulders. "I think you want to be," he said. "Which is just as good."

"But is that honest, Sammy?"

He laughed. "Do you want to be an old maid, Maud?" he demanded. "A sour, bitter old maid?"

She shook her head. "Not particularly," she answered.

"Well?"

"But I am what I am, aren't I, Sammy?"

"Sure. And you will be what you will be."

He was essentially indifferent, of course, but it was only the indifference of one adult for another. It filled her nonetheless with a bleak loneliness.

"I'm an idiot, Sammy," she said abruptly. "And I'm an idiot to think anyone cares whether or not I'm an idiot. I'll go to London. I'll be like the rest of you."

"That's better, Maud. Much better."

8

When she got her next leave she actually did go to London. She left her bag at the Red Cross on Grosvenor Square and walked down the street to Army Headquarters. It was some time before she found Halsted's office, and then she was unable to send a message to him because he was in conference. She waited in the main hall for an hour and a half.

"He may not even come out for lunch," the sergeant told her.

"I'll wait," she said, and he smiled.

When Halsted, now a lieutenant colonel, looking thinner and serious, walked through the hall he was with several other officers, and there was a preoccupation about their quick stride that made her suddenly feel small and unwanted. She was shrinking back in her chair when he spotted her and stopped.

"Maud!" he exclaimed in astonishment. "Well, I'll be damned!"

He went up to her, holding out both arms, and there was a funny little smile on his face.

"I just dropped in to see you," she stammered.

"Been waiting long?"

"Oh, no."

"Like to go out on the town tonight?" he asked. "For auld lang syne?" He looked at his watch. "I guess I can make it."

She nodded eagerly.

"You're at the Red Cross?" he said. "I'll pick you up at ten."

And he was gone. During the rest of the afternoon, as she wandered through the great and empty rooms of the Victoria and Albert Museum, she speculated in vain on the significance of his smile. He did not pick her up that night until long after ten, for he was again in conference. They drove in his jeep to an officers' club which had formerly been a private house, and a rather elaborate one, and sat at a table in a corner of the large Tudor front hall near the stairway, under which a bar had been installed. Halsted did not seem at all nervous, as she was, but he looked tired and older. He talked about the general aspects of the war in a rather learned way and drank a good deal, but she was too excited to take in a word that he said. He was speculating on the possibilities of a revolution within Germany when she interrupted him.

"Halsted, aren't you going to ask about *me*? And the family? I'm dying to tell. And to hear all about you. But not about the war. Please."

He smiled, just a bit wearily. "How have you been, my dear?" he asked.

"Well, not so terribly well," she began nervously. "But better now. Oh, must better, Halsted. I'm not the fool I was."

It was perfectly evident that he had caught the full import of her words, for he frowned and looked away from her. "When you say you're not the fool you were, Maud," he said in a distant, even a superior tone, "does it by any chance mean that you've changed your mind about me?"

She felt the chill in his voice and hesitated. She held her breath for a moment. "Yes," she said.

He turned and looked at her fixedly, but she could not read the expression in his eyes. "Then as far as you're concerned," he said, "it's on again?"

"Oh, no, Halsted," she said hastily. "Of course not! What do you take me for? It's not 'on' again. I have no claim on you. I've had my chance. Making a mess of things hardly entitles me to another."

"Oh, 'entitles.'" He shrugged his shoulders, almost in irritation as he repeated her word. "When women say they're not 'entitled' to something, what they usually mean is that any man who's not an utter heel would make sure that they get it."

The tears started to Maud's eyes. It was the tone that he had sometimes used in court, or to people whom he thought little of, like Lila, or to the world. Never to her.

"Halsted," she protested in a low voice. "That's not fair."

He looked down into his glass. "Maybe not."

"And it's not like you to be unfair," she continued. "It isn't as if I were expecting you to fall all over me. I know it would be a miracle if you had any feeling left."

He looked even more sullen at this. "But you still feel sorry for yourself," he retorted.

Maud put her napkin on the table and reached for her cigarettes. "Good night, Colonel," she said crisply. "There's nothing like auld lang syne, is there?"

"Nothing."

She got up. "You needn't worry about taking me back," she said. "I can find my way."

"Oh, sit down," he said roughly, but in a more human tone. "We've got a whole bottle of whiskey here. I don't suppose you expect me to get through it alone?"

"I'm sure," she said with dignity, "that I don't care how you get through it. There must be plenty of other officers with desk jobs in London who can help you out."

He caught her by the arm and pulled her back into her chair. "Desk jobs, hell," he muttered and poured her a drink. "Now drink that and shut up. I wish to hell I did have a desk job. Would you like to know where I was last week?"

"We're warned," she said, "not to encourage officers who drink too much and start revealing military information."

He finished his drink in a gulp and leaned his head on his hands. "Oh, Christ, Maud," he said.

She said nothing.

"I don't know why you had to come back," he continued. "The same prim little girl. Just a bit older, that's all. I'd gotten over you, you know. I mean it, God damn it. And I was enjoying my melancholy. I liked feeling a hero and thinking of the little girl back home who didn't give a rap about me, and wouldn't she be sorry now? Oh, I could spit." He reached again for the bottle and poured himself another drink. "Now I don't know what I feel. I wish like hell, Maud, that I could say it's all the way it was, but I'm damned if I know."

She believed him, believed him absolutely, but there was no humiliation or pain in it. For her the long uncertainty had ended. In her excitement his doubts seemed almost irrelevant.

"You needn't worry about it, Halsted," she said. "It seems so fair."

He looked at her suspiciously. "Fair?" he repeated. "You must be an icebox, Maud. How else could you talk that way?"

"It's just that I don't know how to talk," she said humbly. "You know that."

He smiled at her. "Oh, you can talk, Maud."

"You can make your life very difficult by being complicated," she went on. "I ought to know something about that. You can think you ought to be feeling all sorts of things that you don't. The people around you don't help. I've been through that. I was a fool."

He stared hard at her for a moment, but as if he were concentrating on something else. He opened his mouth as if he were about to say something and then closed it.

"Maud," he said finally, looking down again at the table, "would you marry me? If I were to ask you again?"

She nodded gravely. "I would."

"After all I've said?"

"After all you've said."

There was a pause, an interminable pause. Then he suddenly smiled and put his hand on hers. "Well, nobody would be able to say," he said, "that we were rushing into this thing without having given it thought. And yet, somehow, I feel that's just what we would be doing."

She took out her handkerchief at last and wiped her eyes. "We've tried waiting," she pointed out. "And that didn't work."

He laughed.

"Well, I'm game," he said. "I'm always taking chances with my future in these days. I might as well take a fling with my past." He put his hand suddenly around her shoulder. "Poor little Maud," he said, smiling. "Poor helpless little Maud. This is only the second time you've trapped your victim. But don't worry. You won't be able to get out of it this time."

"The only thing I'm worrying about," she observed, with an eye on the diminished bottle, "is getting you back to your quarters sober."

"I see you're starting right," he agreed more cheerfully. "Well, I asked for it. Or did I?"

How it would have worked out they never were to know, for Halsted was killed two days later when his reconnaissance plane was shot down over Cherbourg. They had met only once in the interval, at lunch, for Halsted had been in conference or flying day and night in preparation for the great invasion of France that took place only a week after his death. Into the blackness of Maud's heart there is no need to penetrate. It was fortunate for her that her work increased in intensity during those days.

A few weeks later her club mobile unit crossed to France, where it operated just below the front. A friend of Halsted's sent her a note that he had placed in an envelope marked "Maud Spreddon, Red Cross" just before he had taken off on his last flight. It was simply a line: "Maud, dearest, never forget. You're all right, and you're going to be all right. With me or without me." She had folded the note and placed it in a locket which she wore around her neck and which she never afterwards reopened. She did not tell her parents or even Sammy that she had seen Halsted again before his death, or what had passed between them. Such a tale would have made her a worthy object of the pity that she had so despised herself for seeking. It was her sorrow, and Halsted would have admired her for facing it alone.

A Southern Landscape

by ELIZABETH SPENCER

If you're like me and sometimes turn through the paper reading anything and everything because you're too lazy to get up and do what you ought to be doing, then you already know about my home town. There's a church there that has a gilded hand on the steeple, with a finger pointing to Heaven. The hand looks normal size, but it's really as big as a Ford car. At least, that's what they used to say in those little cartoon squares in the newspaper, full of sketches and exclamation points— "Strange As It Seems," "This Curious World," or Ripley's "Believe It or Not." Along with carnivorous tropical flowers, the Rosetta stone, and the cheerful information that the entire human race could be packed into a box a mile square and dumped into the Grand Canyon, there it would be every so often, that old Presbyterian hand the size of a Ford car. It made me feel right in touch with the universe to see it in the paper—something it never did accomplish all by itself. I haven't seen anything about it recently, but then, Ford cars have got bigger, and, come to think of it, maybe they don't even print those cartoons any more. The name of the town, in case you're trying your best to remember and can't is Port Claiborne, Mississippi. Not that I'm *from* there; I'm from *near* there.

Coming down the highway from Vicksburg, you come to Port Claiborne, and then to get to our house you turn off to the right on State Highway No. 202 and follow along the prettiest road. It's just about the way it always was—worn deep down like a tunnel and thick with shade in summer. In spring, it's so full of sweet heavy odors they make you drunk, you can't think of anything—you feel you will faint or go right out of yourself. In fall, there is the rustle of leaves under your tires and the smell of them, all sad and Indian-like. Then in the winter, there are only dust and bare limbs, and mud when it rains, and everything is like an old dirt-dauber's nest up in the corner. Well, any season, you go twisting along this tunnel for a mile or so, then the road breaks down into a flat open run toward a wooden bridge that spans a swampy creek bottom. Tall trees grow up out of the bottom—willow and cypress, gum and sycamore—and there is a jungle of brush and vines—kudzu, Jackson vine, Spanish moss, grapevine, Virginia creeper, and honeysuckle—looping, climbing, and festooning the trees, and harboring every sort of snake and varmint underneath. The wooden bridge clatters when you cross, and down far below you can see water, lying still, not a good step wide. One bank is grassy and the other is a slant of ribbed white sand.

Then you're going to have to stop and ask somebody. Just say, "Can you tell me where to turn to get to the Summerall place?" Everybody knows us. Not that we *are* anybody—I don't mean that. It's just that we've been there forever. When you find the right road, you go right on up through a little wood of oaks, then across a field, across a cattle gap, and you're there. The house is nothing special, just a one-gable affair with a bay window and a front porch—the kind they built back around fifty or sixty years ago. The shrubs around the porch and the privet hedge around the bay window were all grown up too high the last time I was there. They ought to be kept trimmed down. The yard is a nice flat one, not much for growing grass but wonderful for shooting marbles. There were always two or three marble holes out near the pecan trees where I used to play with the colored children.

Benjy Hamilton swore he twisted his ankle in one of those same marble holes once when he came to pick me up for something my senior year in high school. For all I know, they're still there, but Benjy was more than likely drunk and so would hardly have needed a marble hole for an excuse to fall down. Once, before we got the cattle gap, he couldn't open the gate, and fell on the barbed wire trying to cross the fence. I had to pick him out, thread at a time, he was so tangled up. Mama said, "What were you two doing out at the gate so long last night?" "Oh, nothing, just talking," I said. She thought for the longest time that Benjy Hamilton was the nicest boy that ever walked the earth. No matter how drunk he was, the presence of an innocent lady like Mama, who said *"Drinking?"* in the same tone of voice she would have said *"Murder?,"* would bring him around faster than any number of needle showers, massages, ice packs, prairie oysters, or quick dips in December off the northern bank of Lake Ontario. He would straighten up and smile and say, "You made any more peach pickle lately, Miss Sadie?" (He could even say "peach pickle.") And she'd say no, but that there was always some of the old for him whenever he wanted any. And he'd say that was just the sweetest thing he'd ever heard of, but she didn't know what she was promising—anything as good as her peach pickle ought to be guarded like gold. And she'd say, well, for most anybody else she'd think twice before she offered any. And he'd say, if only everybody was as sweet to him as she was. . . . And they'd go on together like that till you'd think that all creation had ground and wound itself down through the vistas of eternity to bring the two of them face to face for exchanging compliments over peach pickle. Then I would put my arm in his so it would look like he was helping me down the porch steps out of the reflexes of his gentlemanly upbringing, and off we'd go.

It didn't happen all the time, like I've made it sound. In fact, it was only a few times when I was in school that I went anywhere with Benjy Hamilton. Benjy isn't his name, either; it's Foster. I sometimes call him "Benjy" to myself, after a big overgrown thirty-three-year-old idiot in *The Sound and the Fury*, by William Faulkner. Not that Foster was so big or overgrown, or even thirty-three years old, back then; but he certainly did behave like an idiot.

I won this prize, see, for writing a paper on the siege of Vicksburg. It was for the United Daughters of the Confederacy's annual contest, and mine was judged the best in the state. So Foster Hamilton came all the way over to the schoolhouse and got me out of class—I felt terribly important—just to "interview" me. He had just graduated from the university and had a job on the paper in Port Claiborne—that was before he started work for the *Times-Picayune*, in New Orleans. We went into an empty classroom and sat down.

He leaned over some blank sheets of coarse-grained paper and scribbled things down with a thick-leaded pencil. I was sitting in the next seat; it was a long bench divided by a number of writing arms, which was why they said that cheating was so prevalent in our school—you could just cheat without meaning to. They kept trying to raise the money for regular desks in every classroom, so as to improve morals. Anyway, I couldn't help seeing what he was writing down, so I said, "'Marilee' is all one word, and with an 'i,' not a 'y.' 'Summerall' is spelled just like it sounds." "Are you a senior?" he asked. "Just a junior," I said. He wore horn-rimmed glasses; that was back before everybody wore them. I thought they looked unusual and very distinguished. Also, I had noticed his shoulders when he went over to let the window down. I thought they were distinguished, too, if a little bit bony. "What is your ambition?" he asked me. "I hope to go to college year after next," I said. "I intend to wait until my junior year in college to choose a career."

He kept looking down at his paper while he wrote, and when he finally looked up at me I was disappointed to see why he hadn't done it before. The reason was, he couldn't keep a straight face. It had happened before that people broke out laughing just when I was being my most earnest and sincere. It must have been what I said, because I don't think I *look* funny. I guess I don't look like much of any one thing. When I see myself in the mirror, no adjective springs right to mind, unless it's "average." I am medium height, I am average weight, I buy "natural"-colored face powder and "medium"-colored lipstick. But I must say for myself, before this goes too far, that every once in a great while I look Just Right. I've never found the combination for making this happen, and no amount of reading the makeup articles in the magazines they have at the beauty parlor will do any good. But sometimes it happens anyway, with no more than soap and water, powder, lipstick, and a damp hairbrush.

My interview took place in the spring, when we were practicing for the senior play every night. Though a junior, I was in it because they always got me, after the eighth grade, to take parts in things. Those of us that lived out in the country Mrs. Arrington would take back home in her car after rehearsal. One night, we went over from the school to get a Coca-Cola before the drugstore closed, and there was Foster Hamilton. He had done a real nice article—what Mama called a "writeup." It was when he was about to walk out that he noticed me and said, "Hey." I said "Hey" back, and since he just stood there, I said, "Thank you for the writeup in the paper."

"Oh, that's all right," he said, not really listening. He wasn't laughing this time. "Are you going home?" he said.

"We are after 'while," I said. "Mrs. Arrington takes us home in her car."

"Why don't you let me take you home?" he said. "It might—it might save Mrs. Arrington an extra trip."

"Well," I said, "I guess I could ask her."

So I went to Mrs. Arrington and said, "Mrs. Arrington, Foster Hamilton said he would be glad to drive me home." She hesitated so long that I put in, "He says it might save you an extra trip." So finally she said, "Well, all right, Marilee." She told Foster to drive carefully. I could tell she was uneasy, but then, my family were known as real good people, very strict, and of course she didn't want them to feel she hadn't done the right thing.

That was the most wonderful night. I'll never forget it. It was full of spring, all restlessness and sweet smells. It was radiant, it was warm, it was serene. It was all the things you want to call it, but no word would ever be the right one, nor any ten words, either. When we got close to our turnoff, after the bridge, I said, "The next road is ours," but Foster drove right on past. I knew where he was going. He was going to Windsor.

Windsor is this big colonial mansion built back before the Civil War. It burned down during the eighteen-nineties sometime, but there were still twenty-five or more Corinthian columns, standing on a big open space of ground that is a pasture now, with cows and mules and calves grazing in it. The columns are enormously high and you can see some of the iron-grillwork railing for the second-story gallery clinging halfway up. Vines cling to the fluted white plaster surfaces, and in some places the plaster has crumbled away, showing the brick underneath. Little trees grow up out of the tops of columns, and chickens have their dust holes among the rubble. Just down the fall of the ground beyond the ruin, there are some Negro houses. A path goes down to them.

It is this ignorant way that the hand of Nature creeps back over Windsor that makes me afraid. I'd rather there'd be ghosts there, but there aren't. Just some old story about lost jewelry that every once in a while sends somebody poking around in all the trash. Still, it is magnificent, and people have compared it to the Parthenon and so on and so on, and even if it makes me feel this undertone of horror, I'm always ready to go and look at it again. When all of it was standing, back in the old days, it was higher even than the columns, and had a cupola, too. You could see the cupola from the river, they say, and the story went that Mark Twain used it to steer by. I've read that book since, *Life on the Mississippi,* and it seems he used everything else to steer by, too—crawfish mounds, old rowboats stuck in the mud, the tassels on somebody's corn patch, and every stump and stob from New Orleans to Cairo, Illinois. But it does kind of connect you up with something to know that Windsor was there, too, like seeing the Presbyterian hand in the newspaper. Some people would say at this point, "Small world," but it isn't a small world. It's an enormous world, bigger than you can imagine, but it's all connected up. What Nature does to Windsor it does to everything, including you and me—there's the horror.

But that night with Foster Hamilton, I wasn't thinking any such doleful thoughts, and though Windsor can be a pretty scary-looking sight by moonlight, it didn't scare me then. I could have got right out of the car, alone, and walked all around among the columns, and whatever I heard walking away through the weeds would not have scared me, either. We sat there, Foster and I, and never said a word. Then, after some time, he turned the car around and took the road back. Before we got to my house, though, he stopped the car by the roadside and kissed me. He held my face up to his, but outside that he didn't touch me. I had never been kissed in any deliberate and accomplished way before, and driving out to Windsor in that accidental way, the whole sweetness of the spring night, the innocence and mystery of the two of us, made me think how simple life was and how easy it was to step into happiness, like walking into your own rightful house.

This frame of mind persisted for two whole days—enough to make a nuisance of itself. I kept thinking that Foster Hamilton would come sooner or later and tell me that he loved me, and I couldn't sleep for thinking about him in various ways, and I had no appetite, and nobody could get me to answer them. I half expected him at play practice or to come to the schoolhouse, and I began to wish he would hurry up and get it over with, when, after play practice on the second night, I saw him uptown, on the corner, with this blonde.

Mrs. Arrington was driving us home, and he and the blonde were standing on the street corner, just about to get in his car. I never saw that blonde before or since, but she is printed eternally on my mind, and to this good day if I'd run into her across the counter from me in the ten-cent store, whichever one of us is selling lipstick to the other one, I'd know her for sure because I saw her for one half of a second in the street light in Port Claiborne with Foster Hamilton. She wasn't any ordinary blonde, either—dyed hair wasn't in it. I didn't know the term "feather-bed blonde" in those days, or I guess I would have thought it. As it was, I didn't really think anything, or say anything, either, but whatever had been galloping along inside me for two solid days and nights came to a screeching halt. Somebody in the car said, being real funny, "Foster Hamilton's got him another girl friend." I just laughed. "Sure has," I said. "Oh, Mari-leee!" they all said, teasing me. I laughed and laughed.

I asked Foster once, a long time later, "Why didn't you come back after that night you drove me out to Windsor?"

He shook his head. "We'd have been married in two weeks," he said. "It scared me half to death."

"Then it's a mercy you didn't," I said. "It scares *me* half to death right now."

Things had changed between us, you realize, between that kiss and that conversation. What happened was—at least, the main thing that happened was—Foster asked me the next year to go to the high-school senior dance with him, so I said all right.

I knew about Foster by then, and that his reputation was not of the best—that it was, in fact, about the worst our county had to offer. I knew he had an uncommon thirst and that on weekends he went helling about the countryside with a fellow that owned the local picture show and worked at a garage in the daytime. His name was A. P. Fortenberry, and he owned a new convertible in a sickening shade of bright maroon. The convertible was always dusty—though you could see A. P. in the garage every afternoon, during the slack hour, hosing it down on the wash rack—because he and Foster were out in it almost every night, harassing the countryside. They knew every bootlegger in a radius of forty miles. They knew girls that lived on the outskirts of town and girls that didn't. I guess "uninhibited" was the word for A. P. Fortenberry, but whatever it was, I couldn't stand him. He called me into the garage one day—to have a word with me about Foster, he said—but when I got inside he backed me into the corner and started trying it on. "Funny little old girl," he kept saying. He rattled his words out real fast. "Funny little old girl." I slapped him as hard as I could, which was pretty hard, but that only seemed to stimulate him. I thought I'd never get away from him—I can't smell the inside of a garage to this good day without thinking about A. P. Fortenberry.

When Foster drove all the way out to see me one day soon after that —we didn't have a telephone in those days—I thought he'd come to apologize for A. P., and I'm not sure yet he didn't intend for me to un- derstand that without saying anything about it. He certainly put him- self out. He sat down and swapped a lot of Port Claiborne talk with Mama—just pleased her to death—and then he went out back with Daddy and looked at the chickens and the peach trees. He even had an opinion on growing peaches, though I reckon he'd given more thought to peach brandy than he'd ever given to orchards. He said when we were walking out to his car that he'd like to take me to the senior dance, so I said O.K. I was pleased; I had to admit it.

Even knowing everything I knew by then (I didn't tell Mama and Daddy), there was something kind of glamorous about Foster Hamilton. He came of a real good family, known for being aristocratic and smart; he had uncles who were college professors and big lawyers and doctors and things. His father had died when he was a babe in arms (tragedy), and he had perfect manners. He had perfect manners, that is, when he was sober, and it was not that he departed from them in any intentional way when he was drunk. Still, you couldn't exactly blame me for being disgusted when, after ten minutes of the dance, I discovered that his face was slightly green around the temples and that whereas he could dance fairly well, he could not stand up by himself at all. He teetered like a baby that has caught on to what walking is, and knows that now is the time to do it, but hasn't had quite enough practice.

"Foster," I whispered, "have you been drinking?"

"Been *drinking*?" he repeated. He looked at me with a sort of wonder, like the national president of the W.C.T.U. might if asked the same question. "It's so close in here," he complained.

It really wasn't that close yet, but it was going to be. The gym doors were open, so that people could walk outside in the night air whenever they wanted to. "Let's go outside," I said. Well, in my many anticipations I had foreseen Foster and me strolling about on the walks outside, me in my glimmering white sheer dress with the blue underskirt (Mama and I had worked for two weeks on that dress), and Foster with his nice broad aristocratic shoulders. Then, lo and behold, he had worn a white dinner jacket! There was never anybody in creation as proud as I was when I first walked into the senior dance that night with Foster Hamilton.

Pride goeth before a fall. The fall must be the one Foster took down the gully back of the boys' privy at the schoolhouse. I still don't know quite how he did it. When we went outside, he put me carefully in his car, helped to tuck in my skirts, and closed the door in the most polite way, and then I saw him heading toward the privy in his white jacket that was swaying like a lantern through the dark, and then he just wasn't there any more. After a while, I got worried that somebody would come out, like us, for air, so I got out and went to the outside wall of the privy and said, "Foster, are you all right?" I didn't get any answer, so I knocked politely on the wall and said, "Foster?" Then I looked around behind and all around, for I was standing very close to the edge of the gully that had eroded right up to the borders of the campus (somebody was always threatening that the whole schoolhouse was going to cave in into it before another school year went by), and there at the bottom of the gully Foster Hamilton was lying face down, like the slain in battle.

What I should have done, I should have walked right off and left him there till doomsday, or till somebody came along who would use him for a model in a statue to our glorious dead in the defense of Port Claiborne against Gen. Ulysses S. Grant in 1863. That battle was over in about ten minutes, too. But I had to consider how things would look —I had my pride, after all. So I took a look around, hiked up my skirts, and went down into the gully. When I shook Foster, he grunted and rolled over, but I couldn't get him up. I wasn't strong enough. Finally, I said, "Foster, Mama's here!," and he soared up like a Roman candle. I never saw anything like it. He walked straight up the side of the gully and gave me a hand up, too. Then I guided him over toward the car and he sat in the door and lighted a cigarette.

"Where is she?" he said.

"Who?" I said.

"Your mother," he said.

"Oh, I just said that, Foster. I had to get you up someway."

At that, his shoulders slumped down and he looked terribly depressed. "I didn't mean to do this, Marilee," he said. "I didn't have any idea it would hit me this way. I'm sure I'll be all right in a minute."

I don't think he ever did fully realize that he had fallen in the gully. "Get inside," I said, and shoved him over. There were one or two couples beginning to come outside and walk around. I squeezed in beside Foster and closed the door. Inside the gym, where the hot lights were, the music was blaring and beating away. We had got a real orchestra specially for that evening, all the way down from Vicksburg, and a brass-voiced girl was singing a nineteen-thirties song. I would have given anything to be in there with it rather than out in the dark with Foster Hamilton.

I got quite a frisky reputation out of that evening. Disappearing after ten minutes of the dance, seen snuggling out in the car, and gone completely by intermission. I drove us away. Foster wouldn't be convinced that anybody would think it at all peculiar if he reappeared inside the gym with red mud smeared all over his dinner jacket. I didn't know how to drive, but I did anyway. I'm convinced you can do anything when you have to—speak French, do a double back flip off the low diving board, play Rachmaninoff on the piano, or fly an airplane. Well, maybe not fly an airplane; it's too technical. Anyway, that's how I learned to drive a car, riding us up and down the highway, holding off Foster with my elbow, marking time till midnight came and I could go home without anybody thinking anything out of the ordinary had happened.

When I got out of the car, I said, "Foster Hamilton, I never want to see you again as long as I live. And I hope you have a wreck on the way home."

Mama was awake, of course. She called out in the dark, "Did you have a good time, Marilee?"

"Oh, yes, Ma'am," I said.

Then I went back to my shed-ceilinged room in the back wing, and cried and cried. And cried.

There was a good bit of traffic coming and going out to our house after that. A. P. Fortenberry came, all pallid and sober, with a tie on and a straw hat in his hand. Then A. P. and Foster came together. Then Foster came by himself.

The story went that Foster had stopped in the garage with A. P. for a drink before the dance, and instead of water in the drink, A. P. had filled it up with grain alcohol. I was asked to believe that he did this because, seeing Foster all dressed up, he got the idea that Foster was going to some family do, and he couldn't stand Foster's family, they were all so stuckup. While Foster was draining the first glass, A. P. had got called out front to put some gas in a car, and while he was gone Foster took just a little tap more whiskey with another glassful of grain alcohol. A. P. wanted me to understand that Foster's condition that night had been all his fault, that instead of three or four ounces of whiskey, Foster had innocently put down eighteen ounces of sheer dynamite, and it was a miracle only to be surpassed by the resurrection of Jesus Christ that he had managed to drive out and get me, converse with Mama about peach pickle, and dance those famous ten minutes at all.

Well, I said I didn't know. I thought to myself I never heard of Foster Hamilton touching anything he even mistook for water.

All these conferences took place at the front gate. "I never saw a girl like you," Mama said. "Why don't you invite the boys to sit on the porch?"

"I'm not too crazy about A. P. Fortenberry," I said. "I don't think he's a very nice boy."

"Uh-*huh*," Mama said, and couldn't imagine what Foster Hamilton was doing running around with him, if he wasn't a nice boy. Mama, to this day, will not hear a word against Foster Hamilton.

I was still giving some thought to the whole matter that summer, sitting now on the front steps, now on the back steps, and now on the side steps, whichever was most in the shade, chewing on pieces of grass and thinking, when one day the mailman stopped in for a glass of Mama's cold buttermilk (it's famous) and told me that Foster and A. P. had had the most awful wreck. They had been up to Vicksburg, and coming home had collided with a whole carload of Negroes. The carnage was awful—so much blood on everybody you couldn't tell black from white. They were both going to live, though. Being so drunk, which in a way had caused the wreck, had also kept them relaxed enough to come out of it alive. I warned the mailman to leave out the drinking part when he told Mama, she thought Foster was such a nice boy.

The next time I saw Foster, he was out of the hospital and had a deep scar on his cheekbone like a sunken star. He looked handsomer and more distinguished than ever. I had gotten a scholarship to Millsaps College in Jackson, and was just about to leave. We had a couple of dates before I left, but things were not the same. We would go to the picture show and ride around afterward, having a conversation that went something like this:

"Marilee, why are you such a nice girl? You're about the only nice girl I know."

"I guess I never learned any different, so I can't help it. Will you teach me how to stop being a nice girl?"

"I certainly will not!" He looked to see how I meant it, and for a minute I thought the world was going to turn over; but it didn't.

"Why won't you, Foster?"

"You're too young. And your mama's a real sweet lady. And your daddy's too good a shot."

"Foster, why do you drink so much?"

"Marilee, I'm going to tell you the honest truth. I drink because I like to drink." He spoke with real conviction.

So I went on up to college in Jackson, where I went in for serious studies and made very good grades. Foster, in time, got a job on the paper in New Orleans, where, during off hours, or so I understood, he continued his investigation of the lower things in life and of the effects of alcohol upon the human system.

It is twenty years later now, and Foster Hamilton is down there yet.

Millions of things have happened; the war has come and gone. I live far away, and everything changes, almost every day. You can't even be sure the moon and stars are going to be the same the day after tomorrow night. So it has become more and more important to me to know that Windsor is still right where it always was, standing pure in its decay, and that the gilded hand on the Presbyterian church in Port Claiborne is still pointing to Heaven and not to Outer Space; and I earnestly feel, too, that Foster Hamilton should go right on drinking. There have got to be some things you can count on, would be an ordinary way to put it. I'd rather say that I feel the need of a land, of a sure terrain, of a sort of permanent landscape of the heart.

Love in the Spring

by JESSE STUART

It was last April when I met Effie. It was over at the Put-Off Ford at the Baptis foot-washing. Effie is a Slab Baptis. She was there having her feet washed. And I can't forget that day in April. It is always work in the spring. Fence to fix. Plowing to do. Cattle to tend to. Seems like everything is to do in the spring on the place. Planting crops is the big job. We don't have no place to go only to church and we don't feel like going there only on Sunday. That is the day we have off and we don't have that day off until we've milked seven cows and slopped the hogs and got in wood and got up water for the day. I can't forget that Sunday in last spring when I met Effie. I just packed in the last load of wood and Mom says to me: "Elster, you are going to fall for a woman sometime so hard that it's going to hurt you. Run around and talk about Mort Anderson being in love and how silly he is. Wait till you fall in love once. The love bug is going to bite you right over the heart."

I went to the baptizing with a clean white starched shirt on and a blue necktie and blue serge pants and black slippers. I looked about as good in them as I can look. I felt good just to get off to the foot-washing. I remember that row of elms along Little Sandy River had just started to leaf out. The rest of the hills just had a few sycamores and poplars down along the creeks that had leafed a little. It was a pretty morning. And down by the ford I never saw as many people in my life gathered at that one place. And I've seen a lot of baptizings there. Horses hitched to the trees with ropes and bridle reins. Wagons here and there with washing-tubs of grub in them and chears where whole families rid miles in them to the foot-washing. And horses eating yaller corn out'n the wagon beds of a lot of the wagons. I just walked down where they's singing "Where the Healing Waters Flow." It was soft music and I wished I was a child of the Lord's then. Good people—the Baptis is—we live neighbors to them. Ain't no better people to help you out in a time of sickness or weedy crops in the spring. Come right in and help you out. Now on this bank and washing feet. I walked down along the edge of the river where the horseweeds had been tromped down. I just wanted to look the crowd over. A whole row up and a whole row down. The row standing up was a-washing the feet of them on the ground. Just setting there on the ground as unconcerned and washing feet. Then they would sing another verse of "Where the Healing Waters Flow."

I looked up in front of me. I couldn't believe my eyes. I saw the prettiest woman I ever saw in my life. She was prettier than a speckled pup. Honest I never saw anything like her. Eyes that just looked at you and melted like yellow butter on hot corn bread—blue kind of eyes—and a face that was smooth as silk and cheeks the color of the peeling on a roman beauty apple in September. Her hair was the color of golden corn silks in August hanging from the shooting corn. Hair pretty and curly waving in the wind. I never saw a woman so pretty in my life. Her hands didn't look to me like no hands that had held to the hoe handle like my mother's hands and my sisters'. Her hands were pretty and soft. Her teeth were white as a bubble of foam in the Sandy River. She was an angel among the sinners trying to come clean. My heart beat faster when I saw her. Some man had his back to me. He was washing her foot. He had an old chipped washpan and a big towel and a bar of homemade soap made from oaktree ashes. He'd put it on her foot like he was putting axle grease on a wagon hub. Then he would smear it with his hands and rub. Then he would take the towel and dry her foot till it would look pink as a wild crab-apple blossom. I just stood there and looked at her. She looked at me. He saw her looking and he looked around. Of all the big ugly devils I ever saw in my life it was this fellow, Jonas Pratt's boy, Tawa Pratt. Lived down on Little Sandy on that big farm in the bend by the grove of cedars. When he turned around and saw me looking he said: "Ain't you a Baptis?"

And I said: "No I ain't no Slab Baptis. I'm a Methodist and I go to Plum Grove to church."

"Go on about your business then," he said, "and leave us Baptis alone. This ain't no side show. We are here worshiping the Lord."

I could see he just didn't want me to see the girl. He didn't like me. I didn't like him. I don't care if he was worshiping the Lord. And I says to him: "If that's the way you feel about it, all right. But I want to know the name of the girl here with you and where she lives."

That burnt him up. His lips just spread out and he showed them big yaller horse-teeth in front. I just thinks to myself: "What woman could kiss that awful mouth behind them big horse-teeth?" He looked at me with them black polecat eyes and his hair was right down over his eyes. He was a sorry-looking devil.

The girl says to me: "I'm Effie Long. I live up on Duck Puddle." I never said a word. I'd go to Duck Puddle. That's just down on Little Sandy four miles and up a hollow that comes into Little Sandy not far from the riffles. I knowed right then and there I'd see that woman again. I said to myself as I walked back from the riverbank over through horseweeds: "That's my wife if I can get her. Pretty as a angel right out of Heaven."

I thought of what Mom told me. I would fall for a skirt. I did like the looks of that woman. I went home. I remember it like it was just one hour ago. The daisies looked good to me. First time flowers ever did look good to me. I pulled off the top of a sweet william and smelt it. It smelt sweet as sugar.

"The love bug's got me right over the heart," I said to Mom as soon as I got in at the door. "I saw my wife at the foot washing—over there among the Baptis today at the Put-Off Ford."

And Mom she says: "Elster, you ain't fell for no Slab Baptis, have you? No Slab Baptis woman can ever come under this Methodist roof until she's been converted into the Methodist faith. That bunch all running around and drinking licker. Won't see no licker in heaven nor no spittoons for that old terbacker."

That's how women are. Right half of the time. When a man is in love, what does he care for spittoons in heaven and bad licker or good licker? What does he care who a Methodist is or a Slab Baptis is? He wants his woman. That's the way I felt. Mom married Pop fifty years ago and she don't know what it is to be young and be in love. I just never said a word.

A week hadn't passed till I heard about church down on Duck Puddle. Slab Baptis holding a pertracted meeting down there. I put on a white starched shirt, a blue necktie and blue serge pants and my black slippers and I went down there. It was a awful walk through the brush and over them ridges. But I followed the fox hunters' paths for more than two miles across through the brush. I walked across the rocks at the riffle and hit the big wagon road up to the church. Meeting was a-going on when I got there. I had to stop and ask four or five times before I found the place. A pretty place after a body gets there but a devil of a time getting to it. I never went inside the house till I peeped in at the winders and looked over the house to see if I could see Effie. I looked and looked. And one time when I looked with my eyes up agin the winderpanes the Slab Baptis preacher said: "A lot of pilferers on the outside of the house tonight. The devil in sheep's clothing is out there. Methodists are snooping around." When I heard this I slipped back in the dark. I'm a Methodist and couldn't be nothing else. Methodist church is good enough for Pa and Mom and Grandpa and Grandma and it's good enough for me. Even if they don't want me, for I bet on chicken fights and play cards once in a while.

I slipped back to the winder. I had looked every place but the amen corner. I looked up there and saw the angel I had seen over at the ford. She was in a mighty good place to be. Me a Methodist and out in the dark. I picked up courage and just walked up and bolted in at the door. I found a empty seat and I saw Effie start looking at me. I started looking at her. And I looked up there and saw old Tawa too. He was in the amen corner. He started showing them teeth soon as he saw me. And I thinks to myself: "Old boy, one of these days I'm going to get me a rock and knock them ugly teeth down your throat. Running around here with a set of horse-teeth in your mouth."

The crowd looked at me. A lot of them had seen me at the Methodist church. A lot of them had seen me at the foot-washing. They all knowed I was a Methodist. They know the Harkreaders are all Methodist—every last devil of them!

I just waited till church was out. I was going to take Effie home. And I had my mind made up. If that horse-toothed thing of a Tawa should come around me and started anything, it would just be too bad. I was going to use my fists long as they would stand it. I got bad bones in my little fingers. And after my fists I was going to knife it with him and after that if he whopped me I was going to use the balance of power. I carried it right in my pocket. The prettiest little .22 you ever saw in your life—could put five balls between your eyes before you could say

"Jack Robinson." I don't go into no strange territory unless I go prepared for the worst. That's the way we got to do here. I don't care if we
are Baptis and Methodist.

The preacher was saying: "Men and women, since you got to work in
your crops tomorrow and I got to work in mine, we'll call the meeting
till tomorrow night at seven. All of you be here and bring your song-
books. Sing "Almost Persuaded," folks, and all who wants to come up
and jine us just come right on." I never saw so many people fall at the
altar.

Church was out and the people already saved—the young people
went home and the old people stayed to pray with the people at the
"mourner's bench." They was just a-going on something awful. A lot of
them were sheep that had left the Methodist flock too. A bunch that
wanted to stay in our church and drink licker and play cards and we
just wouldn't have it in Plum Grove. Effie come right down the aisle
and I said: "Honey, how about seeing you home tonight?" I know my
face got red when she said: "All right." Here was old Tawa right
behind her with that crazy grin showing that big set of yellow horse-
teeth. I thought if he wanted anything he could get it on this night. I
didn't speak to him. No use to hide it. He didn't like me and I didn't
like him.

I got Effie by the arm, and I held it like a leech. We didn't speak.
We just walked out of the house and past a bunch of boys at the door
waiting for their girls and the other fellow's girl. People just looked at
us. Boys lit up their cigarettes and pipes and the old men started spitting their ambeer. A lot of the women lit up their pipes too—old long-
stemmed clay pipes. Something you don't see around our church at
Plum Grove among them already saved. If they done it they went home
or out behind the brush.

I hadn't got out from under the oak trees by the church house till I
had Effie by the hand. And I said: "Honey, I can't eat, drink, work, nor
sleep for thinking about you." And I reached down and got her by the
little soft hand, and she looked up at me and said: "Ain't it funny? I
feel the same way about you. I have felt that way ever since I saw you
at the foot-washing. I can't forget you. I keep thinking about you.
When I saw you tonight I was thinking about you." I just squeezed her
hand a little harder and I said: "Was you, Honey?" Then we went on
out the path without speaking.

We went out past the Duck Puddle graveyard. White tombstones
gleaming there in the moonlight. Lord, it was a sad thing to think
about. I wondered what had become of old Tawa. It was a little dark

even if the moon was shining. I didn't care though. I had Effie. I didn't blame him for loving her, but I just didn't want him to get her.

I guess we went through twenty pairs of drawbars before we come to Effie's place. It was a little log house upon the side of the bank, pretty with flowers in the yard. I'd always thought flowers was for the women-folks. I told Effie I'd never liked flowers till I met her. I told her every-thing like that. We just went up to her door. I said a lot about the crops. Before I started to leave we was standing out at the well-gum. The moon came down upon her old log house there among all them roses and flowers. It was a might pretty place. Effie said: "Guess I'd better get in the house and get to bed. Got to work tomorrow." And I said: "Where, Honey?" "In the terbacker field," she said. And then I said: "W'y, you don't work in no terbacker and stay as white as you are." She said: "That's all you know about it, Elster. I use stocking legs on my arms and a sunbonnet." And I says: "Honey, I love you. I want to marry you." I just pulled her up to me and kissed her there in the moonlight. Soon I left her there and run over the hill like a dog. Tears come into my eyes. Just to think about that. I used to laugh at such stuff. Now, I had six or seven miles to walk home and blue Monday and the plow before me the next day. But seeing Effie was worth a dozen trips like this. When a man is in love he just don't care.

I went to bed that night—must have been morning. It was after the roosters crowed for midnight. Lord, but I was tired. I just could see Effie. I could pull her up to me and kiss her. I could see her eyes, I could see her teeth. I could see her log house in the moonlight. I just couldn't forget it all.

I got up and et my breakfast. Drunk two cups of black coffee and went out to milk the cows. I'd just stop at the barn and look off into the wind. Pa come up to me and he said: "Elster, what in the devil and Tom Walker's got into you here lately—just go around with your head up in the air dreaming. W'y, you even stop when you are shaving your face. If I didn't see you the other day shave half of your face and put the razor up I'm a liar." I never said anything, for it was the truth. I just couldn't help it for thinking about Effie.

I went out to plow corn. I took the mule and the double-shovel plow and went down the path by the barn. I didn't pay any attention but I started the plow on the wrong side of the field and was plowing up the corn. I couldn't think about anything but Effie and how I run away and left that night with my eyes filled with tears. Then I thought: "W'y, I must be crazy to act like this. I'm forgetting everything. I'm not happy as I was. I can't laugh like I did. She didn't say she would marry me.

That's it. That's what's the matter." I just couldn't get back to see Effie that week. I had too much to do. Too much corn to plow and seven cows to milk.

Well, I went out to work Tuesday morning. I couldn't work. I thought I'd go up and see Uncle Tid Porter. He lives right on the bank above us. He gives us boys a lot of advice. Uncle Tid was in the woodyard whacking off a few sticks of stovewood. I walked up and I said: "Uncle Tid, I'm in love with a girl. I can't sleep. I can't work. I can't do anything. I'm going crazy."

You ought to have seen Uncle Tid sling his ax agin the ground and laugh. You know Uncle Tid is a pretty good doctor when we can't get one from town. He uses the yarb remedies and he does pretty well. Used to be the only doctor in this section. Now, he gives us advice along with spring tonics of slipper-elm bark, shoemake bark and ginsang and snakeroot. "Well," said Uncle Tid, shaking his long thin chin whiskers stained with a little terbacker juice—his blue-walled eye squinted a little—"when did you meet this girl and where is she from?"

"I met her last month at the Slab Baptis foot-washing at the Put-Off Ford. She's from Duck Puddle. She's a beauty, too, Uncle Tid. W'y, Uncle Tid, to tell you the truth, I never loved a flower till I met her. Now I notice them. See the wild rose in bloom in the woods. I noticed them this morning. She is with me everywhere I go. I can't sleep. I can't eat."

"It's love in the spring," said Uncle Tid. "Love in the spring is so uncertain I wouldn't trust it. Don't be too sure of yourself and jump in and try to marry. Wait a while. Just go out and watch life in the spring. Go to the house and put the mule in the pasture. Take the afternoon off and go to the pond and watch the frogs. Go find some black snakes in love and watch them. Watch the terrapins and the turtles. Everything is in love now. Listen to the songs of the birds. Listen how they sing to each other. It is time to be in love. All the earth is in love now. And love is so uncertain in the spring."

I just got on the mule and went back home. I took the harness off old Barnie and put it on the stall in the barn and I slapped him with the bridle and made him skiddoo to the pasture. I laid up the drawbars and I made for the pond. There's a lot of bullgrass there and about a foot of water. It's a regular frog and water-snake hangout. Lord, of all the noise! I slipped up by the pond. They all hushed. I never heard another noise only I heard some plump-plumps into the water. I saw that I'd scared them. So I laid down on my belly behind a bunch of bullgrass out of sight from the frogs. It wasn't two minutes before they all started singing. The old frogs didn't do much singing. They'd been in love and out again or they'd just took on some other kind of love after so many springs. The little frogs made up for lost time. They'd get up on a log and jump off and chase each other. I crawled up to the edge of the pond and watched them. If you don't believe young frogs love in the spring when they are doing all of that hollering you just go around the pond and see for yourself.

When I got up to leave there, I heard the birds singing. They sung their love songs to each other and it seemed like I could understand some of the words. But the prettiest thing I saw was two snakes entwined upon the bank in the sun. They were black snakes and very much in love. If it had been before I met Effie I would have picked me up a rock and killed them because Pa says they kill all the birds and young rabbits. I saw two turtles out in the pond on a log. They were bathing in the sun. I just watched them awhile. No wonder I fell in love with Effie, pretty a girl as she is. No wonder I dream of her at night and plan a house to take her to. My mother's bread don't taste as good to me as it used to taste. My bed at home don't look as good as it used to look and home and Mom and Pa don't seem the same. I just can't help feeling that way. I dream of the way Effie is going to bake my bread and fix my bed and clean my shirts and patch my pants. Life is great; and to be in love, love is so much greater. It's about one of the greatest things in the world—to be in love till you can cry. I just went to bed thinking about the house I had in mind and it was altogether different to the house here where we live. Just to see Effie with a blue dress and a little white apron on, lifting big white fluffy biscuits out of the pan—white biscuits with brown tops—and good hot gravy made out of milk—and butter yaller as a daisy eye—and steam off my coffee hot as hell and strong as love!

I just thought: "Well, I'm going to tell Pa and Ma that I am leaving them. That I am going to marry that little Slab Baptis and hunt me a home and help to replenish the earth with a good stock. A body can look at her and tell that she is of good stock and I ain't of such bad stock."

I went to the house. I never got the mule back out of the pasture. I was through. Of course I knowed Pa would hate to see me go and it would break Mom's heart when I told her. Mom is a shouting Methodist and it would kill her to see me marry one of them Slab Baptis that drink licker and bet on chicken fights and play cards. But no use to lie to Mom about it. I would go today and fix everything up. Frogs could fall in love and the birds and snakes and terrapins and lizards—well, why didn't I have the same right? And if Pa put his jib in I would tell him to stay out of my love affair and Uncle Tid Porter too. It may be love in the spring but I loved in the spring.

I'll never forget going into the house. Mom was making biscuit dough. I heard Pa telling her I put the mule up and knocked off for half day. Pa didn't like it and he was worried. "Well," I says to Mom, "I got news for you." And Mom says: "What kind of news, Elster?" And I says: "I am going to leave you. Going to get married."

"Who are you going to marry?" says Pa—his neck and face red as a hen's comb in the spring.

"I am going to marry Effie Long—that little girl I met over at the foot-washing last month," I said to Pa.

"One of them Slab Baptis?" said Pa.

"Yes, one of them Slab Baptis," I said.

"And you been raised under a roof like this one," Mom said, "under a Methodist roof—and then go and marry a Slab Baptis—one that has a religion that believes in drinking and playing poker and betting on roosters fights and spitting at cracks in the crib floor. Then you going to marry one of them kind. Remember, Elster, if you get burnt you got to set on the blister. You are brought up to believe a certain way it is hard to break away from. Elster, your people have been Methodist for nearly a hundred years. And you go marry that infidel. Don't you ever let her darken my door. You can come back when you want to but you be sure you keep her away."

The tears come from Mom's eyes. Pa put his hands up over his eyes. And I said to Mom: "Home here ain't the same any more since I met Effie. Life ain't the same, I tell you. My bed ain't the same upstairs and the good biscuits ain't the same."

"Your Ma's bread is the same. Good as it was twenty years ago. Best cook in the country. Then you talk about the bread and even your bed upstairs. Son, I'm not going to stand for anything like that. You can get out of this house if that is the way you feel about things around here. Get your clothes and go." Pa said it and his voice kinda quivered.

I went upstairs and got my clothes. It didn't take me long, for I don't have many. Lord, it burned me up to think about the whole thing. Life with Effie and I'd never come home to see the boys and Mom and Pa. I'd stay away till they would be glad to see me. That's what I'd do. They'd have to send to Duck Puddle to get me.

I put my clothes into the newspaper and got my work clothes—my heavy shoes and my Sunday shoes and my .22 pistol. I thought it might come in handy about a home of my own. I went down through the front room. Mom was crying. "Ain't you going to eat a bite before you leave?" Mom said. And I said: "Nope, I don't believe I care for anything to eat."

"Take a piece of hot corn bread and butter it and eat a piece of smoked ham as you go."

I took it. Lord, but it tasted good. I had et Mom's cooking for eighteen years and it was good. But I went out of the house. I wasn't going to wait till fall. Couldn't plant any ground that late. I was going to marry early enough to rent some ground and get out a late crop and pray for a late fall so they would ripen. I could make it all right.

I walked out into the sunlight. It was a pretty day in May. I never felt so good in all my life. Had my clothes under my arm and going to get my sweet Effie—sweeter than the wild red rose. I went down past the barn and I said farewell to the milk cows, Boss, Fern, Star, Daisy, Little Bitty, Roan and Blacky. I waved my hands to them and to Pete and Barnie in the pasture—mules I'd worked many a day. Barnie nickered at me. He walked along the pasture fence far as he could follow me. I'd been his master ever since he was a colt. Now he would get another master. I said good-by to the trees, the barn, to everything. I was going to a new country.

Sky was pretty above me. The birds never sung any sweeter for me. The wind had music in it. Flowers bloomed so pretty by the road, whole hillsides covered with wild roses. Well, when I got to the riffles the sun was getting pretty low on tother hill. I knowed it would soon be time for them to come from the fields. I'd just get in there a little after suppertime. Lord, but I was hungry. I got across the rocks at the riffle all right, and I went right up the creek till I come to the church house. I was moving fast to get there before dark. A little moon in the sky already.

I crossed the ditch by the church and took out toward the first pair of bars. If I ever go over a road once I never forget it. I soon came to the second pair of bars. The moon was a little bigger in the sky. One of them quarter moons. And a dry moon at that. One edge kinda turned up. Darkness had come at last but here was the house. Light in the front room. So I goes up and looks in. There was old Tawa. He was setting on the couch beside of my Effie. I knocked on the door. Effie come to the door. I said: "How are you, Honey?" and I just closed her in my arms. Old Tawa showed them big horse-teeth with that funny grin— them polecat eyes just a-snapping.

"Come here, Mart Long," Tawa hollered.

"Come where?" said a voice from upstairs. I heard him getting out of the bed. Sounded like the whole loft was coming in. Must 'a' been a big feller. "What are you coming here for?" said Tawa.

"If it's any your business," I said, "I'm coming here to marry Effie. That's why I've come."

"You ain't getting Effie," said Tawa. "She belongs to me. I'm one of her kind. I am a Slab Baptis. I ain't no damned infidental."

I thought I'd take my .22 out and blow his lights out. Calling me a infidental. I never did like the Methodists so much as I did now. And I said: "Who in the hell are you calling a infidental? You polecat you. I'll clean this floor with you." I started to turn Effie loose and get him. Just then in stepped Sourwood Long, Effie's pap.

"There's that infidental Methodist," said Tawa to Sourwood.

And Sourwood said: "W'y, he just looks like the rest of us. Got eyes like us and a mouth and talks. W'y, he's like the rest of us only I don't want Effie marrying you until you repent and get into our church."

"I have come after Effie right now," I said. "Besides, I am a Methodist. I don't intend to repent neither. Why can't she get into the Methodist church? What's wrong with us?"

"And what's wrong with us?" said Sourwood. Black beard covering his face. His arms were big as fence posts and hairy as a brier thicket around a old fence row. He kept them folded upon his big hairy chest. He didn't have many teeth. Had a lot of snags in his mouth—a big nose and he was dark as a wet piece of chestnut bark.

"Nothing ain't wrong with us," said Tawa. "We are the only people right. You know we got a lot of them Methodists in our church when the pertracted meeting was going on. Left your church for ours."

"You got a lot that couldn't stay in our church," I said. I was ready to fight. I still had Effie in my arms. I hadn't turned her loose yet.

"You ain't going to marry Effie. I wouldn't have one of you fellers in my house for dinner let alone in my family to put up with you a lifetime. Get out of here right now."

Another voice from upstairs. "Sourwood, what's going on down there?"

"Malinda, what are you doing up there? A Methodist has come to get Effie. Come on down here."

"Better let a Methodist have her than that thing down there. That Tawa. Get 'em both out of here. Get 'em out quick."

I never saw Effie's mother. I don't know how it was done. It was done so quick. Old Tawa must 'a' come around the back side of the house and upon the front porch and hit me over the head with something. I remember I waked up out in the yard. My clothes were under my head for a piller. The moon was in the sky. It just seemed like I'd been asleep and had slept a little too long. Seemed like a dream. Lights all out of the house just like nothing had ever happened. They's all in bed, I guess. Don't know what ever become of Tawa. Have never seen him from that day to this. I can hardly tell you how I got home. I was about half crazy from that lick. I remember I was so hungry. I remember, too, the chickens were crowing for the daylight. I didn't have my .22 on me. It was gone.

Mom was getting breakfast. I went in and I said: "Mom, your biscuits are all right. Lord, I can eat twenty-two this morning. I'm so hungry."

"Where's your wife?" Mom said.

"I took another notion," I said. "I remembered what you said. I didn't want one of them infidentals after we've been Methodists so long. I thought it over and changed my mind."

"I thought you would," said Mom. "A boy with your raising and get into a mix-up like that. Couldn't bring her home. You'll do better marrying one of your own kind. I'm making you some good strong coffee."

"Good strong coffee is what I need. Strong as love but not love in the spring. Love in the fall. Coffee hot as hell too."

Lord, but Mom did look good to me in that apron. She just looked the best I ever saw her. And her biscuits tasted right too. "Mom, you are the best girl I've ever had," I said and I kinda give Mom a bear hug and she says to this day I cracked a couple of her ribs. She says she can hardly get her breath at times ever since I hugged her.

This has been a day in September. Uncle Tid Porter was down today. He said to me: "Now is the kind of weather to fall in love—now while the chill winds blow and the leaves fly—now while the frost has come. The spring is the time to marry and go on a gay carousal like the frog. Like the snakes and the flowers and all living things. Spring is the time to marry—not the time to fall in love. Love in the spring is fickle as the wind."

"I have often wondered what has become of Tawa," I said to Uncle Tid, "the fellow that loved the girl I loved last spring—w'y, he's the ugliest human being I ever saw for to love as pretty a woman as Effie——"

"She's married him, I guess," said Uncle Tid. "That's the way of a woman. They do the unexpected thing—not knowing which way the wind will blow and if there will be snow or rain tomorrow. That's what a man likes—he likes the unexpected thing."

The wind blows outside. The wind is cool. Pa is out at the barn putting a roof over the fattening hog pen. Mom is still complaining of her ribs: "I never heard of that but once before in my life. A teacher come to this deestrict to teach school and he hugged one of Mort Giggin's girls—it was Ester, I believe—and he broke three of her ribs. I tell you he never got another school in this deestrict."

The Apple Tree

by JOHN GALSWORTHY

"The Apple-tree, the singing and the gold."

Murray's "Hippolytus of Euripides."

On their silver-wedding day Ashurst and his wife were motoring along
the outskirts of the moor, intending to crown the festival by stopping
the night at Torquay, where they had first met. This was the idea of
Stella Ashurst, whose character contained a streak of sentiment. If she
had long lost the blue-eyed, flower-like charm, the cool slim purity of
face and form, the apple-blossom colouring, that had so swiftly and so
oddly affected Ashurst twenty-six years ago, she was still at forty-three a
comely and faithful companion, whose cheeks were faintly mottled, and
whose grey-blue eyes had acquired a certain fullness.

It was she who had stopped the car where the common rose steeply to
the left, and a narrow strip of larch and beech, with here and there a
pine, stretched out to the right, towards the valley between the road
and the first long high hill of the full moor. She was looking for a place
where they might lunch, for Ashurst never looked for anything; and
this, between the golden furze and the feathery green larches smelling

of lemons in the last sun of April—this, with a view into the deep valley
and up to the long moor heights, seemed fitting to the decisive nature
of one who sketched in water-colours, and loved romantic spots. Grasp-
ing her paint box, she got out.

"Won't this do, Frank?"

Ashurst, rather like a bearded Schiller, grey in the wings, tall, long-
legged, with large remote grey eyes that sometimes filled with meaning
and became almost beautiful, with nose a little to one side, and bearded
lips just open—Ashurst, forty-eight, and silent, grasped the luncheon
basket, and got out too.

"Oh! Look, Frank! A grave!"

By the side of the road, where the track from the top of the common
crossed it at right angles and ran through a gate past the narrow wood,
was a thin mound of turf, six feet by one, with a moorstone to the west,
and on it someone had thrown a blackthorn spray and a handful of
bluebells. Ashurst looked, and the poet in him moved. At cross-roads—a
suicide's grave! Poor mortals with their superstitions! Whoever lay
there, though, had the best of it—no clammy sepulchre among other hideous graves carved with futilities—just a rough stone, the wide sky, and
wayside blessings! And, without comment, for he had learned not to be
a philosopher in the bosom of his family, he strode away up on to the
common, dropped the luncheon basket under a wall, spread a rug for
his wife to sit on—she would turn up from her sketching when she was
hungry—and took from his pocket Murray's translation of the
"Hyppolytus." He had soon finished reading of "The Cyprian" and her
revenge, and looked at the sky instead. And watching the white clouds
so bright against the intense blue, Ashurst, on his silver-wedding day,
longed for—he knew not what. Mal-adjusted to life—man's organism!
One's mode of life might be high and scrupulous, but there was always
an undercurrent of greediness, a hankering, and sense of waste. Did
women have it too? Who could tell? And yet, men who gave vent to
their appetites for novelty, their riotous longings for new adventures,
new risks, new pleasures, these suffered, no doubt, from the reverse side
of starvation, from surfeit. No getting out of it—a mal-adjusted animal,
civilised man! There could be no garden of his choosing, of "the Apple-
tree, the singing, and the gold," in the words of that lovely Greek chorus, no achievable elysium in life, or lasting haven of happiness for any
man with a sense of beauty—nothing that could compare with the captured loveliness in a work of art, set down for ever, so that to look on it
or read was always to have the same precious sense of exaltation and
restful inebriety. Life no doubt had moments with that quality of

beauty, of unbidden flying rapture, but the trouble was, they lasted no longer than the span of a cloud's flight over the sun; impossible to keep them with you, as Art caught beauty and held it fast. They were as fleeting as one of the glimmering or golden visions one had of the soul in nature, glimpses of its remote and brooding spirit. Here, with the sun hot on his face, a cuckoo calling from a thorn tree, and in the air the honey savour of gorse—here among the little fronds of the young fern, the starry blackthorn, while the bright clouds drifted by high above the hills and dreamy valleys—here and now was such a glimpse. But in a moment it would pass—as the face of Pan, that looks round the corner of a rock, vanishes at your stare. And suddenly he sat up. Surely there was something familiar about this view, this bit of common, that ribbon of road, the old wall behind him. While they were driving he had not been taking notice—never did; thinking of far things or of nothing—but now he saw! Twenty-six years ago, just at this time of year, from the farmhouse within half a mile of this very spot he had started for that day in Torquay whence it might be said he had never returned. And a sudden ache beset his heart; he had stumbled on just one of those past moments in his life, whose beauty and rapture he had failed to arrest, whose wings had fluttered away into the unknown; he had stumbled on a buried memory, a wild sweet time, swiftly choked and ended. And, turning on his face, he rested his chin on his hands, and stared at the short grass where the little blue milkwort was growing. . . .

And this is what he remembered.

1

On the first of May, after their last year together at college, Frank Ashurst and his friend Robert Garton were on a tramp. They had walked that day from Brent, intending to make Chagford, but Ashurst's football knee had given out, and according to their map they had still some seven miles to go. They were sitting on a bank beside the road, where a track crossed alongside a wood, resting the knee and talking of the universe, as young men will. Both were over six feet, and as thin as rails; Ashurst pale, idealistic, full of absence; Garton queer, round-the-corner, knotted, curly, like some primeval beast. Both had a literary bent; neither wore a hat. Ashurst's hair was smooth, pale, wavy, and had a way of rising on either side of his brow, as if always being flung back; Garton's was a kind of dark unfathomed mop. They had not met a soul for miles.

"My dear fellow," Garton was saying, "pity's only the effect of self-consciousness; it's a disease of the last five thousand years. The world was happier without."

Ashurst, following the clouds with his eyes, answered:

"It's the pearl in the oyster, anyway."

"My dear chap, all our modern unhappiness comes from pity. Look at animals, and Red Indians, limited to feeling their own occasional misfortunes; then look at ourselves—never free from feeling the tooth-aches of others. Let's get back to feeling for nobody, and have a better time."

"You'll never practise that."

Garton pensively stirred the hotch-potch of his hair.

"To attain full growth, one mustn't be squeamish. To starve oneself emotionally's a mistake. All emotion is to the good—enriches life."

"Yes, and when it runs up against chivalry?"

"Ah! That's so English! If you speak of emotion the English always think you want something physical, and are shocked. They're afraid of passion, but not of lust—oh, no!—so long as they can keep it secret."

Ashurst did not answer; he had plucked a blue floweret, and was twiddling it against the sky. A cuckoo began calling from a thorn-tree. The sky, the flowers, the songs of birds! Robert was talking through his hat! And he said:

"Well, let's go on, and find some farm where we can put up." In uttering those words, he was conscious of a girl coming down from the common just above them. She was outlined against the sky, carrying a basket, and you could see that sky through the crook of her arm. And Ashurst, who saw beauty without wondering how it could advantage him, thought: 'How pretty!' The wind, blowing her dark frieze skirt against her legs, lifted her battered peacock tam-o'-shanter; her greyish blouse was worn and old, her shoes were split, her little hands rough and red, her neck browned. Her dark hair waved untidy across her broad forehead, her face was short, her upper lip short, showing a glint of teeth, her brows were straight and dark, her lashes long and dark, her nose straight; but her grey eyes were the wonder—as dewy as if opened for the first time that day. She looked at Ashurst—perhaps he struck her as strange, limping along without a hat, with his large eyes on her, and his hair flung back. He could not take off what was not on his head, but put up his hand in a salute, and said:

"Can you tell us if there's a farm near here where we could stay the night? I've gone lame."

"There's only our farm near, sir." She spoke without shyness, in a pretty soft crisp voice.

"And where is that?"

"Down here, sir."

"Would you put us up?"

"Oh! I think we would."

"Will you show us the way?"

"Yes, sir."

He limped on, silent, and Garton took up the catechism.

"Are you a Devonshire girl?"

"No, sir."

"What then?"

"From Wales."

"Ah! I *thought* you were a Celt; so it's not your farm?"

"My aunt's, sir."

"And your uncle's?"

"He is dead."

"Who farms it, then?"

"My aunt, and my three cousins."

"But your uncle was a Devonshire man?"

"Yes, sir."

"Have you lived here long?"

"Seven years."

"And how d'you like it after Wales?"

"I don't know, sir."

"I suppose you don't remember?"

"Oh, yes! But it is different."

"I believe you!"

Ashurst broke in suddenly:

"How old are you?"

"Seventeen, sir."

"And what's your name?"

"Megan David."

"This is Robert Garton, and I am Frank Ashurst. We wanted to get on to Chagford."

"It is a pity your leg is hurting you."

Ashurst smiled, and when he smiled his face was rather beautiful.

Descending past the narrow wood, they came on the farm suddenly— a long, low, stone-built, dwelling with casement windows, in a farmyard where pigs and fowls and an old mare were straying. A short steep-up grass hill behind was crowned with a few Scotch firs, and in front, an old

orchard of apple trees, just breaking into flower, stretched down to a
stream and a long wild meadow. A little boy with oblique dark eyes was
shepherding a pig, and by the house door stood a woman, who came towards them. The girl said:

"It is Mrs. Narracombe, my aunt."

"Mrs. Narracombe, my aunt," had a quick, dark eye, like a mother
wild-duck's, and something of the same snaky turn about her neck.

"We met your niece on the road," said Ashurst; "she thought you
might perhaps put us up for the night."

Mrs. Narracombe, taking them in from head to heel, answered:

"Well, I can, if you don't mind one room. Megan, get the spare
room ready, and a bowl of cream. You'll be wanting tea, I suppose."

Passing through a sort of porch made by two yew trees and some
flowering currant bushes, the girl disappeared into the house, her
peacock tam-o'-shanter bright athwart that rosy-pink and the dark green
of the yews.

"Will you come into the parlour and rest your leg? You'll be from
college, perhaps?"

"We were, but we've gone down now."

Mrs. Narracombe nodded sagely.

The parlour, brick-floored, with bare table and shiny chairs and sofa
stuffed with horsehair, seemed never to have been used, it was so terribly clean. Ashurst sat down at once on the sofa, holding his lame knee
between his hands, and Mrs. Narracombe gazed at him. He was the
only son of a late professor of chemistry, but people found a certain
lordliness in one who was often so sublimely unconscious of them.

"Is there a stream where we could bathe?"

"There's the strame at the bottom of the orchard, but sittin' down
you'll not be covered!"

"How deep?"

"Well, 'tis about a foot and a half, maybe."

"Oh! That'll do fine. Which way?"

"Down the lane, through the second gate on the right, an' the pool's
by the big apple tree that stands by itself. There's trout there, if you
can tickle them."

"They're more likely to tickle us!"

Mrs. Narracombe smiled. "There'll be the tea ready when you come
back."

The pool, formed by the damming of a rock, had a sandy bottom;
and the big apple tree, lowest in the orchard, grew so close that its
boughs almost overhung the water; it was in leaf, and all but in flower—

its crimson buds just bursting. There was not room for more than one at a time in that narrow bath, and Ashurst waited his turn, rubbing his knee and gazing at the wild meadow, all rocks and thorn trees and field flowers, with a grove of beeches beyond, raised up on a flat mound. Every bough was swinging in the wind, every spring bird calling, and a slanting sunlight dappled the grass. He thought of Theocritus, and the river Cherwell, of the moon, and the maiden with the dewy eyes; of so many things that he seemed to think of nothing; and he felt absurdly happy.

2

During a late and sumptuous tea with eggs to it, cream and jam, and thin, fresh cakes touched with saffron, Garton descanted on the Celts. It was about the period of the Celtic awakening, and the discovery that there was Celtic blood about this family had excited one who believed that he was a Celt himself. Sprawling on a horsehair chair, with a hand-made cigarette dribbling from the corner of his curly lips, he had been plunging his cold pin-points of eyes into Ashurst's and praising the refinement of the Welsh. To come out of Wales into England was like the change from china to earthenware! Frank, as a d——d Englishman, had not of course perceived the exquisite refinement and emotional capacity of that Welsh girl! And, delicately stirring in the dark mat of his still wet hair, he explained how exactly she illustrated the writings of the Welsh bard Morgan-ap-Something in the twelfth century.

Ashurst, full length on the horsehair sofa, and jutting far beyond its end, smoked a deeply-coloured pipe, and did not listen, thinking of the girl's face when she brought in a relay of cakes. It had been exactly like looking at a flower, or some other pretty sight in Nature—till, with a funny little shiver, she had lowered her glance and gone out, quiet as a mouse.

"Let's go to the kitchen," said Garton, "and see some more of her."

The kitchen was a white-washed room with rafters, to which were attached smoked hams; there were flower-pots on the window-sill, and guns hanging on nails, queer mugs, china and pewter, and portraits of Queen Victoria. A long, narrow table of plain wood was set with bowls and spoons, under a string of high-hung onions; two sheep-dogs and three cats lay here and there. On one side of the recessed fireplace sat two small boys, idle, and good as gold; on the other sat a stout, light-eyed, red-faced youth with hair and lashes the colour of the tow he was running through the barrel of a gun; between them Mrs. Narracombe dreamily stirred some savoury-scented stew in a large pot. Two other youths, oblique-eyed, dark-haired, rather sly-faced, like the two little boys, were talking together and lolling against the wall; and a short, elderly, clean-shaven man in corduroys, seated in the window, was conning a battered journal. The girl Megan seemed the only active creature—drawing cider and passing with the jugs from cask to table. Seeing them thus about to eat, Garton said:

"Ah! If you'll let us, we'll come back when supper's over," and without waiting for an answer they withdrew again to the parlour. But the colour in the kitchen, the warmth, the scents, and all those faces, heightened the bleakness of their shiny room, and they resumed their seats moodily.

"Regular gipsy type, those boys. There was only one Saxon—the fellow cleaning the gun. That girl is a very subtle study psychologically."

Ashurst's lips twitched. Garton seemed to him an ass just then. Subtle study! She was a wild flower. A creature it did you good to look at. Study!

Garton went on:

"Emotionally she would be wonderful. She wants awakening."

"Are you going to awaken her?"

Garton looked at him and smiled. "How coarse and English you are!" that curly smile seemed saying.

And Ashurst puffed his pipe. Awaken her! That fool had the best opinion of himself! He threw up the window and leaned out. Dusk had gathered thick. The farm buildings and the wheel-house were all dim and blueish, the apple trees but a blurred wilderness; the air smelled of wood-smoke from the kitchen fire. One bird going to bed later than the others was uttering a half-hearted twitter, as though surprised at the darkness. From the stable came the snuffle and stamp of a feeding horse. And away over there was the loom of the moor, and away and away the shy stars that had not as yet full light, pricking white through the deep blue heavens. A quavering owl hooted. Ashurst drew a deep breath. What a night to wander out in! A padding of unshod hoofs came up the lane, and three dim, dark shapes passed—ponies on an evening march. Their heads, black and fuzzy, showed above the gate. At the tap of his pipe, and a shower of little sparks, they shied round and scampered. A bat went fluttering past, uttering its almost inaudible "chip, chip." Ashurst held out his hand; on the upturned palm he could feel the dew. Suddenly from overhead he heard little burring boys' voices, little thumps of boots thrown down, and another voice, crisp and soft—the girl's, putting them to bed, no doubt; and nine clear words: "No, Rick, you can't have the cat in bed"; then came a skirmish of giggles and gurgles, a soft slap, a laugh so low and pretty that it made him shiver a little. A blowing sound, and the glim of the candle that was fingering the dusk above, went out; silence reigned. Ashurst withdrew into the room and sat down; his knee pained him, and his soul felt gloomy.

"You go to the kitchen," he said; "I'm going to bed."

3

For Ashurst the wheel of slumber was wont to turn noiseless and slick and swift, but though he seemed sunk in sleep when his companion came up, he was really wide awake; and long after Garton, smothered in the other bed of that low-roofed room, was worshipping darkness with his upturned nose, he heard the owls. Barring the discomfort of his knee, it was not unpleasant—the cares of life did not loom large in night watches for this young man. In fact he had none; just enrolled a barrister, with literary aspirations, the world before him, no father or mother, and four hundred a year of his own. Did it matter where he went, what he did, or when he did it? His bed, too, was hard, and this preserved him from fever. He lay, sniffing the scent of the night that drifted into the low room through the open casement close to his head. Except for a definite irritation with his friend, natural when you have tramped with a man for three days, Ashurst's memories and visions that sleepless night were kindly and wistful and exciting. One vision, specially clear and unreasonable, for he had not even been conscious of noting it, was the face of the youth cleaning the gun; its intent, stolid, yet startled uplook at the kitchen doorway, quickly shifted to the girl carrying the cider jug. This red, blue-eyed, light-lashed, tow-haired face stuck as firmly in his memory as the girl's own face, so dewy and simple. But at last, in the square of darkness through the uncurtained casement, he saw day coming, and heard one hoarse and sleepy caw. Then followed silence, dead as ever, till the song of a blackbird, not properly awake, adventured into the hush. And, from staring at the framed brightening light, Ashurst fell asleep.

Next day his knee was badly swollen; the walking tour was obviously over. Garton, due back in London on the morrow, departed at midday with an ironical smile which left a scar of irritation—healed the moment his loping figure vanished round the corner of the steep lane. All day Ashurst rested his knee, in a green-painted wooden chair on the patch of grass by the yew-tree porch, where the sunlight distilled the scent of stocks and gilly-flowers, and a ghost of scent from the flowering currant bushes. Beatifically he smoked, dreamed, watched.

A farm in spring is all birth—young things coming out of bud and shell, and human beings watching over the process with faint excitement, feeding and tending what has been born. So still the young man sat, that a mother-goose, with stately cross-footed waddle, brought her six yellow-necked grey-backed goslings to strop their little beaks against the grass blades at his feet. Now and again Mrs. Narracombe or the girl Megan would come and ask if he wanted anything, and he would smile and say: "Nothing, thanks. It's splendid here." Towards tea-time they came out together, bearing a long poultice of some dark stuff in a bowl, and after a long and solemn scrutiny of his swollen knee, bound it on. When they were gone, he thought of the girl's soft "Oh!"—of her pitying eyes, and the little wrinkle in her brow. And again he felt that unreasoning irritation against his departed friend, who had talked such rot about her. When she brought out his tea, he said:

"How did you like my friend, Megan?"

She forced down her upper lip, as if afraid that to smile was not polite. "He was a funny gentleman; he made us laugh. I think he is very clever."

"What did he say to make you laugh?"

"He said I was a daughter of the bards. What are they?"

"Welsh poets, who lived hundreds of years ago."

"Why am I their daughter, please?"

"He meant that you were the sort of girl they sang about."

She wrinkled her brows. "I think he likes to joke. Am I?"

"Would you believe me, if I told you?"

"Oh, yes!"

"Well, I think he was right."

She smiled.

And Ashurst thought: 'You *are* a pretty thing!'

"He said, too, that Joe was a Saxon type. What would that be?"

"Which is Joe? With the blue eyes and red face?"

"Yes. My uncle's nephew."

"Not your cousin, then?"

"No."

"Well, he meant that Joe was like the men who came over to England about fourteen hundred years ago, and conquered it."

"Oh! I know about them; but is he?"

"Garton's crazy about that sort of thing; but I must say Joe does look a bit Early Saxon."

"Yes."

That "Yes" tickled Ashurst. It was so crisp and graceful, so conclusive, and politely acquiescent in what was evidently Greek to her.

"He said that all the other boys were regular gipsies. He should not have said that. My aunt laughed, but she didn't like it, of course, and my cousins were angry. Uncle was a farmer—farmers are not gipsies. It is wrong to hurt people."

Ashurst wanted to take her hand and give it a squeeze, but he only answered:

"Quite right, Megan. By the way, I heard you putting the little ones to bed last night."

She flushed a little. "Please to drink your tea—it is getting cold. Shall I get you some fresh?"

"Do you ever have time to do anything for yourself?"

"Oh! Yes."

"I've been watching, but I haven't seen it yet."

She wrinkled her brows in a puzzled frown, and her colour deepened.

When she was gone, Ashurst thought: 'Did she think I was chaffing her? I wouldn't for the world!' He was at that age when to some men "Beauty's a flower," as the poet says, and inspires in them the thoughts of chivalry. Never very conscious of his surroundings, it was some time before he was aware that the youth whom Garton had called "a Saxon type" was standing outside the stable door; and a fine bit of colour he made in his soiled brown velvet-cords, muddy gaiters, and blue shirt; red-armed, red-faced, the sun turning his hair from tow to flax; immovably stolid, persistent, unsmiling he stood. Then, seeing Ashurst looking at him, he crossed the yard at that gait of the young countryman always ashamed not to be slow and heavy-dwelling on each leg, and disappeared round the end of the house towards the kitchen entrance. A chill came over Ashurst's mood. Clods? With all the good will in the world, how impossible to get on terms with them. And yet—see that girl! Her shoes were split, her hands rough; but—what was it? Was it really her Celtic blood, as Garton had said?—she was a lady born, a jewel, though probably she could do no more than just read and write!

The elderly, clean-shaved man he had seen last night in the kitchen had come into the yard with a dog, driving the cows to their milking. Ashurst saw that he was lame.

"You've got some good ones there!"

The lame man's face brightened. He had the upward look in his eyes that prolonged suffering often brings.

"Yeas; they'm praaper buties; gude milkers tu."

"I bet they are."

" 'Ope as yure leg's better, zurr."

"Thank you, it's getting on."

The lame man touched his own: "I know what 'tes, meself; 'tes a main worritin' thing, the knee. I've a—'ad mine bad this ten year."

Ashurst made the sound of sympathy that comes so readily from those who have an independent income, and the lame man smiled again.

"Mustn't complain, though—they mighty near 'ad it off."

"Ho!"

"Yeas; an' compared with what 'twas, 'tes almost so gude as nu."

"They've put a bandage of splendid stuff on mine."

"The maid she picks et. She'm a gude maid wi' the flowers. There's folks zeem to know the healin' in things. My mother was a rare one for that. 'Ope as yu'll zune be better, zurr. Goo ahn, therr!"

Ashurst smiled. "Wi' the flowers!" A flower herself!

That evening, after his supper of cold duck, junket, and cider, the girl came in.

"Please, auntie says—will you try a piece of our Mayday cake?"

"If I may come to the kitchen for it."

"Oh, yes! You'll be missing your friend."

"Not I. But are you sure no one minds?"

"Who would mind? We shall be very pleased."

Ashurst rose too suddenly for his stiff knee, staggered, and subsided. The girl gave a little gasp, and held out her hands. Ashurst took them, small, rough, brown; checked his impulse to put them to his lips, and let her pull him up. She came close beside him, offering her shoulder. And leaning on her he walked across the room. That shoulder seemed quite the pleasantest thing he had ever touched. But he had presence of mind enough to catch his stick out of the rack, and withdraw his hand before arriving at the kitchen.

That night he slept like a top, and woke with his knee of almost normal size. He again spent the morning in his chair on the grass patch, scribbling down verses; but in the afternoon he wandered about with the two little boys Nick and Rick. It was Saturday, so they were early home from school; quick, shy, dark little rascals of seven and six, soon talkative, for Ashurst had a way with children. They had shown him all their methods of destroying life by four o'clock, except the tickling of trout; and with breeches tucked up, lay on their stomachs over the trout stream, pretending they had this accomplishment also. They tickled nothing, of course, for their giggling and shouting scared every spotted thing away. Ashurst, on a rock at the edge of the beech clump, watched them, and listened to the cuckoos, till Nick, the elder and less persevering, came up and stood beside him.

"The gipsy bogle zets on that stone," he said.

"What gipsy bogle?"

"Dunno; never zeen 'e. Megan zays 'e zets there; an' old Jim zeed 'e once. 'E was zettin' there naight afore our pony kicked-in father's 'ead. 'E plays the viddle."

"What tune does he play?"

"Dunno."

"What's he like?"

"'E's black. Old Jim zays 'e's all over 'air. 'E's praaper bogle. 'E don' come only at naight." The little boy's oblique dark eyes slid round. "D'yu think 'e might want to take me away? Megan's feared of 'e."

"Has she seen him?"

"No. She's not afeared o' yu."

"I should think not. Why should she be?"

"She zays a prayer for yu."

"How do you know that, you little rascal?"

"When I was asleep, she said: 'God bless us all, an' Mr. Ashes.' I yeard 'er whisperin'."

"You're a little ruffian to tell what you hear when you're not meant to hear it!"

The little boy was silent. Then he said aggressively:

"I can skin rabbets. Megan, she can't bear skinnin' 'em. I like blood."

"Oh! you do; you little monster!"

"What's that?"

"A creature that likes hurting others."

The little boy scowled. "They'm only dead rabbets, what us eats."

"Quite right, Nick. I beg your pardon."

"I can skin frogs, tu."

But Ashurst had become absent. "God bless us all, and Mr. Ashes!" And puzzled by that sudden inaccessibility, Nick ran back to the stream, where the giggling and shouts again uprose at once.

When Megan brought his tea, he said:

"What's the gipsy bogle, Megan?"

She looked up, startled.

"He brings bad things."

"Surely you don't believe in ghosts?"

"I hope I will never see him."

"Of course you won't. There aren't such things. What old Jim saw was a pony."

"No! There are bogles in the rocks; they are the men that lived long ago."

"They aren't gipsies, anyway; those old men were dead long before gipsies came."

She said simply: "They are all bad."

"Why? If there are any, they're only wild, like the rabbits. The flowers aren't bad for being wild; the thorn trees were never planted—and you don't mind them. I shall go down at night and look for your bogle, and have a talk with him."

"Oh, no! Oh, no!"

"Oh, yes! I shall go and sit on his rock."

She clasped her hands together: "Oh, please!"

"Why! What does it matter if anything happens to me?"

She did not answer; and in a sort of pet he added:

"Well, I daresay I shan't see him, because I suppose I must be off soon."

"Soon?"

"Your aunt won't want to keep me here."

"Oh, yes! We always let lodgings in summer."

Fixing his eyes on her face, he asked:

"Would you like me to stay?"

"Yes."

"I'm going to say a prayer for *you* to-night!"

She flushed crimson, frowned, and went out of the room. He sat, cursing himself, till his tea was stewed. It was as if he had hacked with his thick boots at a clump of bluebells. Why had he said such a silly thing? Was he just a towny college ass like Robert Garton, as far from understanding this girl?

4

Ashurst spent the next week confirming the restoration of his leg, by exploration of the country within easy reach. Spring was a revelation to him this year. In a kind of intoxication he would watch the pink-white buds of some backward beech tree sprayed up in the sunlight against the deep blue sky, or the trunks and limbs of the few Scotch firs, tawny in violent light, or again, on the moor, the gale-bent larches that had such a look of life when the wind streamed in their young green, above the rusty black under-boughs. Or he would lie on the banks, gazing at the clusters of dog-violets, or up in the dead bracken, fingering the pink, transparent buds of the dewberry, while the cuckoos called and yaffles laughed, or a lark, from very high, dripped its beads of song. It was certainly different from any spring he had ever known, for spring was within him, not without. In the daytime he hardly saw the family; and when Megan brought in his meals she always seemed too busy in the house or among the young things in the yard to stay talking long. But in the evenings he installed himself in the window seat in the kitchen, smoking and chatting with the lame man Jim, or Mrs. Narracombe, while the girl sewed, or moved about, clearing the supper things away. And sometimes, with the sensation a cat must feel when it purrs, he would become conscious that Megan's eyes—those dew-grey eyes—were fixed on him with a sort of lingering soft look that was strangely flattering.

It was on Sunday week in the evening, when he was lying in the orchard listening to a blackbird and composing a love poem, that he heard the gate swing to, and saw the girl come running among the trees, with the red-cheeked, stolid Joe in swift pursuit. About twenty yards away the chase ended, and the two stood fronting each other, not noticing the stranger in the grass—the boy pressing on, the girl fending him off. Ashurst could see her face, angry, disturbed; and the youth's— who would have thought that red-faced yokel could look so distraught! And painfully affected by that sight, he jumped up. They saw him then. Megan dropped her hands, and shrunk behind a tree-trunk; the boy gave an angry grunt, rushed at the bank, scrambled over and vanished. Ashurst went slowly up to her. She was standing quite still, biting her lip—very pretty, with her fine, dark hair blown loose about her face, and her eyes cast down.

"I beg your pardon," he said.

She gave him one upward look, from eyes much dilated; then, catching her breath, turned away. Ashurst followed.

"Megan!"

But she went on; and taking hold of her arm, he turned her gently round to him.

"Stop and speak to me."

"Why do you beg my pardon? It is not to me you should do that."

"Well, then, to Joe."

"How dare he come after me?"

"In love with you, I suppose."

She stamped her foot.

Ashurst uttered a short laugh. "Would you like me to punch his head?"

She cried with sudden passion:

"You laugh at me—you laugh at us!"

He caught hold of her hands, but she shrank back, till her passionate little face and loose dark hair were caught among the pink clusters of the apple blossom. Ashurst raised one of her imprisoned hands and put his lips to it. He felt how chivalrous he was, and superior to that clod Joe—just brushing that small, rough hand with his mouth! Her shrinking ceased suddenly; she seemed to tremble towards him. A sweet warmth overtook Ashurst from top to toe. This slim maiden, so simple and fine and pretty, was pleased, then, at the touch of his lips! And, yielding to a swift impulse, he put his arms round her, pressed her to him, and kissed her forehead. Then he was frightened—she went so pale, closing her eyes, so that the long, dark lashes lay on her pale cheeks; her hands, too, lay inert at her sides. The touch of her breast sent a quiver through him. "Megan!" he sighed out, and let her go. In the utter silence a blackbird shouted. Then the girl seized his hand, put it to her cheek, her heart, her lips, kissed it passionately, and fled away among the mossy trunks of the apple trees, till they hid her from him.

Ashurst sat down on a twisted old tree that grew almost along the ground, and, all throbbing and bewildered, gazed vacantly at the blossom which had crowned her hair—those pink buds with one white open apple star. What had he done? How had he let himself be thus stampeded by beauty—pity—or—just the spring! He felt curiously happy, all the same; happy and triumphant, with shivers running through his limbs, and a vague alarm. This was the beginning of—what? The midges bit him, the dancing gnats tried to fly into his mouth, and all the spring around him seemed to grow more lovely and alive; the songs of the cuckoos and the blackbirds, the laughter of the yaffles, the level-slanting sunlight, the apple blossom that had crowned her head——! He got up from the old trunk and strode out of the orchard, wanting space, an open sky, to get on terms with these new sensations. He made for the moor, and from an ash tree in the hedge a magpie flew out to herald him.

Of man—at any age from five years on—who can say he has never been in love? Ashurst had loved his partners at his dancing class; loved his nursery governess; girls in school-holidays; perhaps never been quite out of love, cherishing always some more or less remote admiration. But this was different, not remote at all. Quite a new sensation, terribly delightful, bringing a sense of completed manhood. To be holding in his fingers such a wild flower, to be able to put it to his lips, and feel it tremble with delight against them! What intoxication, and—embarrassment! What to do with it—how meet her next time? His first caress had been cool, pitiful; but the next could not be, now that, by her burning little kiss on his hand, by her pressure of it to her heart, he knew that she loved him. Some natures are coarsened by love bestowed on them; others, like Ashurst's, are swayed and drawn, warmed and softened, almost exalted, by what they feel to be a sort of miracle.

And up there among the tors he was torn between the passionate desire to revel in this new sensation of spring fulfilled within him, and a vague but very real uneasiness. At one moment he gave himself completely to his pride at having captured this pretty, trustful, soft-eyed thing! At the next he thought with factitious solemnity: 'Yes, my boy! But look out what you're doing! You know what comes of it!'

Dusk dropped down without his noticing—dusk on the carved syrian-looking masses of the rocks. And the voice of Nature said: "This is a new world for you!" As when a man gets up at four o'clock and goes out into a summer morning, and beasts, birds, trees stare at him and he feels as if all had been made new.

He stayed up there for hours, till it grew cold, then groped his way down the stones and heather roots to the road, back into the lane, and came again past the wild meadow to the orchard. There he struck a match and looked at his watch. Nearly twelve! It was black and unstirring in there now, very different from the lingering, bird-befriended brightness of six hours ago! And suddenly he saw this idyll of his with the eyes of the outer world—had mental vision of Mrs. Narracombe's snake-like neck turned, her quick dark glance taking it all in, her shrewd face hardening; saw the gipsy-like cousins coarsely mocking and distrustful; Joe stolid and furious; only the lame man, Jim, with the suffering eyes, seemed tolerable to his mind. And the village pub!—the gossiping matrons he passed on his walks; and then—his own friends—Robert Garton's smile when he went off that morning ten days ago; so ironical and knowing! Disgusting! For a minute he literally hated this earthy, cynical world that one belonged to, willy-nilly. The gate where he was leaning grew grey, a sort of shimmer passed before him and spread into the blueish darkness. The moon! He could just see it over the bank behind; red, nearly round—a strange moon! And turning away, he went up the lane that smelled of the night and cow-dung and young leaves. In the straw-yard he could see the dark shapes of cattle, broken by the pale sickles of their horns, like so many thin moons, fallen ends-up. He unlatched the farm gate stealthily. All was dark in the house. Muffling his footsteps, he gained the porch, and, blotted against one of the yew trees, looked up at Megan's window. It was open. Was she sleeping, or lying awake perhaps, disturbed—unhappy at his absence? An owl hooted while he stood there peering up, and the sound seemed to fill the whole night, so quiet was all else, save for the never-ending murmur of the stream running below the orchard. The cuckoos by day, and now the owls—how wonderfully they voiced this troubled ecstasy within him! And suddenly he saw her at her window, looking out. He moved little from the yew tree, and whispered: "Megan!" She drew back, vanished, reappeared, leaning far down. He stole forward on the grass, hit his shin against the green-painted chair, and held his breath at the sound. The pale blur of her stretched-down arm and face did not stir; he moved the chair, and noiselessly mounted it. By reaching up his arm he could just reach. Her hand held the huge key of the front door, and he clasped that burning hand with the cold key in it. He could just see her face, the glint of teeth between her lips, her tumbled hair. She was still dressed—poor child; sitting up for him, no doubt! "Pretty Megan!" Her hot, roughened fingers clung to his; her face had a strange, lost look. To have been able to reach it—even with cold steel! The owl hooted, a scent of sweetbriar crept into his nostrils. Then one of the farm dogs barked; her grasp relaxed, she shrank back. "Good-night, Megan!"

"Good-night, sir!" She was gone! With a sigh he dropped back to earth, and sitting on that chair, took off his boots. Nothing for it but to creep in and go to bed; yet for a long while he sat unmoving, his feet wet in the dew, drunk on the memory of her lost, half-smiling face, and the clinging grip of her burning fingers, pressing the cold key into his hand.

5

He woke feeling as if he had eaten heavily overnight, instead of having eaten nothing. And far off, unreal, seemed yesterday's romance! Yet it was a golden morning. Full spring had burst at last—in one night the "milk-cups," as the little boys called them, seemed to have made the meadows their own, and from his window he could see apple blossom covering the orchard as with a rose and white quilt. He went down almost dreading to see Megan; and yet, when not she but Mrs. Narracombe brought in his breakfast, he felt vexed and disappointed. The woman's quick eye and snaky neck seemed to have a new alacrity this morning. Had she noticed?

"So you an' the moon went walkin' last night, Mr. Ashurst! Did ye have your supper anywheres?"

Ashurst shook his head.

"We kept it for you, but I suppose you was too busy in your brain to think o' such a thing as that?"

Was she mocking him, in that voice of hers, which still kept some Welsh crispness against the invading burr of the West Country? If she knew! And at that moment he thought: 'No, no; I'll clear out. I won't put myself in such a beastly false position.'

But, after breakfast, the longing to see Megan began and increased with every minute, together with fear lest something should have been said to her which had spoiled everything. Sinister that she had not appeared, not given him even a glimpse of her! And the love poem, whose manufacture had been so important and absorbing yesterday afternoon under the apple trees, now seemed so paltry that he tore it up and rolled it into pipe spills. What had he known of love, till she seized his hand and kissed it! And now—what did he not know? But to write of it seemed mere insipidity! He went up to his bedroom to get a book, and his heart began to beat violently, for she was in there making the bed. He stood in the doorway watching; and suddenly, with turbulent joy, he saw her stoop and kiss his pillow, just at the hollow made by his head last night. How let her know he had seen that pretty act of devotion? And yet, if she heard him stealing away, it would be even worse. She took the pillow up, holding it as if reluctant to shake out the impress of his cheek, dropped it, and turned round.

"Megan!"

She put her hands up to her cheeks, but her eyes seemed to look right into him. He had never before realised the depth and purity and touching faithfulness in those dew-bright eyes, and he stammered:

"It was sweet of you to wait up for me last night."

She still said nothing, and he stammered on:

"I was wandering about on the moor; it was such a jolly night. I—I've just come up for a book."

Then, the kiss he had seen her give the pillow afflicted him with sudden headiness, and he went up to her. Touching her eyes with his lips, he thought with queer excitement: "I've done it! Yesterday all was sudden—anyhow; but now—I've done it!" The girl let her forehead rest against his lips, which moved downward till they reached hers. That first real lover's kiss—strange, wonderful, still almost innocent—in which heart did it make the most disturbance?

"Come to the big apple tree to-night, after they've gone to bed. Megan—promise!"

She whispered back: "I promise."

Then, scared at her white face, scared at everything, he let her go, and went downstairs again. Yes! he had done it now! Accepted her love, declared his own! He went out to the green chair as devoid of a book as ever; and there he sat staring vacantly before him, triumphant and re-morseful, while under his nose and behind his back the work of the farm went on. How long he had been sitting in that curious state of vacancy he had no notion when he saw Joe standing a little behind him to the right. The youth had evidently come from hard work in the fields, and stood shifting his feet, breathing loudly, his face coloured like a setting sun, and his arms, below the rolled-up sleeves of his blue shirt, showing the hue and furry sheen of ripe peaches. His red lips were open, his blue eyes with their flaxen lashes stared fixedly at Ashurst, who said ironically:

"Well, Joe, anything I can do for you?"

"Yeas."

"What, then?"

"Yu can goo away from yere. Us don' want yu."

Ashurst's face, never too humble, assumed its most lordly look.

"Very good of you, but, do you know, I prefer the others should speak for themselves."

The youth moved a pace or two nearer, and the scent of his honest heat afflicted Ashurst's nostrils.

"What d'yu stay yere for?"

"Because it pleases me."

" 'Twon't please yu when I've bashed yure 'ead in!"

"Indeed! When would you like to begin that?"

Joe answered only with the loudness of his breathing, but his eyes looked like those of a young and angry bull. Then a sort of spasm seemed to convulse his face.

"Megan don' want yu."

A rush of jealousy, of contempt, and anger with this thick, loud-breathing rustic got the better of Ashurst's self-possession; he jumped up, and pushed back his chair.

"You can go to the devil!"

And as he said those simple words, he saw Megan in the doorway with a tiny brown puppy spaniel in her arms. She came up to him quickly.

"Its eyes are blue!" she said.

Joe turned away; the back of his neck was literally crimson.

Ashurst put his finger to the mouth of the tiny brown bull-frog of a creature in her arms. How cosy it looked against her!

"It's fond of you already. Ah! Megan, everything is fond of *you*."

"What was Joe saying to you, please?"

"Telling me to go away, because you didn't want me here."

She stamped her foot; then looked up at Ashurst. At that adoring look he felt his nerves quiver, just as if he had seen a moth scorching its wings.

"To-night!" he said. "Don't forget!"

"No." And smothering her face against the puppy's little fat, brown body, she slipped back into the house.

Ashurst wandered down the lane. And at the gate of the wild meadow he came on the lame man and his cows.

"Beautiful day, Jim!"

"Ah! 'Tes brave weather for the grass. The ashes be later than th' oaks this year. 'When th' oak before th' ash——' "

Ashurst said idly: "Where were you standing when you saw the gipsy bogle, Jim?"

"It might be under that big apple tree, as you might say."

"And you really do think it was there?"

The lame man answered cautiously:

"I shouldn't like to say rightly that 't *was* there. 'Twas in my mind as 'twas there."

"What do you make of it?"

The lame man lowered his voice.

"They du zay old master, Mist' Narracombe, come o' gipsy stock. But that's tellin'. They'm a wonderful people, yu know, for claimin' their own. Maybe they knu 'e was goin', an' sent this feller along for company. That's what I've a-thought about it."

"What was he like?"

" 'E 'ad 'air all over 'is face, an' goin' like this, he was, zame as if 'e 'ad a viddle. They zay there's no such thing as bogles, but I've a-zeen the 'air on this dog standin' up of a dark naight, when I couldn' zee nothin', meself."

"Was there a moon?"

"Yeas, very near full, but 'twas on'y just risen, gold-like be'ind them trees."

"And you think a ghost means trouble, do you?"

The lame man pushed his hat up; his aspiring eyes looked at Ashurst more earnestly than ever.

"'Tes not for me to zay that—but 'tes they bein' so unrestin'-like. There's things us don' understand, that's zartin, for zure. There's people that zee things, tu, an' others that don' never zee nothin'. Now, our Joe—yu might putt anything under 'is eyes an' 'e'd never zee it; and them other boys, tu, they'm rattlin' fellers. But yu take an' putt our Megan where there's suthin', she'll zee it, an' more tu, or I'm mistaken."

"She's sensitive, that's why."

"What's that?"

"I mean, she feels everything."

"Ah! She'm very lovin'-'earted."

Ashurst, who felt colour coming into his cheeks, held out his tobacco pouch.

"Have a fill, Jim?"

"Thank 'ee, sir. She'm one in an 'underd, I think."

"I expect so," said Ashurst shortly, and folding up his pouch, walked on.

"Lovin'-'earted!" Yes! And what was he doing? What were his intentions—as they say—towards this loving-hearted girl? The thought dogged him, wandering through fields bright with buttercups, where the little red calves were feeding, and the swallows flying high. Yes, the oaks were before the ashes, brown-gold already; every tree in different stage and hue. The cuckoos and a thousand birds were singing; the little streams were very bright. The ancients believed in a Golden Age, in the garden of the Hesperides! . . . A queen wasp settled on his sleeve. Each queen wasp killed meant two thousand fewer wasps to thieve the apples that would grow from that blossom in the orchard; but who, with love in his heart, could kill anything on a day like this? He entered a field where a young red bull was feeding. It seemed to Ashurst that he looked like Joe. But the young bull took no notice of this visitor, a little drunk himself, perhaps, on the singing and the glamour of the golden pasture under his short legs. Ashurst crossed out unchallenged to the hillside above the stream. From that slope a tor mounted to its crown of rocks. The ground there was covered with a mist of bluebells, and nearly a score of crab-apple trees were in full bloom. He threw himself down on the grass. The change from the buttercup glory and oak-goldened glamour of the fields to this ethereal beauty under the grey tor filled him with a sort of wonder; nothing the same, save the sound of running water and the songs of the cuckoos. He lay there a long time, watching the sunlight wheel till the crab-trees threw shadows over the bluebells, his only companions a few wild bees. He was not quite sane, thinking of that morning's kiss, and of to-night under the apple tree. In such a spot as this, fauns and dryads surely lived; nymphs, white as the crab-apple blossom, retired within those trees; fauns, brown as the dead bracken, with pointed ears, lay in wait for them. The cuckoos were still calling when he woke, there was the sound of running water; but the sun had couched behind the tor, the hillside was cool, and some rabbits had come out. 'To-night!' he thought. Just as from the earth everything was pushing up, unfolding under the soft insistent fingers of an unseen hand, so were his heart and senses being pushed, unfolded. He got up and broke off a spray from a crab-apple tree. The buds were like Megan —shell-like, rose-pink, wild, and fresh; and so, too, the opening flowers, white, and wild, and touching. He put the spray into his coat. And all the rush of the spring within him escaped in a triumphant sigh. But the rabbits scurried away.

6

It was nearly eleven that night when Ashurst put down the pocket "Odyssey" which for half an hour he had held in his hands without reading, and slipped through the yard down to the orchard. The moon had just risen, very golden, over the hill, and like a bright, powerful, watching spirit peered through the bars of an ash tree's half-naked boughs. In among the apple trees it was still dark, and he stood making sure of his direction, feeling the rough grass with his feet. A black mass close behind him stirred with a heavy grunting sound, and three large pigs settled down again close to each other, under the wall. He listened. There was no wind, but the stream's burbling whispering chuckle had gained twice its daytime strength. One bird, he could not tell what, cried "Pip—pip," "Pip—pip," with perfect monotony; he could hear a night-jar spinning very far off; an owl hooting. Ashurst moved a step or two, and again halted, aware of a dim living whiteness all round his head. On the dark unstirring trees innumerable flowers and buds all soft and blurred were being bewitched to life by the creeping moonlight. He had the oddest feeling of actual companionship, as if a million white moths or spirits had floated in and settled between dark sky and darker ground, and were opening and shutting their wings on a level with his eyes. In the bewildering, still, scentless beauty of that moment he almost lost memory of why he had come to the orchard. The flying glamour that had clothed the earth all day had not gone now that night had fallen, but only changed into this new form. He moved on through the thicket of stems and boughs covered with that live powdering whiteness, till he reached the big apple tree. No mistaking that, even in the dark; nearly twice the height and size of any other, and leaning out towards the open meadow and the stream. Under its thick branches he stood still again, to listen. The same sounds exactly, and a faint grunting from the sleepy pigs. He put his hands on the dry, almost warm tree trunk, whose rough mossy surface gave forth a peaty scent at his touch. Would she come—would she? And among these quivering, haunted, moon-witched trees he was seized with doubts of everything! All was other-worldly here, fit for no earthly lovers; fit only for god and goddess, faun and nymph—not for him and this little country girl. Would it not be almost a relief if she did not come? But all the time he was listening. And still that unknown bird went "Pip—pip," "Pip—pip," and there rose the busy chatter of the little trout stream, whereon the moon was flinging glances through the bars of her tree-prison. The blossom on a level with his eyes seemed to grow more living every moment, seemed with its mysterious white beauty more and more a part of his suspense. He plucked a fragment and held it close—three blossoms. Sacrilege to pluck fruit-tree blossom—soft, sacred, young blossom—and throw it away! Then suddenly he heard the gate close, the pigs stirring again and grunting; and leaning against the trunk, he pressed his hands to its mossy sides behind him, and held his breath. She might have been a spirit threading the trees, for all the noise she made! Then he saw her quite close—her dark form part of a little tree, her white face part of its blossom; so still and peering towards him. He whispered: "Megan!" and held out his hands. She ran forward, straight to his breast. When he felt her heart beating against him, Ashurst knew to the full the sensation of chivalry and passion. Because she was not of his world, because she was so simple and young and headlong, adoring and defenceless, how could he be other than her protector, in the dark! Because she was all simple, loving nature and beauty, as much a part of this spring night as was the living blossom, how should he not take all that she would give him—how not fulfil the spring in her heart and his! And torn between these two emotions he clasped her close, and kissed her hair. How long they stood there without speaking he knew not. The stream went on chattering, the owls hooting, the moon kept stealing up and growing whiter; the blossom all round them and above brightened in suspense of living beauty. Their lips had sought each other's, and they did not speak. The moment speech began all would be unreal! Spring has no speech, nothing but rustling and whispering. Spring has so much more than speech in its unfolding flowers and leaves, and the coursing of its streams, and in its sweet restless seeking! And sometimes spring will come alive, and, like a mysterious Presence stand, encircling lovers with its arms, laying on them the fingers of enchantment, so that, standing lips to lips, they forget everything but just a kiss. While her heart beat against him, and her lips quivered on his, Ashurst felt nothing but simple rapture— Destiny meant her for his arms, Love could not be flouted! But when their lips parted for breath, division began again at once. Only, passion now was so much the stronger, and he sighed:

"Oh! Megan! Why did you come?"

She looked up, hurt, amazed.

"Sir, you asked me to."

"Don't call me 'sir,' my pretty sweet."

"What should I be callin' you?"

"Frank."

"I could not. Oh, no!"

"But you love me—don't you?"

"I could not help lovin' you. I want to be with you—that's all."

"All!"

So faint that he hardly heard, she whispered:

"I shall die if I can't be with you."

Ashurst took a mighty breath.

"Come and be with me, then!"

"Oh!"

Intoxicated by the awe and rapture in that "Oh!" he went on, whispering:

"We'll go to London. I'll show you the world. And I *will* take care of you, I promise, Megan. I won't be a brute to you!"

"If I can be with you—that is all."

He stroked her hair, and whispered on:

"To-morrow I'll go to Torquay and get some money, and get you some clothes that won't be noticed, and then we'll steal away. And when we get to London, soon perhaps, if you love me well enough, we'll be married."

He could feel her hair shiver with the shake of her head.

"Oh, no! I could not. I only want to be with you!"

Drunk on his own chivalry, Ashurst went on murmuring:

"It's I who am not good enough for you. Oh! Megan, when did you begin to love me?"

"When I saw you in the road, and you looked at me. The first night I loved you; but I never thought you would want me."

She slipped down suddenly to her knees, trying to kiss his feet.

A shiver of horror went through Ashurst; he lifted her up bodily and held her fast—too upset to speak.

She whispered: "Why won't you let me?"

"It's I who will kiss your feet!"

Her smile brought tears into his eyes. The whiteness of her moonlit face so close to his, the faint pink of her opened lips, had the living unearthly beauty of the apple blossom.

And then, suddenly, her eyes widened and stared past him painfully; she writhed out of his arms, and whispered: "Look!"

Ashurst saw nothing but the brightened stream, the furze faintly gilded, the beech trees glistening, and behind them all the wide loom of the moonlit hill. Behind him came her frozen whisper: "The gipsy bogle!"

"Where?"

"There—by the stone—under the trees!"

Exasperated, he leaped the stream, and strode towards the beech clump. Prank of the moonlight! Nothing! In and out of the boulders and thorn trees, muttering and cursing, yet with a kind of terror, he rushed and stumbled. Absurd! Silly! Then he went back to the apple tree. But she was gone; he could hear a rustle, the grunting of the pigs, the sound of a gate closing. Instead of her, only this old apple tree! He flung his arms round the trunk. What a substitute for her soft body; the rough moss against his face—what a substitute for her soft cheek; only the scent, as of the woods, a little the same! And above him, and around, the blossoms, more living, more moonlit than ever, seemed to glow and breathe.

7

Descending from the train at Torquay station, Ashurst wandered uncertainly along the front, for he did not know this particular queen of English watering places. Having little sense of what he had on, he was quite unconscious of being remarkable among its inhabitants, and strode along in his rough Norfolk jacket, dusty boots, and battered hat, without observing that people gazed at him rather blankly. He was seeking a branch of his London Bank, and having found one, found also the first obstacle to his mood. Did he know anyone in Torquay? No. In that case, if he would wire to his Bank in London, they would be happy to oblige him on receipt of the reply. That suspicious breath from the matter-of-fact world somewhat tarnished the brightness of his visions. But he sent the telegram.

Nearly opposite to the post office he saw a shop full of ladies' garments, and examined the window with strange sensations. To have to undertake the clothing of his rustic love was more than a little disturbing. He went in. A young woman came forward; she had blue eyes and a faintly puzzled forehead. Ashurst stared at her in silence.

"Yes, sir?"

"I want a dress for a young lady."

The young woman smiled. Ashurst frowned—the peculiarity of his request struck him with sudden force.

The young woman added hastily:

"What style would you like—something modish?"

"No. Simple."

"What figure would the young lady be?"

"I don't know; about two inches shorter than you, I should say."

"Could you give me her waist measurement?"

Megan's waist!

"Oh! anything usual!"

"Quite!"

While she was gone he stood disconsolately eyeing the models in the window, and suddenly it seemed to him incredible that Megan—his Megan—could ever be dressed save in the rough tweed skirt, coarse blouse, and tam-o'-shanter cap he was wont to see her in. The young woman had come back with several dresses in her arms, and Ashurst eyed her laying them against her own modish figure. There was one whose colour he liked, a dove-grey, but to imagine Megan clothed in it was beyond him. The young woman went away, and brought some more. But on Ashurst there had now come a feeling of paralysis. How choose? She would want a hat too, and shoes, and gloves; and, suppose, when he had got them all, they commonised her, as Sunday clothes always commonised village folk! Why should she not travel as she was? Ah! but conspicuousness would matter; this was a serious elopement. And, staring at the young woman, he thought: 'I wonder if she guesses, and thinks me a blackguard?'

"Do you mind putting aside that grey one for me?" he said desperately at last. "I can't decide now; I'll come in again this afternoon."

The young woman sighed.

"Oh! certainly. It's a very tasteful costume. I don't think you'll get anything that will suit your purpose better."

"I expect not," Ashurst murmured, and went out.

Freed again from the suspicious matter-of-factness of the world, he took a long breath, and went back to visions. In fancy he saw the trustful, pretty creature who was going to join her life to his; saw himself and her stealing forth at night, walking over the moor under the moon, he with his arm round her, and carrying her new garments, till, in some far-off wood, when dawn was coming, she would slip off her old things and put on these, and an early train at a distant station would bear them away on their honeymoon journey, till London swallowed them up, and the dreams of love came true.

"Frank Ashurst! Haven't seen you since Rugby, old chap!"

Ashurst's frown dissolved; the face, close to his own, was blue-eyed, suffused with sun—one of those faces where sun from within and without joins in a sort of lustre. And he answered:

"Phil Halliday, by Jove!"

"What are you doing here?"

"Oh! nothing. Just looking round, and getting some money. I'm staying on the moor."

"Are you lunching anywhere? Come and lunch with us; I'm here with my young sisters. They've had measles."

Hooked in by that friendly arm Ashurst went along, up a hill, down a hill, away out of the town, while the voice of Halliday, redolent of optimism as his face was of sun, explained how "in this mouldy place the only decent things were the bathing and boating," and so on, till presently they came to a crescent of houses a little above and back from the sea, and into the centre one—an hotel—made their way.

"Come up to my room and have a wash. Lunch'll be ready in a jiffy."

Ashurst contemplated his visage in a looking-glass. After his farmhouse bedroom, the comb and one spare shirt *régime* of the last fortnight, this room littered with clothes and brushes was a sort of Capua; and he thought: 'Queer—one doesn't realize——' But what—he did not quite know.

When he followed Halliday into the sitting room for lunch, three faces, very fair and blue-eyed, were turned suddenly at the words: "This is Frank Ashurst—my young sisters."

Two were indeed young, about eleven and ten. The third was perhaps seventeen, tall and fair-haired too, with pink-and-white cheeks just touched by the sun, and eyebrows, rather darker than the hair, running a little upward from her nose to their outer points. The voices of all three were like Halliday's, high and cheerful; they stood up straight, shook hands with a quick movement, looked at Ashurst critically, away again at once, and began to talk of what they were going to do in the afternoon. A regular Diana and attendant nymphs! After the farm this crisp, slangy, eager talk, this cool, clean, off-hand refinement, was queer at first, and then so natural that what he had come from became suddenly remote. The names of the two little ones seemed to be Sabina and Freda; of the eldest, Stella.

Presently the one called Sabina turned to him and said:

"I say, will you come shrimping with us?—it's awful fun!"

Surprised by this unexpected friendliness, Ashurst murmured:

"I'm afraid I've got to get back this afternoon."

"Oh!"

"Can't you put it off?"

Ashurst turned to the new speaker, Stella, shook his head, and smiled. She was very pretty! Sabina said regretfully: "You might!" Then the talk switched off to caves and swimming.

"Can you swim far?"

"About two miles."

"Oh!"

"I say!"

"How jolly!"

The three pairs of blue eyes, fixed on him, made him conscious of his new importance. The sensation was agreeable. Halliday said:

"I say, you simply must stop and have a bathe. You'd better stay the night."

"Yes, do!"

But again Ashurst smiled and shook his head. Then suddenly he found himself being catechised about his physical achievements. He had rowed—it seemed—in his college boat, played in his college football team, won his college mile; and he rose from table a sort of hero. The two little girls insisted that he must see "their" cave, and they set forth chattering like magpies, Ashurst between them, Stella and her brother a little behind. In the cave, damp and darkish like any other cave, the great feature was a pool with possibility of creatures that might be caught and put into bottles. Sabina and Freda, who wore no stockings on their shapely brown legs, exhorted Ashurst to join them in the middle of it, and help sieve the water. He too was soon bootless and sockless. Time goes fast for one who has a sense of beauty, when there are pretty children in a pool and a young Diana on the edge, to receive with wonder anything you can catch! Ashurst never had much sense of time. It was a shock when, pulling out his watch, he saw it was well past three. No cashing his cheque to-day—the Bank would be closed before he could get there. Watching his expression, the little girls cried out at once:

"Hurrah! Now you'll have to stay!"

Ashurst did not answer. He was seeing again Megan's face, when at breakfast time he had whispered: "I'm going to Torquay, darling, to get everything. I shall be back this evening. If it's fine we can go to-night. Be ready." He was seeing again how she quivered and hung on his words. What would she think? Then he pulled himself together, conscious suddenly of the calm scrutiny of this other young girl, so tall and fair and Diana-like, at the edge of the pool, of her wondering blue eyes under those brows that slanted up a little. If they knew what was in his mind—if they knew that this very night he had meant——! Well, there would be a little sound of disgust, and he would be alone in the cave. And with a curious mixture of anger, chagrin, and shame, he put his watch back into his pocket and said abruptly:

"Yes; I'm dished for to-day."

"Hurrah! Now you can bathe with us."

It was impossible not to succumb a little to the contentment of these pretty children, to the smile on Stella's lips, to Halliday's "Ripping, old chap! I can lend you things for the night!" But again a spasm of longing and remorse throbbed through Ashurst, and he said moodily:

"I must send a wire!"

The attractions of the pool palling, they went back to the hotel. Ashurst sent his wire, addressing it to Mrs. Narracombe: "Sorry, detained for the night, back to-morrow." Surely Megan would understand that he had too much to do; and his heart grew lighter. It was a lovely afternoon, warm, the sea calm and blue, and swimming his great passion; the favour of these pretty children flattered him, the pleasure of looking at them, at Stella, at Halliday's sunny face; the slight unreality, yet extreme naturalness of it all—as of a last peep at normality before he took this plunge with Megan! He got his borrowed bathing dress, and they all set forth. Halliday and he undressed behind one rock, the three girls behind another. He was first into the sea, and at once swam out with the bravado of justifying his self-given reputation. When he turned he could see Halliday swimming along shore, and the girls flopping and dipping, and riding the little waves, in the way he was accustomed to despise, but now thought pretty and sensible, since it gave him the distinction of the only deep-water fish. But drawing near, he wondered if they would like him, a stranger, to come into their splashing group; he felt shy, approaching that slim nymph. Then Sabina summoned him to teach her to float, and between them the little girls kept him so busy that he had no time even to notice whether Stella was accustomed to his presence, till suddenly he heard a startled sound from her. She was standing submerged to the waist, leaning a little forward, her slim white arms stretched out and pointing, her wet face puckered by the sun and an expression of fear.

"Look at Phil! Is he all right? Oh, look!"

Ashurst saw at once that Phil was not all right. He was splashing and struggling, out of his depth, perhaps a hundred yards away; suddenly he gave a cry, threw up his arms, and went down. Ashurst saw the girl launch herself towards him, and crying out: "Go back, Stella! Go back!" he dashed out. He had never swum so fast, and reached Halliday just as he was coming up a second time. It was a case of cramp, but to get him in was not difficult, for he did not struggle. The girl, who had stopped where Ashurst told her to, helped as soon as he was in her depth, and once on the beach they sat down one on each side of him to rub his limbs, while the little ones stood by with scared faces. Halliday was soon smiling. It was—he said—rotten of him, absolutely rotten! If Frank would give him an arm, he could get to his clothes all right now. Ashurst gave him the arm, and as he did so caught sight of Stella's face, wet and flushed and tearful, all broken up out of its calm; and he thought: 'I called her Stella! Wonder if she minded?'

While they were dressing, Halliday said quietly:

"You saved my life, old chap!"

"Rot!"

Clothed, but not quite in their right minds, they went up all together to the hotel and sat down to tea, except Halliday, who was lying down in his room. After some slices of bread and jam, Sabina said:

"I say, you know, you *are* a brick!" And Freda chimed in:

"Rather!"

Ashurst saw Stella looking down; he got up in confusion, and went to the window. From there he heard Sabina mutter: "I say, let's swear blood bond. Where's your knife, Freda?" and out of the corner of his eye could see each of them solemnly prick herself, squeeze out a drop of blood and dabble on a bit of paper. He turned and made for the door.

"Don't be a stoat! Come back!" His arms were seized; imprisoned between the little girls he was brought back to the table. On it lay a piece of paper with an effigy drawn in blood, and the three names Stella

Halliday, Sabina Halliday, Freda Halliday—also in blood, running towards it like the rays of a star. Sabina said:

"That's you. We shall have to kiss you, you know."

And Freda echoed:

"Oh! Blow—Yes!"

Before Ashurst could escape, some wettish hair dangled against his face, something like a bite descended on his nose, he felt his left arm pinched, and other teeth softly searching his cheek. Then he was released, and Freda said:

"Now, Stella."

Ashurst, red and rigid, looked across the table at a red and rigid Stella. Sabina giggled; Freda cried:

"Buck up—it spoils everything!"

A queer, ashamed eagerness shot through Ashurst; then he said quietly:

"Shut up, you little demons!"

Again Sabina giggled.

"Well, then, she can kiss her hand, and you can put it against your nose. It *is* on one side!"

To his amazement the girl did kiss her hand and stretch it out. Solemnly he took that cool, slim hand and laid it to his cheek. The two little girls broke into clapping, and Freda said:

"Now, then, we shall have to save your life at any time; that's settled. Can I have another cup, Stella, not so beastly weak?"

Tea was resumed, and Ashurst, folding up the paper, put it in his pocket. The talk turned on the advantages of measles, tangerine oranges, honey in a spoon, no lessons, and so forth. Ashurst listened, silent, exchanging friendly looks with Stella, whose face was again of its normal sun-touched pink and white. It was soothing to be so taken to the heart of this jolly family, fascinating to watch their faces. And after tea, while the two little girls pressed seaweed, he talked to Stella in the window seat and looked at her watercolour sketches. The whole thing was like a pleasurable dream; time and incident hung up, importance and reality suspended. To-morrow he would go back to Megan, with nothing of all this left save the paper with the blood of these children, in his pocket. Children! Stella was not quite that—as old as Megan! Her talk—quick, rather hard and shy, yet friendly—seemed to flourish on his silences, and about her there was something cool and virginal—a maiden in a bower. At dinner, to which Halliday, who had swallowed too much sea-water, did not come, Sabina said:

"I'm going to call you Frank."

Freda echoed:

"Frank, Frank, Franky."

Ashurst grinned and bowed.

"Every time Stella calls you Mr. Ashurst, she's got to pay a forfeit. It's ridiculous."

Ashurst looked at Stella, who grew slowly red. Sabina giggled; Freda cried:

"She's 'smoking'—'smoking!'—Yah!"

Ashurst reached out to right and left, and grasped some fair hair in each hand.

"Look here," he said, "you two! Leave Stella alone, or I'll tie you together!"

Freda gurgled:

"Ouch! You *are* a beast!"

Sabina murmured cautiously:

"*You* call *her* Stella, you see!"

"Why shouldn't I? It's a jolly name!"

"All right; we give you leave to!"

Ashurst released the hair. Stella! What would she call him—after this? But she called him nothing; till at bedtime he said, deliberately:

"Good-night, Stella!"

"Good-night, Mr. —— Good-night, Frank! It *was* jolly of you, you know!"

"Oh—that! Bosh!"

Her quick, straight handshake tightened suddenly, and as suddenly became slack.

Ashurst stood motionless in the empty sitting-room. Only last night, under the apple tree and the living blossom, he had held Megan to him, kissing her eyes and lips. And he gasped, swept by that rush of remembrance. To-night it should have begun—his life with her who only wanted to be with him! And now, twenty-four hours and more must pass, because—of not looking at his watch! Why had he made friends with this family of innocents just when he was saying good-bye to innocence, and all the rest of it? 'But I mean to marry her,' he thought; 'I told her so!'

He took a candle, lighted it, and went to his bedroom, which was next to Halliday's. His friend's voice called, as he was passing:

"Is that you, old chap? I say, come in."

He was sitting up in bed, smoking a pipe and reading.

"Sit down a bit."

Ashurst sat down by the open window.

"I've been thinking about this afternoon, you know," said Halliday rather suddenly. "They say you go through all your past. I didn't. I suppose I wasn't far enough gone."

"What did you think of?"

Halliday was silent for a little, then said quietly:

"Well, I did think of one thing—rather odd—of a girl at Cambridge that I might have—you know; I was glad I hadn't got her on my mind. Anyhow, old chap, I owe it to you that I'm here; I should have been in the big dark by now. No more bed, or baccy; no more anything. I say, what d'you suppose happens to us?"

Ashurst murmured:

"Go out like flames, I expect."

"Phew!"

"We may flicker, and cling about a bit, perhaps."

"H'm! I think that's rather gloomy. I say, I hope my young sisters have been decent to you?"

"Awfully decent."

Halliday put his pipe down, crossed his hands behind his neck, and turned his face towards the window. "They're not bad kids!" he said.

Watching his friend, lying there, with that smile, and the candle-light on his face, Ashurst shuddered. Quite true! He might have been lying there with no smile, with all that sunny look gone out for ever! He might not have been lying there at all, but "sanded" at the bottom of the sea, waiting for resurrection on the—ninth day, was it? And that smile of Halliday's seemed to him suddenly something wonderful, as if in it were all the difference between life and death—the little flame—the all! He got up, and said softly:

"Well, you ought to sleep, I expect. Shall I blow out?"

Halliday caught his hand.

"I can't say it, you know; but it must be rotten to be dead. Good-night, old boy!"

Stirred and moved, Ashurst squeezed the hand, and went downstairs. The hall door was still open, and he passed out on to the lawn before the Crescent. The stars were bright in a very dark blue sky, and by their light some lilacs had that mysterious colour of flowers by night which no one can describe. Ashurst pressed his face against a spray; and before his closed eyes Megan started up, with the tiny brown spaniel pup against her breast. "I thought of a girl that I might have—you know. I was glad I hadn't got her on my mind!" He jerked his head away from the lilac, and began pacing up and down over the grass, a grey phantom coming to substance for a moment in the light from the lamp at either end. He was with her again under the living, breathing whiteness of the blossom, the stream chattering by, the moon glinting steel-blue on the bathing-pool; back in the rapture of his kisses on her upturned face of innocence and humble passion, back in the suspense and beauty of that pagan night. He stood still once more in the shadow of the lilacs. Here the sea, not the stream, was Night's voice; the sea with its sigh and rustle; no little bird, no owl, no night-jar called or spun; but a piano tinkled, and the white houses cut the sky with solid curve, and the scent from the lilacs filled the air. A window of the hotel, high up, was lighted; he saw a shadow move across the blind. And most queer sensations stirred within him, a sort of churning, and twining, and turning of a single emotion on itself, as though spring and love, bewildered and confused, seeking the way, were baffled. This girl, who had called him Frank, whose hand had given his that sudden little clutch, this girl so cool and pure—what would *she* think of such wild, unlawful loving? He sank down on the grass, sitting there cross-legged, with his back to the house, motionless as some carved Buddha. Was he really going to break through innocence, and steal? Sniff the scent out of a wild flower, and—perhaps—throw it away? "Of a girl at Cambridge that I might have—you know!" He put his hands to the grass, one on each side, palms downward, and pressed; it was just warm still—the grass, barely moist, soft and firm and friendly. 'What am I going to do?' he thought. Perhaps Megan was at her window, looking out at the blossom, thinking of him! Poor little Megan! 'Why not?' he thought. 'I love her! But do I—really love her? or do I only want her because she is so pretty, and loves me? What am I going to do?' The piano tinkled on, the stars winked; and Ashurst gazed out before him at the dark sea, as if spell-bound. He got up at last, cramped and rather chilly. There was no longer light in any window. And he went in to bed.

8

Out of a deep and dreamless sleep he was awakened by the sound of thumping on the door. A shrill voice called:

"Hi! Breakfast's ready."

He jumped up. Where was he——? Ah!

He found them already eating marmalade, and sat down in the empty place between Stella and Sabina, who, after watching him a little, said:

"I say, do buck up; we're going to start at half-past nine."

"We're going to Berry Head, old chap; you *must* come!"

Ashurst thought: 'Come! Impossible. I shall be getting things and going back.' He looked at Stella. She said quickly:

"Do come!"

Sabina chimed in:

"It'll be no fun without you."

Freda got up and stood behind his chair.

"You've got to come, or else I'll pull your hair!"

Ashurst thought: 'Well—one day more—to think it over! One day more!' And he said:

"All right! You needn't tweak my mane!"

"Hurrah!"

At the station he wrote a second telegram to the farm, and then— tore it up; he could not have explained why. From Brixham they drove in a very little wagonette. There, squeezed between Sabina and Freda, with his knees touching Stella's, they played "Up, Jenkins"; and the gloom he was feeling gave way to frolic. In this one day more to think it over, he did not want to think! They ran races, wrestled, paddled—for to-day nobody wanted to bathe—they sang catches, played games, and ate all they had brought. The little girls fell asleep against him on the way back, and his knees still touched Stella's in the narrow wagonette. It seemed incredible that thirty hours ago he had never set eyes on any of those three flaxen heads. In the train he talked to Stella of poetry, discovering her favourites, and telling her his own with a pleasing sense of superiority; till suddenly she said, rather low:

"Phil says you don't believe in a future life, Frank. I think that's dreadful."

Disconcerted, Ashurst muttered:

"I don't either believe or not believe—I simply don't know."

She said quickly:

"I couldn't bear that. What would be the use of living?"

Watching the frown of those pretty oblique brows, Ashurst answered:

"I don't believe in believing things because one wants to."

"But why should one *wish* to live again, if one isn't going to?"

And she looked full at him.

He did not want to hurt her, but an itch to dominate pushed him on to say:

"While one's alive one naturally wants to go on living for ever; that's part of being alive. But it probably isn't anything more."

"Don't you believe in the Bible at all, then?"

Ashurst thought: 'Now I shall really hurt her!'

"I believe in the Sermon on the Mount, because it's beautiful and good for all time."

"But don't you believe Christ was divine?"

He shook his head.

She turned her face quickly to the window, and there sprang into his mind Megan's prayer, repeated by little Nick: "God bless us all, and Mr. Ashes!" Who else would ever say a prayer for him, like her who at this moment must be waiting—waiting to see him come down the lane? And he thought suddenly: 'What a scoundrel I am!'

All that evening this thought kept coming back; but, as is not unusual, each time with less poignancy, till it seemed almost a matter of course to be a scoundrel. And—strange!—he did not know whether he was a scoundrel if he meant to go back to Megan, or if he did not mean to go back to her.

They played cards till the children were sent off to bed; then Stella went to the piano. From over on the window seat, where it was nearly dark, Ashurst watched her between the candles—that fair head on the long, white neck bending to the movement of her hands. She played fluently, without much expression; but what a picture she made, the faint golden radiance, a sort of angelic atmosphere—hovering about her! Who could have passionate thoughts or wild desires in the presence of that swaying, white-clothed girl with the seraphic head? She played a thing of Schumann's, called "Warum?" Then Halliday brought out a flute, and the spell was broken. After this they made Ashurst sing, Stella playing his accompaniments from a book of Schumann songs, till, in the middle of "Ich grolle nicht," two small figures clad in blue dressing gowns crept in and tried to conceal themselves beneath the piano. The evening broke up in confusion, and what Sabina called "a splendid rag."

That night Ashurst hardly slept at all. He was thinking, only too hard, and tossed and turned. The intense domestic intimacy of these last two days, the strength of this Halliday atmosphere, seemed to ring him round, and make the farm and Megan—even Megan—seem unreal. Had he really made love to her—really promised to take her away to live with him? He must have been bewitched by the spring, the night, the apple blossom! This May madness could but destroy them both! The notion that he was going to make her his mistress—that simple child not yet eighteen—now filled him with a sort of horror, even while it still stung and whipped his blood. He muttered to himself: "It's awful, what I've done—awful!" And the sound of Schumann's music throbbed and mingled with his fevered thoughts, and he saw again Stella's cool, white, fair-haired figure and bending neck, the queer, angelic radiance about her. 'I must have been—I must be—mad!' he thought. 'What came into me? Poor little Megan! "God bless us all, and Mr. Ashes!" "I want to be with you—only to be with you!"' And burying his face in his pillow, he smothered down a fit of sobbing. Not to go back was awful! To go back—more awful still!

Emotion, when you are young, and give real vent to it, loses its power of torture. And he fell asleep, thinking: 'What was it—a few kisses—all forgotten in a month!'

Next morning he got his cheque cashed, but avoided the shop of the dove-grey dress like the plague; and, instead, bought himself some necessaries. He spent the whole day in a queer mood, cherishing a kind of sullenness against himself. Instead of the hankering of the last two days, he felt nothing but a blank—all passionate longing gone, as if quenched in that outburst of tears. After tea Stella put a book down beside him, and said shyly:

"Have you read that, Frank?"

It was Farrar's "Life of Christ." Ashurst smiled. Her anxiety about his beliefs seemed to him comic, but touching. Infectious too, perhaps, for he began to have an itch to justify himself, if not to convert her. And in the evening, when the children and Halliday were mending their shrimping nets, he said:

"At the back of orthodox religion, so far as I can see, there's always the idea of reward—what you can get for being good; a kind of begging for favours. I think it all starts in fear."

She was sitting on the sofa, making reefer knots with a bit of string. She looked up quickly:

"I think it's much deeper than that."

Ashurst felt again that wish to dominate.

"You think so," he said; "but wanting the '*quid pro quo*' is about the deepest thing in all of us! It's jolly hard to get to the bottom of it!"

She wrinkled her brows in a puzzled frown.

"I don't think I understand."

He went on obstinately:

"Well, think, and see if the most religious people aren't those who feel that this life doesn't give them all they want. I believe in being good because to be good is good in itself."

"Then you do believe in being good?"

How pretty she looked now—it was easy to be good with her! And he nodded and said:

"I say, show me how to make that knot!"

With her fingers touching his, in manœuvring of the bit of string, he felt soothed and happy. And when he went to bed he wilfully kept his thoughts on her, wrapping himself in her fair, cool sisterly radiance, as in some garment of protection.

Next day he found they had arranged to go by train to Totnes, and picnic at Berry Pomeroy Castle. Still in that resolute oblivion of the past, he took his place with them in the landau beside Halliday, back to the horses. And, then, along the sea front, nearly at the turning to the railway station, his heart almost leaped into his mouth. Megan—Megan herself!—was walking on the far pathway, in her old skirt and jacket and her tam-o'-shanter, looking up into the faces of the passers-by. Instinctively he threw his hand up for cover, then made a feint of clearing dust out of his eyes; but between his fingers he could see her still, moving, not with her free country step, but wavering, lost-looking, pitiful—like some little dog that has missed its master and does not know whether to run on, to run back—where to run. How had she come like this?—what excuse had she found to get away?—what did she hope for? But with every turn of the wheels that bore him away from her, his heart revolted and cried to him to stop them, to get out, and go to her! When the landau turned the corner to the station he could bear no more, and opening the carriage door, muttered: "I've forgotten something! Go on—don't wait for me! I'll join you at the castle by the next train!" He jumped, stumbled, spun round, recovered his balance, and walked forward, while the carriage with the astonished Hallidays rolled on.

From the corner he could only just see Megan, a long way ahead now. He ran a few steps, checked himself, and dropped into a walk. With each step nearer to her, further from the Hallidays, he walked more and more slowly. How did it alter anything—this sight of her? How make the going to her, and that which must come of it, less ugly? For there was no hiding it—since he had met the Hallidays he had become gradually sure that he would not marry Megan. It would only be a wild love-time, a troubled, remorseful, difficult time—and then—well, then he would get tired, just because she gave him everything, was so simple, and so trustful, so dewy. And dew—wears off! The little spot of faded colour, her tam-o'-shanter cap, wavered on far in front of him, as she looked up into every face, and at the house windows. Had any man ever such a cruel moment to go through? Whatever he did, he felt he would be a beast. And he uttered a groan that made a nursemaid turn and stare. He saw Megan stop and lean against the sea-wall, looking at

the sea; and he too stopped. Quite likely she had never seen the sea before, and even in her distress could not resist that sight. 'Yes—she's at
the threshold,' he thought; 'everything's before her. And just for a few
weeks' passion, I shall be cutting her life to ribbons. I'd better go and
hang myself rather than do it!' And suddenly he seemed to see Stella's
calm eyes looking into his, the wave of fluffy hair on her forehead
stirred by the wind. Ah! it would be madness, would mean giving up all
that he respected, and his own self-respect. He turned and walked
quickly back towards the station. But memory of that poor, bewildered
little figure, those anxious eyes searching the passers-by, smote him too
hard again, and once more he turned towards the sea. The cap was no
longer visible; that little spot of colour had vanished in the stream of
the noon promenaders. And impelled by the passion of longing, the
dearth which comes on one when life seems to be whirling something
out of reach, he hurried forward. She was nowhere to be seen; for half
an hour he looked for her; then on the beach flung himself face downward in the sand. To find her again he knew he had only to go to the
station and wait till she returned from her fruitless quest, to take her
train home; or to take train himself and go back to the farm, so that
she found him there when she returned. But he lay inert in the sand,
among the indifferent groups of children with their spades and buckets.
Pity at her little figure wandering, seeking, was well-nigh merged in the
spring-running of his blood; for it was all wild feeling now—the chivalrous part, what there had been of it, was gone. He wanted her again,
wanted her kisses, her soft, little body, her abandonment, all her quick,
warm, pagan emotion; wanted the wonderful feeling of that night
under the moonlit apple boughs; wanted it all with a horrible intensity,
as the faun wants the nymph. The quick chatter of the little bright
trout-stream, the dazzle of the buttercups, the rocks of the old "wild
men"; the calling of the cuckoos and yaffles, the hooting of the owls;
and the red moon peeping out of the velvet dark at the living whiteness
of the blossom; and her face just out of reach at her window, lost in its
love-look; and her heart against his, her lips answering his, under the
apple tree—all this besieged him. Yet he lay inert. What was it that
struggled against pity and this feverish longing, and kept him there
paralysed in the warm sand? Three flaxen heads—a fair face with
friendly blue-grey eyes, a slim hand pressing his, a quick voice speaking
his name—"So you do believe in being good?" Yes, and a sort of atmosphere as of some old walled-in English garden, with pinks, and
cornflowers, and roses, and scents of lavender and lilac—cool and fair,
untouched, almost holy—all that he had been brought up to feel was

clean and good. And suddenly he thought: 'She might come along the front again and see me!' and he got up and made his way to the rock at the far end of the beach. There, with the spray lifting into his face, he could think more coolly. To go back to the farm and love Megan out in the woods, among the rocks, with everything around wild and fitting— that, he knew, was impossible, utterly. To transplant her to a great town, to keep in some little flat or rooms, one who belonged so wholly to Nature—the poet in him shrank from it. His passion would be a mere sensuous revel, soon gone; in London, her very simplicity, her lack of all intellectual quality, would make her his secret plaything—nothing else. The longer he sat on the rock, with his feet dangling over a greenish pool from which the sea was ebbing, the more clearly he saw this; but it was as if her arms and all of her were slipping slowly, slowly down from him, into the pool, to be carried away out to sea; and her face looking up, her lost face with beseeching eyes, and dark, wet hair— possessed, haunted, tortured him! He got up at last, scaled the low rock-cliff, and made his way down into a sheltered cove. Perhaps in the sea he could get back his control—lose this fever! And stripping off his clothes, he swam out. He wanted to tire himself so that nothing mattered, and swam recklessly, fast and far; then suddenly, for no reason, felt afraid. Suppose he could not reach shore again—suppose the current set him out—or he got cramp, like Halliday! He turned to swim in. The red cliffs looked a long way off. If he were drowned they would find his clothes. The Hallidays would know; but Megan perhaps never —they took no newspaper at the farm. And Phil Halliday's words came back to him again: "A girl at Cambridge I might have—— Glad I hadn't got her on my mind!" And in that moment of unreasoning fear he vowed he would not have her on his mind. Then his fear left him; he swam in easily enough, dried himself in the sun, and put on his clothes. His heart felt sore, but no longer ached; his body cool and refreshed.

When one is as young as Ashurst, pity is not a violent emotion. And, back in the Hallidays' sitting-room, ravenously eating, he felt much like a man recovered from fever. Everything seemed new and clear; the tea, the buttered toast and jam tasted absurdly good; tobacco had never smelt so nice. And walking up and down the empty room, he stopped here and there to touch or look. He took up Stella's work-basket, fingered the cotton reels and a gaily-coloured plait of sewing silks, smelt at the little bag filled with woodroffe she kept among them. He sat down at the piano, playing tunes with one finger, thinking: 'To-night she'll play; I shall watch her while she's playing; it does me good to watch her.' He took up the book, which still lay where she had placed it beside him, and tried to read. But Megan's little, sad figure began to haunt him at once, and he got up and leaned in the window, listening to the thrushes in the Crescent gardens, gazing at the sea, dreamy and blue below the trees. A servant came in and cleared the tea away, and he still stood, inhaling the evening air, trying not to think. Then he saw the Hallidays coming through the gate of the Crescent, Stella a little in front of Phil and the children, with their baskets, and instinctively he drew back. His heart, too sore and discomfited, shrank from this encounter, yet wanted its friendly solace—bore a grudge against this influence, yet craved its cool innocence, and the pleasure of watching Stella's face. From against the wall behind the piano he saw her come in and stand looking a little blank as though disappointed; then she saw him and smiled, a swift, brilliant smile that warmed yet irritated Ashurst.

"You never came after us, Frank."

"No; I found I couldn't."

"Look! We picked such lovely late violets!" She held out a bunch. Ashurst put his nose to them, and there stirred within him vague longings, chilled instantly by a vision of Megan's anxious face lifted to the faces of the passers-by.

He said shortly: "How jolly!" and turned away. He went up to his room, and avoiding the children, who were coming up the stairs, threw himself on his bed, and lay there with his arms crossed over his face. Now that he felt the die really cast, and Megan given up, he hated himself, and almost hated the Hallidays and their atmosphere of healthy, happy English homes. Why should they have chanced here, to drive away first love—to show him that he was going to be no better than a common seducer? What right had Stella, with her fair, shy beauty, to make him know for certain that he would never marry Megan; and, tarnishing it all, bring him such bitterness of regretful longing and such pity? Megan would be back by now, worn out by her miserable seeking —poor little thing!—expecting, perhaps, to find him there when she reached home. Ashurst bit at his sleeve, to stifle a groan of remorseful longing. He went to dinner glum and silent, and his mood threw a dinge even over the children. It was a melancholy, rather ill-tempered evening, for they were all tired; several times he caught Stella looking at him with a hurt, puzzled expression, and this pleased his evil mood. He slept miserably; got up quite early, and wandered out. He went down to the beach. Alone there with the serene, the blue, the sunlit sea, his heart relaxed a little. Conceited fool—to think that Megan would take it so hard! In a week or two she would almost have forgotten! And he—well, he would have the reward of virtue! A good young man! If Stella knew, she would give him her blessing for resisting that devil she believed in; and he uttered a hard laugh. But slowly the peace and beauty of sea and sky, the flight of the lonely seagulls, made him feel ashamed. He bathed, and turned homeward.

In the Crescent gardens Stella herself was sitting on a camp stool, sketching. He stole up close behind. How fair and pretty she was, bent diligently, holding up her brush, measuring, wrinkling her brows.

He said gently:

"Sorry I was such a beast last night, Stella."

She turned round, startled, flushed very pink, and said in her quick way:

"It's all right. I knew there was something. Between friends it doesn't matter, does it?"

Ashurst answered:

"Between friends—and we are, aren't we?"

She looked up at him, nodded vehemently, and her upper teeth gleamed again in that swift, brilliant smile.

Three days later he went back to London, travelling with the Hallidays. He had not written to the farm. What was there he could say?

On the last day of April in the following year he and Stella were married. . . .

Such were Ashurst's memories, sitting against the wall among the gorse, on his silver-wedding day. At this very spot, where he had laid out the lunch, Megan must have stood outlined against the sky when he had first caught sight of her. Of all queer coincidences! And there moved in him a longing to go down and see again the farm and the orchard, and the meadow of the gipsy bogle. It would not take long; Stella would be an hour yet, perhaps.

How well he remembered it all—the little crowning group of pine trees, the steep-up grass hill behind! He paused at the farm gate. The low stone house, the yew-tree porch, the flowering currants—not changed a bit; even the old green chair was out there on the grass under the window, where he had reached up to her that night to take the key. Then he turned down the lane, and stood leaning on the orchard gate—grey skeleton of a gate, as then. A black pig even was wandering in there among the trees. Was it true that twenty-six years had passed, or had he dreamed and awakened to find Megan waiting for him by the big apple tree? Unconsciously he put up his hand to his grizzled beard and brought himself back to reality. Opening the gate, he made his way down through the docks and nettles till he came to the stream, and the old apple tree itself. Unchanged! A little more of the grey-green lichen, a dead branch or two, and for the rest it might have been only last night that he had embraced that mossy trunk after Megan's flight and inhaled its woody savour, while above his head the moonlit blossom had seemed to breathe and live. In that early spring a few buds were showing already; the blackbirds shouting their songs, a cuckoo calling, the sunlight bright and warm. Incredibly the same—the chattering trout-stream, the narrow pool he had lain in every morning, splashing the water over his flanks and chest; and out there in the wild meadow the beech clump and the stone where the gipsy bogle was supposed to sit. And an ache for lost youth, a hankering, a sense of wasted love and sweetness, gripped Ashurst by the throat. Surely, on this earth of such wild beauty, one was meant to hold rapture to one's heart, as this earth and sky held it! And yet, one could not!

He went to the edge of the stream, and looking down at the little pool, thought: 'Youth and spring! What has become of them all, I wonder?' And then, in sudden fear of having this memory jarred by human encounter, he went back to the lane, and pensively retraced his steps to the cross-roads.

Beside the car an old, grey-bearded labourer was leaning on a stick, talking to the chauffeur. He broke off at once, as though guilty of disrespect, and touching his hat, prepared to limp on down the lane.

Ashurst pointed to the narrow green mound. "Can you tell me what this is?"

The old fellow stopped; on his face had come a look as though he were thinking: 'You've come to the right shop, mister!'

" 'Tes a grave," he said.

"But why out here?"

The old man smiled. "That's a tale, as yu may say. An' not the first time as I've a-told et—there's plenty folks asks 'bout that bit o' turf. 'Maid's Grave' us calls et, 'ereabouts."

Ashurst held out his pouch. "Have a fill?"

The old man touched his hat again, and slowly filled an old clay pipe. His eyes, looking upward out of a mass of wrinkles and hair, were still quite bright.

"If yu don' mind, zurr, I'll zet down—my leg's 'urtin' a bit to-day." And he sat down on the mound of turf.

"There's always a vlower on this grave. An' 'tain't so very lonesome, neither; brave lot o' folks goes by now, in they new motor cars an' things—not as 'twas in th' old days. She've a got company up 'ere. 'Twas a poor soul killed 'erself."

"I see!" said Ashurst. "Cross-roads burial. I didn't know that custom was kept up."

"Ah! but 'twas a main long time ago. Us 'ad a parson as was very God-fearin' then. Let me see, I've a 'ad my pension six year come Michaelmas, an' I were just on fifty when t'appened. There's no one livin' knows more about et than I du. She belonged close 'ere; same farm as where I used to work along o' Mrs. Narracombe—'tes Nick Narracombe's now; I dus a bit for 'im still, odd times."

Ashurst, who was leaning against the gate, lighting his pipe, left his curved hands before his face for long after the flame of the match had gone out.

"Yes?" he said, and to himself his voice sounded hoarse and queer.

"She was one in an 'underd, poor maid! I putts a vlower 'ere every time I passes. Pretty maid an' gude maid she was, though they wouldn't burry 'er up tu th' church, nor where she wanted to be burried neither." The old labourer paused, and put his hairy, twisted hand flat down on the turf beside the bluebells.

"Yes?" said Ashurst.

"In a manner of speakin'," the old man went on, "I think as 'twas a love-story—though there's no one never knu for zartin. Yu can't tell what's in a maid's 'ead—but that's wot I think about it." He drew his hand along the turf. "I was fond o' that maid—don' know as there was anyone as wasn' fond of 'er. But she was tu lovin'-'earted—that's where 'twas, I think." He looked up. And Ashurst, whose lips were trembling in the cover of his beard, murmured again: "Yes?"

"'Twas in the spring, 'bout now as 't might be, or a little later—blossom time—an' we 'ad one o' they young college gentlemen stayin' at the farm—nice feller tu, with 'is 'ead in the air. I liked 'e very well, an' I never see nothin' between 'em, but to my thinkin' 'e turned the maid's fancy." The old man took the pipe out of his mouth, spat, and went on:

"Yu see, 'e went away sudden one day, an' never come back. They got 'is knapsack and bits o' things down there still. That's what stuck in my mind—'is never sendin' for 'em. 'Is name was Ashes, or somethen' like that."

"Yes?" said Ashurst once more.

The old man licked his lips.

"'Er never said nothin', but from that day 'er went kind of dazed lukin'; didn't seem rightly therr at all. I never knu a 'uman creature so changed in me life—never. There was another young feller at the farm —Joe Biddaford 'is name wer', that was praaperly sweet on 'er, tu; I guess 'e used to plague 'er wi' 'is attentions. She got to luke quite wild. I'd zee her sometimes of an avenin' when I was bringin' up the calves; ther' she'd stand in th' orchard, under the big apple tree, lukin' straight before 'er. 'Well,' I used t' think, 'I dunno what 'tes that's the matter wi' yu, but yu'm lukin' pitiful, that yu are.'"

The old man relit his pipe, and sucked at it reflectively.

"Yes?" said Ashurst.

"I remembers one day I said to 'er: 'What's the matter, Megan?'—'er name was Megan David, she come from Wales same as 'er aunt, ol' Missis Narracombe. 'Yu'm frettin' about somethin',' I says. 'No, Jim,' she says, 'I'm not frettin'.' 'Yes, yu are!' I says. 'No,' she says, and tu tears cam' rollin' out. 'Yu'm cryin'—what's that, then?' I says. She putts 'er 'and over 'er 'eart: 'It 'urts me,' she says; 'but 'twill sune be better,' she says. 'But if anything shude 'appen to me, Jim, I wants to be burried under this 'ere apple tree.' I laughed. 'What's goin' to 'appen to yu?' I says; 'don't 'ee be fulish.' 'No,' she says, 'I won't be fulish.' Well, I know what maids are, an' I never thought no more about et, till tu days arter that, 'bout six in the avenin' I was comin' up wi' the calves, when I see somethin' dark lyin' in the strame, close to that big apple tree. I says to meself: 'Is that a pig—funny place for a pig to get to!' an' I goes up to et, an' I see what 'twas."

The old man stopped; his eyes, turned upward, had a bright, suffering look.

"'Twas the maid, in a little narrer pool ther' that's made by the stoppin' of a rock—where I see the young gentleman bathin' once or twice. 'Er was lyin' on 'er face in the watter. There was a plant o' goldie-cups growin' out o' the stone just above 'er 'ead. An' when I come to luke at 'er face, 'twas luvly, butiful, so calm's a baby's—wonderful butiful et was. When the doctor saw 'er, 'e said: 'She culdn' never a-done it in that little bit o' watter ef 'er 'adn't a-been in an extarsy.' Ah! an' judgin' from 'er face, that was just 'ow she was. Et made me cry praaper—butiful et was! 'Twas June then, but she'd a-found a little bit of apple blossom left over somewheres, and stuck et in 'er 'air. That's why I thinks 'er must a-been in an extarsy, to go to et gay, like that. Why! there wasn't more than a fute and a 'arf o' watter. But I tell 'ee one thing—that meadder's 'arnted; I knu et, an' she knu et; an' no one'll persuade me as 'tesn't. I told 'em what she said to me 'bout bein' burried under th' apple tree. But I think that turned 'em—made et luke tu much 's ef she'd 'ad it in 'er mind deliberate; an' so they burried 'er up 'ere. Parson we 'ad then was very particular, 'e was."

Again the old man drew his hand over the turf.

"'Tes wonderful, et seems," he added slowly, "what maids'll du for love. She 'ad a lovin' 'eart; I guess 'twas broken. But us never *knu* nothin'!"

He looked up as if for approval of his story, but Ashurst had walked past him as if he were not there.

Up on the top of the hill, beyond where he had spread the lunch, over, out of sight, he lay down on his face. So had his virtue been rewarded, and "The Cyprian," goddess of love, taken her revenge! And before his eyes, dim with tears, came Megan's face with the sprig of apple blossom in her dark, wet hair. 'What did I do that was wrong?' he thought. 'What *did* I do?' But he could not answer. Spring, with its rush of passion, its flowers and song—the spring in his heart and Megan's! Was it just Love seeking a victim! The Greek was right, then —the words of the "Hippolytus" as true to-day!

> "For mad is the heart of Love,
>   And gold the gleam of his wing;
>   And all to the spell thereof
>   Bend when he makes his spring.
>   All life that is wild and young
>   In mountain and wave and stream
>   All that of earth is sprung,
>   Or breathes in the red sunbeam;
> Yea, and Mankind. O'er all a royal throne,
>   Cyprian, Cyprian, is thine alone!"

The Greek was right! Megan! Poor little Megan—coming over the hill! Megan under the old apple tree waiting and looking! Megan dead, with beauty printed on her! . . .

A voice said:

"Oh, there you are! Look!"

Ashurst rose, took his wife's sketch, and stared at it in silence.

"Is the foreground right, Frank?"

"Yes."

"But there's something wanting, isn't there?"

Ashurst nodded. Wanting? The apple tree, the singing, and the gold!

And solemnly he put his lips to her forehead. It was his silver-wedding day.

1916.

Permissions Acknowledgments